Love&Lies

LOVE and LIES by MUSAWO

CONTENTS

Chapter 27: Love Upon a Star

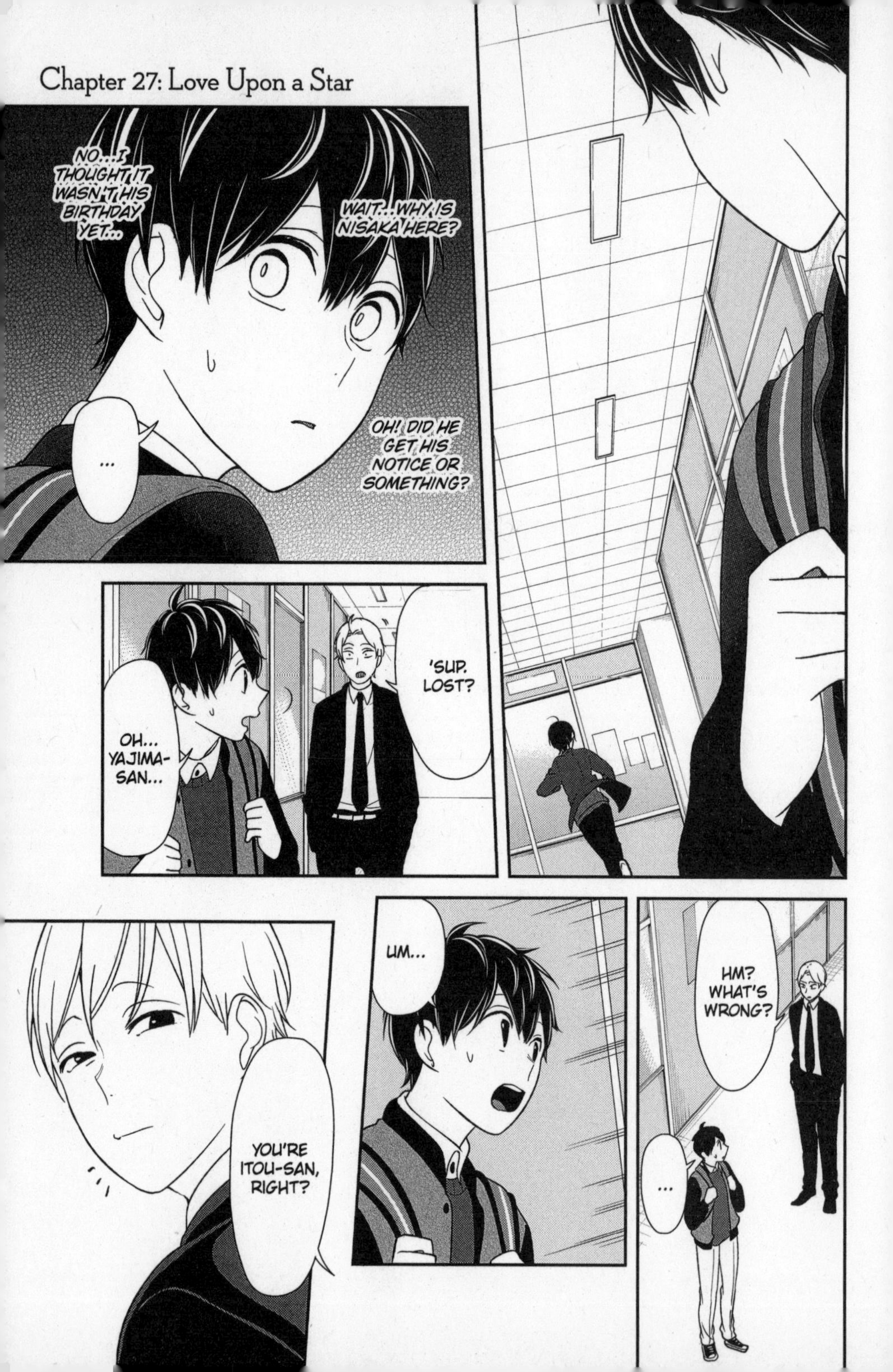
WAIT...WHY IS NISAKA HERE?
NO...I THOUGHT IT WASN'T HIS BIRTHDAY YET...
OH! DID HE GET HIS NOTICE OR SOMETHING?
...
'SUP. LOST?
OH... YAJIMA-SAN...
HM? WHAT'S WRONG?
...
UM...
YOU'RE ITOU-SAN, RIGHT?

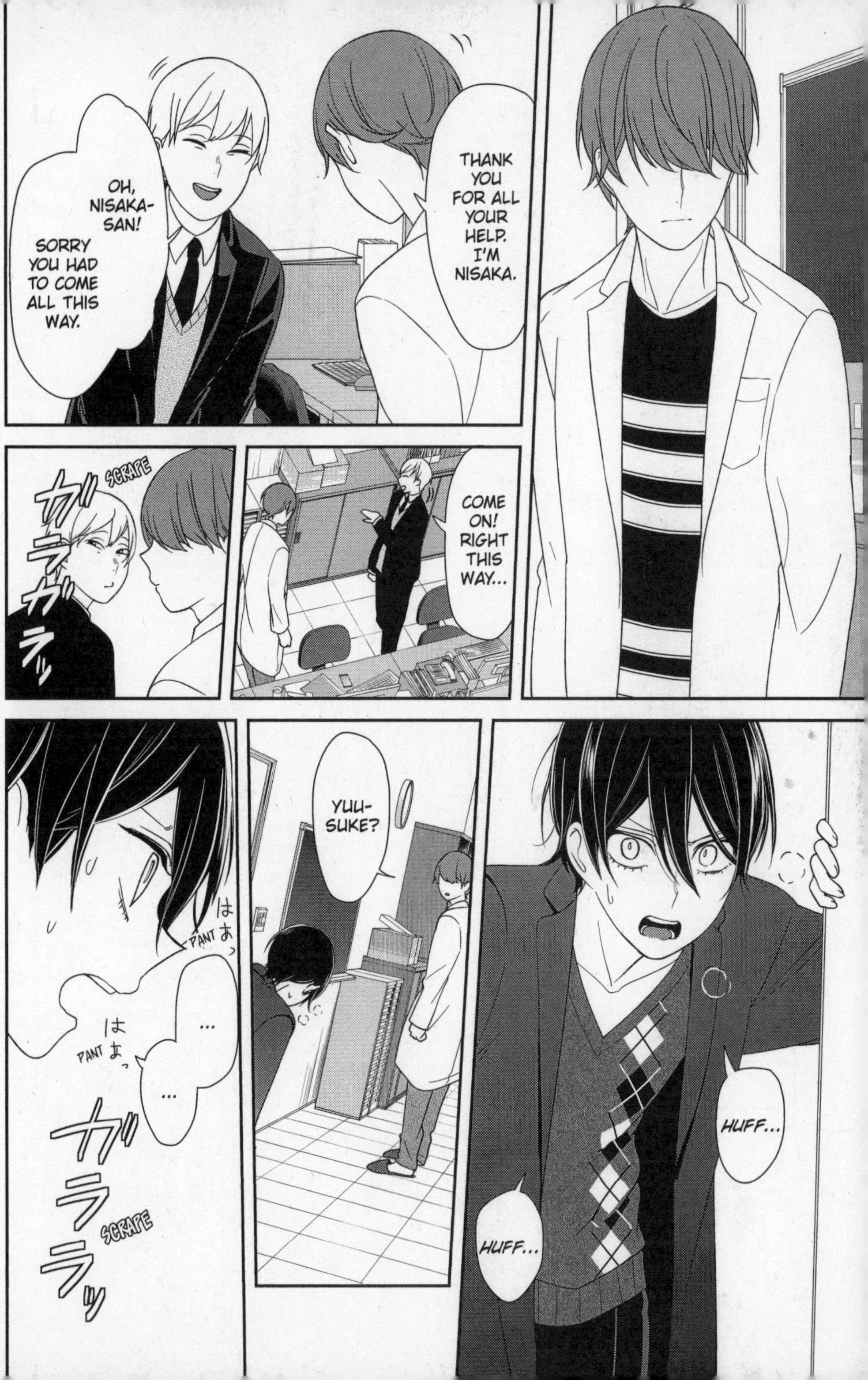
THANK YOU FOR ALL YOUR HELP. I'M NISAKA.
OH, NISAKA-SAN!
SORRY YOU HAD TO COME ALL THIS WAY.
COME ON! RIGHT THIS WAY...
ガラガラッ
SCRAPE
HUFF...
HUFF...
YUU-SUKE?
はぁっ
PANT
はぁっ
PANT
...
...
ガララッ
SCRAPE

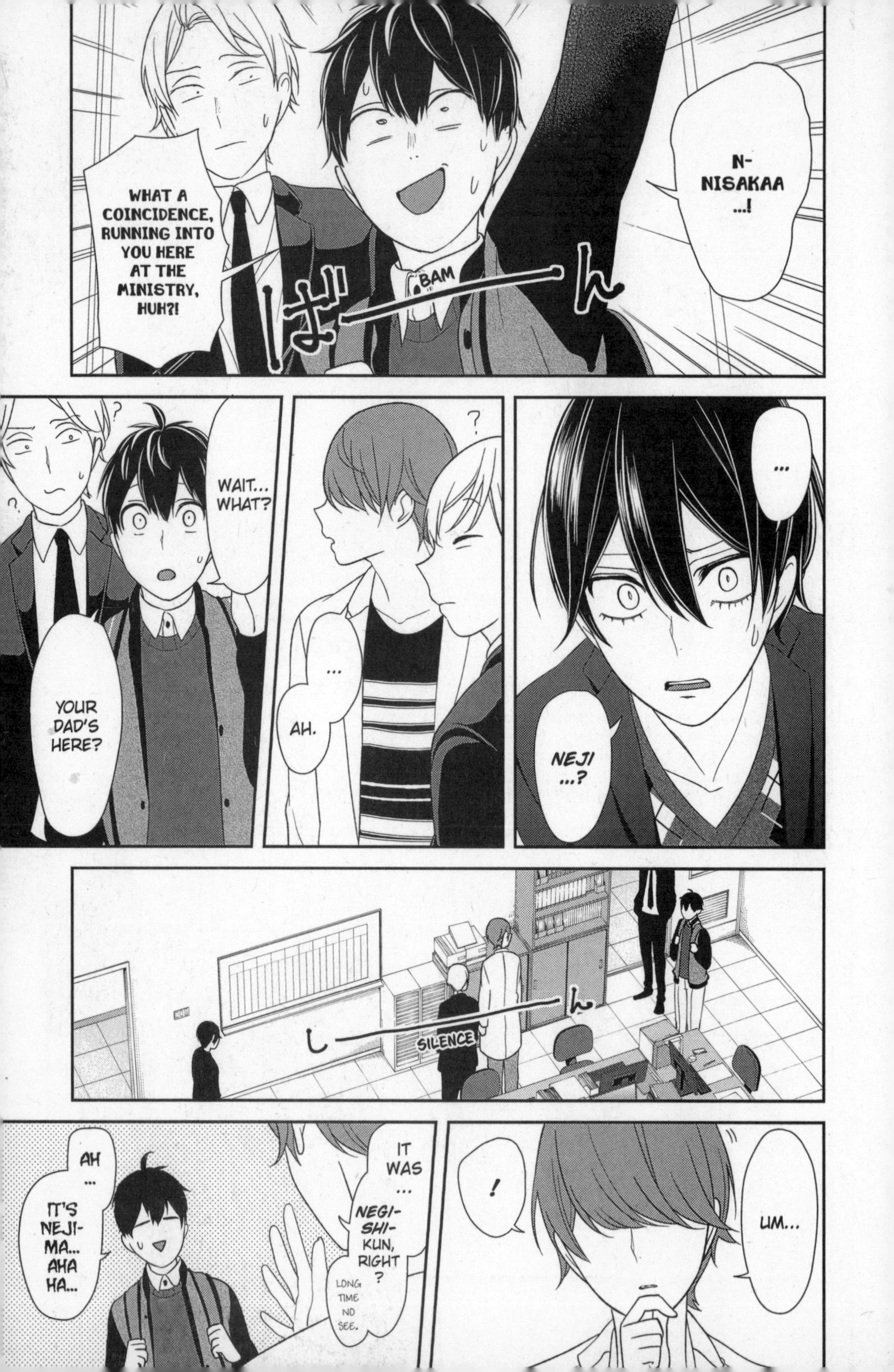
N-NISAKAA ...!
WHAT A COINCIDENCE, RUNNING INTO YOU HERE AT THE MINISTRY, HUH?!
BAM
...
NEJI ...?
...
AH.
WAIT... WHAT?
YOUR DAD'S HERE?
SILENCE
UM...
!
IT WAS ... NEGISHI-KUN, RIGHT?
LONG TIME NO SEE.
AH ... IT'S NEJIMA... AHA HA...

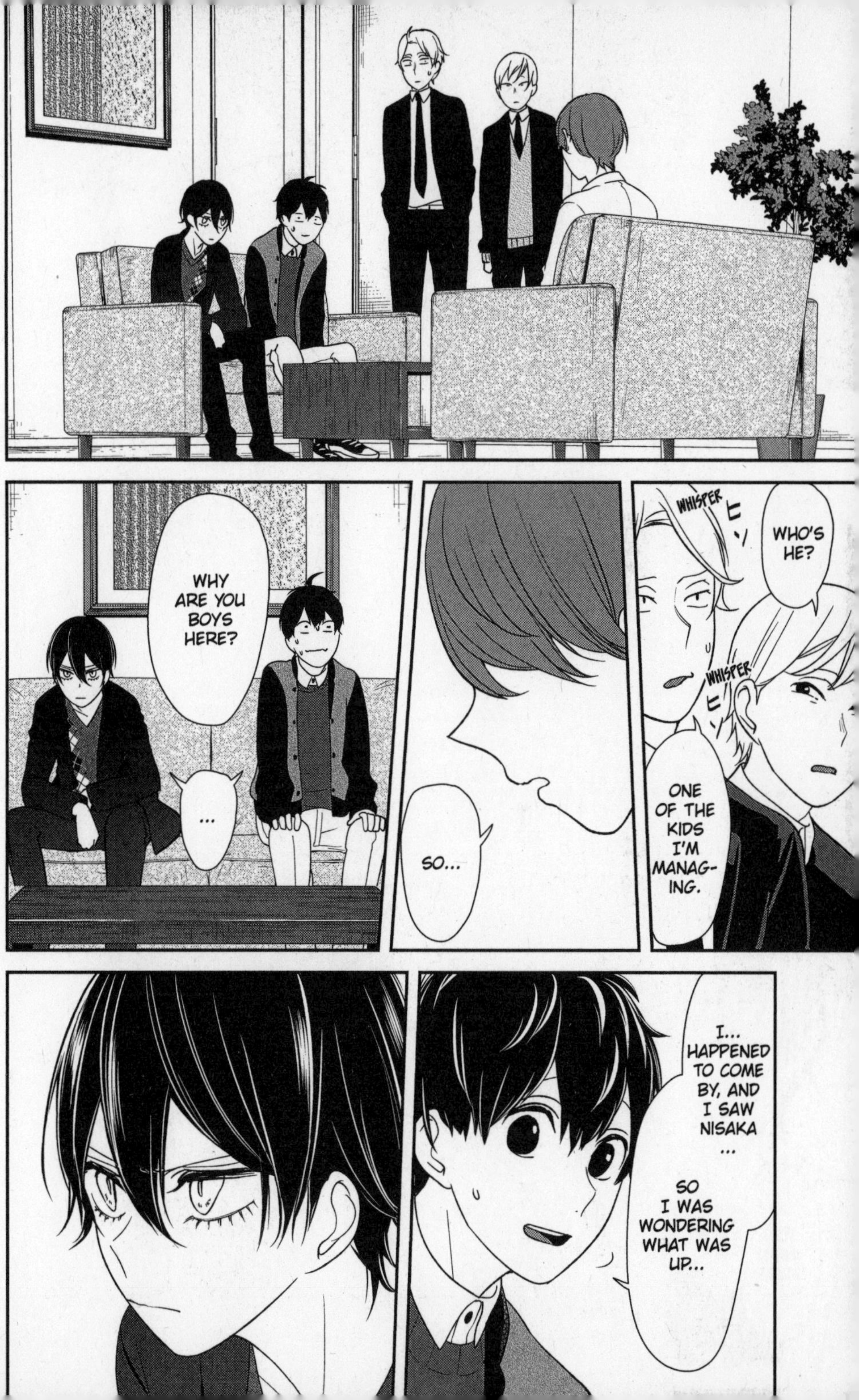
WHISPER
WHO'S HE?
WHISPER
ONE OF THE KIDS I'M MANAGING.
SO...
WHY ARE YOU BOYS HERE?
...
I... HAPPENED TO COME BY, AND I SAW NISAKA ...
SO I WAS WONDERING WHAT WAS UP...

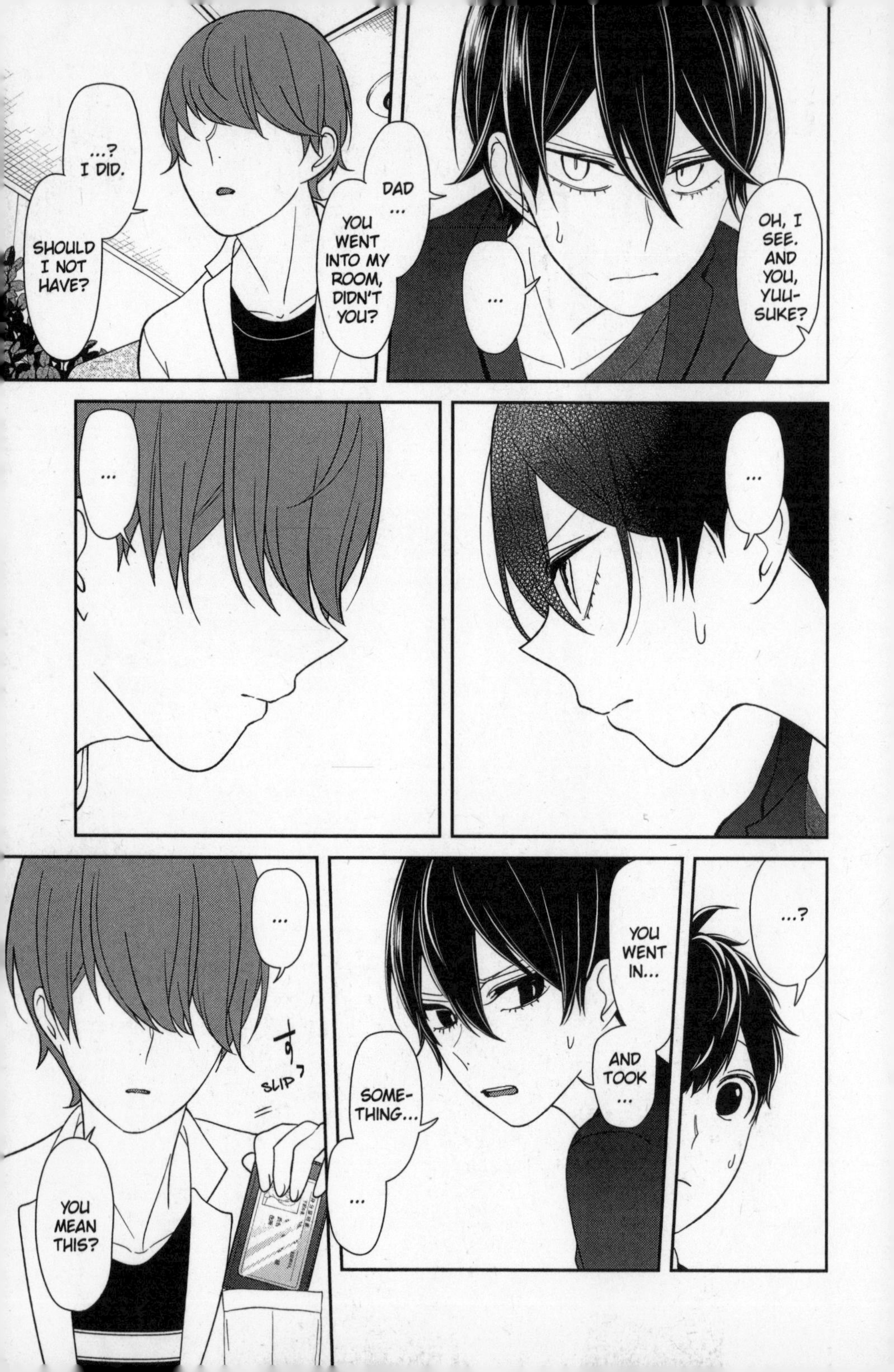
OH, I SEE. AND YOU, YUU-SUKE?
...
DAD ...
YOU WENT INTO MY ROOM, DIDN'T YOU?
...? I DID.
SHOULD I NOT HAVE?
...
...
...?
YOU WENT IN...
AND TOOK ...
SOME-THING...
...
...
すっ
SLIP
YOU MEAN THIS?

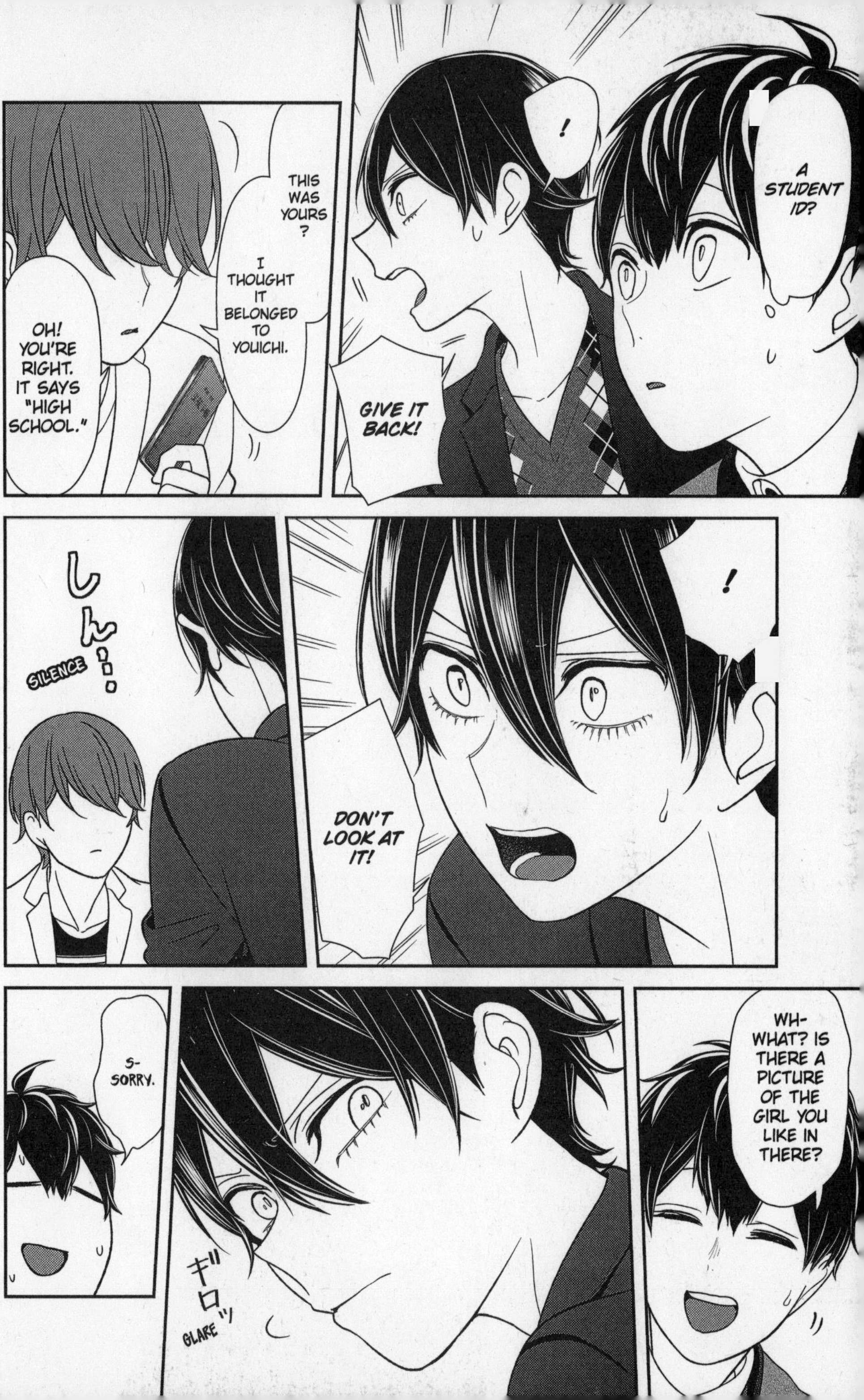
A STUDENT ID?
!
GIVE IT BACK!
THIS WAS YOURS?
I THOUGHT IT BELONGED TO YOUICHI.
OH! YOU'RE RIGHT. IT SAYS "HIGH SCHOOL."
!
DON'T LOOK AT IT!
しん…
SILENCE
WH-WHAT? IS THERE A PICTURE OF THE GIRL YOU LIKE IN THERE?
ギロッ
GLARE
S-SORRY.

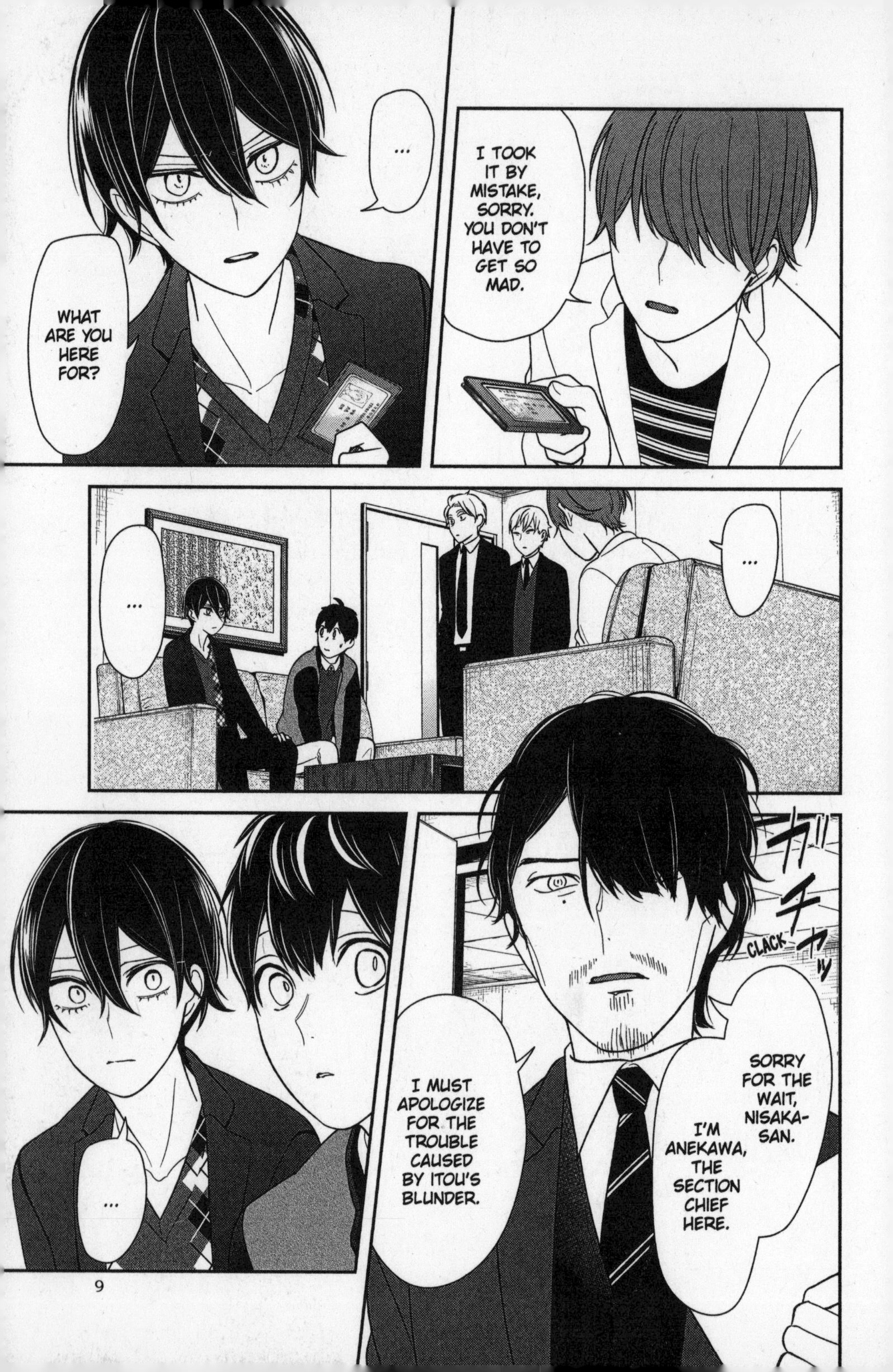
I TOOK IT BY MISTAKE, SORRY. YOU DON'T HAVE TO GET SO MAD.
...
WHAT ARE YOU HERE FOR?
...
...
CLACK
SORRY FOR THE WAIT, NISAKA-SAN.
I'M ANEKAWA, THE SECTION CHIEF HERE.
I MUST APOLOGIZE FOR THE TROUBLE CAUSED BY ITOU'S BLUNDER.
...

*PERSONAL STAMP: IN JAPAN, OFFICIALLY REGISTERED, CUSTOM-CARVED INK STAMPS ARE USED ON MOST OFFICIAL DOCUMENTS, RATHER THAN HANDWRITTEN SIGNATURES.

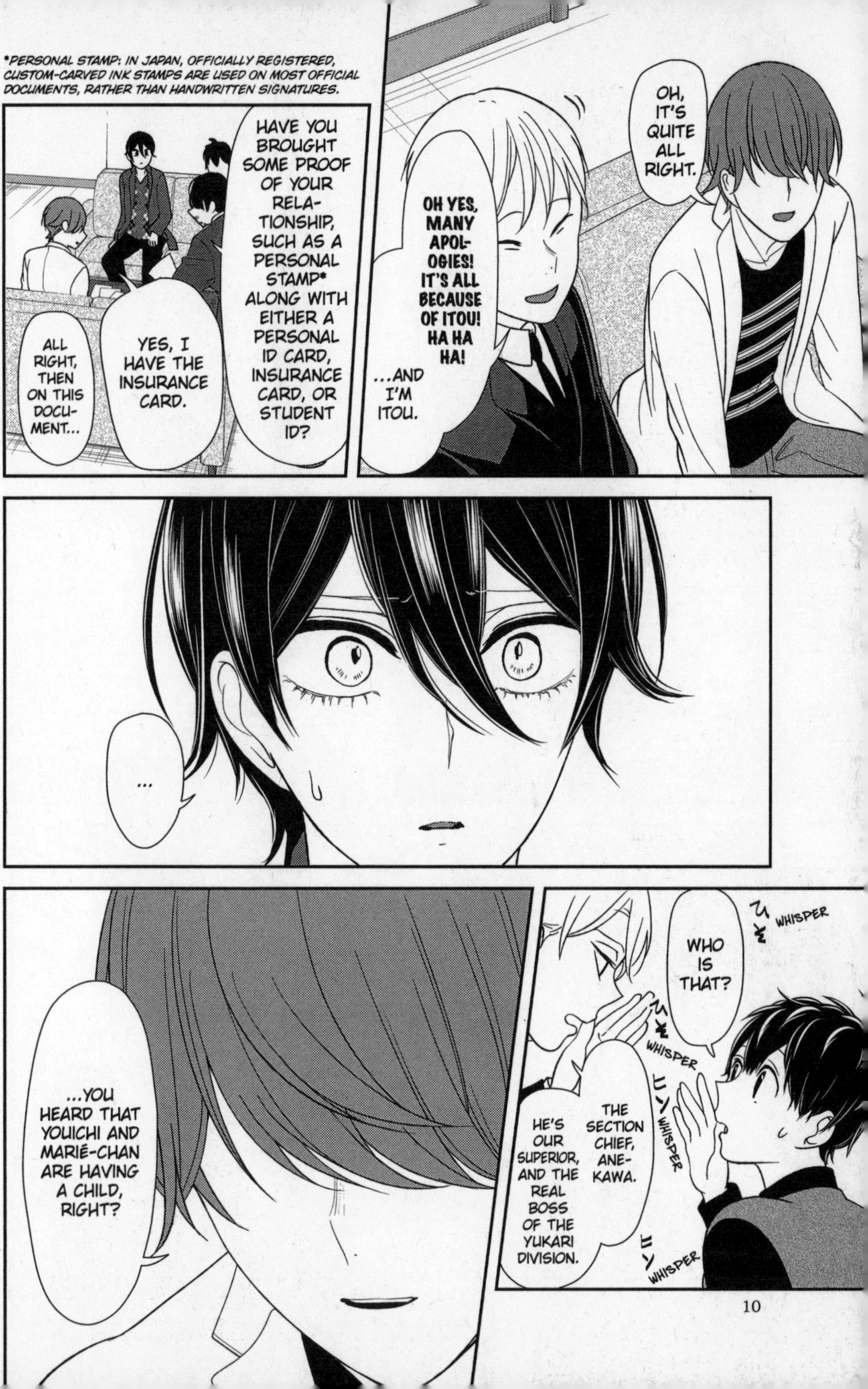
OH, IT'S QUITE ALL RIGHT.
OH YES, MANY APOLOGIES! IT'S ALL BECAUSE OF ITOU! HA HA HA!
...AND I'M ITOU.
HAVE YOU BROUGHT SOME PROOF OF YOUR RELATIONSHIP, SUCH AS A PERSONAL STAMP* ALONG WITH EITHER A PERSONAL ID CARD, INSURANCE CARD, OR STUDENT ID?
YES, I HAVE THE INSURANCE CARD.
ALL RIGHT, THEN ON THIS DOCUMENT...
...
WHISPER
WHO IS THAT?
WHISPER
THE SECTION CHIEF, ANEKAWA.
WHISPER
HE'S OUR SUPERIOR, AND THE REAL BOSS OF THE YUKARI DIVISION.
WHISPER
...YOU HEARD THAT YOUICHI AND MARIÉ-CHAN ARE HAVING A CHILD, RIGHT?

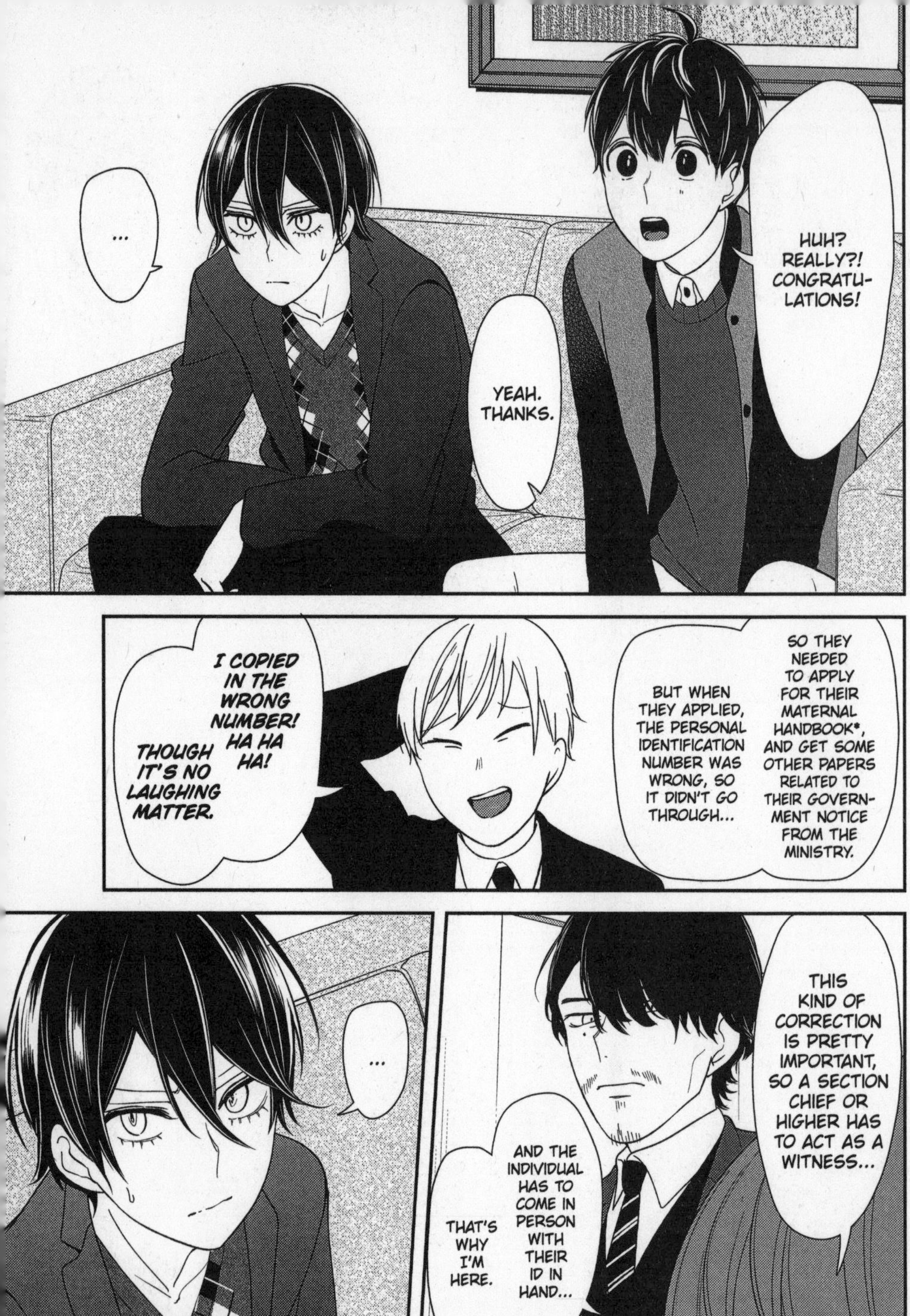
HUH? REALLY?! CONGRATULATIONS!
YEAH. THANKS.
...
SO THEY NEEDED TO APPLY FOR THEIR MATERNAL HANDBOOK*, AND GET SOME OTHER PAPERS RELATED TO THEIR GOVERNMENT NOTICE FROM THE MINISTRY.
BUT WHEN THEY APPLIED, THE PERSONAL IDENTIFICATION NUMBER WAS WRONG, SO IT DIDN'T GO THROUGH...
I COPIED IN THE WRONG NUMBER! HA HA HA!
THOUGH IT'S NO LAUGHING MATTER.
THIS KIND OF CORRECTION IS PRETTY IMPORTANT, SO A SECTION CHIEF OR HIGHER HAS TO ACT AS A WITNESS...
AND THE INDIVIDUAL HAS TO COME IN PERSON WITH THEIR ID IN HAND...
THAT'S WHY I'M HERE.
...

*MATERNAL & CHILD HEALTH HANDBOOK: THIS IS AN OFFICIAL DOCUMENT THAT MUST BE PRESENTED TO HEALTH CARE PROVIDER FOR ALL MATERNAL INFANT MEDICAL VISITS, INCLUDING ULTRASOUNDS, CHILDBIRTH, CHILD VACCINATIONS, ETC.

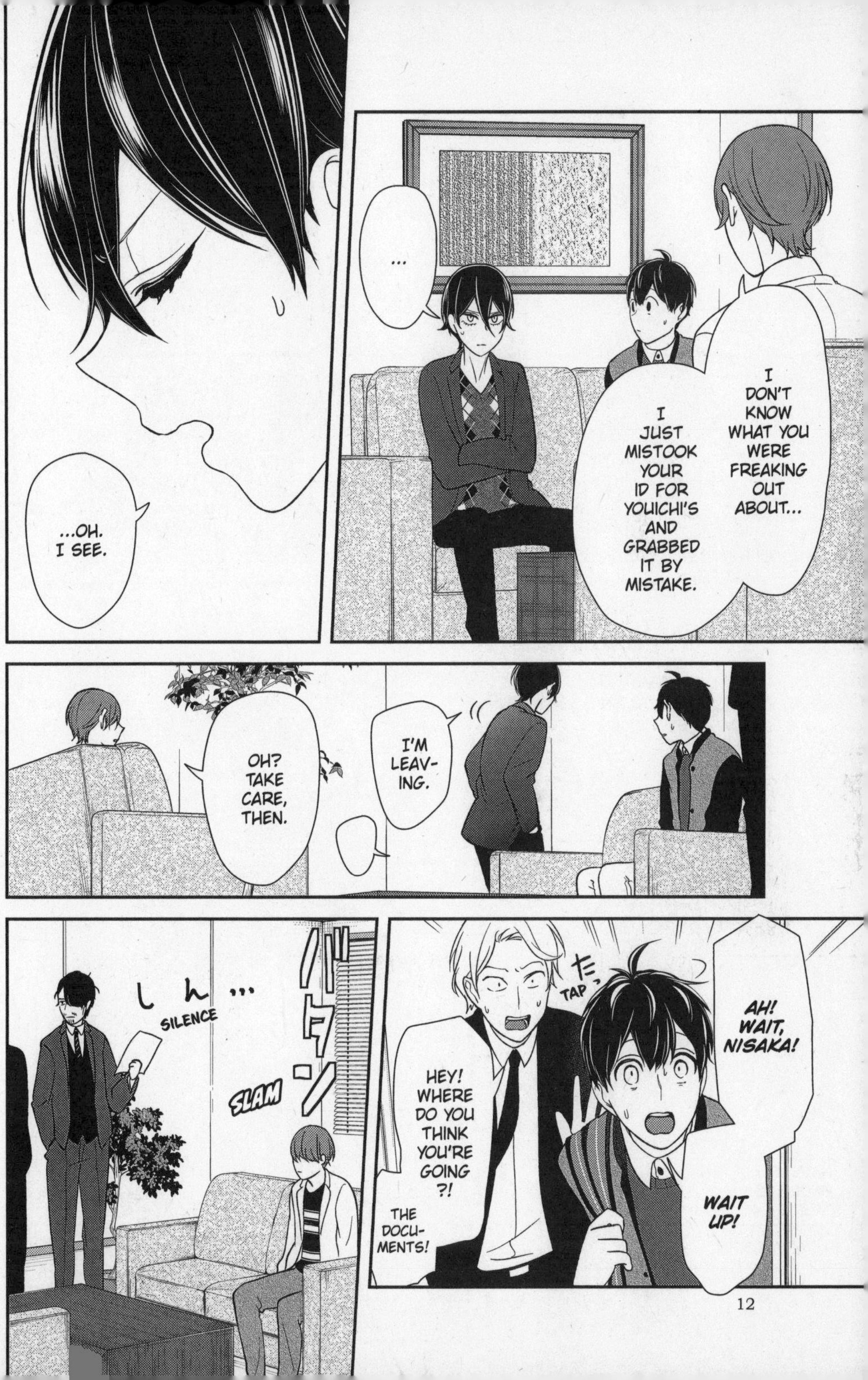
I DON'T KNOW WHAT YOU WERE FREAKING OUT ABOUT...
I JUST MISTOOK YOUR ID FOR YOUICHI'S AND GRABBED IT BY MISTAKE.
...
...OH. I SEE.
I'M LEAVING.
OH? TAKE CARE, THEN.
AH! WAIT, NISAKA!
TAP
HEY! WHERE DO YOU THINK YOU'RE GOING?!
THE DOCUMENTS!
WAIT UP!
SLAM
SILENCE

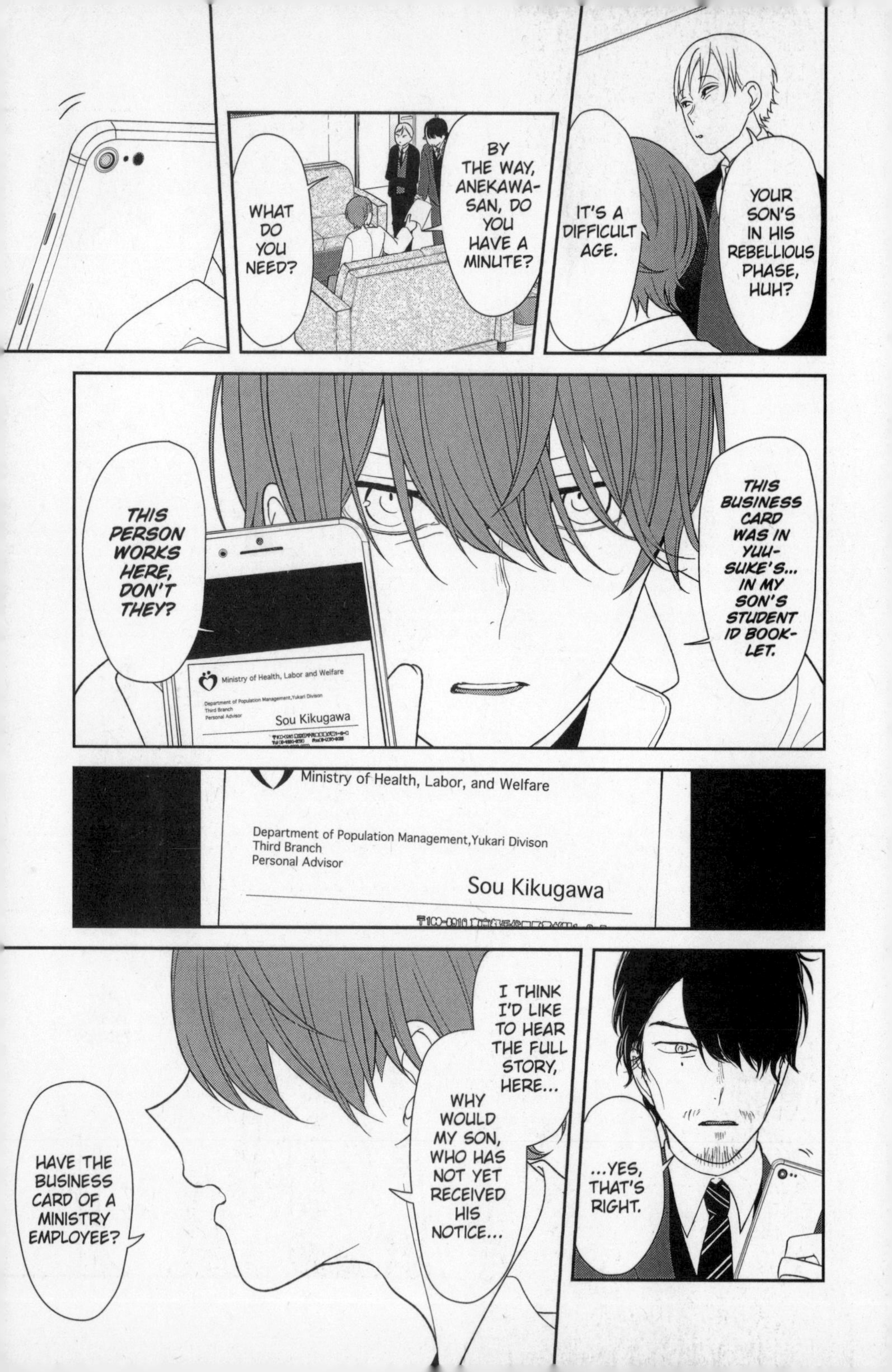
YOUR SON'S IN HIS REBELLIOUS PHASE, HUH?
IT'S A DIFFICULT AGE.
BY THE WAY, ANEKAWA-SAN, DO YOU HAVE A MINUTE?
WHAT DO YOU NEED?
THIS BUSINESS CARD WAS IN YUU-SUKE'S... IN MY SON'S STUDENT ID BOOK-LET.
THIS PERSON WORKS HERE, DON'T THEY?
Ministry of Health, Labor and Welfare
Department of Population Management,Yukari Division
Third Branch
Personal Advisor
Sou Kikugawa
Ministry of Health, Labor, and Welfare
Department of Population Management,Yukari Divison
Third Branch
Personal Advisor
Sou Kikugawa
...YES, THAT'S RIGHT.
I THINK I'D LIKE TO HEAR THE FULL STORY, HERE...
WHY WOULD MY SON, WHO HAS NOT YET RECEIVED HIS NOTICE...
HAVE THE BUSINESS CARD OF A MINISTRY EMPLOYEE?

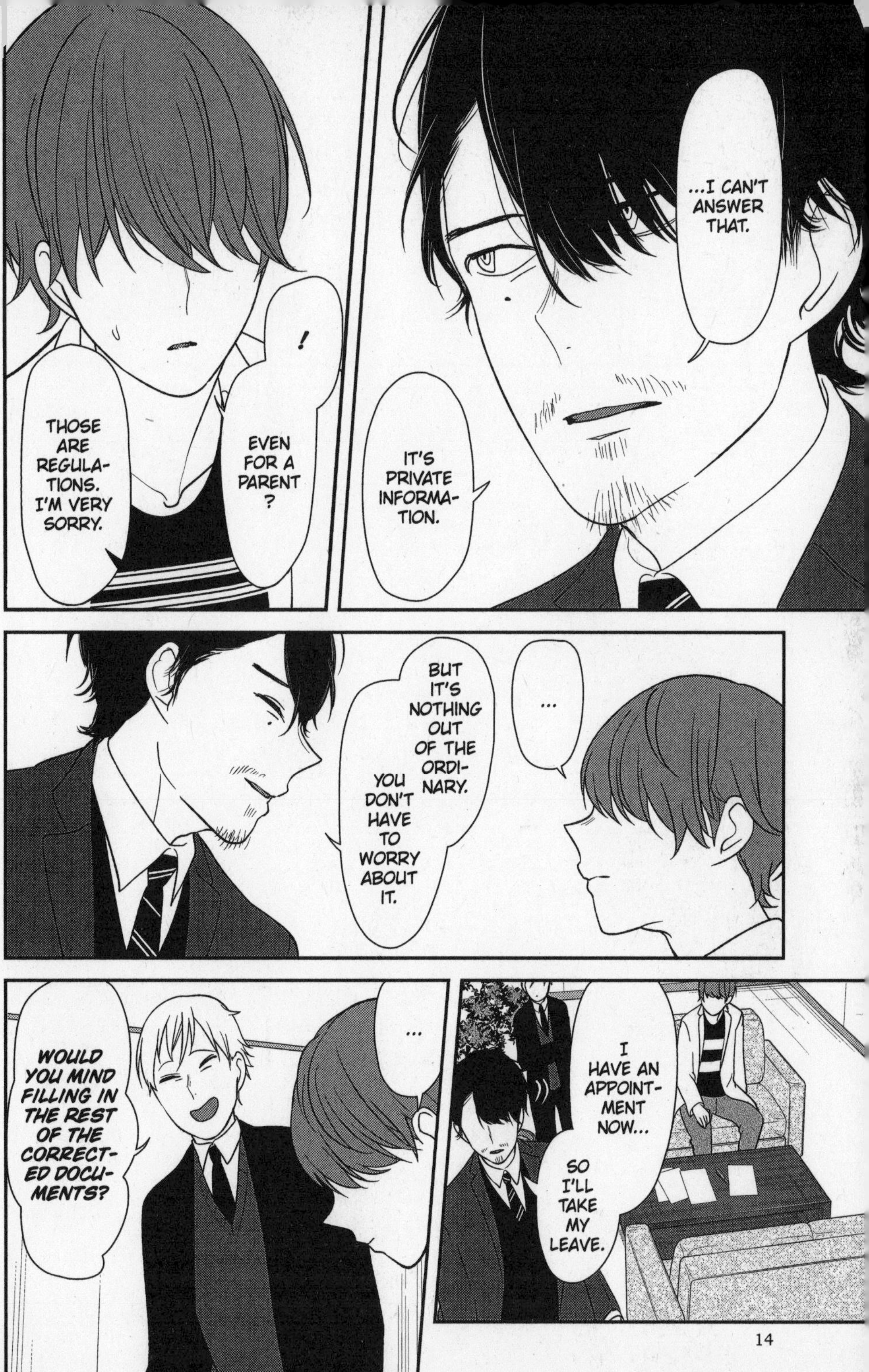
...I CAN'T ANSWER THAT.
IT'S PRIVATE INFORMATION.
!
EVEN FOR A PARENT?
THOSE ARE REGULATIONS. I'M VERY SORRY.
...
BUT IT'S NOTHING OUT OF THE ORDINARY.
YOU DON'T HAVE TO WORRY ABOUT IT.
I HAVE AN APPOINTMENT NOW...
SO I'LL TAKE MY LEAVE.
...
WOULD YOU MIND FILLING IN THE REST OF THE CORRECTED DOCUMENTS?

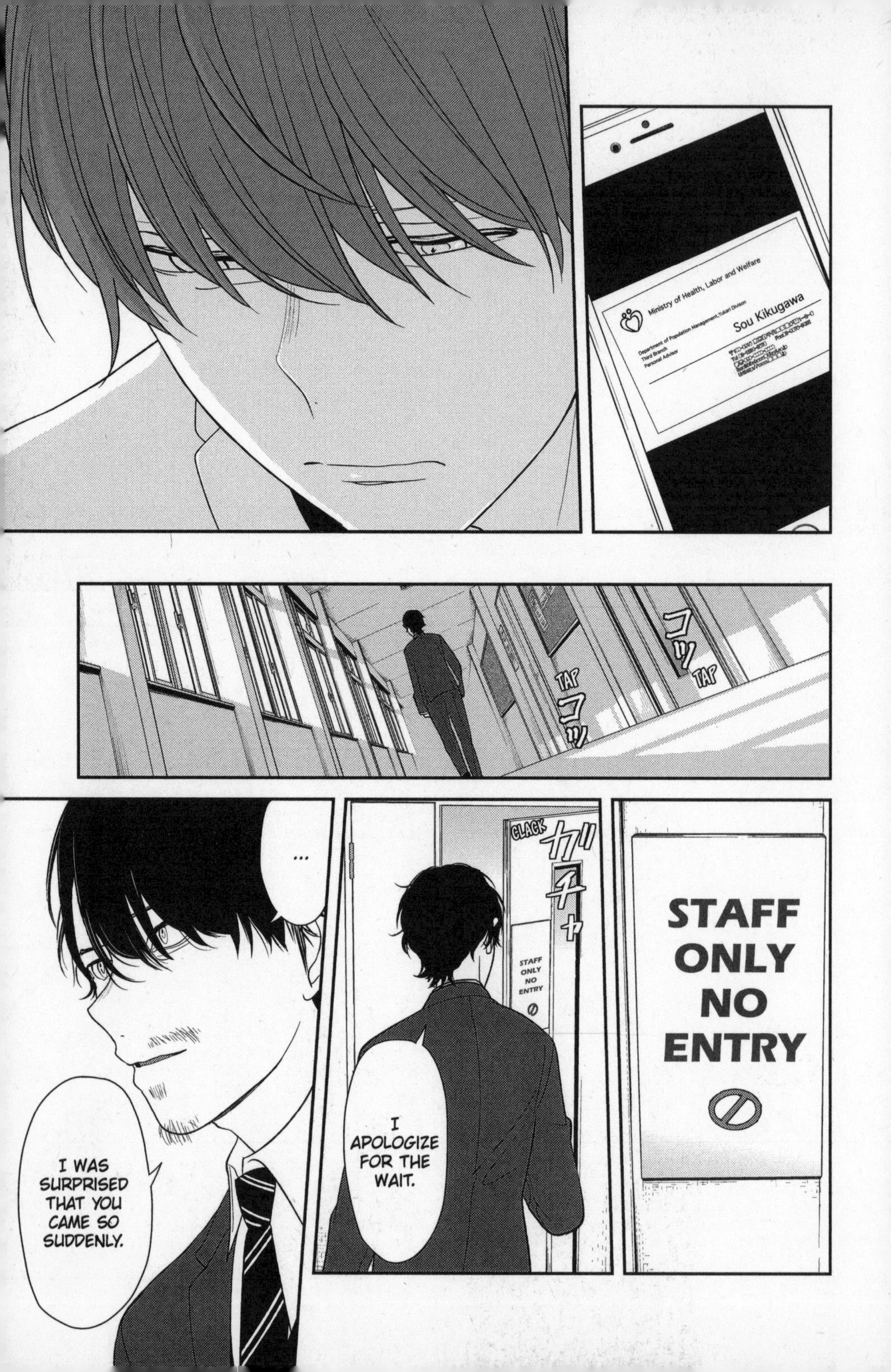
Ministry of Health, Labor and Welfare
Sou Kikugawa
Department of Population Management, Yukari Division
Third Branch
Personal Advisor
コツ TAP
コツ TAP
STAFF ONLY NO ENTRY
GLACK ガチャ
STAFF ONLY NO ENTRY
I APOLOGIZE FOR THE WAIT.
...
I WAS SURPRISED THAT YOU CAME SO SUDDENLY.

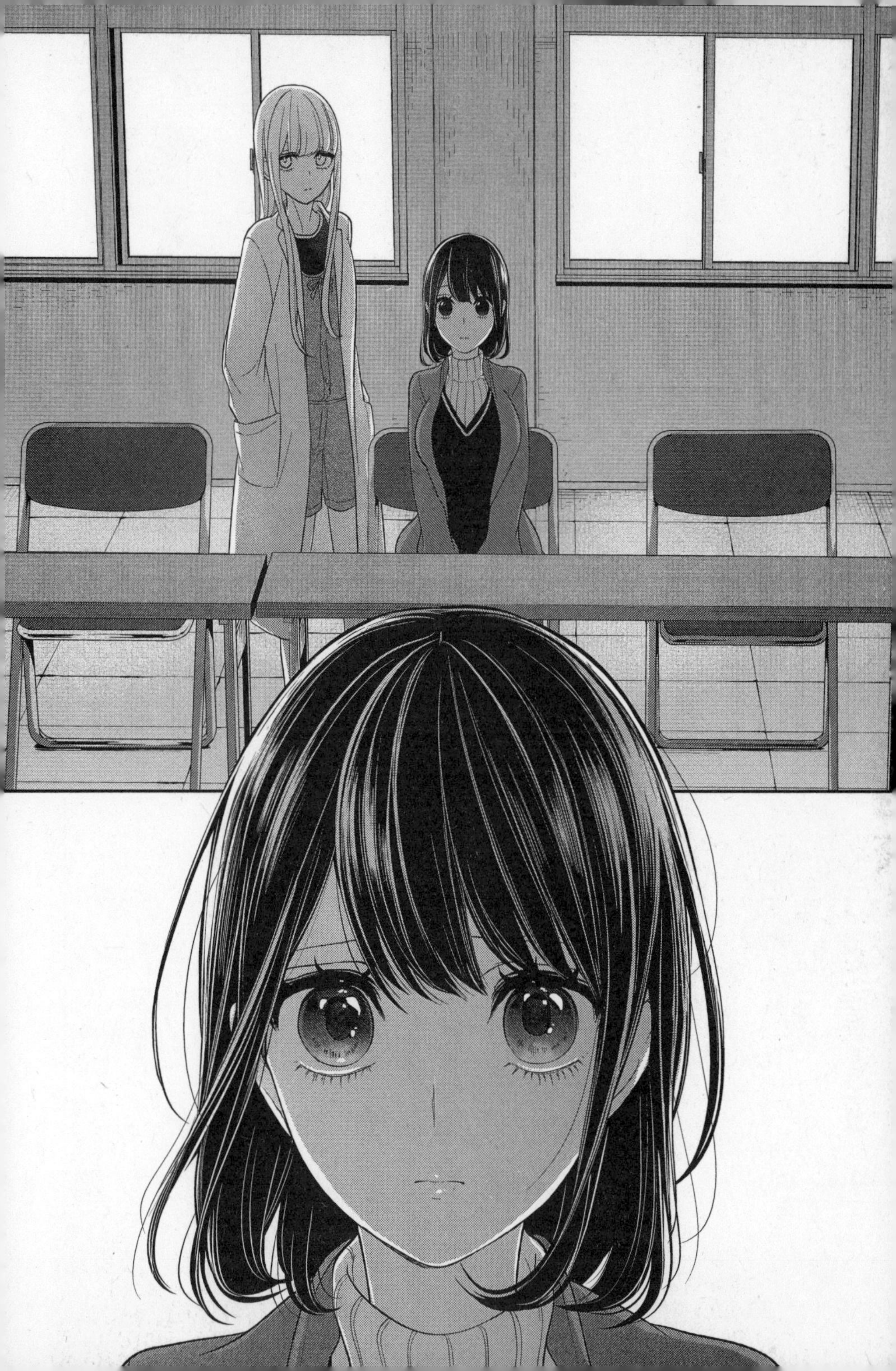

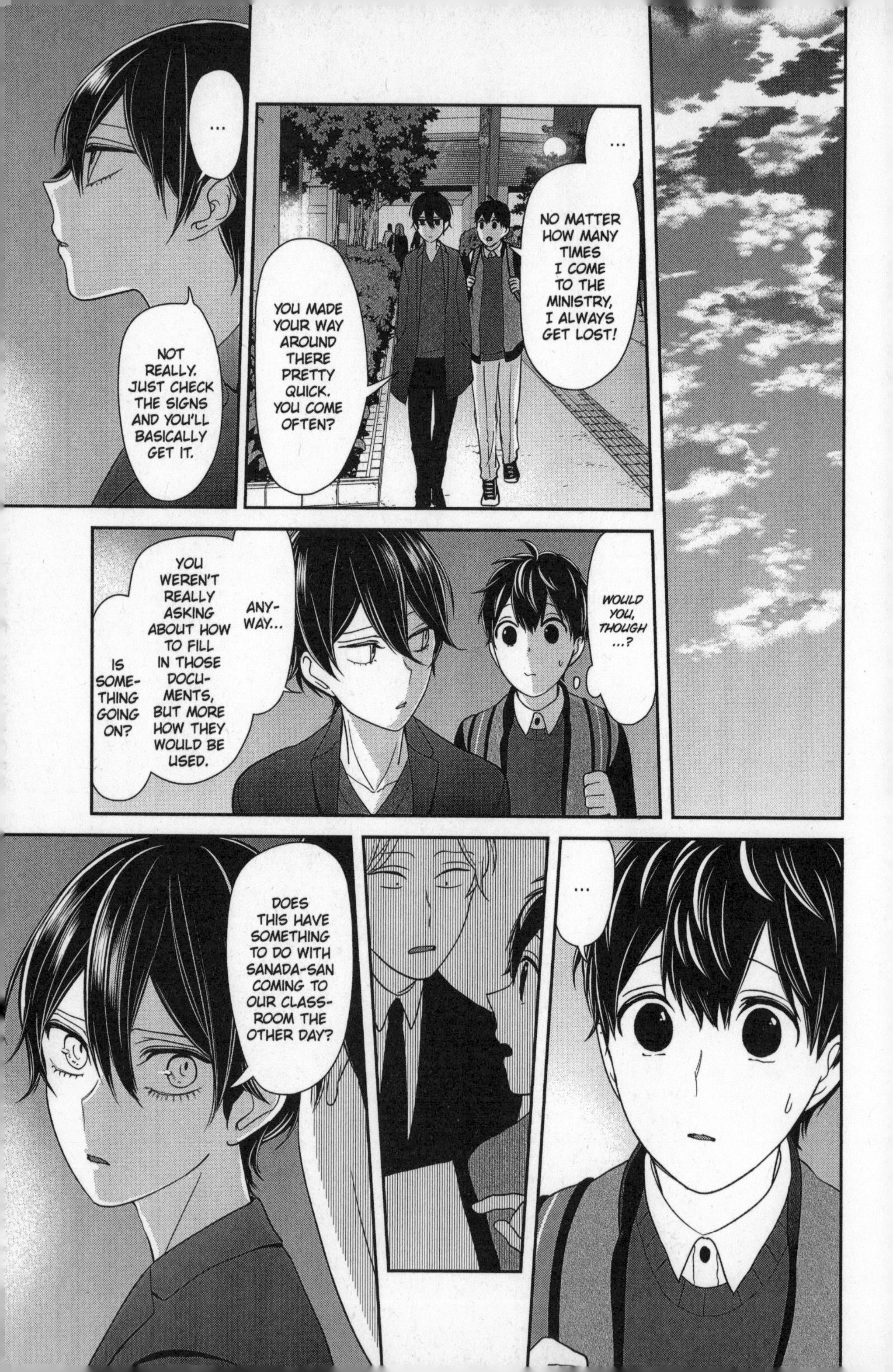
...
NO MATTER HOW MANY TIMES I COME TO THE MINISTRY, I ALWAYS GET LOST!
YOU MADE YOUR WAY AROUND THERE PRETTY QUICK. YOU COME OFTEN?
...
NOT REALLY. JUST CHECK THE SIGNS AND YOU'LL BASICALLY GET IT.
WOULD YOU, THOUGH...?
ANY-WAY...
YOU WEREN'T REALLY ASKING ABOUT HOW TO FILL IN THOSE DOCU-MENTS, BUT MORE HOW THEY WOULD BE USED.
IS SOME-THING GOING ON?
...
DOES THIS HAVE SOMETHING TO DO WITH SANADA-SAN COMING TO OUR CLASS-ROOM THE OTHER DAY?

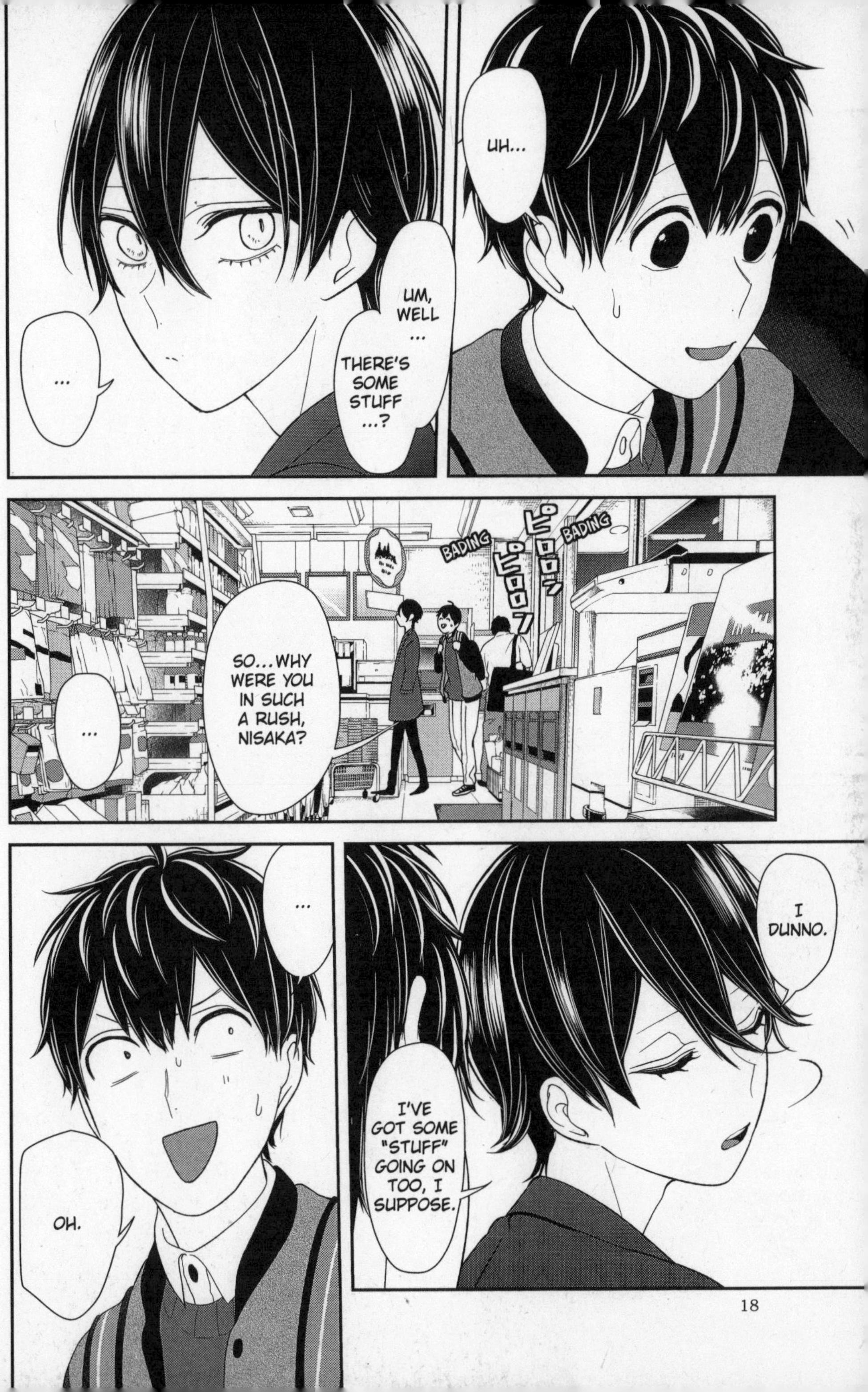
UH...
UM, WELL ... THERE'S SOME STUFF ...?
...
BADING
BADING
SO...WHY WERE YOU IN SUCH A RUSH, NISAKA?
...
I DUNNO.
I'VE GOT SOME "STUFF" GOING ON TOO, I SUPPOSE.
...
OH.

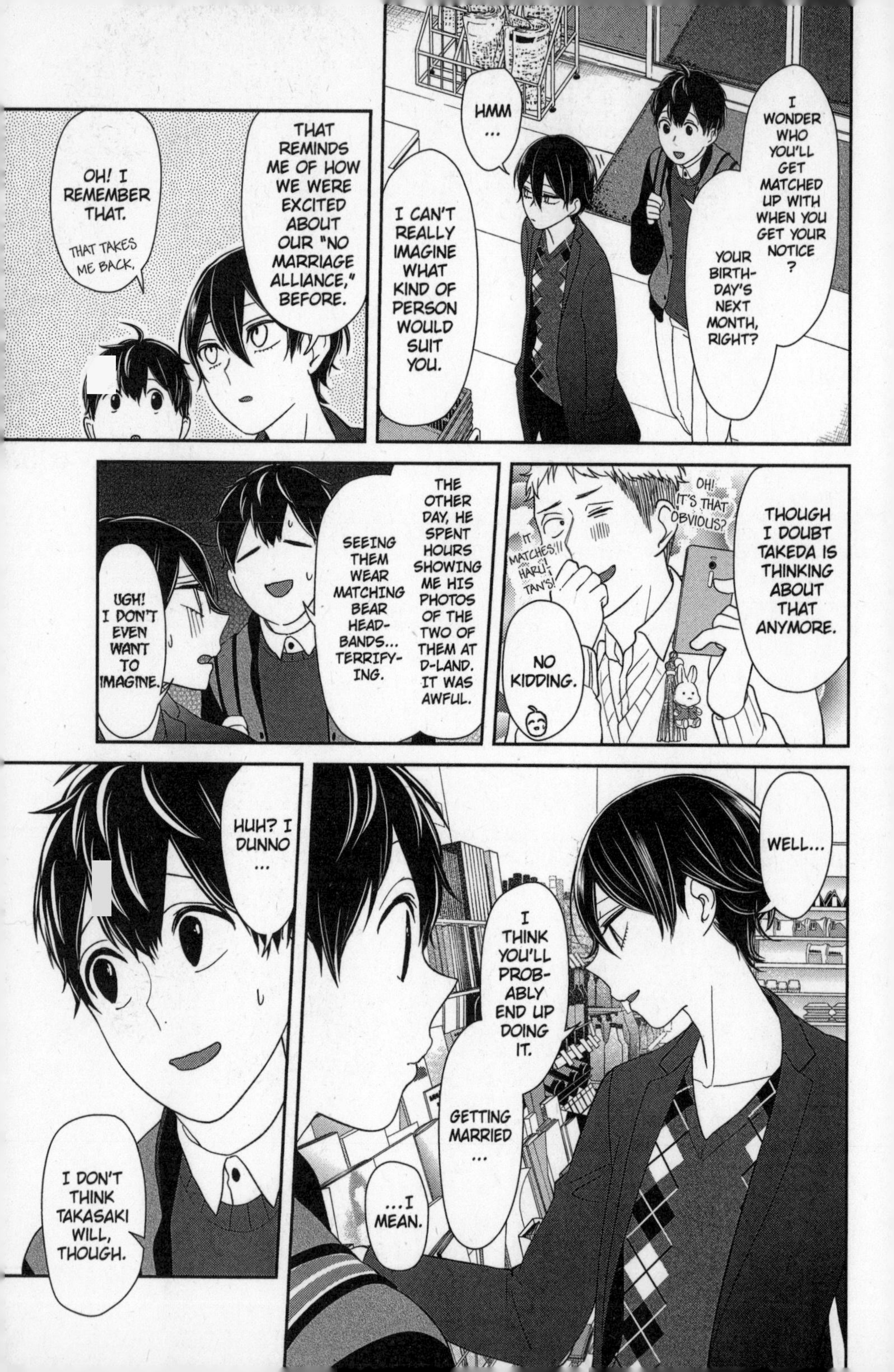
I WONDER WHO YOU'LL GET MATCHED UP WITH WHEN YOU GET YOUR NOTICE?
YOUR BIRTHDAY'S NEXT MONTH, RIGHT?
HMM...
I CAN'T REALLY IMAGINE WHAT KIND OF PERSON WOULD SUIT YOU.
THAT REMINDS ME OF HOW WE WERE EXCITED ABOUT OUR "NO MARRIAGE ALLIANCE," BEFORE.
OH! I REMEMBER THAT.
THAT TAKES ME BACK.
THOUGH I DOUBT TAKEDA IS THINKING ABOUT THAT ANYMORE.
OH! IT'S THAT OBVIOUS?
IT MATCHES HARU-TAN'S!
NO KIDDING.
THE OTHER DAY, HE SPENT HOURS SHOWING ME HIS PHOTOS OF THE TWO OF THEM AT D-LAND. IT WAS AWFUL.
SEEING THEM WEAR MATCHING BEAR HEADBANDS... TERRIFYING.
UGH! I DON'T EVEN WANT TO IMAGINE.
WELL...
I THINK YOU'LL PROBABLY END UP DOING IT.
GETTING MARRIED...
...I MEAN.
HUH? I DUNNO...
I DON'T THINK TAKASAKI WILL, THOUGH.

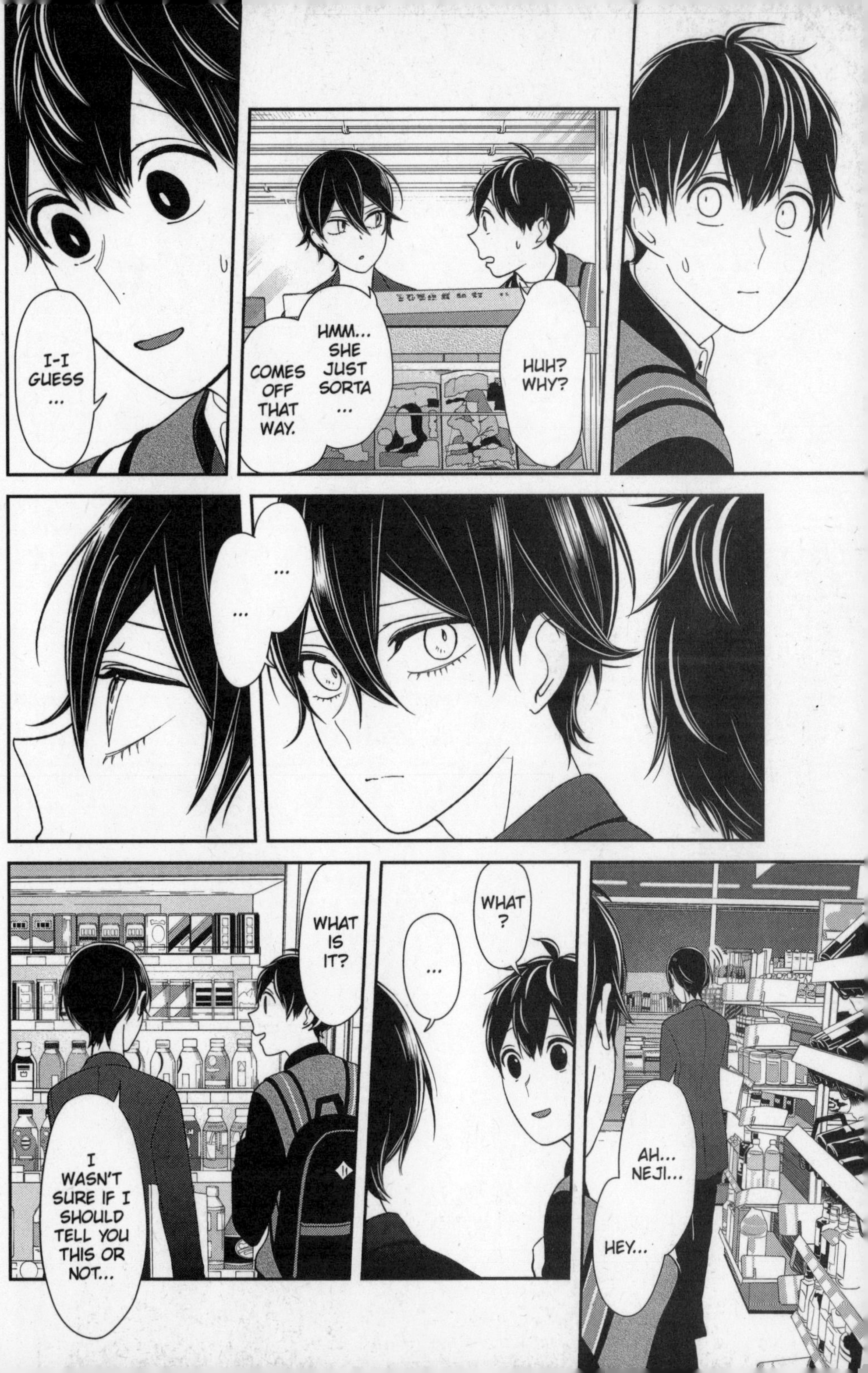
HUH? WHY?
HMM... SHE JUST SORTA ... COMES OFF THAT WAY.
I-I GUESS ...
...
...
AH... NEJI...
HEY...
WHAT ?
...
WHAT IS IT?
I WASN'T SURE IF I SHOULD TELL YOU THIS OR NOT...

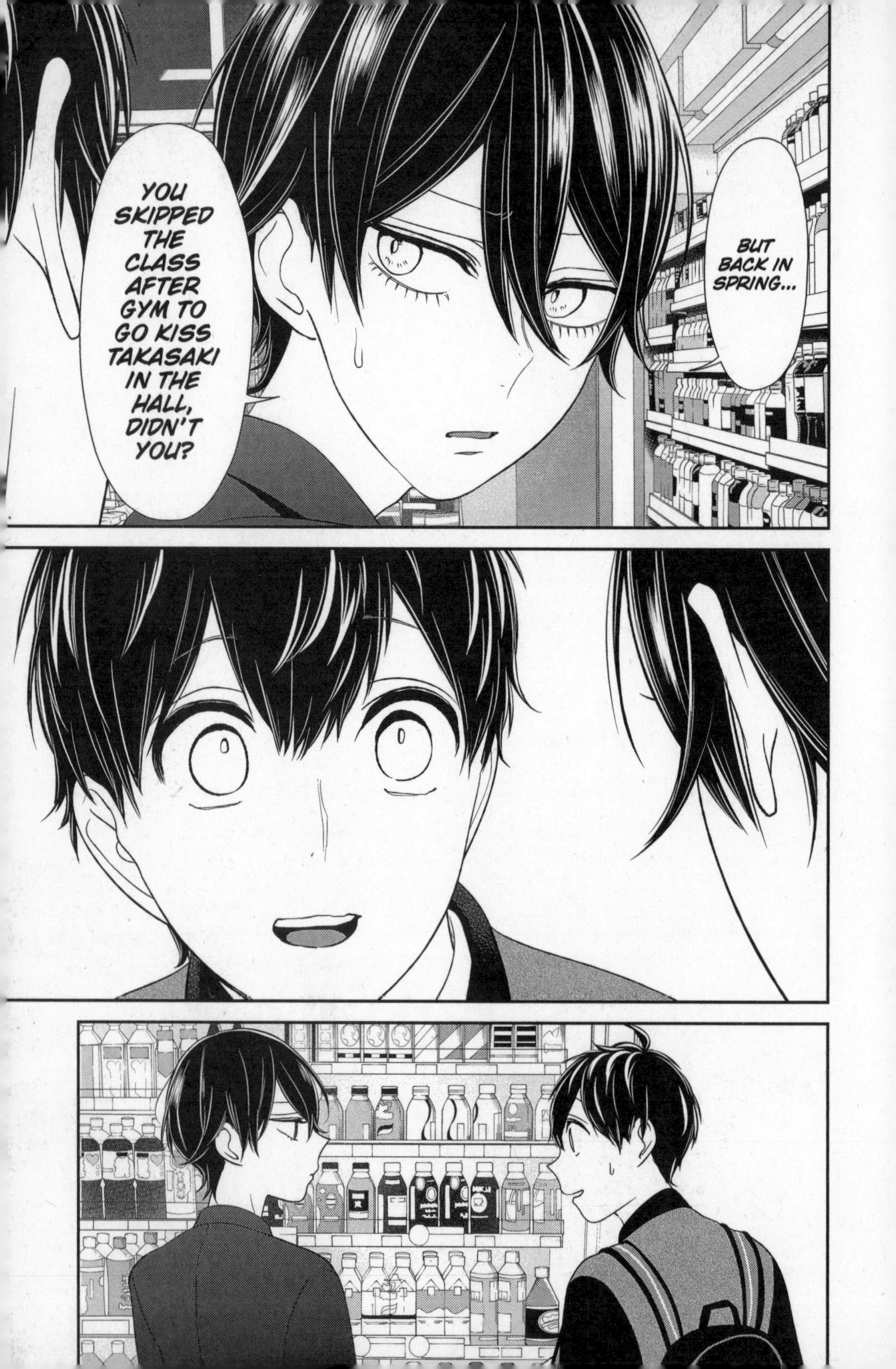
BUT BACK IN SPRING...
YOU SKIPPED THE CLASS AFTER GYM TO GO KISS TAKASAKI IN THE HALL, DIDN'T YOU?

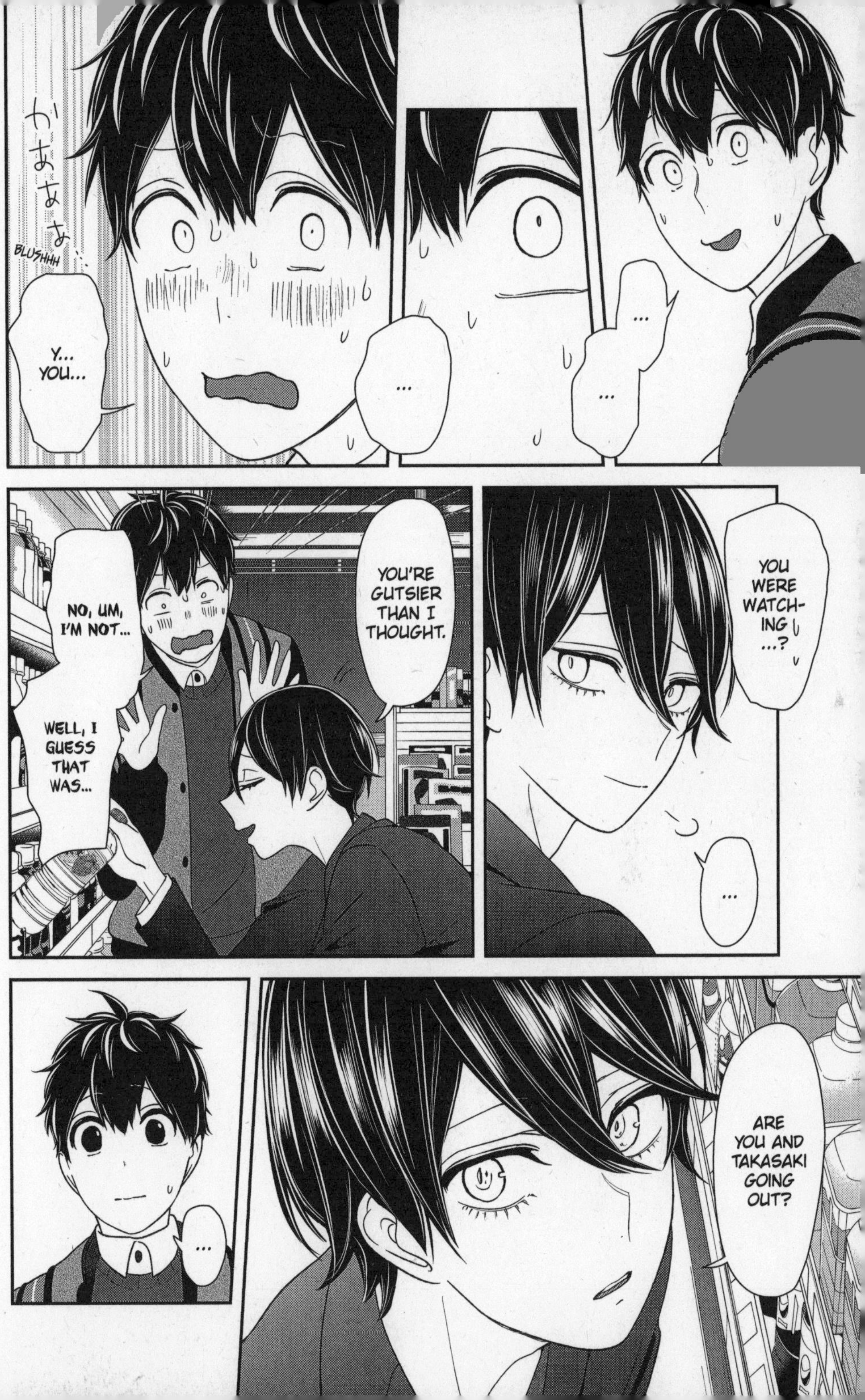
...
...
...
かあああ
BLUSHHH
Y... YOU...
YOU WERE WATCHING...?
...
YOU'RE GUTSIER THAN I THOUGHT.
NO, UM, I'M NOT...
WELL, I GUESS THAT WAS...
ARE YOU AND TAKASAKI GOING OUT?
...

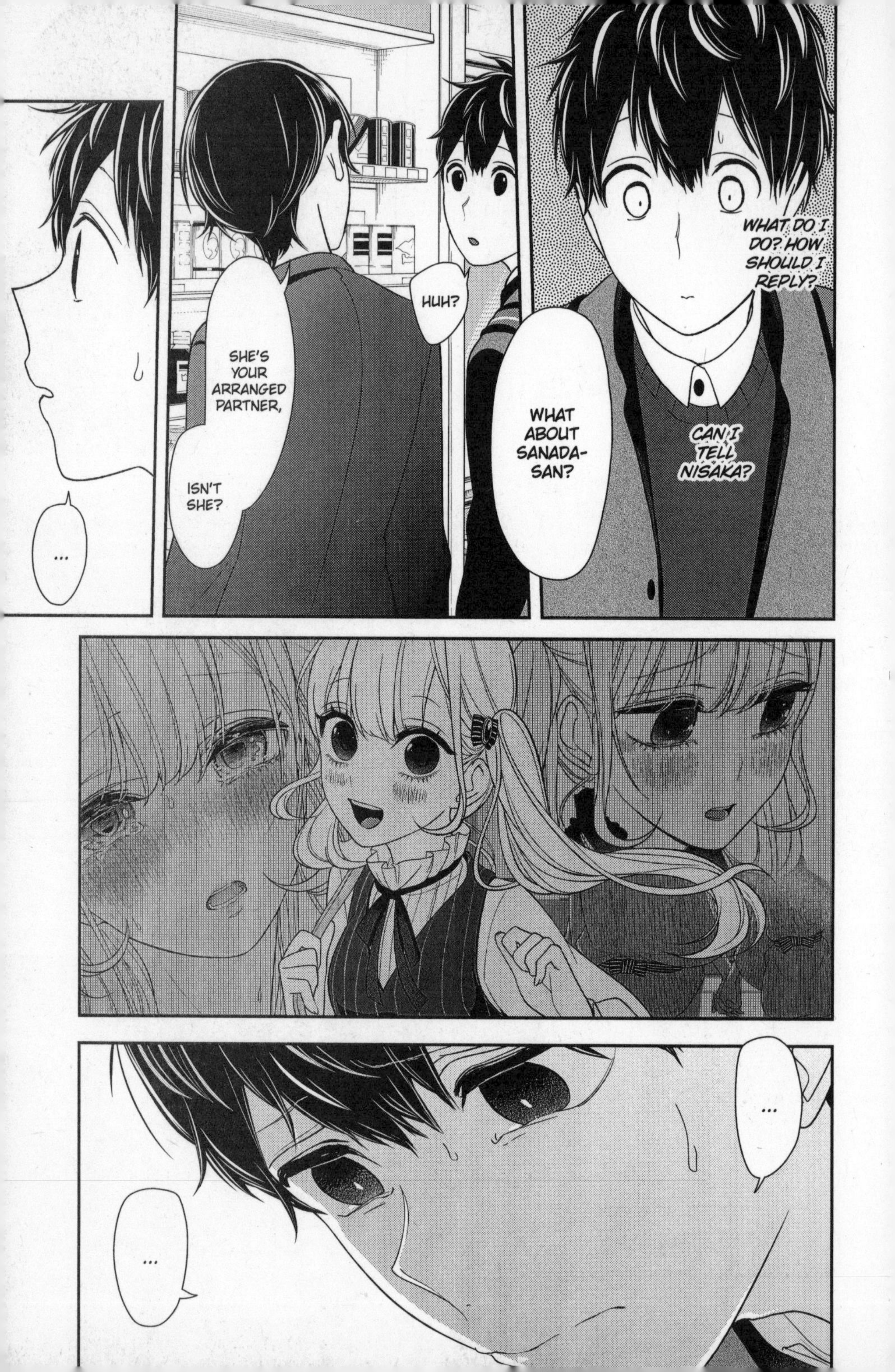
WHAT DO I DO? HOW SHOULD I REPLY?
CAN I TELL NISAKA?
WHAT ABOUT SANADA-SAN?
HUH?
SHE'S YOUR ARRANGED PARTNER,
ISN'T SHE?
...
...
...

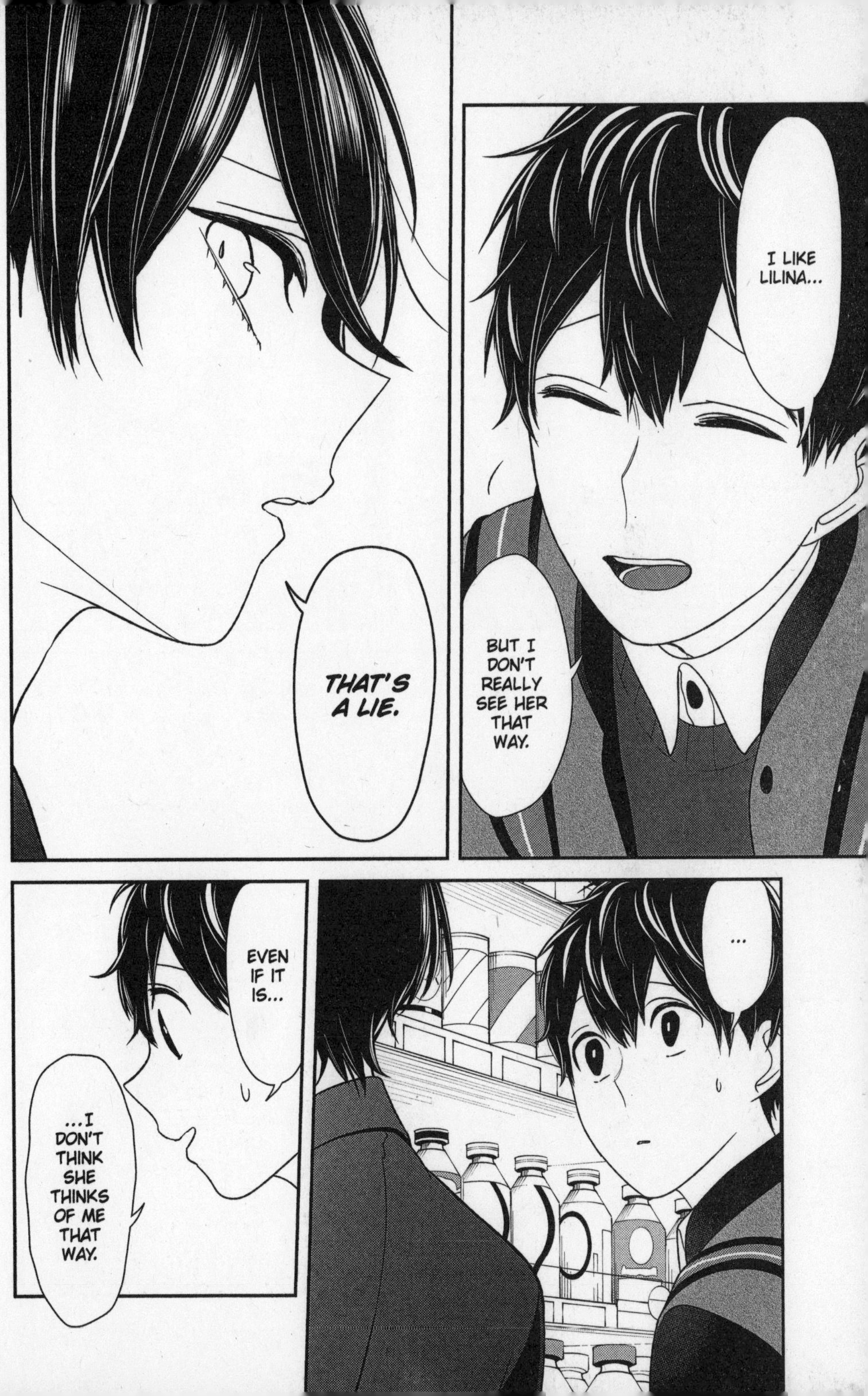
I LIKE LILINA...
BUT I DON'T REALLY SEE HER THAT WAY.
THAT'S A LIE.
...
EVEN IF IT IS...
...I DON'T THINK SHE THINKS OF ME THAT WAY.

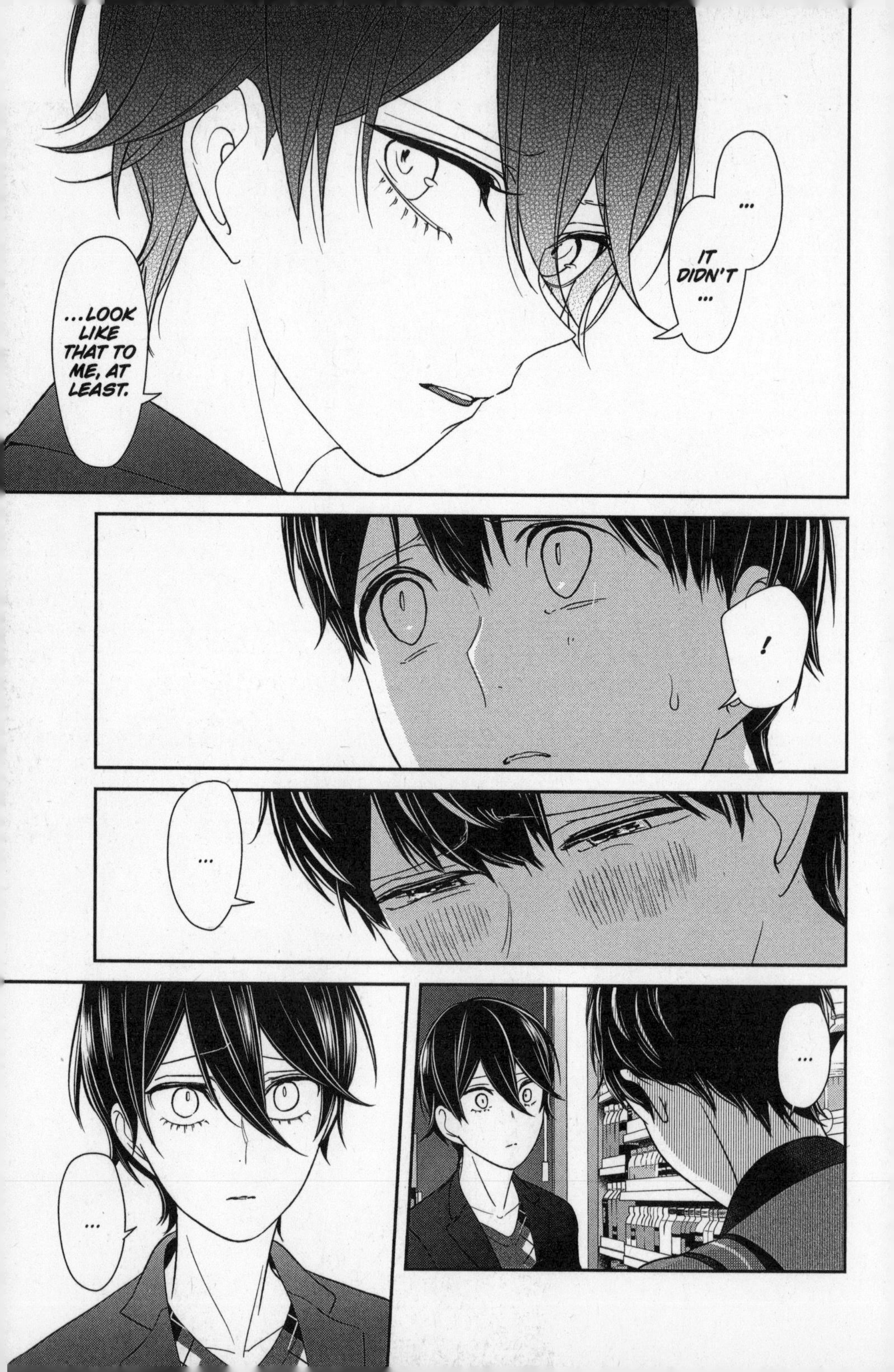
... IT DIDN'T ...
...LOOK LIKE THAT TO ME, AT LEAST.
!
...
...
...

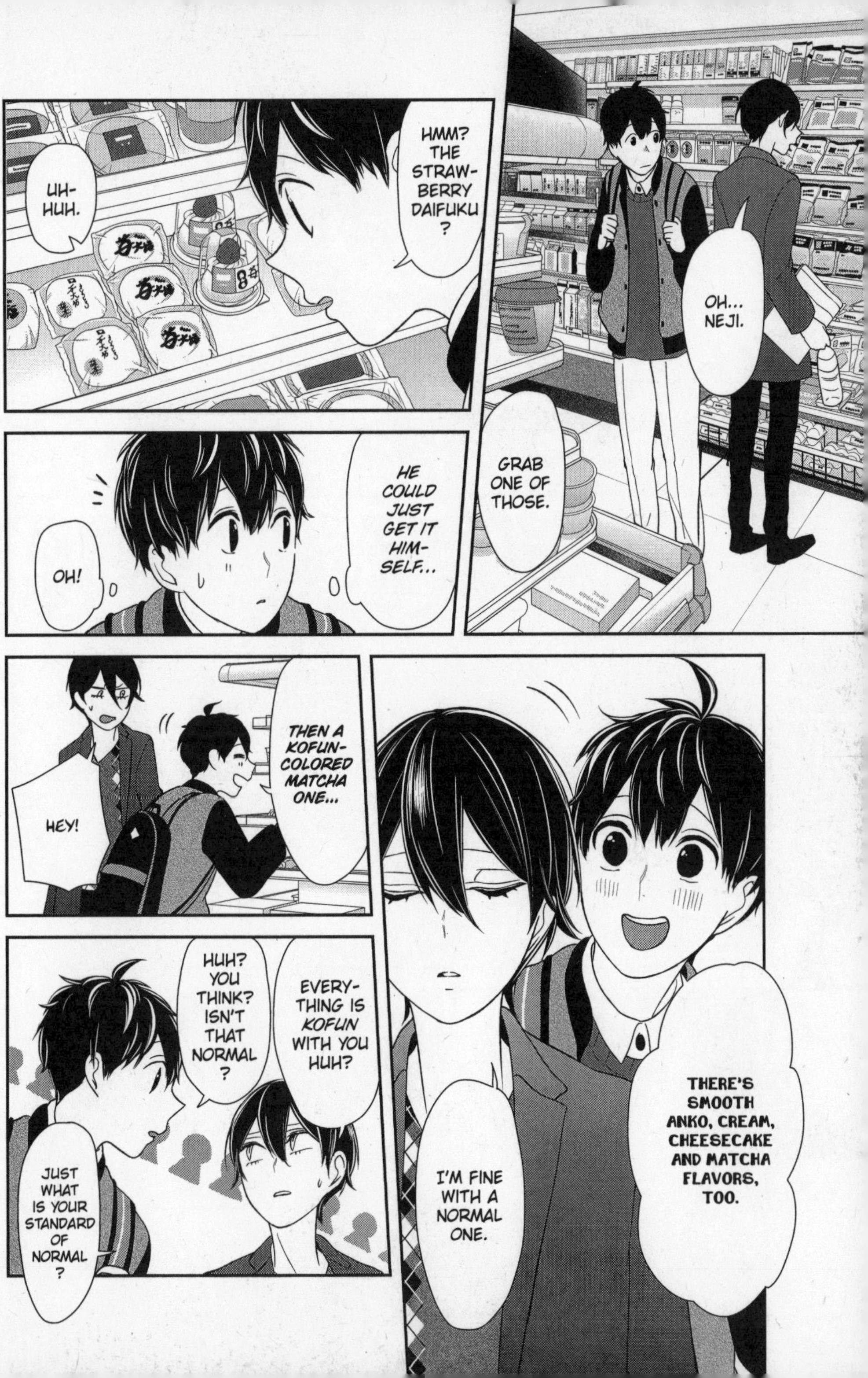
OH... NEJI.
GRAB ONE OF THOSE.
HMM? THE STRAWBERRY DAIFUKU?
UH-HUH.
HE COULD JUST GET IT HIMSELF...
OH!
THERE'S SMOOTH ANKO, CREAM, CHEESECAKE AND MATCHA FLAVORS, TOO.
I'M FINE WITH A NORMAL ONE.
THEN A KOFUN-COLORED MATCHA ONE...
HEY!
EVERYTHING IS KOFUN WITH YOU HUH?
HUH? YOU THINK? ISN'T THAT NORMAL?
JUST WHAT IS YOUR STANDARD OF NORMAL?

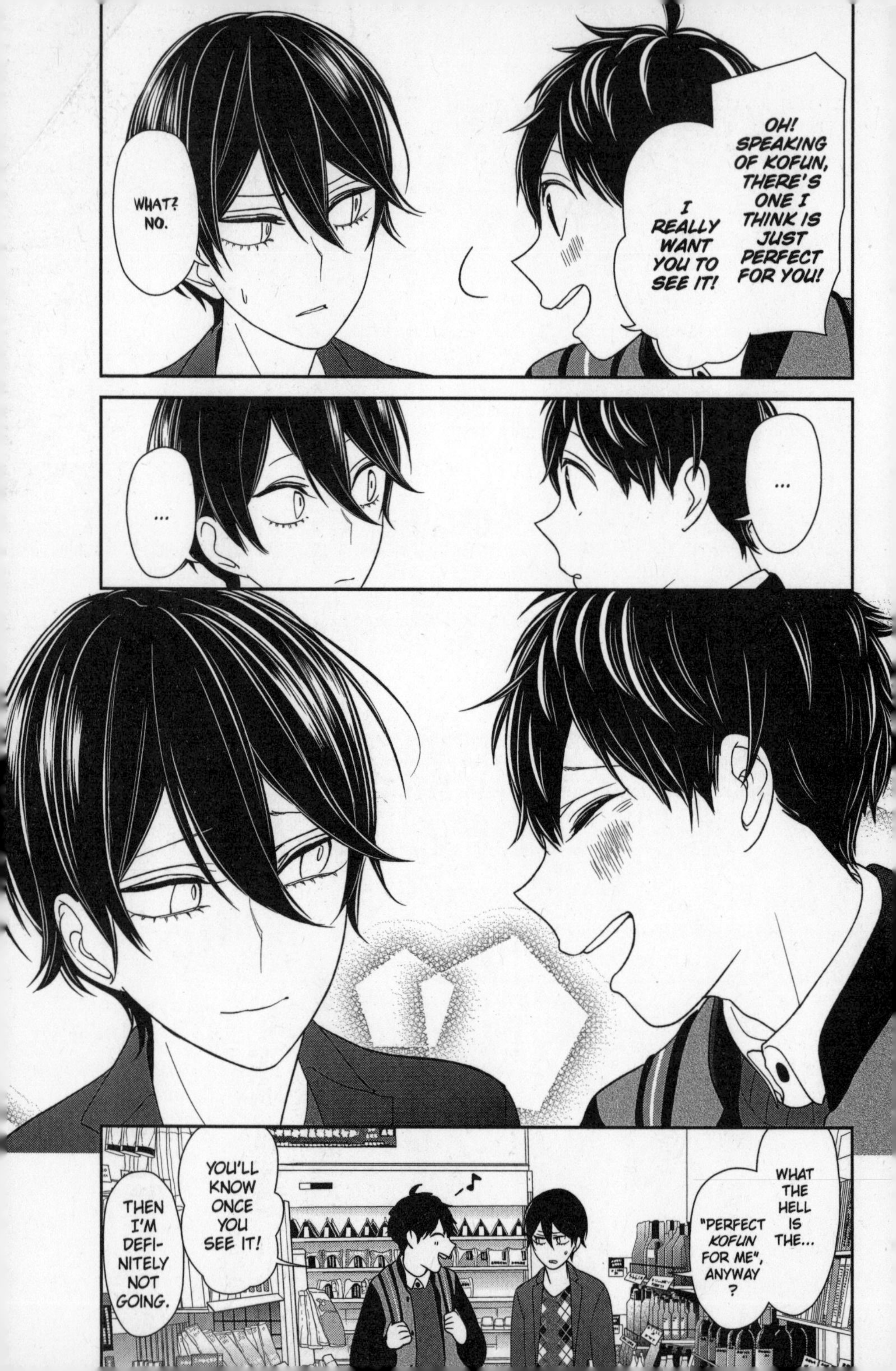
OH! SPEAKING OF KOFUN, THERE'S ONE I THINK IS JUST PERFECT FOR YOU!
I REALLY WANT YOU TO SEE IT!
WHAT? NO.
...
...
WHAT THE HELL IS THE... "PERFECT KOFUN FOR ME", ANYWAY?
YOU'LL KNOW ONCE YOU SEE IT!
THEN I'M DEFI-NITELY NOT GOING.

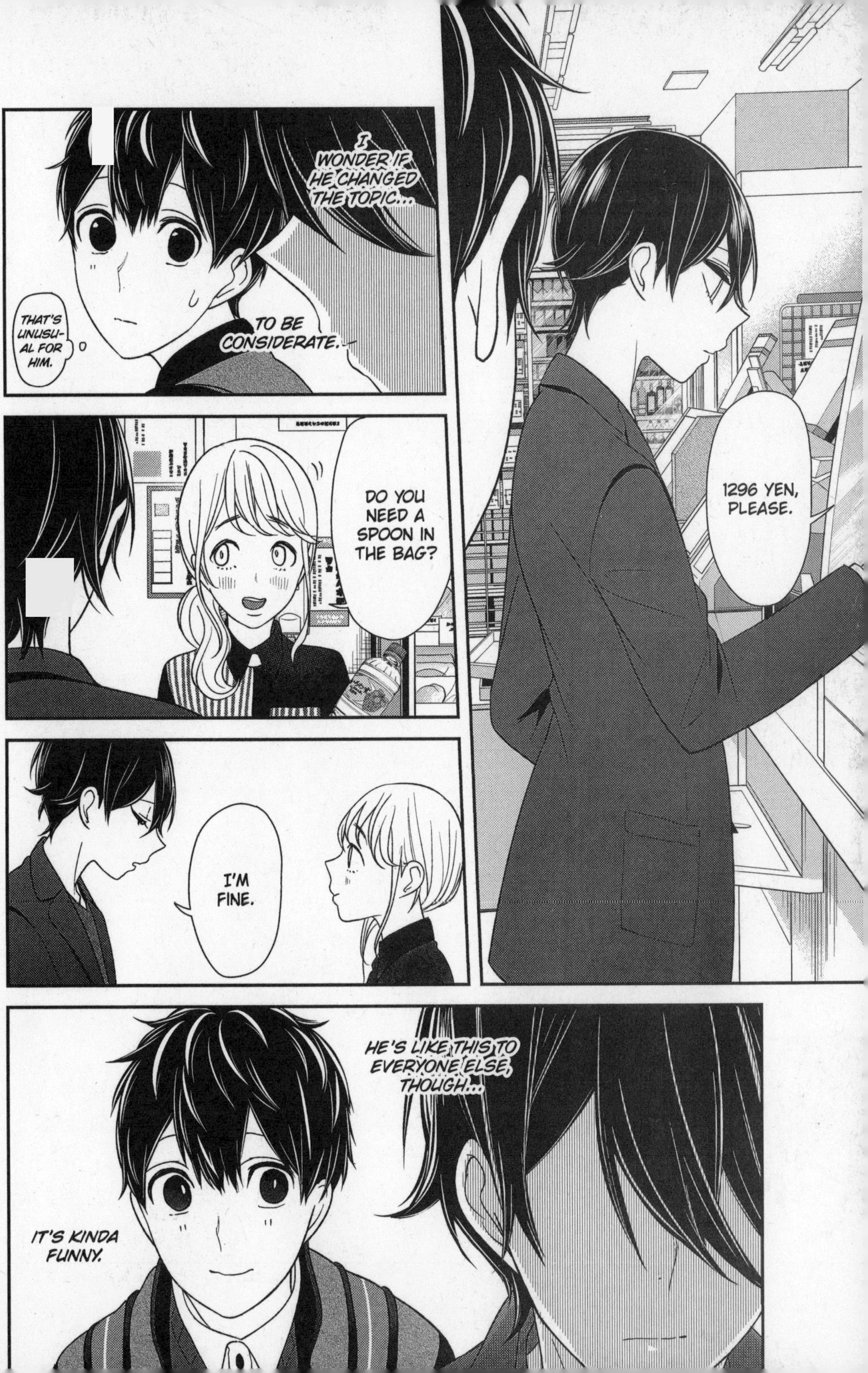
1296 YEN, PLEASE.
I WONDER IF HE CHANGED THE TOPIC...
TO BE CONSIDERATE...
THAT'S UNUSU-AL FOR HIM.
DO YOU NEED A SPOON IN THE BAG?
I'M FINE.
HE'S LIKE THIS TO EVERYONE ELSE, THOUGH...
IT'S KINDA FUNNY.

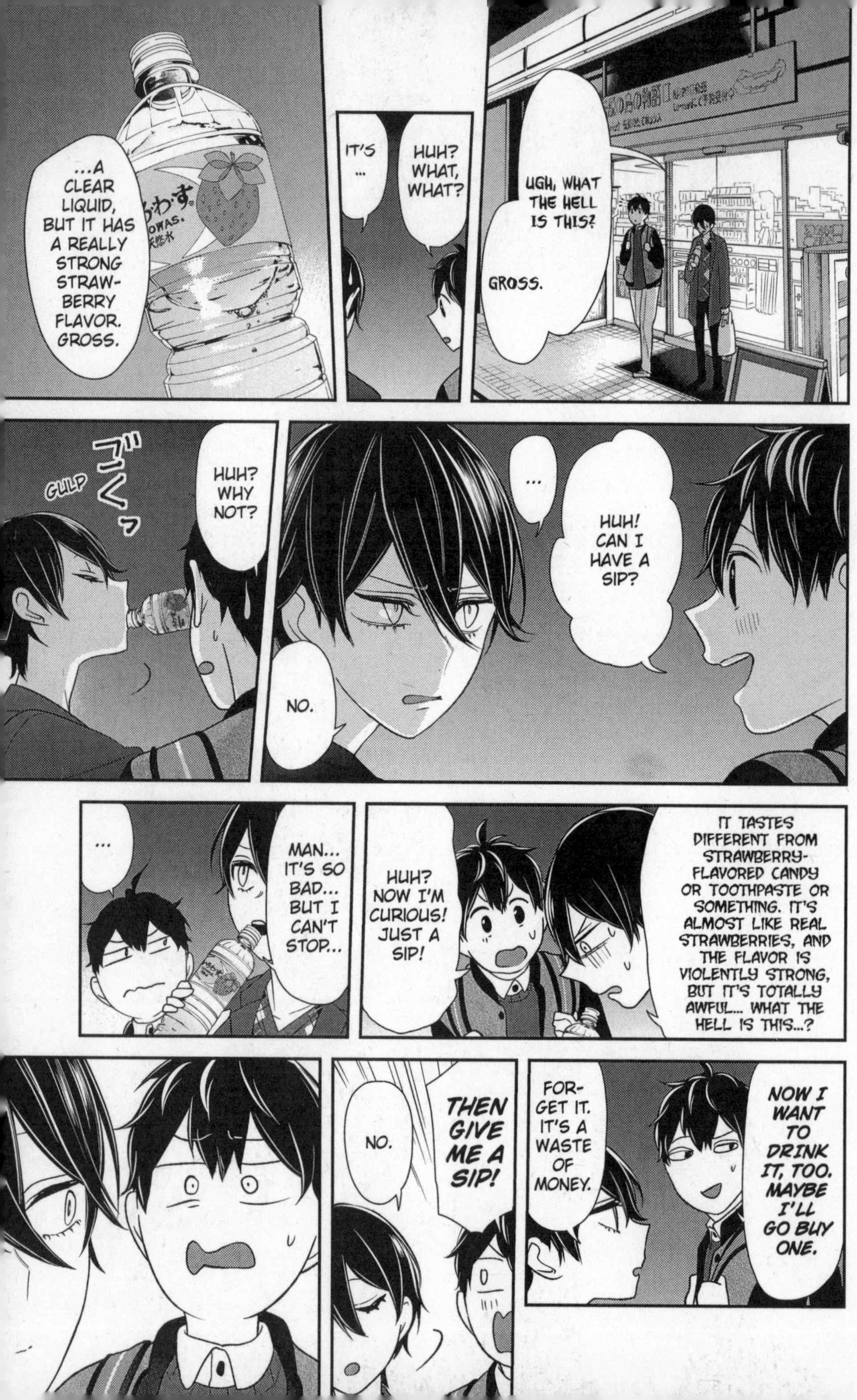
UGH, WHAT THE HELL IS THIS?
GROSS.
HUH? WHAT, WHAT?
IT'S ...
...A CLEAR LIQUID, BUT IT HAS A REALLY STRONG STRAW-BERRY FLAVOR. GROSS.
HUH! CAN I HAVE A SIP?
...
NO.
HUH? WHY NOT?
ゴくっ
GULP
IT TASTES DIFFERENT FROM STRAWBERRY-FLAVORED CANDY OR TOOTHPASTE OR SOMETHING. IT'S ALMOST LIKE REAL STRAWBERRIES, AND THE FLAVOR IS VIOLENTLY STRONG, BUT IT'S TOTALLY AWFUL... WHAT THE HELL IS THIS...?
HUH? NOW I'M CURIOUS! JUST A SIP!
MAN... IT'S SO BAD... BUT I CAN'T STOP...
...
NOW I WANT TO DRINK IT, TOO. MAYBE I'LL GO BUY ONE.
FOR-GET IT. IT'S A WASTE OF MONEY.
THEN GIVE ME A SIP!
NO.

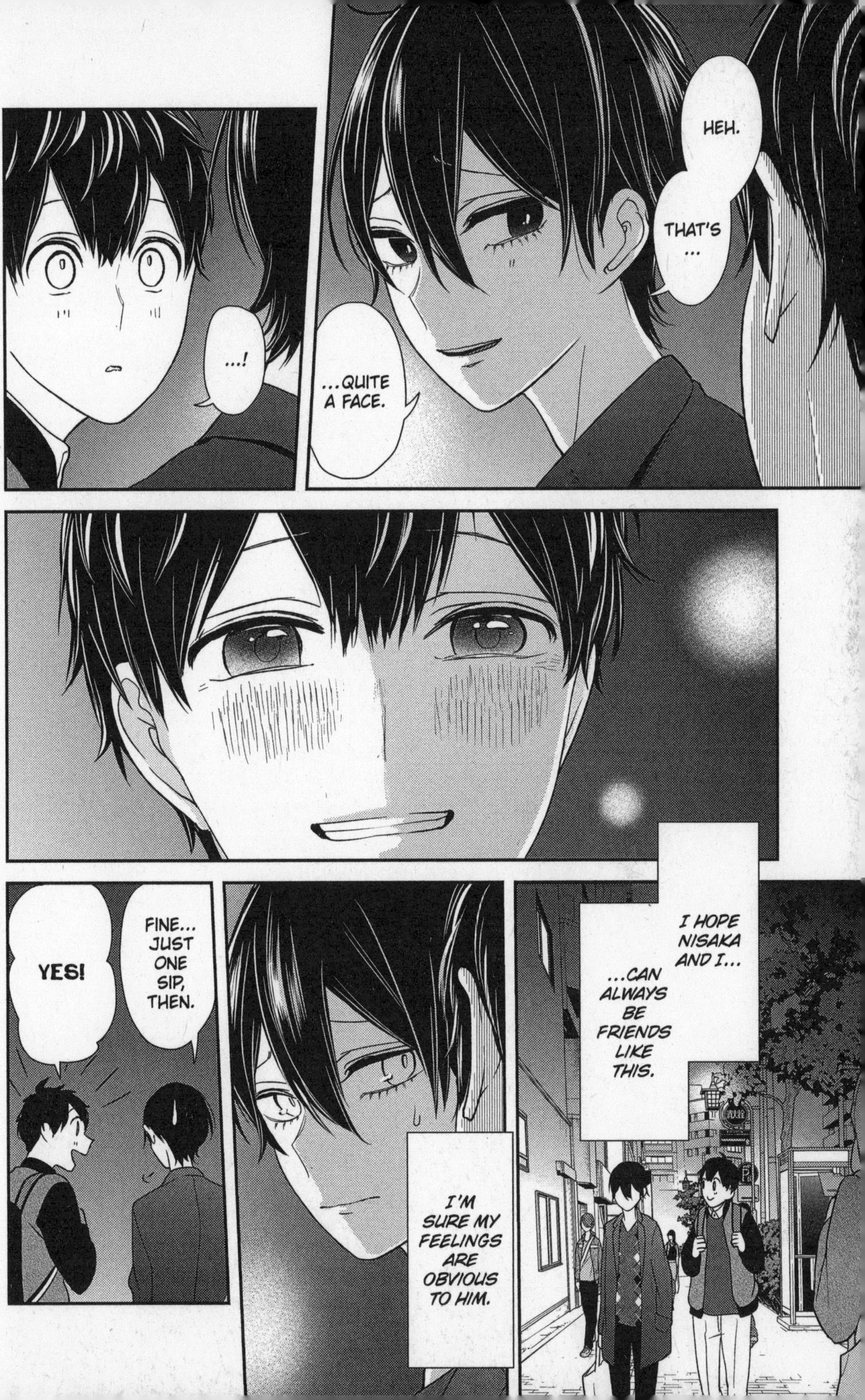
HEH.
THAT'S...
...QUITE A FACE.
...!
I HOPE NISAKA AND I...
...CAN ALWAYS BE FRIENDS LIKE THIS.
I'M SURE MY FEELINGS ARE OBVIOUS TO HIM.
FINE... JUST ONE SIP, THEN.
YES!

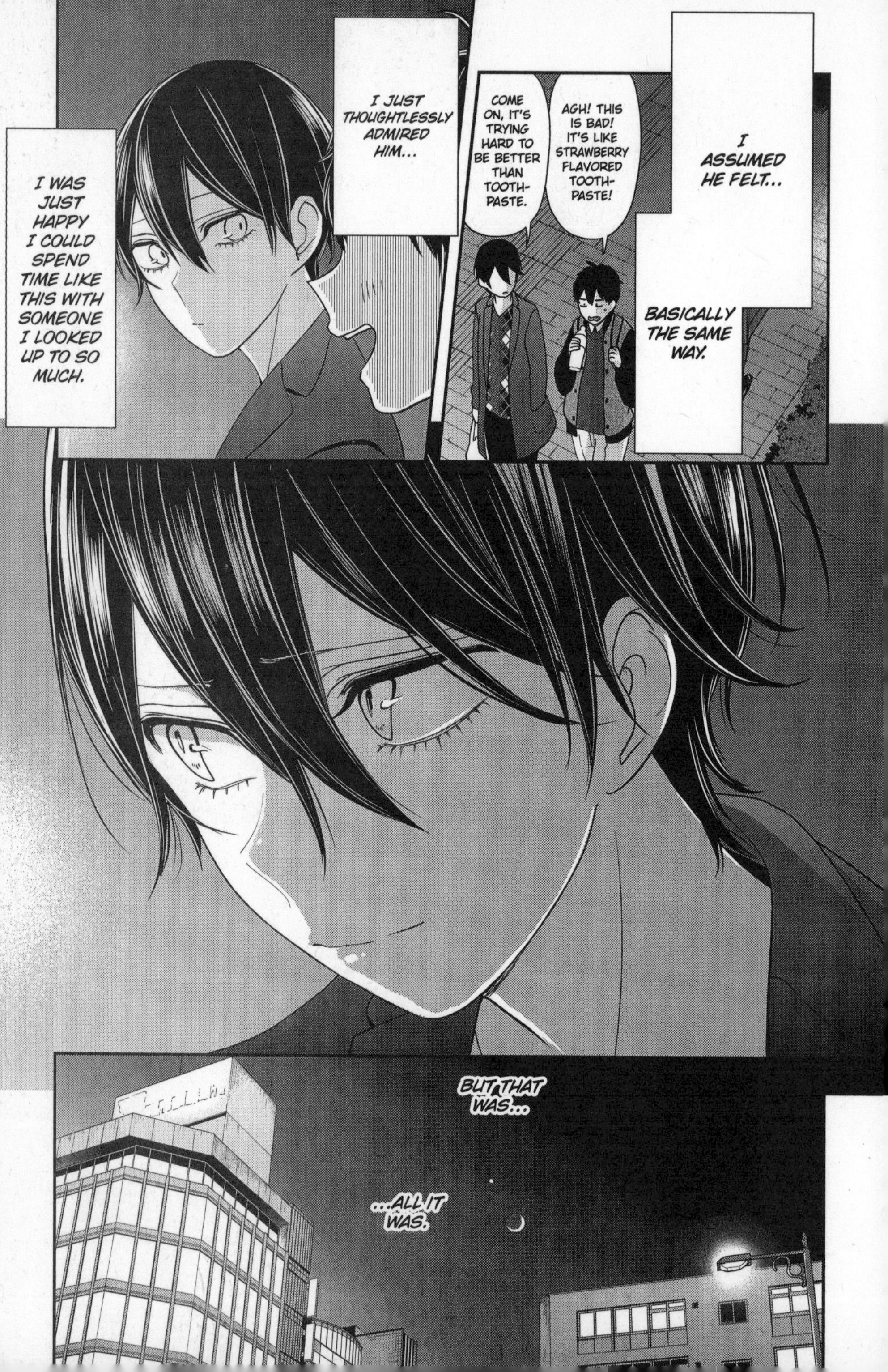
I ASSUMED HE FELT...
AGH! THIS IS BAD! IT'S LIKE STRAWBERRY FLAVORED TOOTH-PASTE!
COME ON, IT'S TRYING HARD TO BE BETTER THAN TOOTH-PASTE.
BASICALLY THE SAME WAY.
I JUST THOUGHTLESSLY ADMIRED HIM...
I WAS JUST HAPPY I COULD SPEND TIME LIKE THIS WITH SOMEONE I LOOKED UP TO SO MUCH.
BUT THAT WAS...
...ALL IT WAS.

Love & Lies

Chapter 28: A Lie Confessed

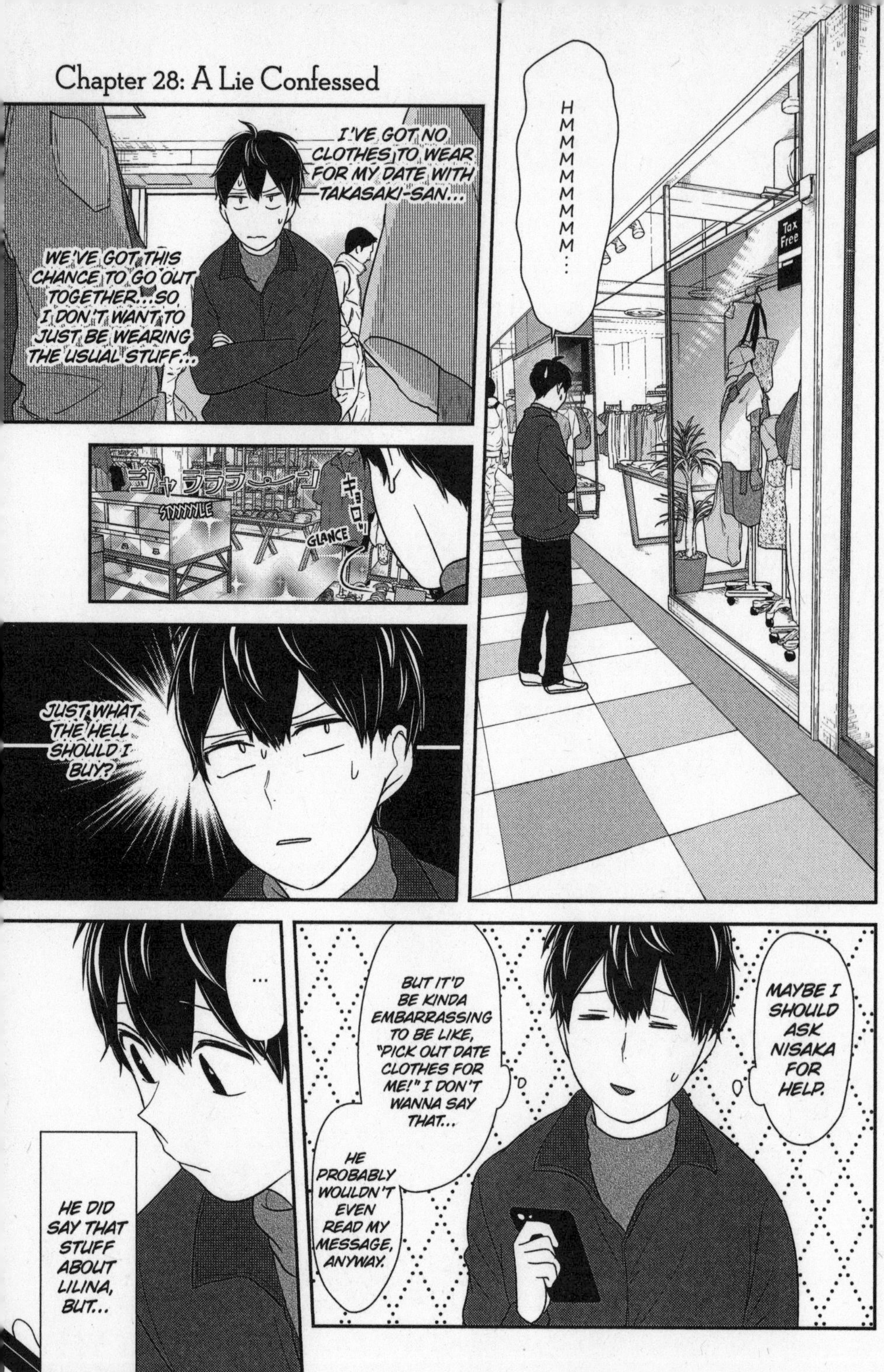
HMMMMMMMM...
I'VE GOT NO CLOTHES TO WEAR FOR MY DATE WITH TAKASAKI-SAN...
WE'VE GOT THIS CHANCE TO GO OUT TOGETHER... SO, I DON'T WANT TO JUST BE WEARING THE USUAL STUFF...
キョロッ
GLANCE
シャラララ〜ン
STYYYYLE
JUST WHAT THE HELL SHOULD I BUY?
MAYBE I SHOULD ASK NISAKA FOR HELP.
BUT IT'D BE KINDA EMBARRASSING TO BE LIKE, "PICK OUT DATE CLOTHES FOR ME!" I DON'T WANNA SAY THAT...
HE PROBABLY WOULDN'T EVEN READ MY MESSAGE, ANYWAY.
...
HE DID SAY THAT STUFF ABOUT LILINA, BUT...

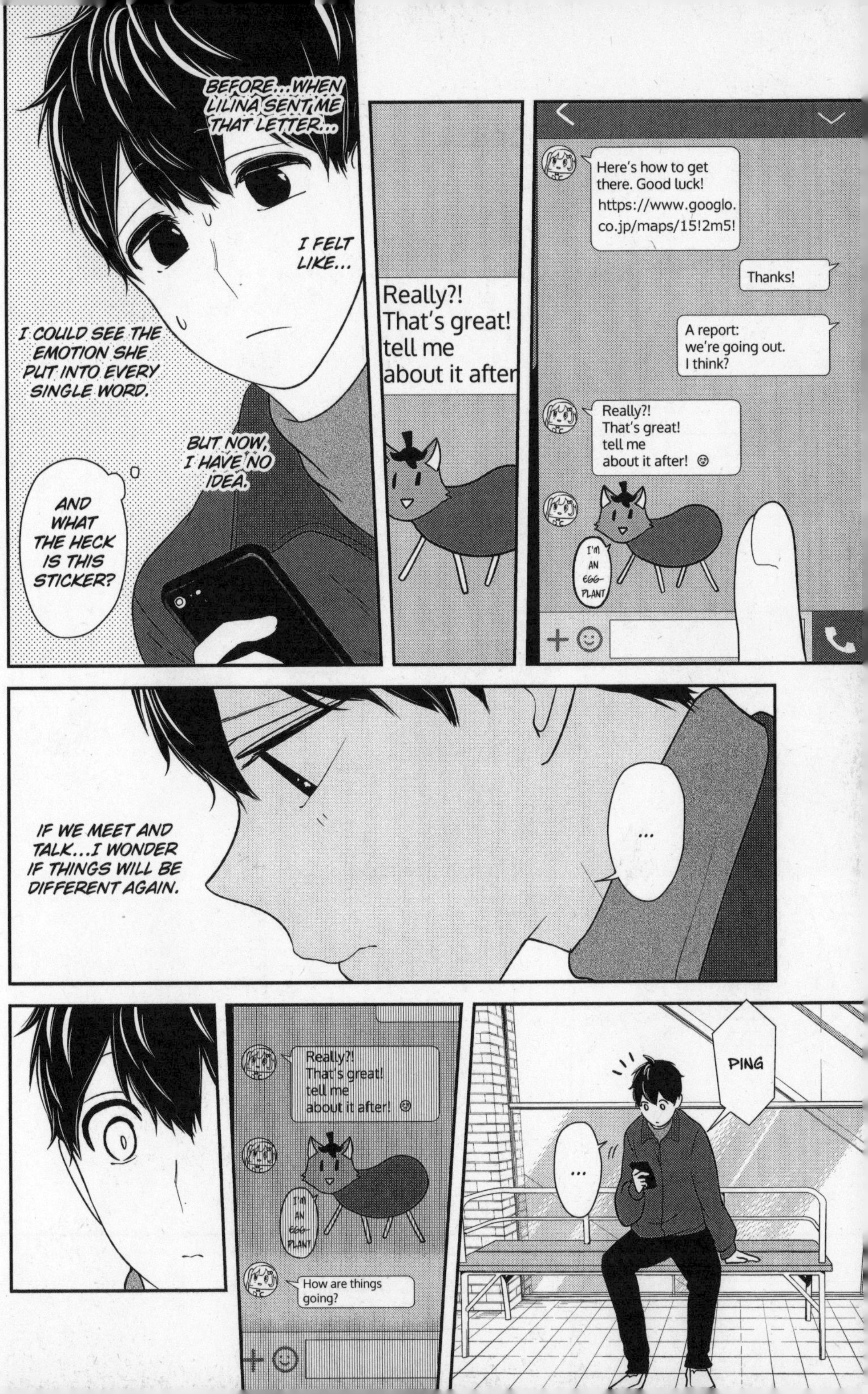
Here's how to get there. Good luck!
https://www.googlo.co.jp/maps/15!2m5!
Thanks!
A report: we're going out. I think?
Really?! That's great! tell me about it after!
I'M AN EGG-PLANT
Really?! That's great! tell me about it after
BEFORE...WHEN LILINA SENT ME THAT LETTER...
I FELT LIKE...
I COULD SEE THE EMOTION SHE PUT INTO EVERY SINGLE WORD.
BUT NOW, I HAVE NO IDEA.
AND WHAT THE HECK IS THIS STICKER?
...
IF WE MEET AND TALK...I WONDER IF THINGS WILL BE DIFFERENT AGAIN.
PING
...
Really?! That's great! tell me about it after!
I'M AN EGG-PLANT
How are things going?

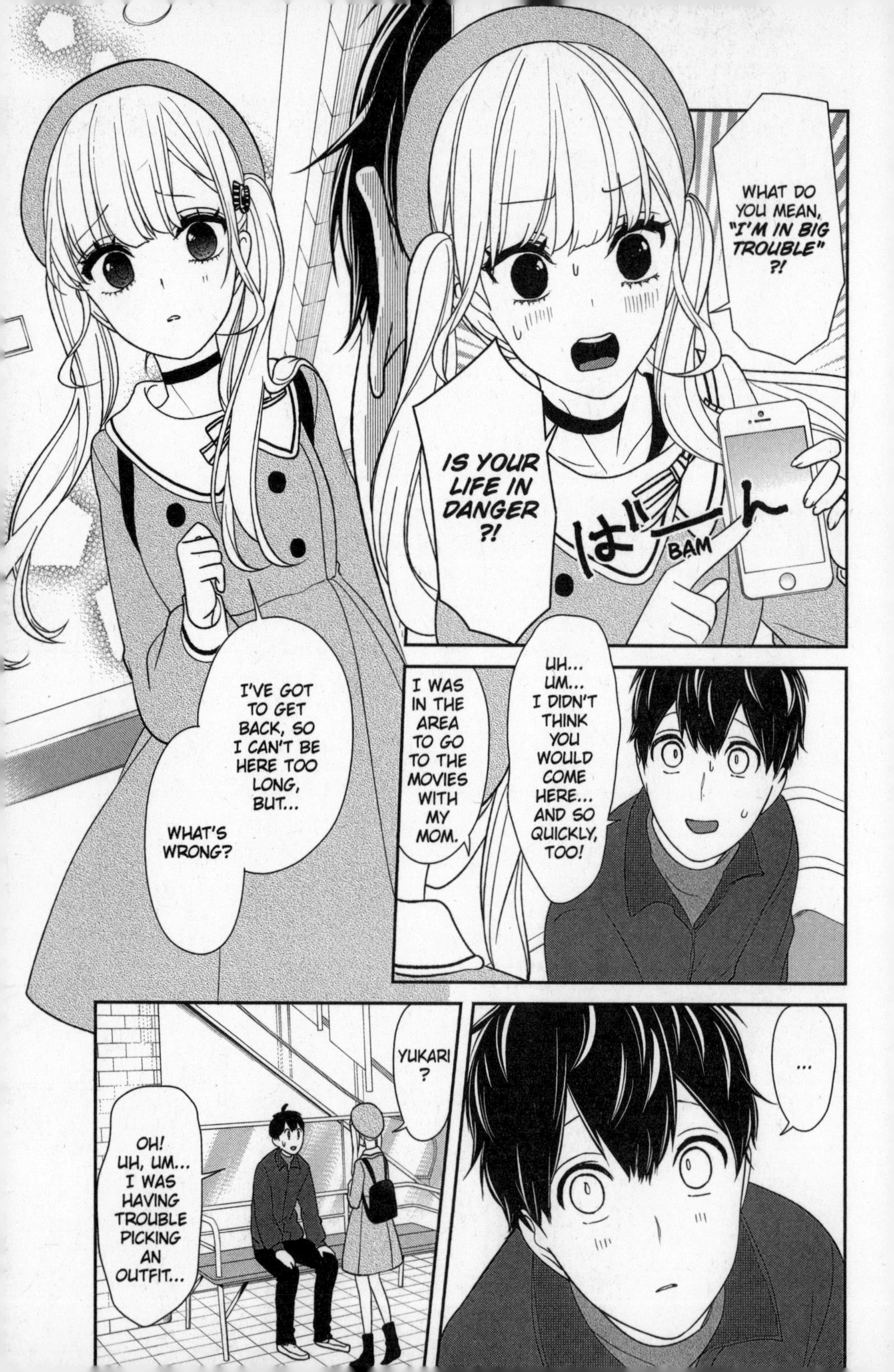
WHAT DO YOU MEAN, "I'M IN BIG TROUBLE"?!
IS YOUR LIFE IN DANGER?!
ばーん
BAM
UH... UM... I DIDN'T THINK YOU WOULD COME HERE... AND SO QUICKLY, TOO!
I WAS IN THE AREA TO GO TO THE MOVIES WITH MY MOM.
I'VE GOT TO GET BACK, SO I CAN'T BE HERE TOO LONG, BUT...
WHAT'S WRONG?
...
YUKARI?
OH! UH, UM... I WAS HAVING TROUBLE PICKING AN OUTFIT...

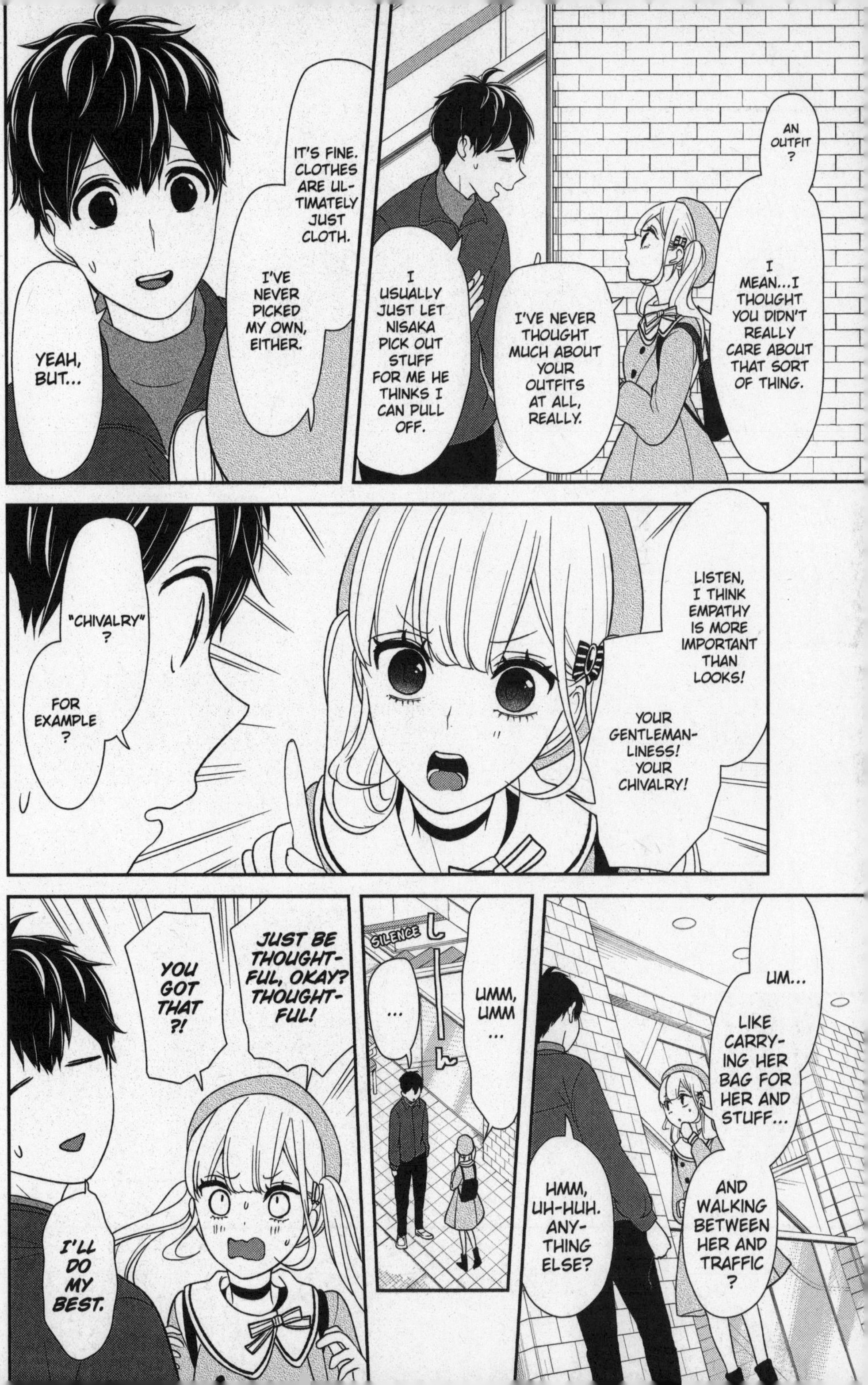
AN OUTFIT?
I MEAN...I THOUGHT YOU DIDN'T REALLY CARE ABOUT THAT SORT OF THING.
I'VE NEVER THOUGHT MUCH ABOUT YOUR OUTFITS AT ALL, REALLY.
I USUALLY JUST LET NISAKA PICK OUT STUFF FOR ME HE THINKS I CAN PULL OFF.
IT'S FINE. CLOTHES ARE ULTIMATELY JUST CLOTH.
I'VE NEVER PICKED MY OWN, EITHER.
YEAH, BUT...
LISTEN, I THINK EMPATHY IS MORE IMPORTANT THAN LOOKS!
YOUR GENTLEMANLINESS! YOUR CHIVALRY!
"CHIVALRY"?
FOR EXAMPLE?
UM...
LIKE CARRYING HER BAG FOR HER AND STUFF...
AND WALKING BETWEEN HER AND TRAFFIC?
HMM, UH-HUH. ANYTHING ELSE?
SILENCE
UMM, UMM...
...
JUST BE THOUGHTFUL, OKAY? THOUGHTFUL!
YOU GOT THAT?!
I'LL DO MY BEST.

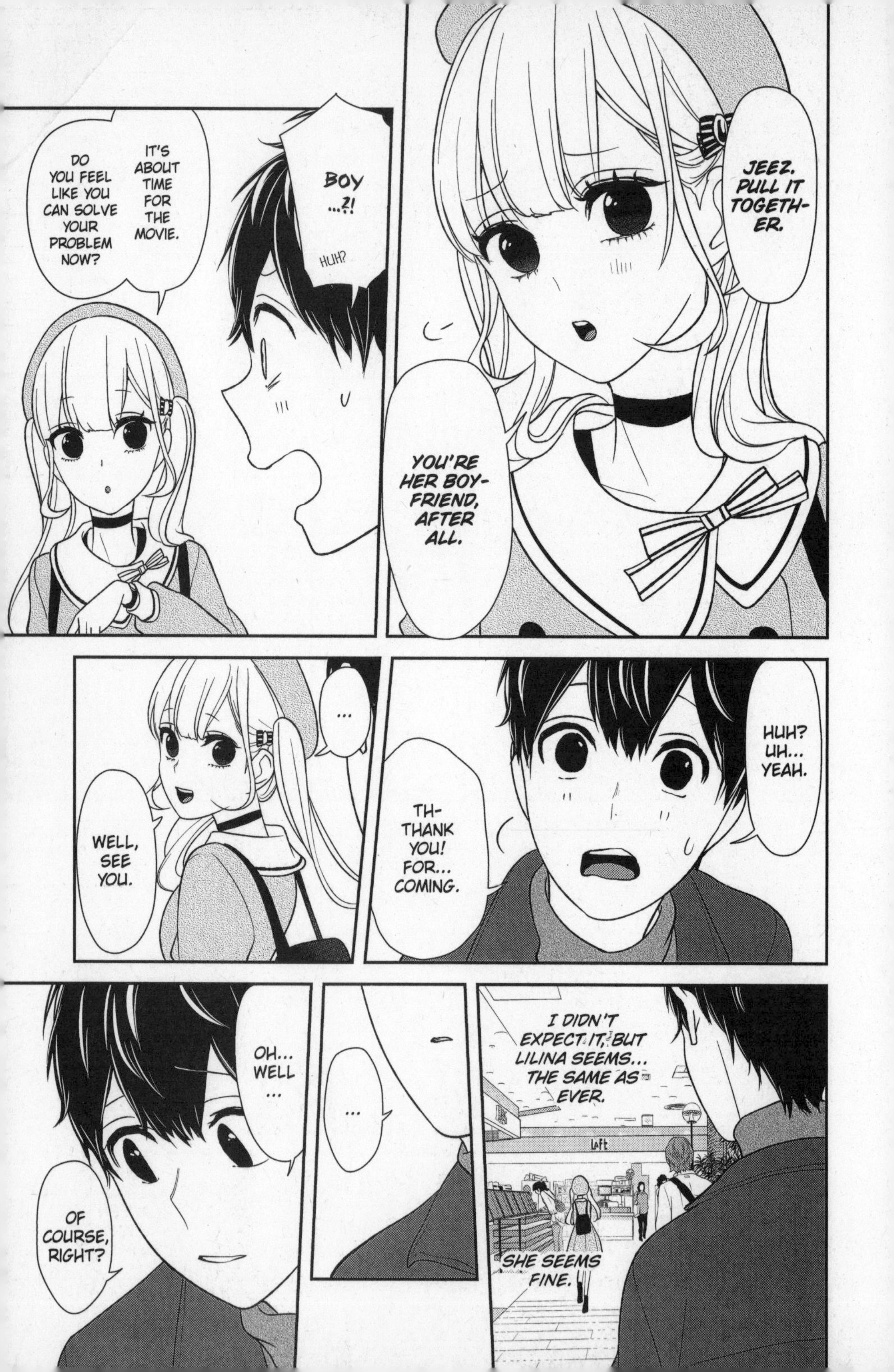
JEEZ. PULL IT TOGETHER.
YOU'RE HER BOYFRIEND, AFTER ALL.
BOY ...?!
HUH?
IT'S ABOUT TIME FOR THE MOVIE.
DO YOU FEEL LIKE YOU CAN SOLVE YOUR PROBLEM NOW?
HUH? UH... YEAH.
TH-THANK YOU! FOR... COMING.
...
WELL, SEE YOU.
I DIDN'T EXPECT IT, BUT LILINA SEEMS... THE SAME AS EVER.
SHE SEEMS FINE.
...
OH... WELL ...
OF COURSE, RIGHT?

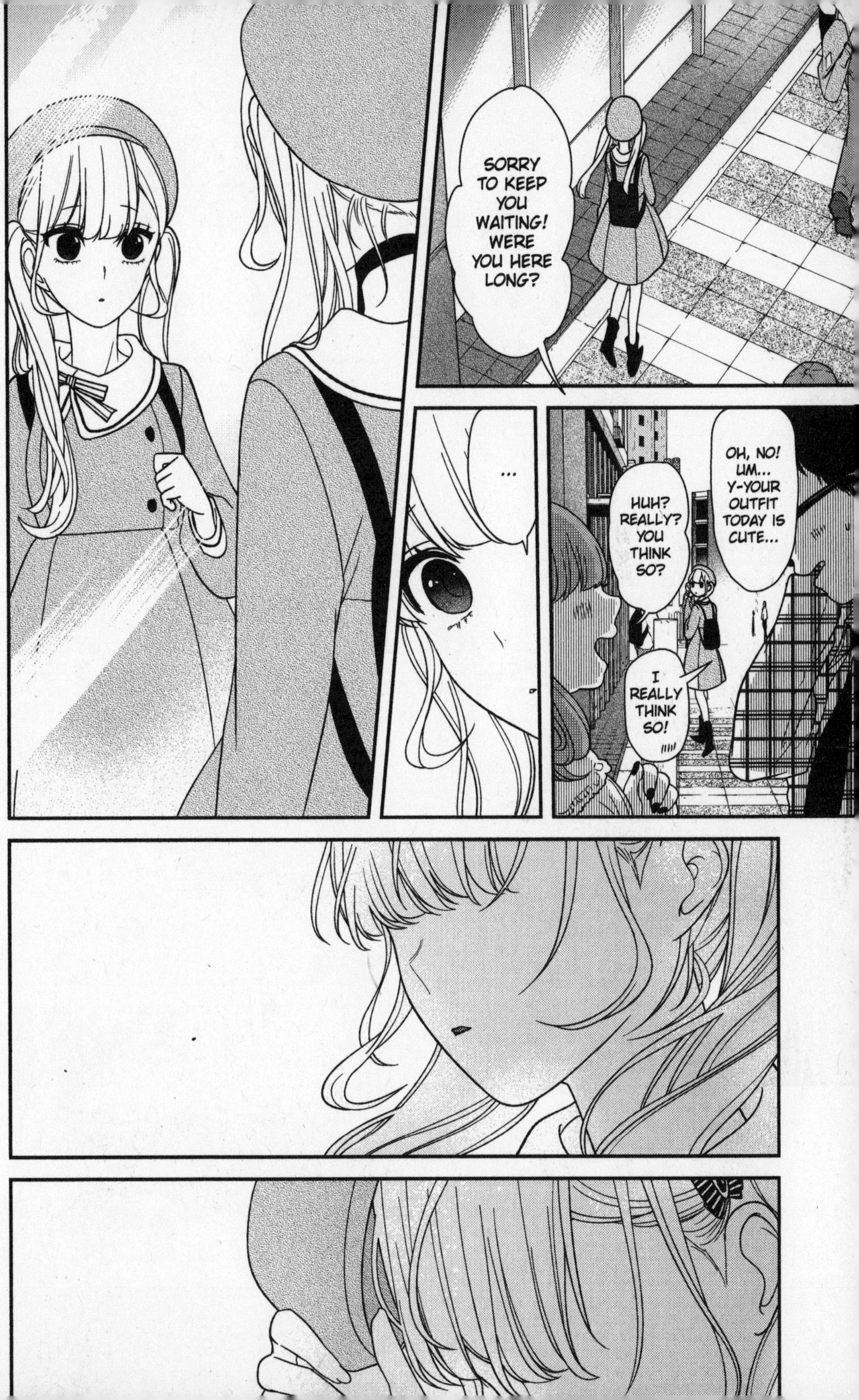
SORRY TO KEEP YOU WAITING! WERE YOU HERE LONG?
OH, NO! UM... Y-YOUR OUTFIT TODAY IS CUTE...
HUH? REALLY? YOU THINK SO?
I REALLY THINK SO!
...

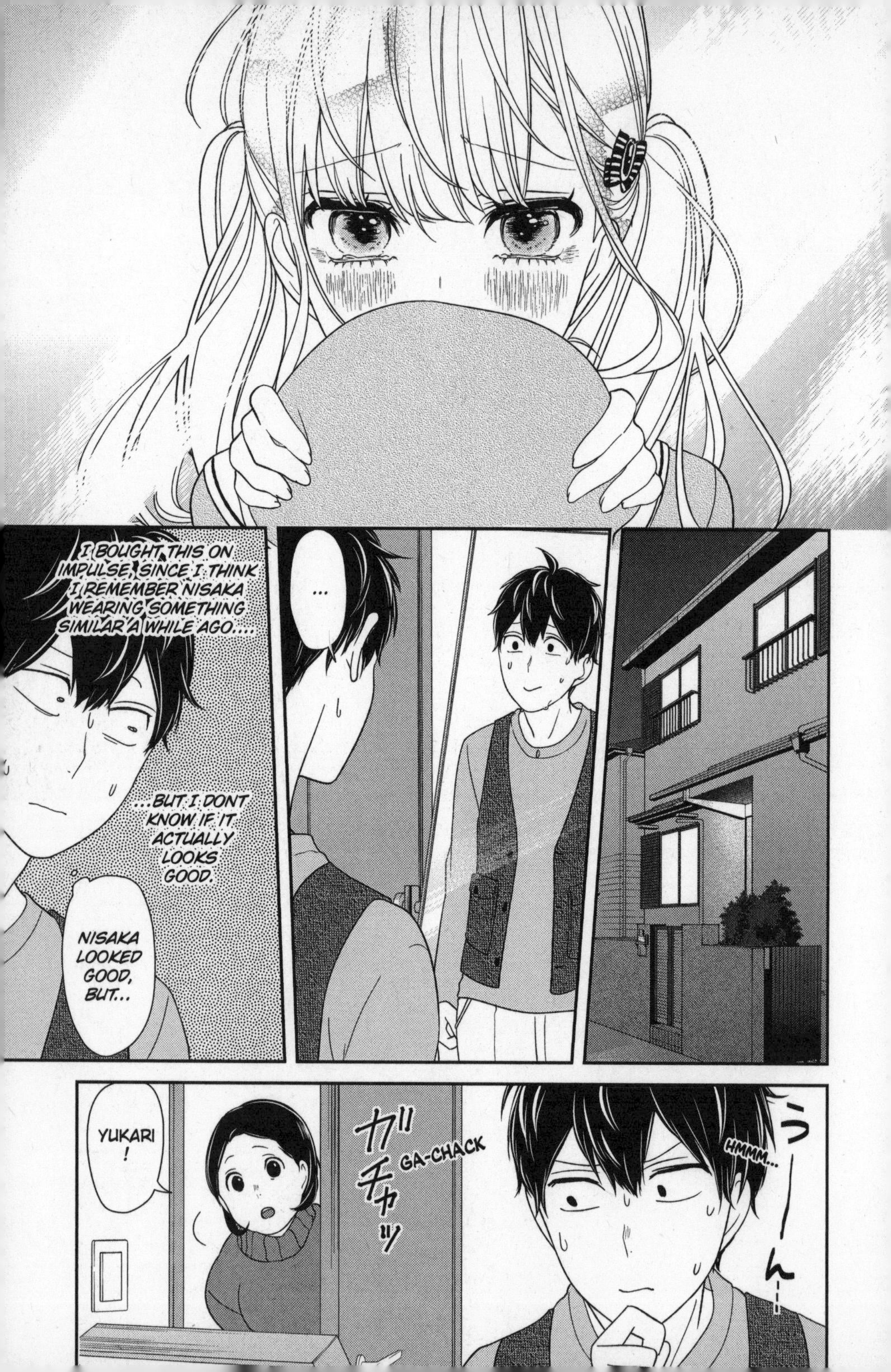
...
I BOUGHT THIS ON IMPULSE, SINCE I THINK I REMEMBER NISAKA WEARING SOMETHING SIMILAR A WHILE AGO....
...BUT I DONT KNOW IF IT ACTUALLY LOOKS GOOD.
NISAKA LOOKED GOOD, BUT...
うーんー
HMMM...
ガチャッ
GA-CHACK
YUKARI!

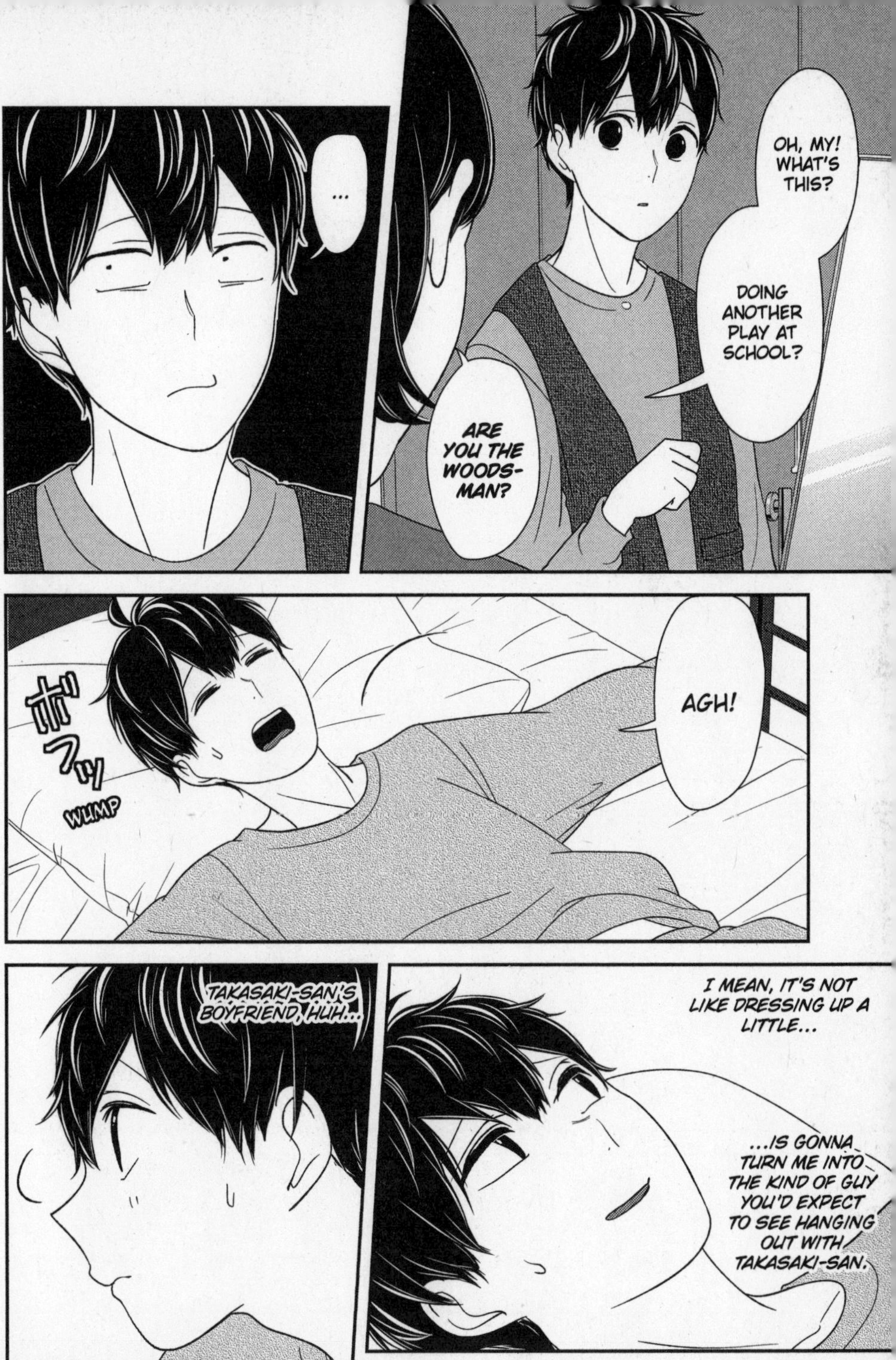
OH, MY! WHAT'S THIS?
DOING ANOTHER PLAY AT SCHOOL?
ARE YOU THE WOODSMAN?
...
AGH!
ボフッ
WUMP
I MEAN, IT'S NOT LIKE DRESSING UP A LITTLE...
...IS GONNA TURN ME INTO THE KIND OF GUY YOU'D EXPECT TO SEE HANGING OUT WITH TAKASAKI-SAN.
TAKASAKI-SAN'S BOYFRIEND, HUH...
BOYFRIEND...

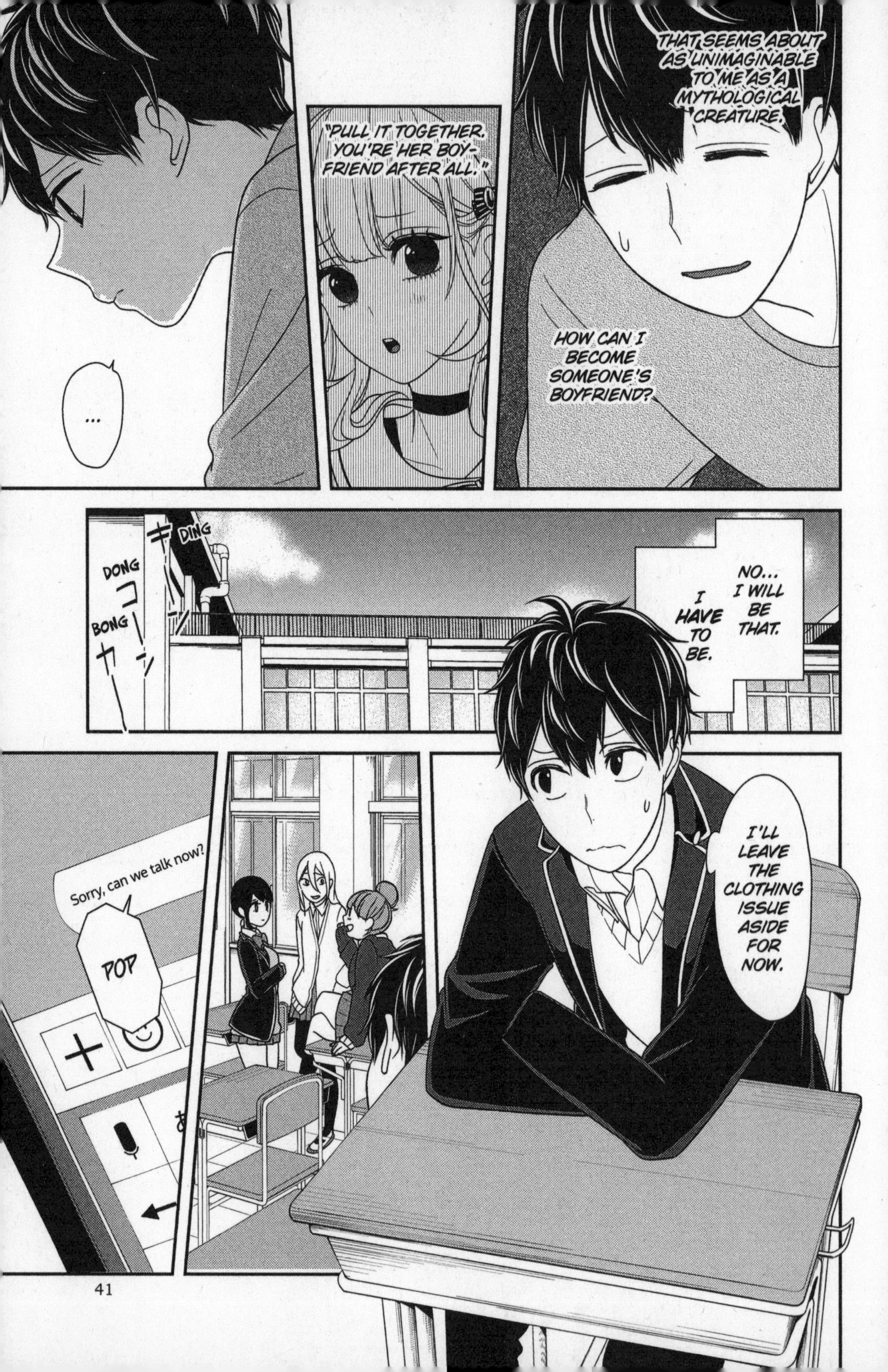
THAT SEEMS ABOUT AS UNIMAGINABLE TO ME AS A MYTHOLOGICAL CREATURE.
HOW CAN I BECOME SOMEONE'S BOYFRIEND?
"PULL IT TOGETHER. YOU'RE HER BOY-FRIEND AFTER ALL."
...
NO... I WILL BE THAT.
I HAVE TO BE.
DING
DONG
BONG
I'LL LEAVE THE CLOTHING ISSUE ASIDE FOR NOW.
Sorry, can we talk now?
POP

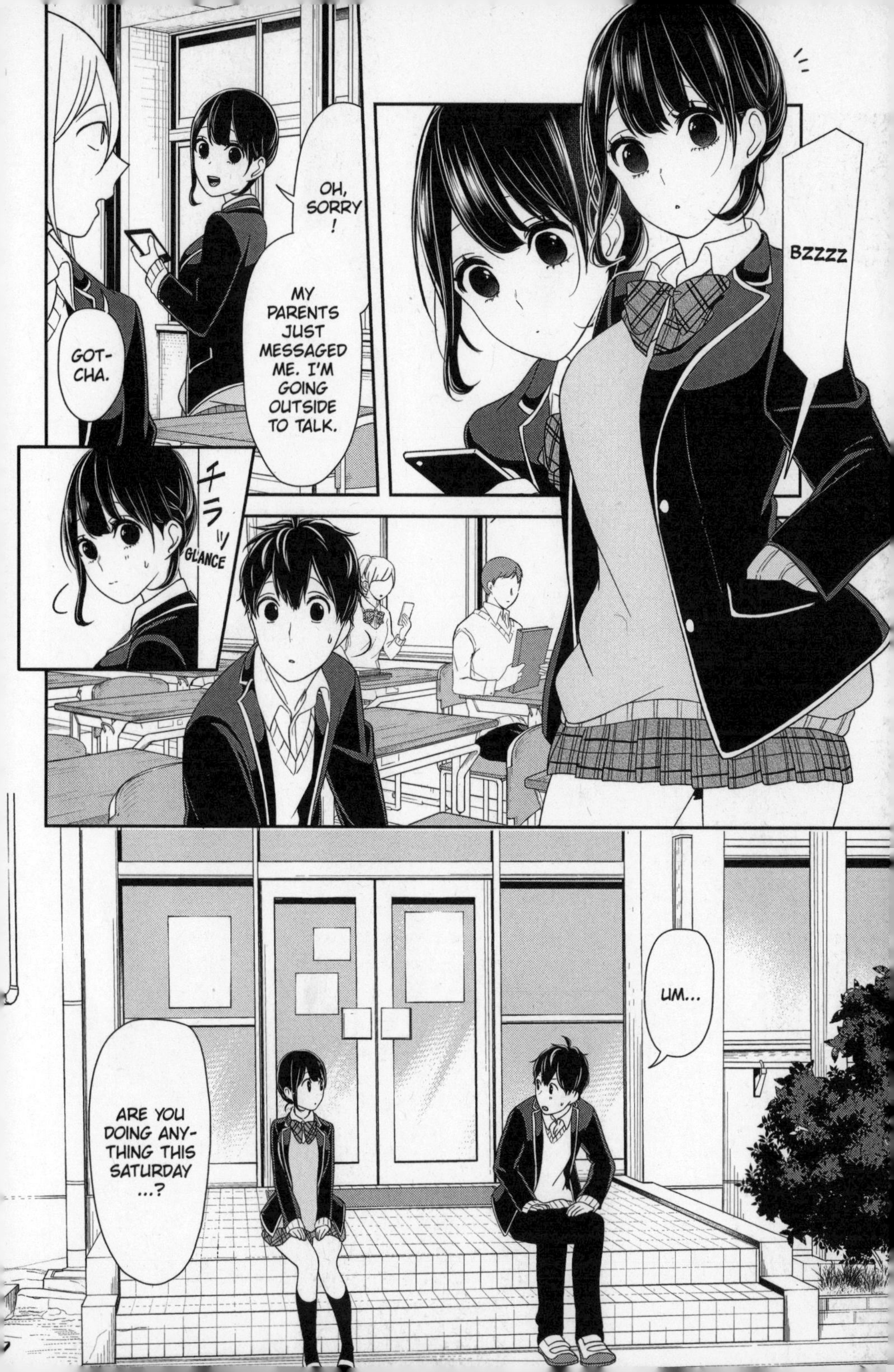
BZZZZ
OH, SORRY!
MY PARENTS JUST MESSAGED ME. I'M GOING OUTSIDE TO TALK.
GOT-CHA.
チラッ
GLANCE
UM...
ARE YOU DOING ANYTHING THIS SATURDAY ...?

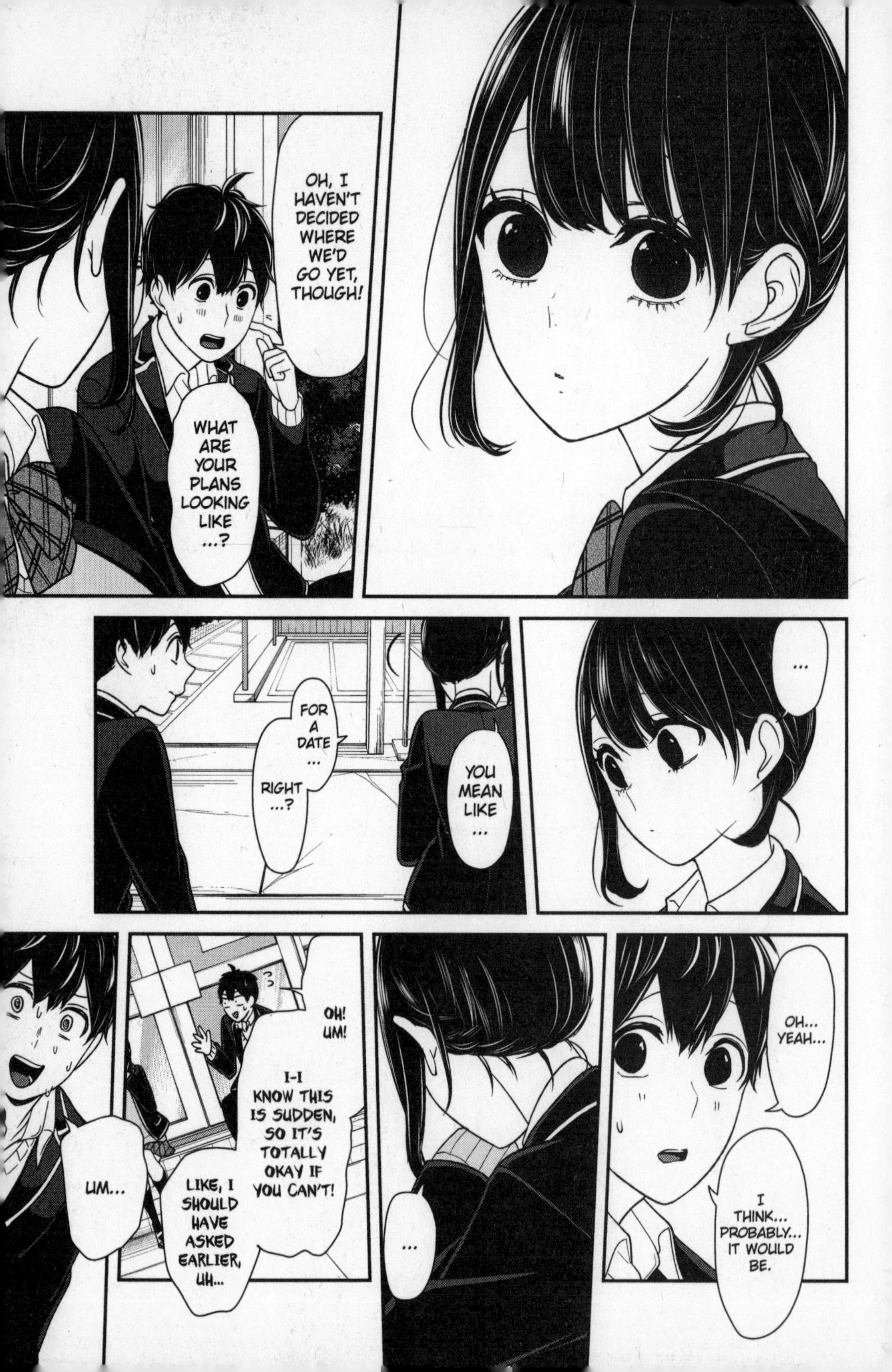
OH, I HAVEN'T DECIDED WHERE WE'D GO YET, THOUGH!
WHAT ARE YOUR PLANS LOOKING LIKE ...?
...
YOU MEAN LIKE ...
FOR A DATE ... RIGHT ...?
OH... YEAH...
I THINK... PROBABLY... IT WOULD BE.
...
OH! UM!
I-I KNOW THIS IS SUDDEN, SO IT'S TOTALLY OKAY IF YOU CAN'T!
LIKE, I SHOULD HAVE ASKED EARLIER, UH...
UM...

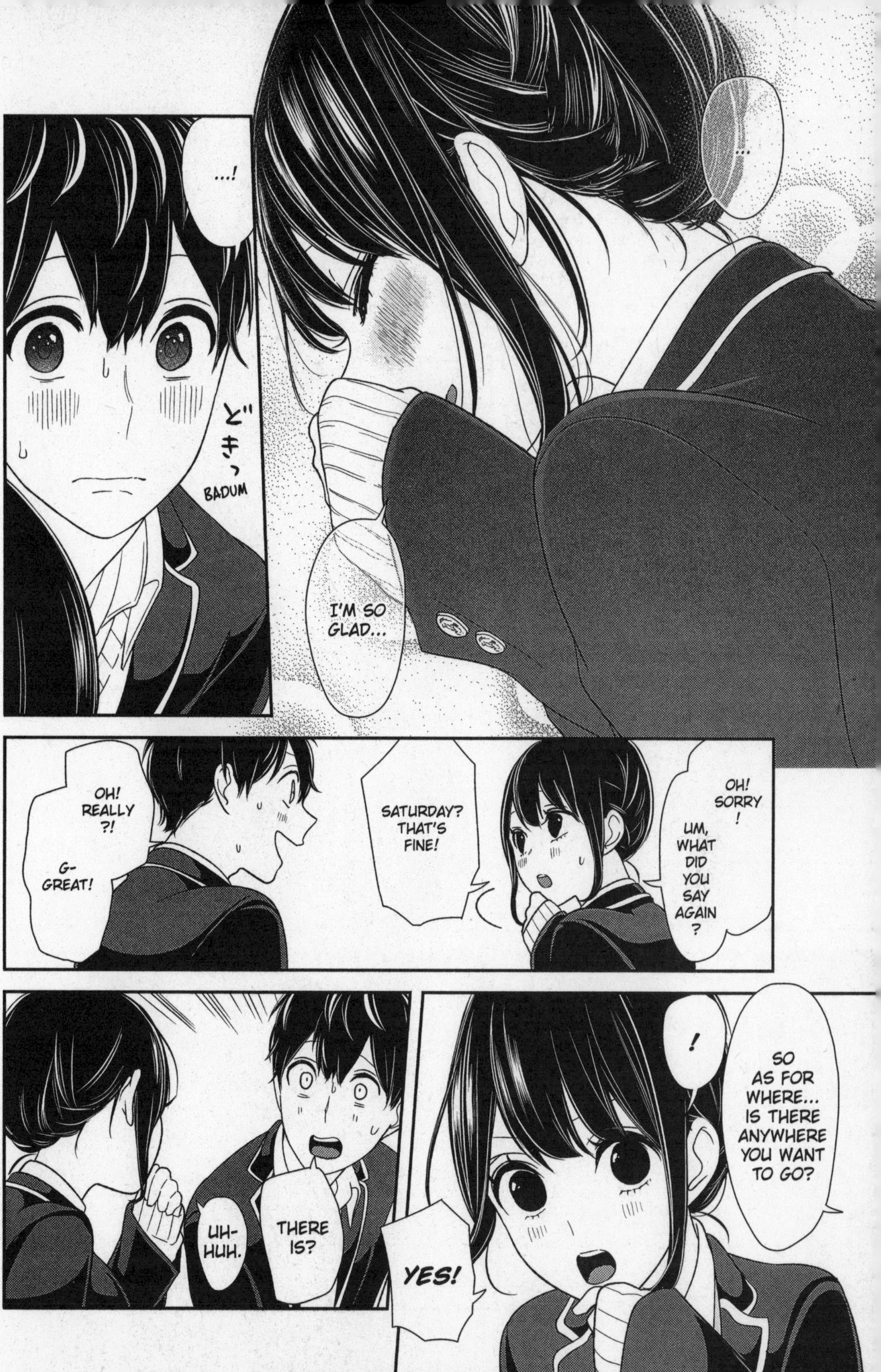
...
I'M SO GLAD...
...!
どきっ
BADUM
OH! SORRY! UM, WHAT DID YOU SAY AGAIN?
SATURDAY? THAT'S FINE!
OH! REALLY?!
G-GREAT!
SO AS FOR WHERE... IS THERE ANYWHERE YOU WANT TO GO?
!
THERE IS?
UH-HUH.
YES!

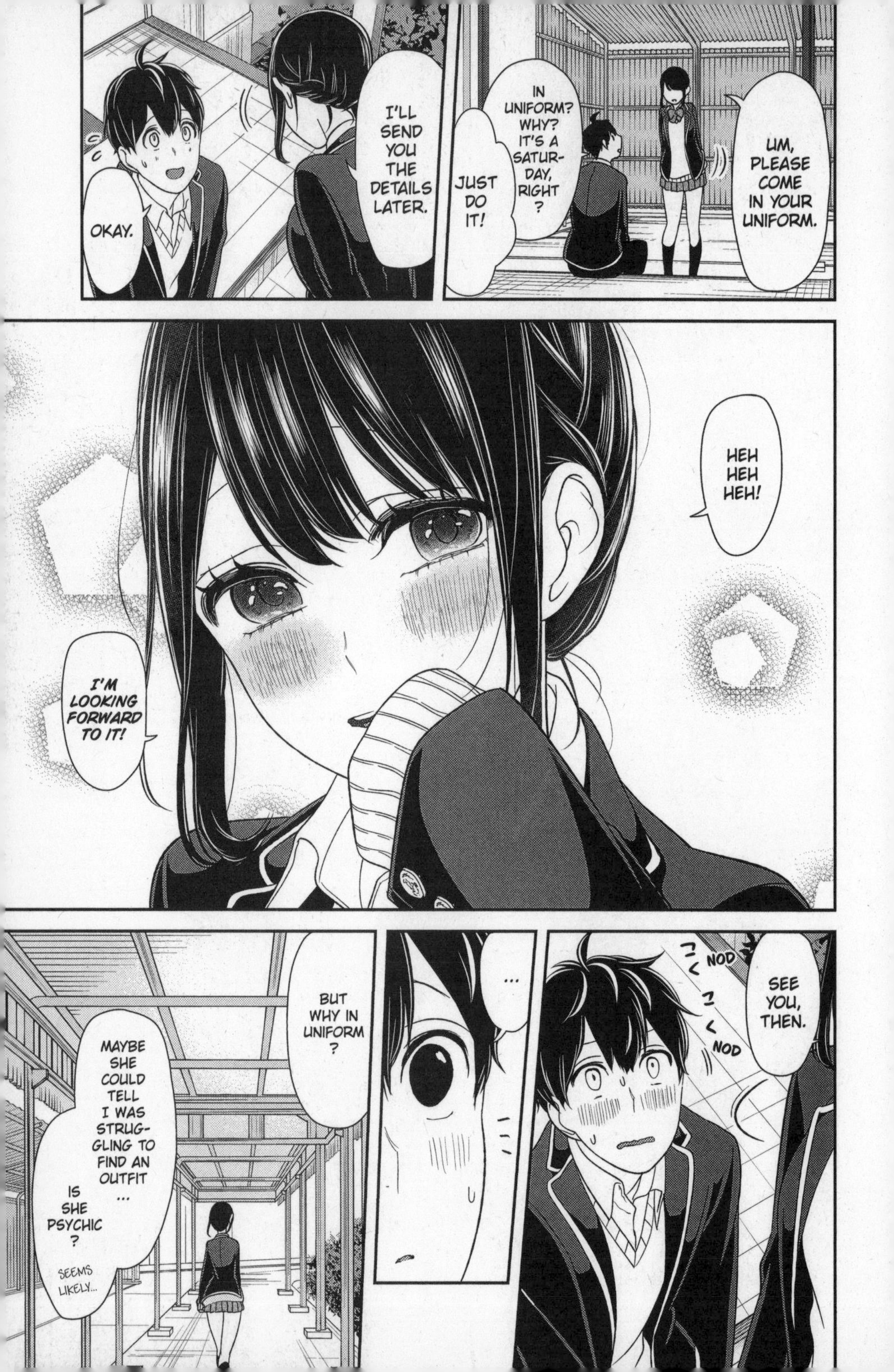
UM, PLEASE COME IN YOUR UNIFORM.
IN UNIFORM? WHY? IT'S A SATUR-DAY, RIGHT?
JUST DO IT!
I'LL SEND YOU THE DETAILS LATER.
OKAY.
HEH HEH HEH!
I'M LOOKING FORWARD TO IT!
SEE YOU, THEN.
NOD
NOD
...
BUT WHY IN UNIFORM?
MAYBE SHE COULD TELL I WAS STRUG-GLING TO FIND AN OUTFIT...
IS SHE PSYCHIC?
SEEMS LIKELY...

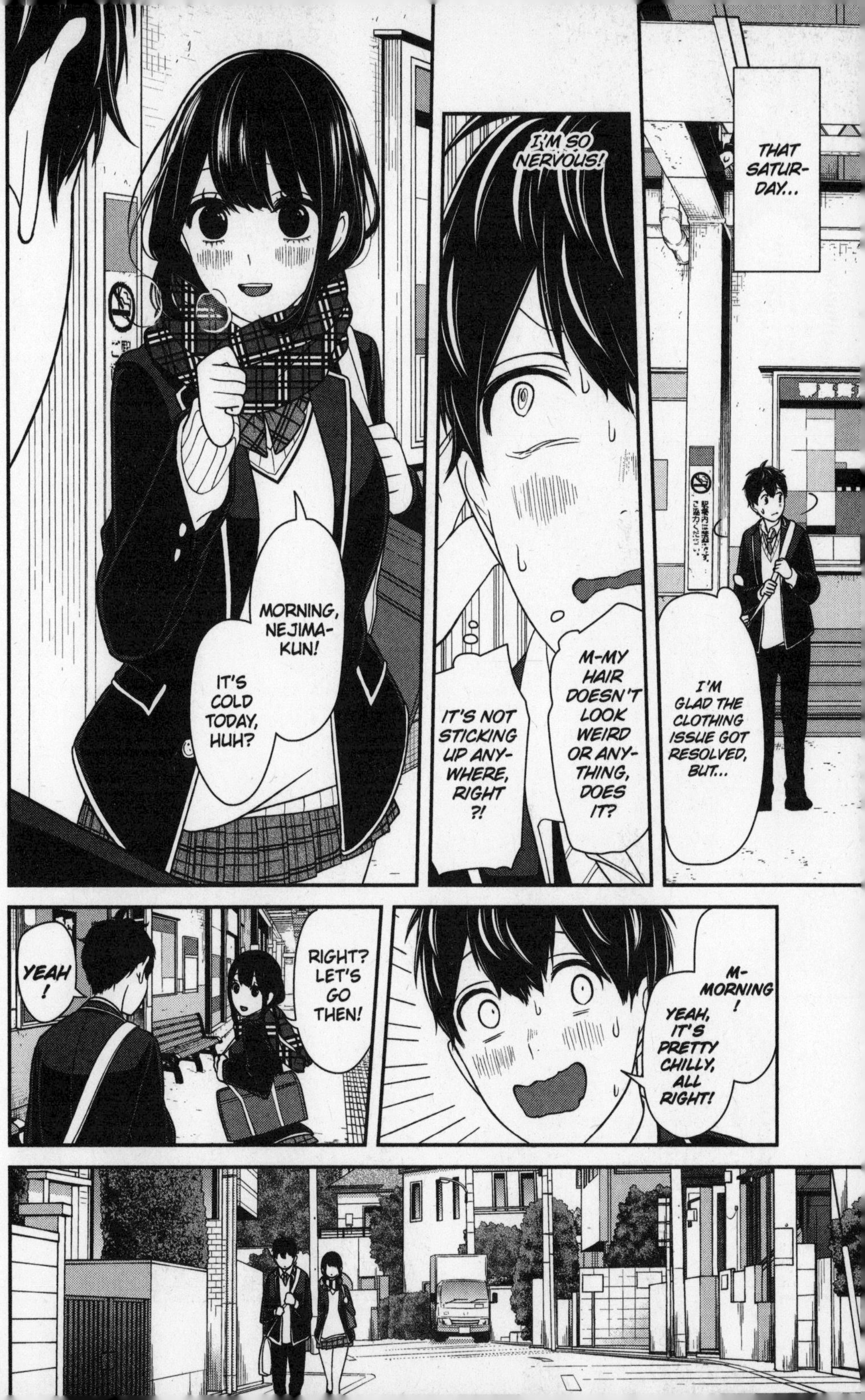
THAT SATURDAY...
I'M GLAD THE CLOTHING ISSUE GOT RESOLVED, BUT...
I'M SO NERVOUS!
M-MY HAIR DOESN'T LOOK WEIRD OR ANYTHING, DOES IT?
IT'S NOT STICKING UP ANYWHERE, RIGHT?!
MORNING, NEJIMA-KUN!
IT'S COLD TODAY, HUH?
M-MORNING!
YEAH, IT'S PRETTY CHILLY, ALL RIGHT!
RIGHT? LET'S GO THEN!
YEAH!

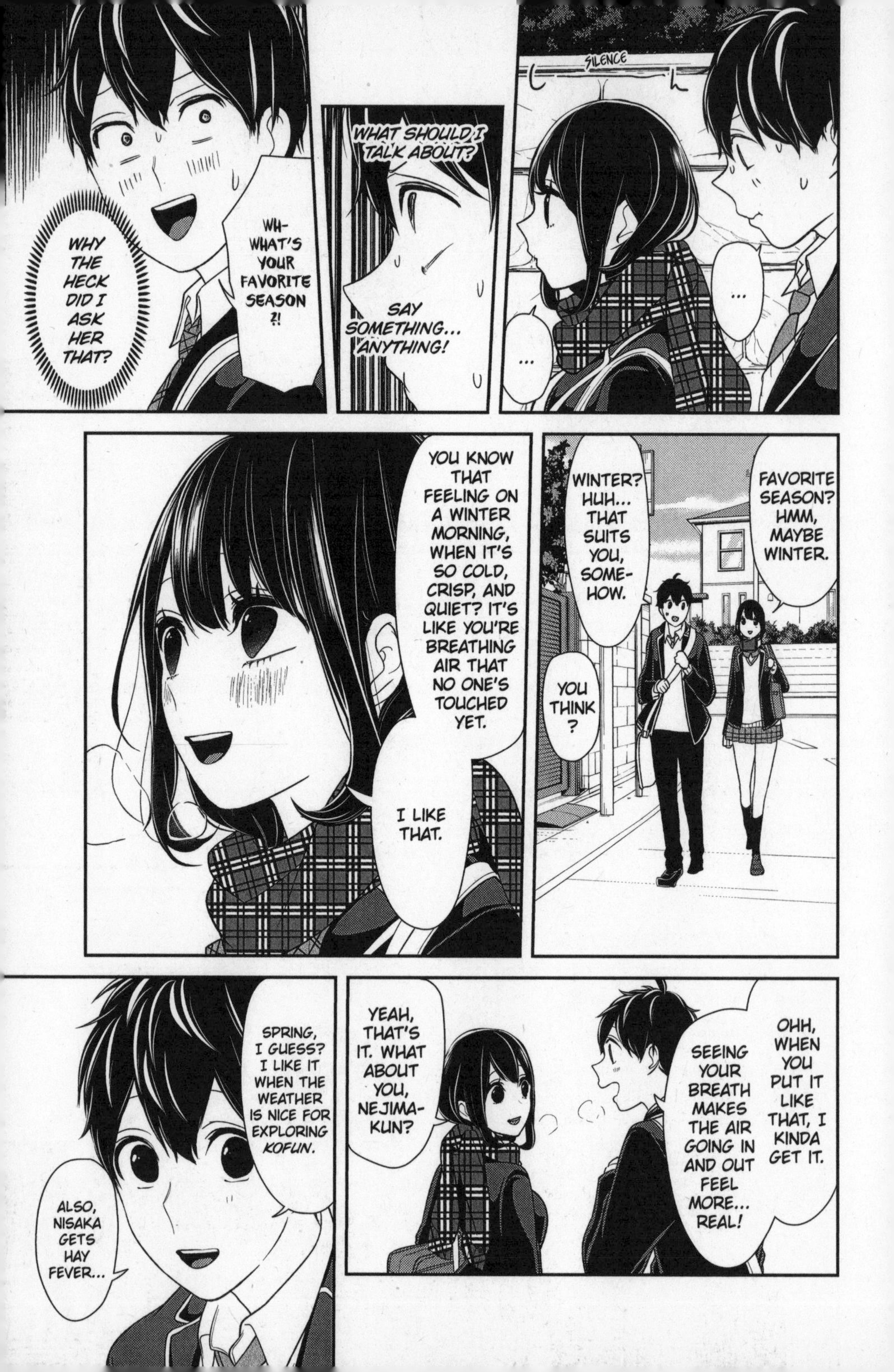
SILENCE
...
...
WHAT SHOULD I TALK ABOUT?
SAY SOMETHING... ANYTHING!
WH-WHAT'S YOUR FAVORITE SEASON?!
WHY THE HECK DID I ASK HER THAT?
FAVORITE SEASON? HMM, MAYBE WINTER.
WINTER? HUH... THAT SUITS YOU, SOMEHOW.
YOU THINK?
YOU KNOW THAT FEELING ON A WINTER MORNING, WHEN IT'S SO COLD, CRISP, AND QUIET? IT'S LIKE YOU'RE BREATHING AIR THAT NO ONE'S TOUCHED YET.
I LIKE THAT.
OHH, WHEN YOU PUT IT LIKE THAT, I KINDA GET IT.
SEEING YOUR BREATH MAKES THE AIR GOING IN AND OUT FEEL MORE... REAL!
YEAH, THAT'S IT. WHAT ABOUT YOU, NEJIMA-KUN?
SPRING, I GUESS? I LIKE IT WHEN THE WEATHER IS NICE FOR EXPLORING *KOFUN*.
ALSO, NISAKA GETS HAY FEVER...

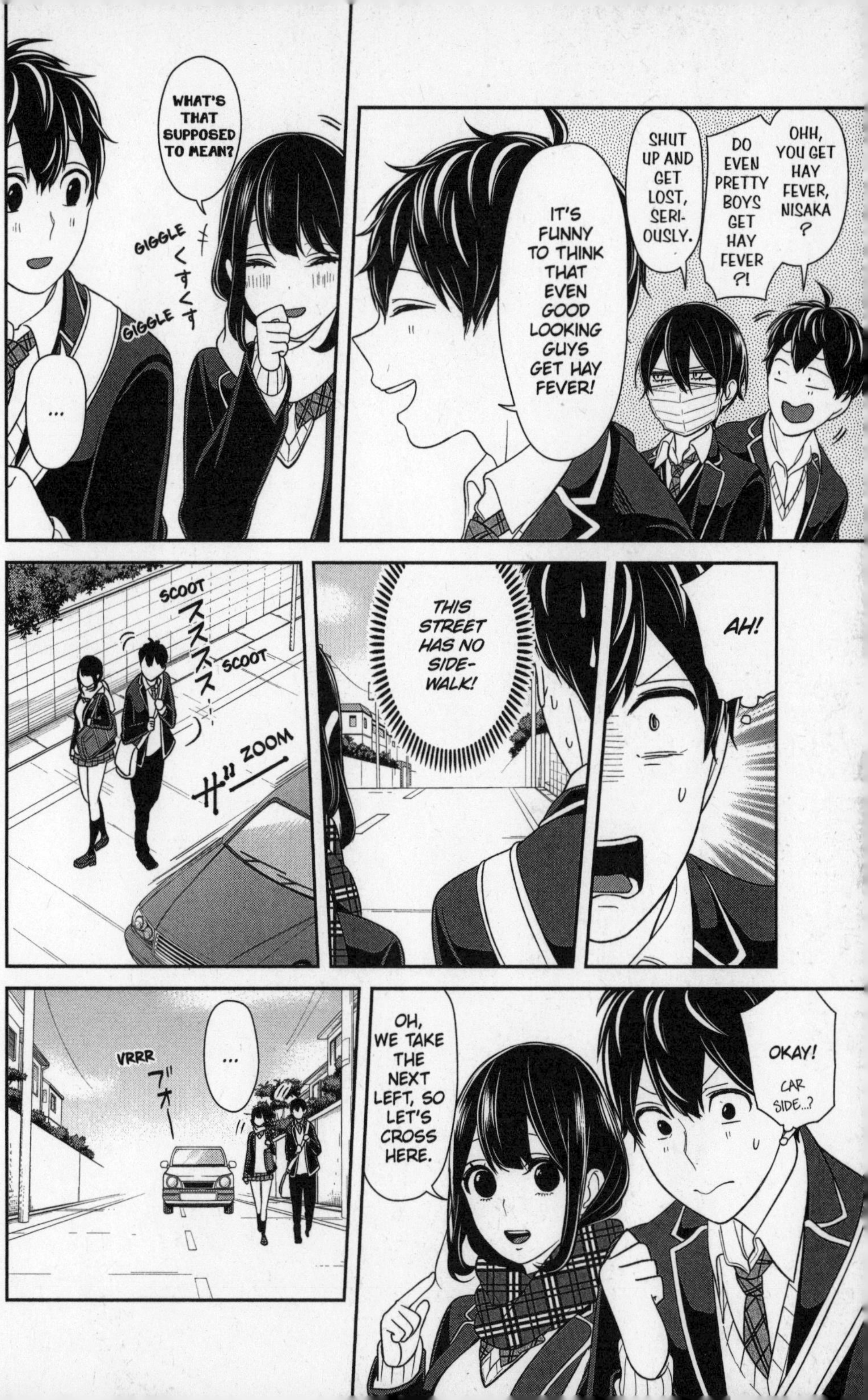
OHH, YOU GET HAY FEVER, NISAKA?
DO EVEN PRETTY BOYS GET HAY FEVER?!
SHUT UP AND GET LOST, SERIOUSLY.
IT'S FUNNY TO THINK THAT EVEN GOOD LOOKING GUYS GET HAY FEVER!
WHAT'S THAT SUPPOSED TO MEAN?
GIGGLE くすくす GIGGLE
...
AH!
THIS STREET HAS NO SIDE-WALK!
SCOOT ススス SCOOT
ZOOM
OKAY!
CAR SIDE...?
OH, WE TAKE THE NEXT LEFT, SO LET'S CROSS HERE.
...
VRRR ブオー

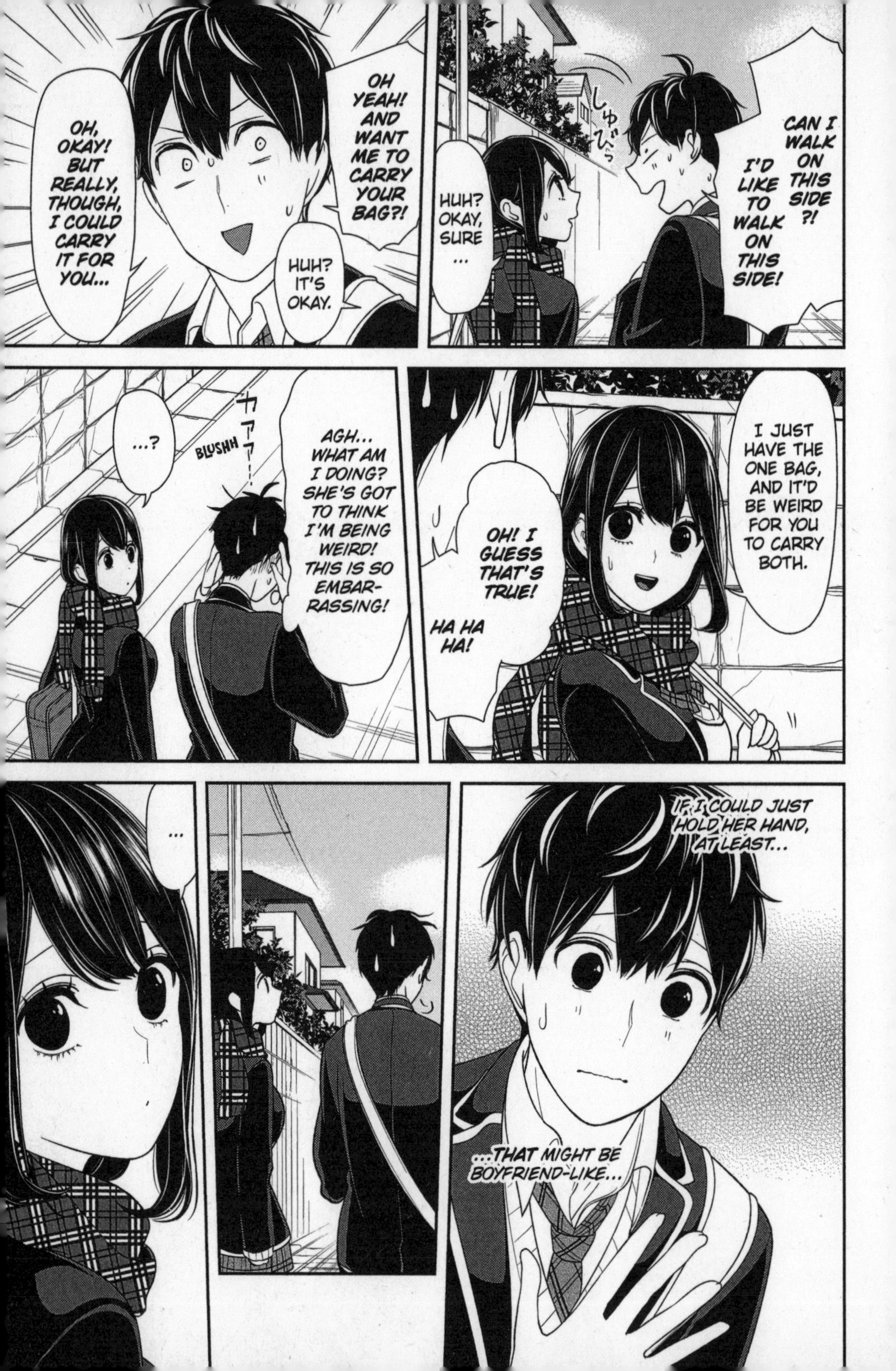
CAN I WALK ON THIS SIDE?!
I'D LIKE TO WALK ON THIS SIDE!
HUH? OKAY, SURE ...
OH YEAH! AND WANT ME TO CARRY YOUR BAG?!
HUH? IT'S OKAY.
OH, OKAY! BUT REALLY, THOUGH, I COULD CARRY IT FOR YOU...
I JUST HAVE THE ONE BAG, AND IT'D BE WEIRD FOR YOU TO CARRY BOTH.
OH! I GUESS THAT'S TRUE!
HA HA HA!
AGH... WHAT AM I DOING? SHE'S GOT TO THINK I'M BEING WEIRD! THIS IS SO EMBARRASSING!
BLUSHH
...?
IF I COULD JUST HOLD HER HAND, AT LEAST...
...THAT MIGHT BE BOYFRIEND-LIKE...
...

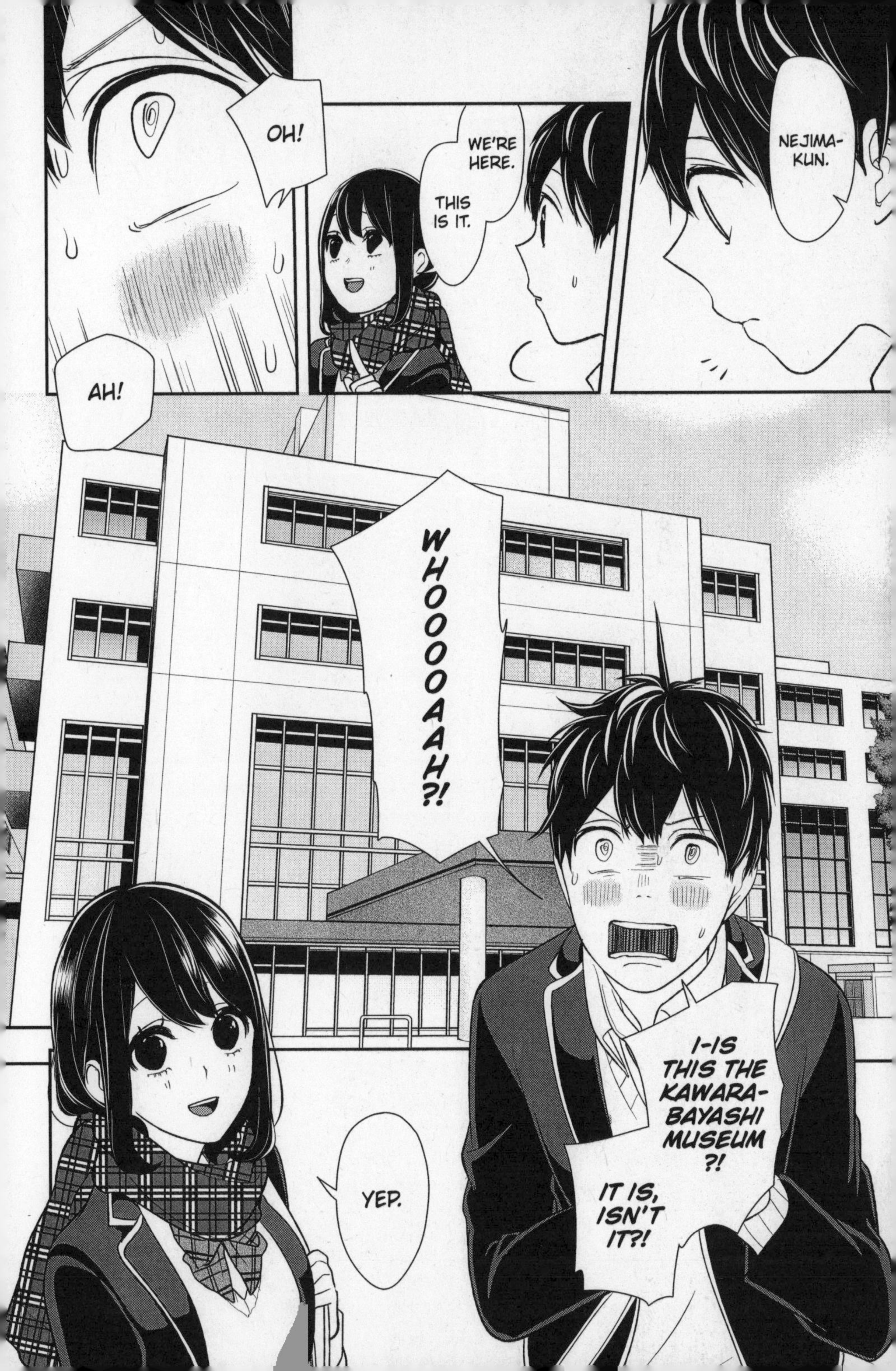
NEJIMA-KUN.
WE'RE HERE.
THIS IS IT.
OH!
AH!
WHOOOOAAAH?!
I-IS THIS THE KAWARA-BAYASHI MUSEUM?!
IT IS, ISN'T IT?!
YEP.

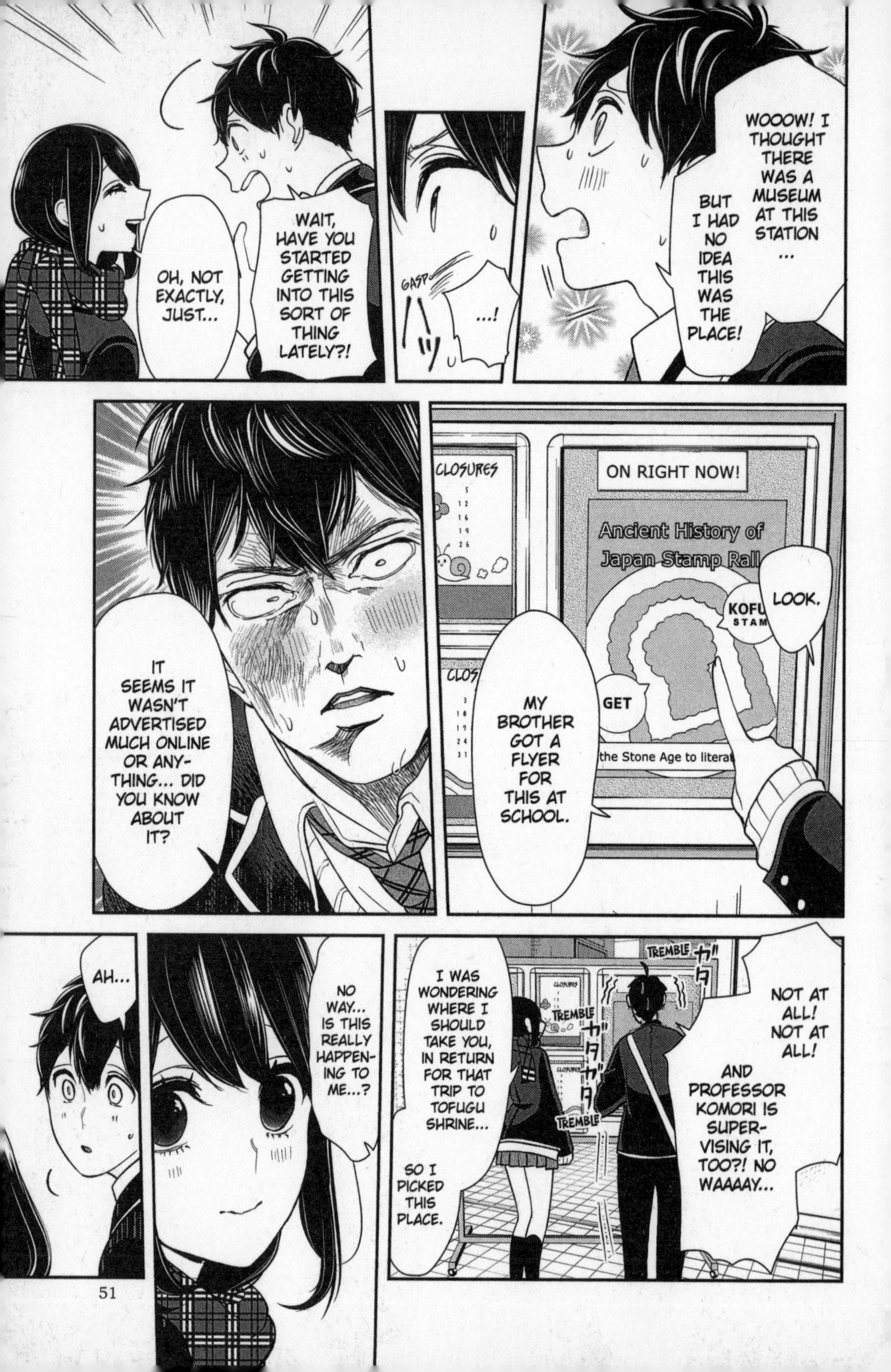
WOOOW! I THOUGHT THERE WAS A MUSEUM AT THIS STATION ...
BUT I HAD NO IDEA THIS WAS THE PLACE!
GASP
...!
WAIT, HAVE YOU STARTED GETTING INTO THIS SORT OF THING LATELY?!
OH, NOT EXACTLY, JUST...
LOOK.
ON RIGHT NOW!
Ancient History of Japan Stamp Rall
KOFU STAM
GET
the Stone Age to literat
CLOSURES
MY BROTHER GOT A FLYER FOR THIS AT SCHOOL.
IT SEEMS IT WASN'T ADVERTISED MUCH ONLINE OR ANY-THING... DID YOU KNOW ABOUT IT?
NOT AT ALL! NOT AT ALL!
AND PROFESSOR KOMORI IS SUPER-VISING IT, TOO?! NO WAAAAY...
TREMBLE
TREMBLE
TREMBLE
I WAS WONDERING WHERE I SHOULD TAKE YOU, IN RETURN FOR THAT TRIP TO TOFUGU SHRINE...
SO I PICKED THIS PLACE.
NO WAY... IS THIS REALLY HAPPEN-ING TO ME...?
AH...

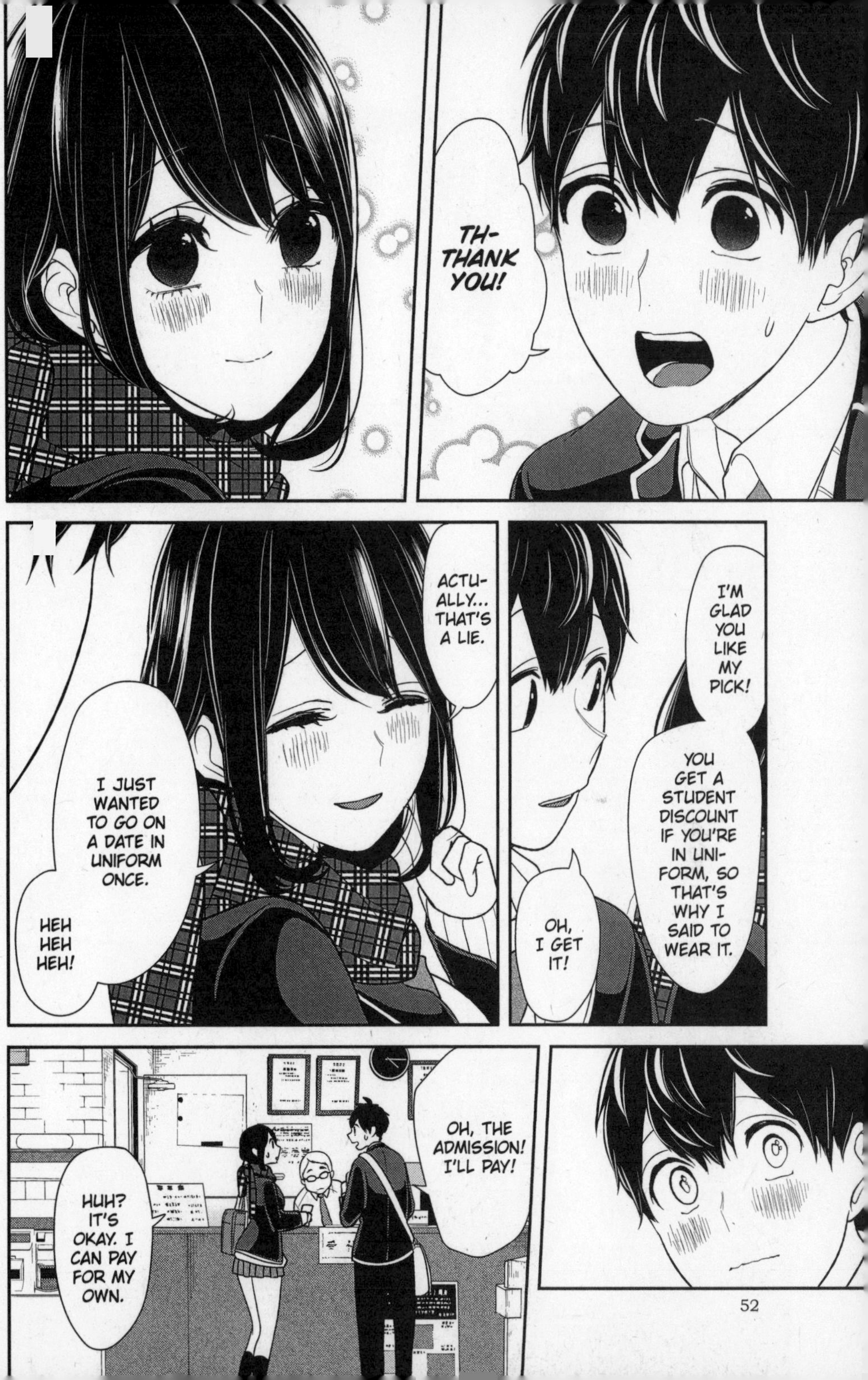
TH-THANK YOU!
I'M GLAD YOU LIKE MY PICK!
YOU GET A STUDENT DISCOUNT IF YOU'RE IN UNI-FORM, SO THAT'S WHY I SAID TO WEAR IT.
OH, I GET IT!
ACTU-ALLY... THAT'S A LIE.
I JUST WANTED TO GO ON A DATE IN UNIFORM ONCE.
HEH HEH HEH!
OH, THE ADMISSION! I'LL PAY!
HUH? IT'S OKAY. I CAN PAY FOR MY OWN.

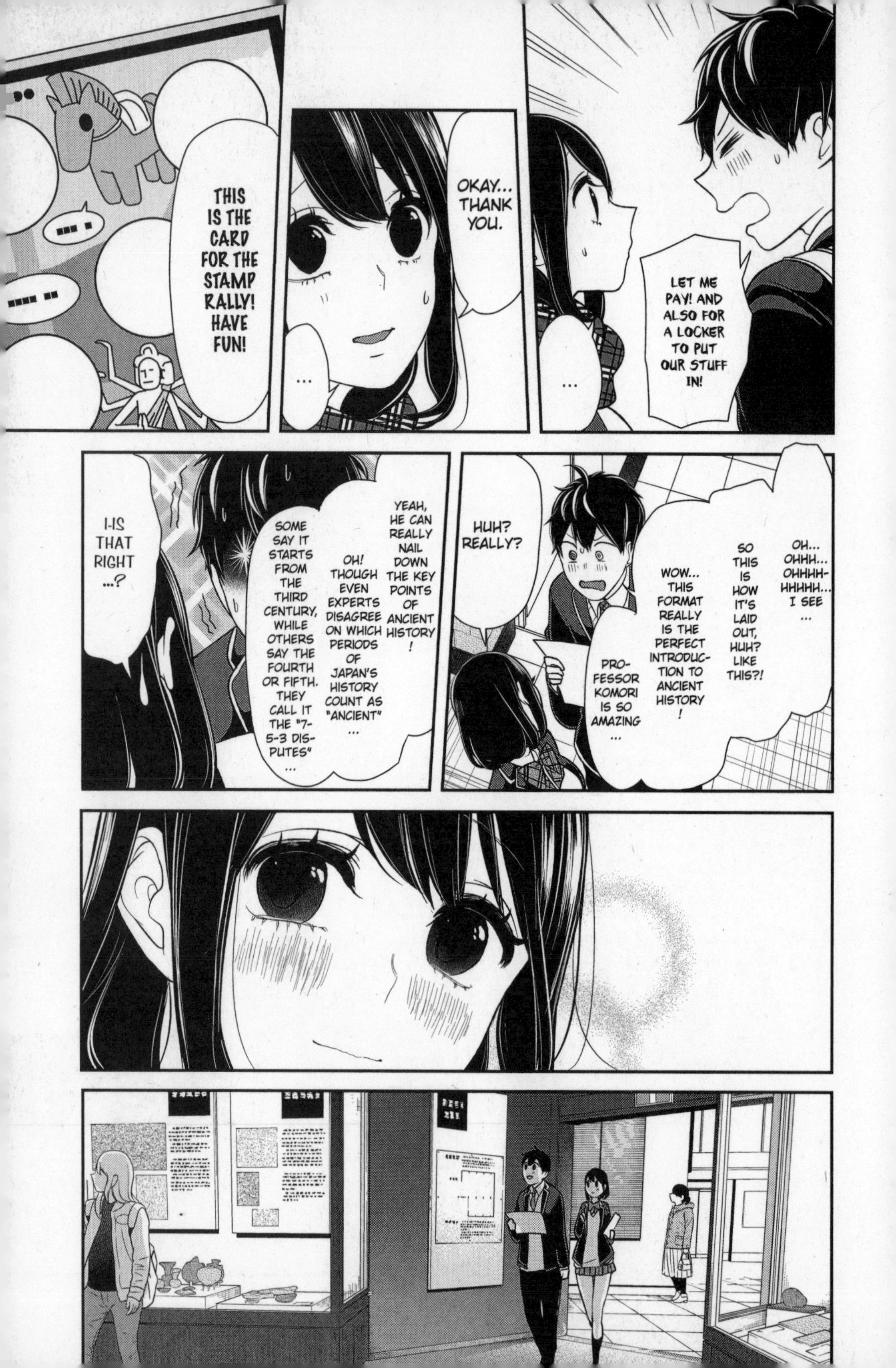
LET ME PAY! AND ALSO FOR A LOCKER TO PUT OUR STUFF IN!
...
OKAY... THANK YOU.
...
THIS IS THE CARD FOR THE STAMP RALLY! HAVE FUN!
OH... OHHH... OHHHHHHHH... I SEE...
SO THIS IS HOW IT'S LAID OUT, HUH? LIKE THIS?!
WOW... THIS FORMAT REALLY IS THE PERFECT INTRODUCTION TO ANCIENT HISTORY!
PROFESSOR KOMORI IS SO AMAZING...
HUH? REALLY?
YEAH, HE CAN REALLY NAIL DOWN THE KEY POINTS OF ANCIENT HISTORY!
OH! THOUGH EVEN EXPERTS DISAGREE ON WHICH PERIODS OF JAPAN'S HISTORY COUNT AS "ANCIENT"...
SOME SAY IT STARTS FROM THE THIRD CENTURY, WHILE OTHERS SAY THE FOURTH OR FIFTH. THEY CALL IT THE "7-5-3 DISPUTES"...
I-IS THAT RIGHT...?

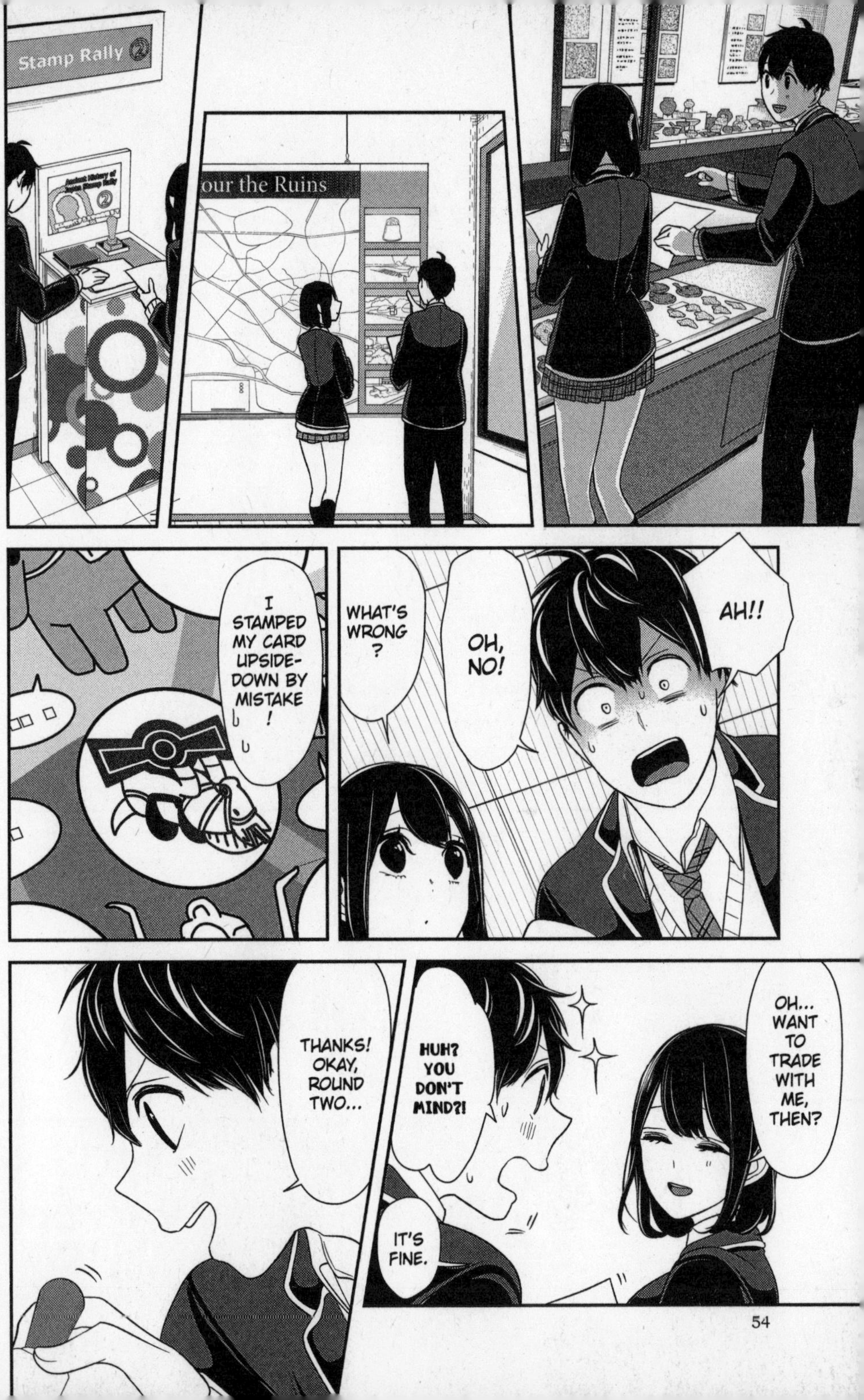

our the Ruins
Stamp Rally ②
AH!!
OH, NO!
WHAT'S WRONG?
I STAMPED MY CARD UPSIDE-DOWN BY MISTAKE!
OH... WANT TO TRADE WITH ME, THEN?
HUH? YOU DON'T MIND?!
IT'S FINE.
THANKS! OKAY, ROUND TWO...

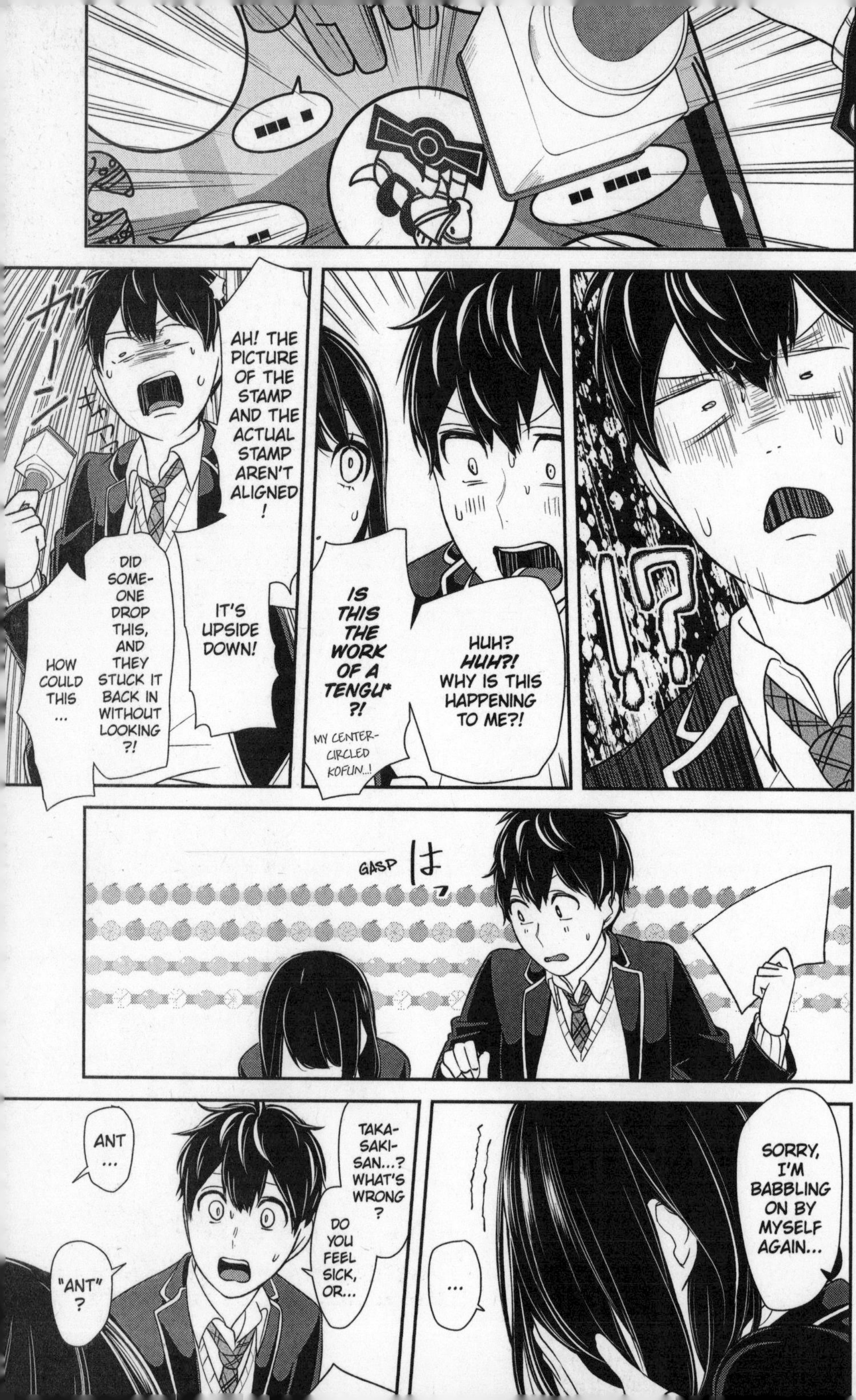
!?
HUH? HUH?! WHY IS THIS HAPPENING TO ME?!
IS THIS THE WORK OF A TENGU* ?!
MY CENTER-CIRCLED KOFUN...!
AH! THE PICTURE OF THE STAMP AND THE ACTUAL STAMP AREN'T ALIGNED!
IT'S UPSIDE DOWN!
DID SOME-ONE DROP THIS, AND THEY STUCK IT BACK IN WITHOUT LOOKING?!
HOW COULD THIS...
GASP
はっ
SORRY, I'M BABBLING ON BY MYSELF AGAIN...
......
...
TAKA-SAKI-SAN...? WHAT'S WRONG?
DO YOU FEEL SICK, OR...
ANT...
"ANT"?

*TENGU: A MYTHOLOGICAL CREATURE WITH A LONG NOSE AND WINGS, THEY'RE SAID TO GET UP TO A WIDE VARIETY OF MISCHIEF.

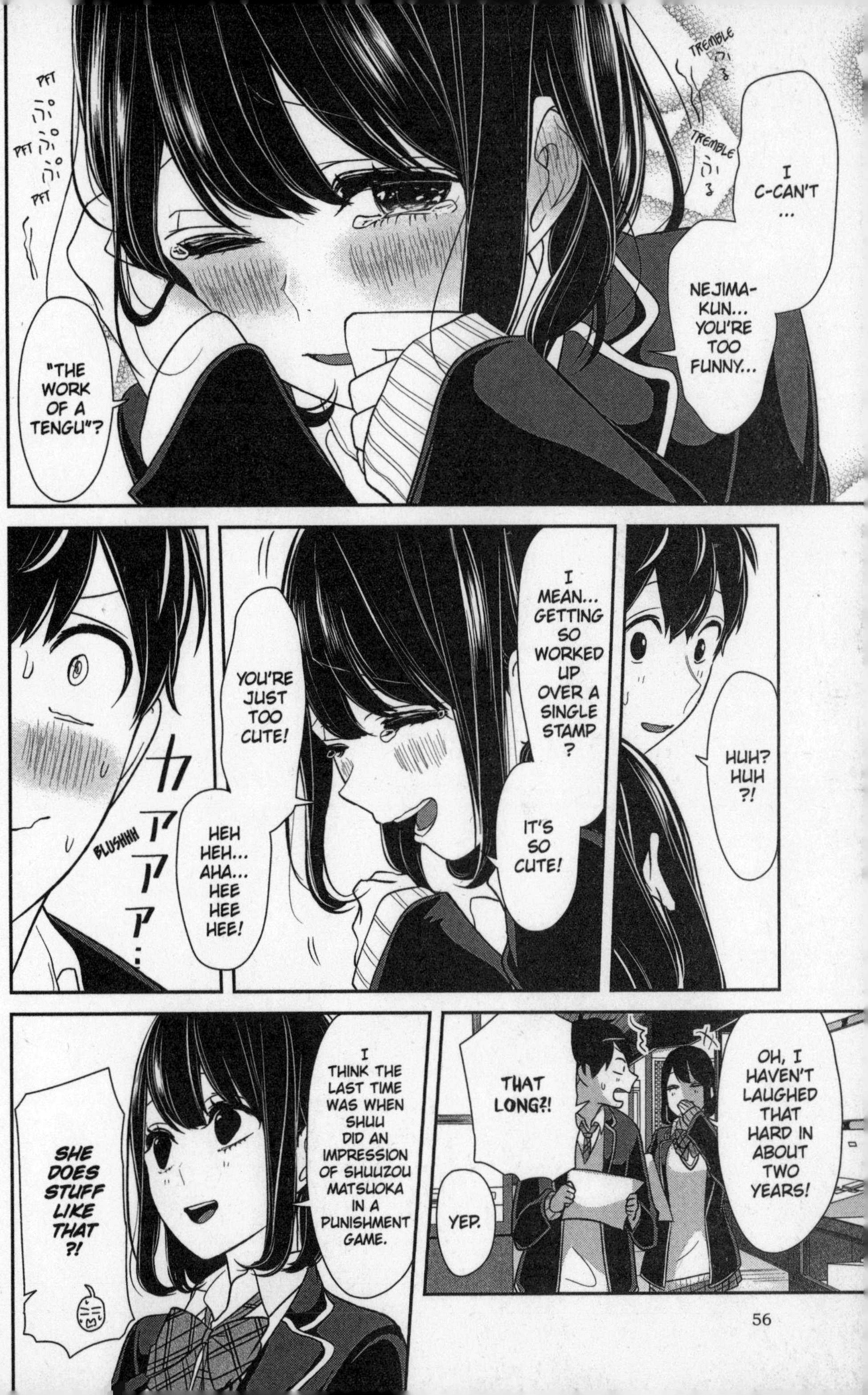
TREMBLE
TREMBLE
I C-CAN'T ...
NEJIMA-KUN... YOU'RE TOO FUNNY...
PFT
PFT
PFT
"THE WORK OF A TENGU"?
HUH? HUH ?!
I MEAN... GETTING SO WORKED UP OVER A SINGLE STAMP ?
IT'S SO CUTE!
YOU'RE JUST TOO CUTE!
HEH HEH... AHA... HEE HEE HEE!
BLUSHHH
OH, I HAVEN'T LAUGHED THAT HARD IN ABOUT TWO YEARS!
THAT LONG?!
YEP.
I THINK THE LAST TIME WAS WHEN SHUU DID AN IMPRESSION OF SHUUZOU MATSUOKA IN A PUNISHMENT GAME.
SHE DOES STUFF LIKE THAT?!

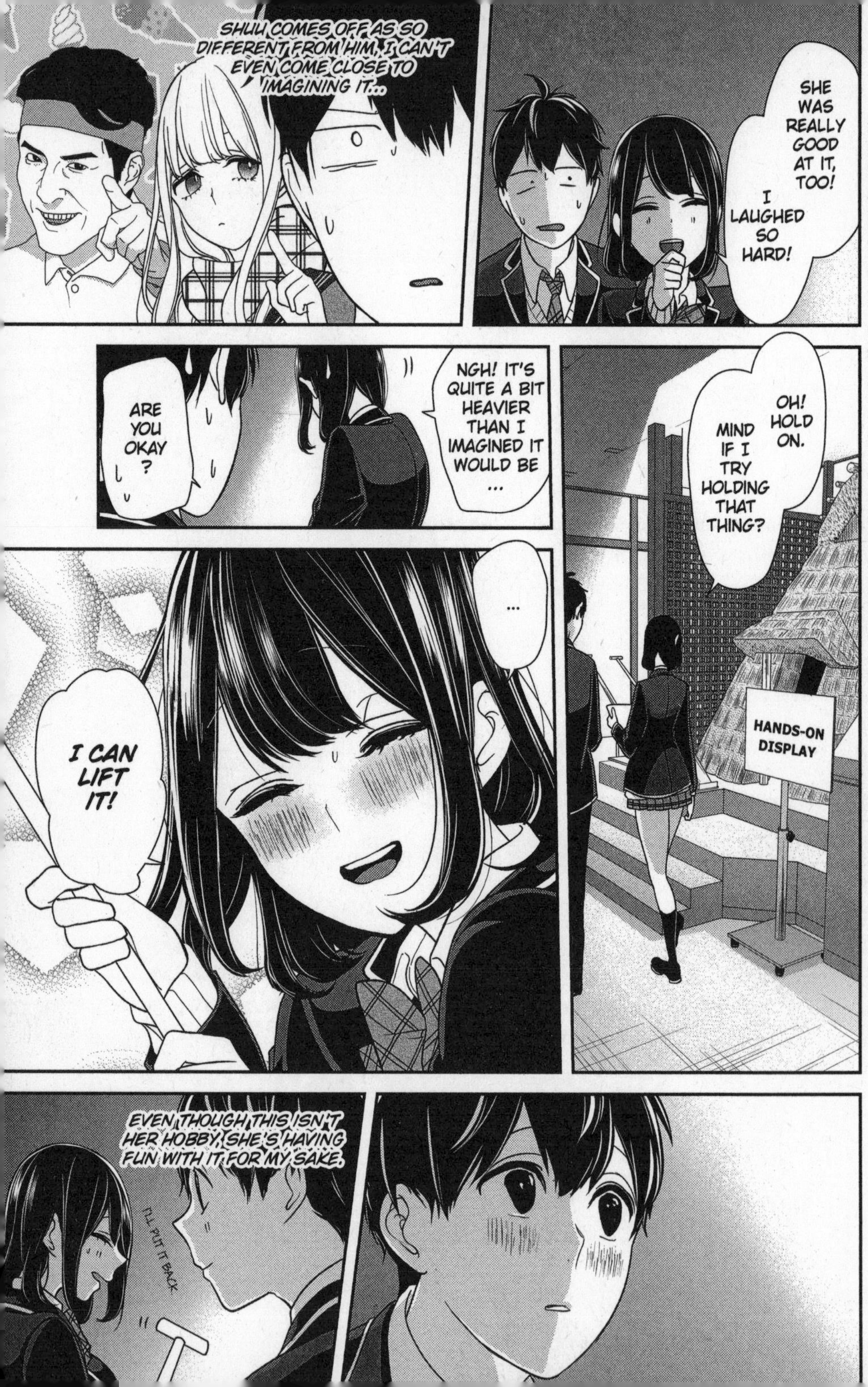
SHE WAS REALLY GOOD AT IT, TOO!
I LAUGHED SO HARD!
SHUU COMES OFF AS SO DIFFERENT FROM HIM, I CAN'T EVEN COME CLOSE TO IMAGINING IT...
OH! HOLD ON.
MIND IF I TRY HOLDING THAT THING?
HANDS-ON DISPLAY
NGH! IT'S QUITE A BIT HEAVIER THAN I IMAGINED IT WOULD BE ...
ARE YOU OKAY ?
...
I CAN LIFT IT!
EVEN THOUGH THIS ISN'T HER HOBBY, SHE'S HAVING FUN WITH IT FOR MY SAKE.
I'LL PUT IT BACK

*SHUUZOU MATSUOKA IS A PRO TENNIS PLAYER NOTORIOUS FOR TALKING WITH LOTS OF POINTING AND AGGRESSIVE GESTURES.

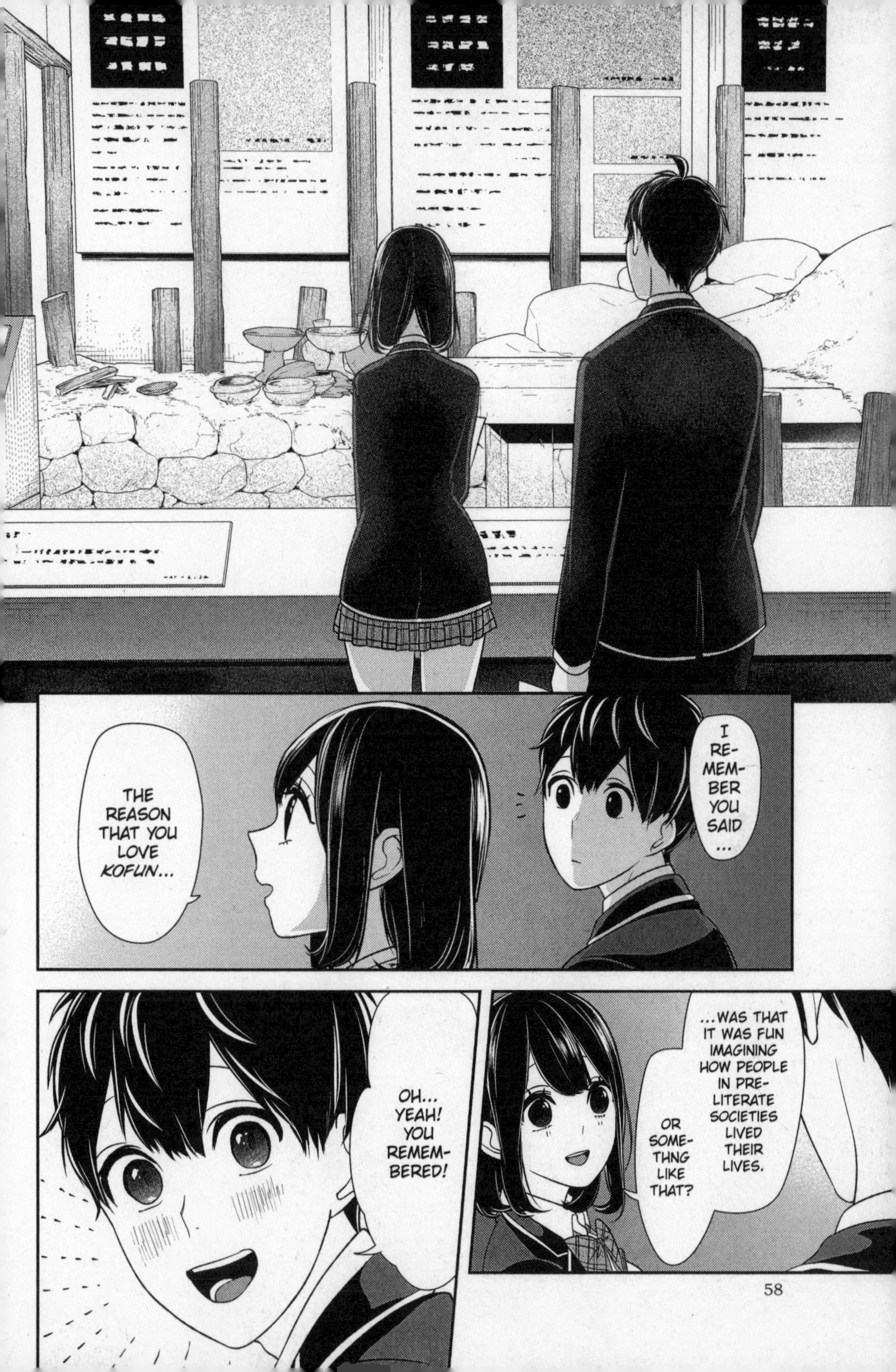
I RE-MEM-BER YOU SAID...
THE REASON THAT YOU LOVE *KOFUN*...
...WAS THAT IT WAS FUN IMAGINING HOW PEOPLE IN PRE-LITERATE SOCIETIES LIVED THEIR LIVES.
OR SOME-THNG LIKE THAT?
OH... YEAH! YOU REMEM-BERED!

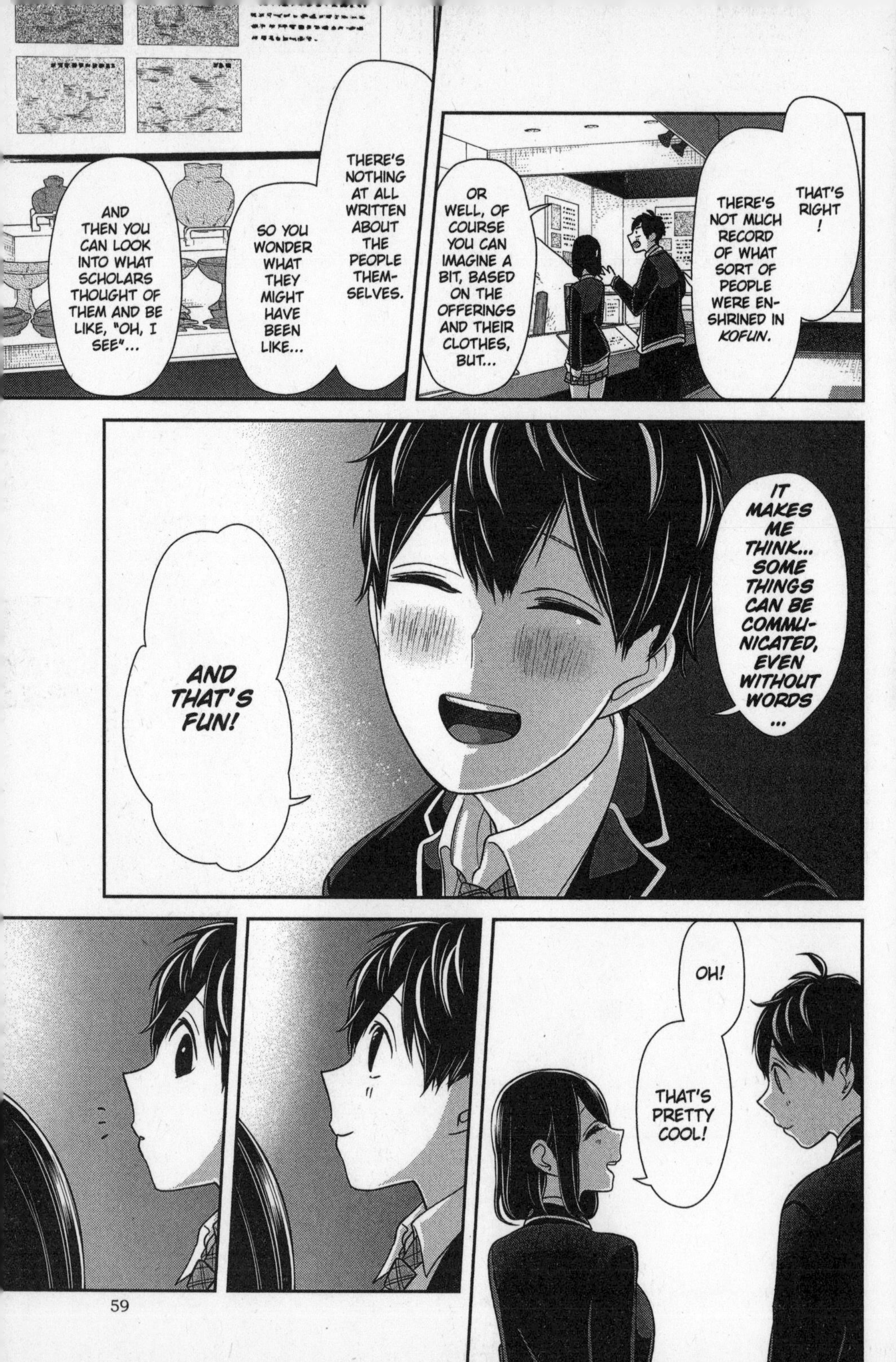
THAT'S RIGHT!
THERE'S NOT MUCH RECORD OF WHAT SORT OF PEOPLE WERE ENSHRINED IN KOFUN.
OR WELL, OF COURSE YOU CAN IMAGINE A BIT, BASED ON THE OFFERINGS AND THEIR CLOTHES, BUT...
THERE'S NOTHING AT ALL WRITTEN ABOUT THE PEOPLE THEMSELVES.
SO YOU WONDER WHAT THEY MIGHT HAVE BEEN LIKE...
AND THEN YOU CAN LOOK INTO WHAT SCHOLARS THOUGHT OF THEM AND BE LIKE, "OH, I SEE"...
IT MAKES ME THINK... SOME THINGS CAN BE COMMUNICATED, EVEN WITHOUT WORDS...
AND THAT'S FUN!
OH!
THAT'S PRETTY COOL!

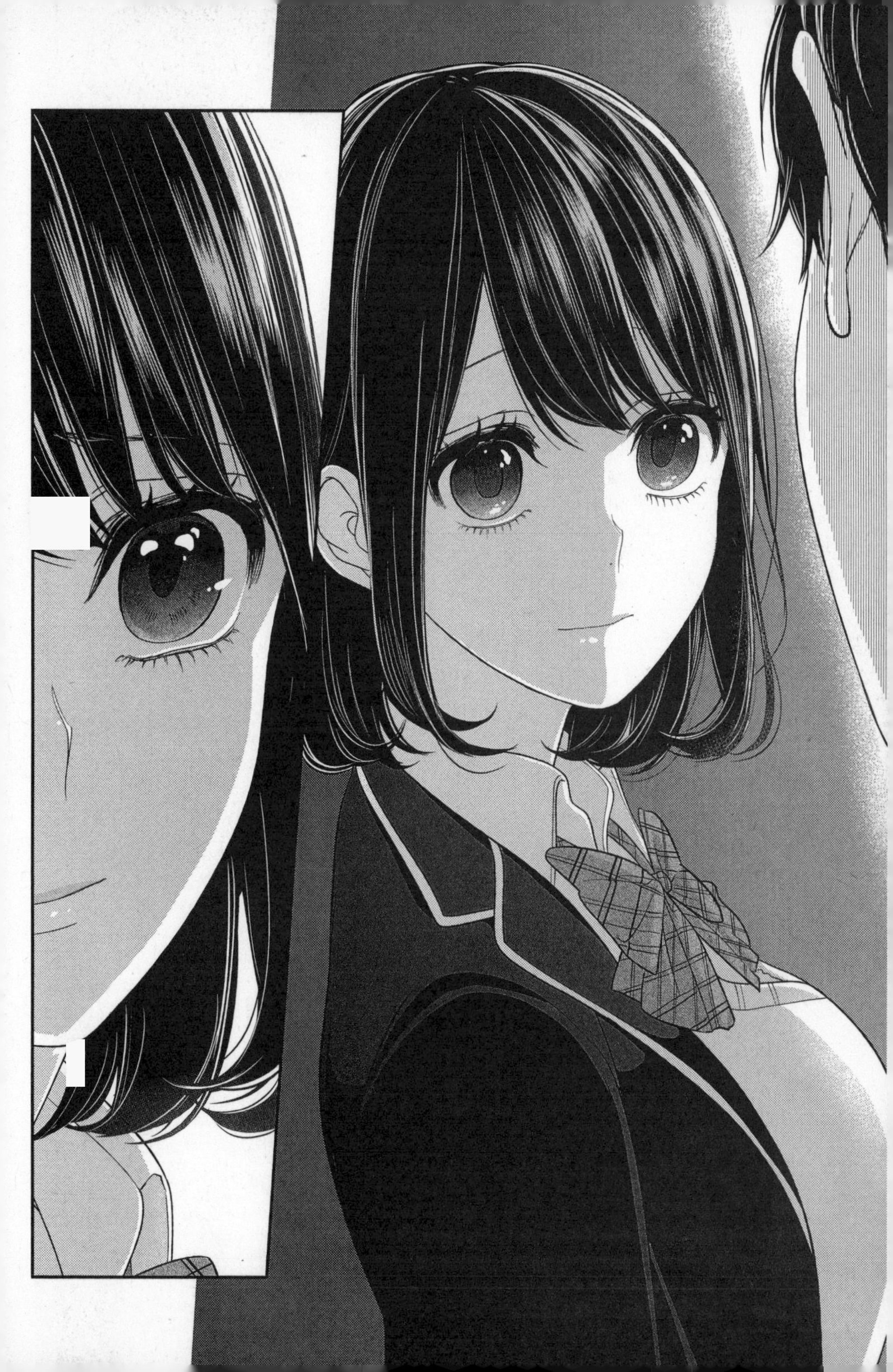

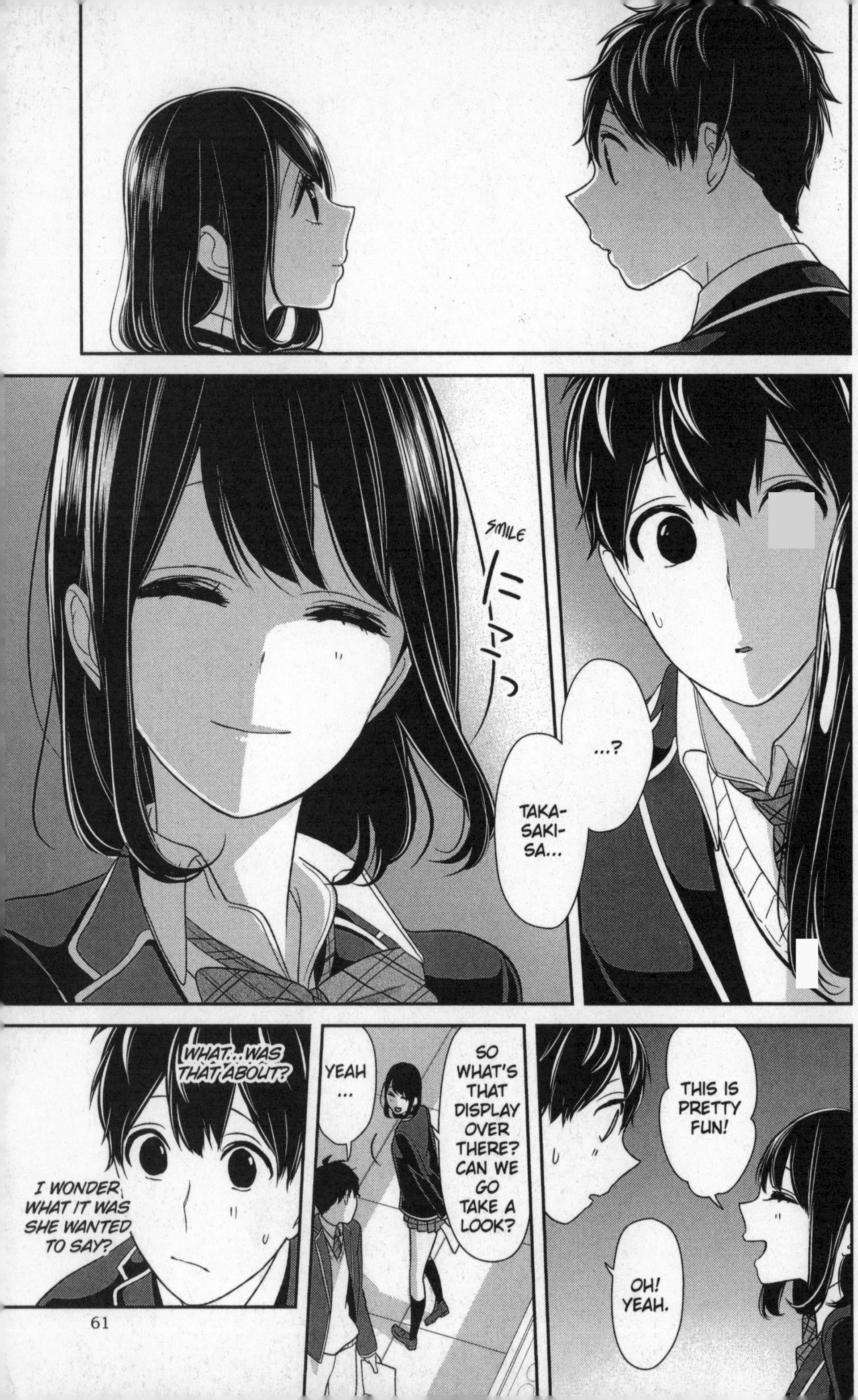
...?
TAKA-SAKI-SA...
SMILE
THIS IS PRETTY FUN!
OH! YEAH.
SO WHAT'S THAT DISPLAY OVER THERE? CAN WE GO TAKE A LOOK?
YEAH ...
WHAT...WAS THAT ABOUT?
I WONDER WHAT IT WAS SHE WANTED TO SAY?

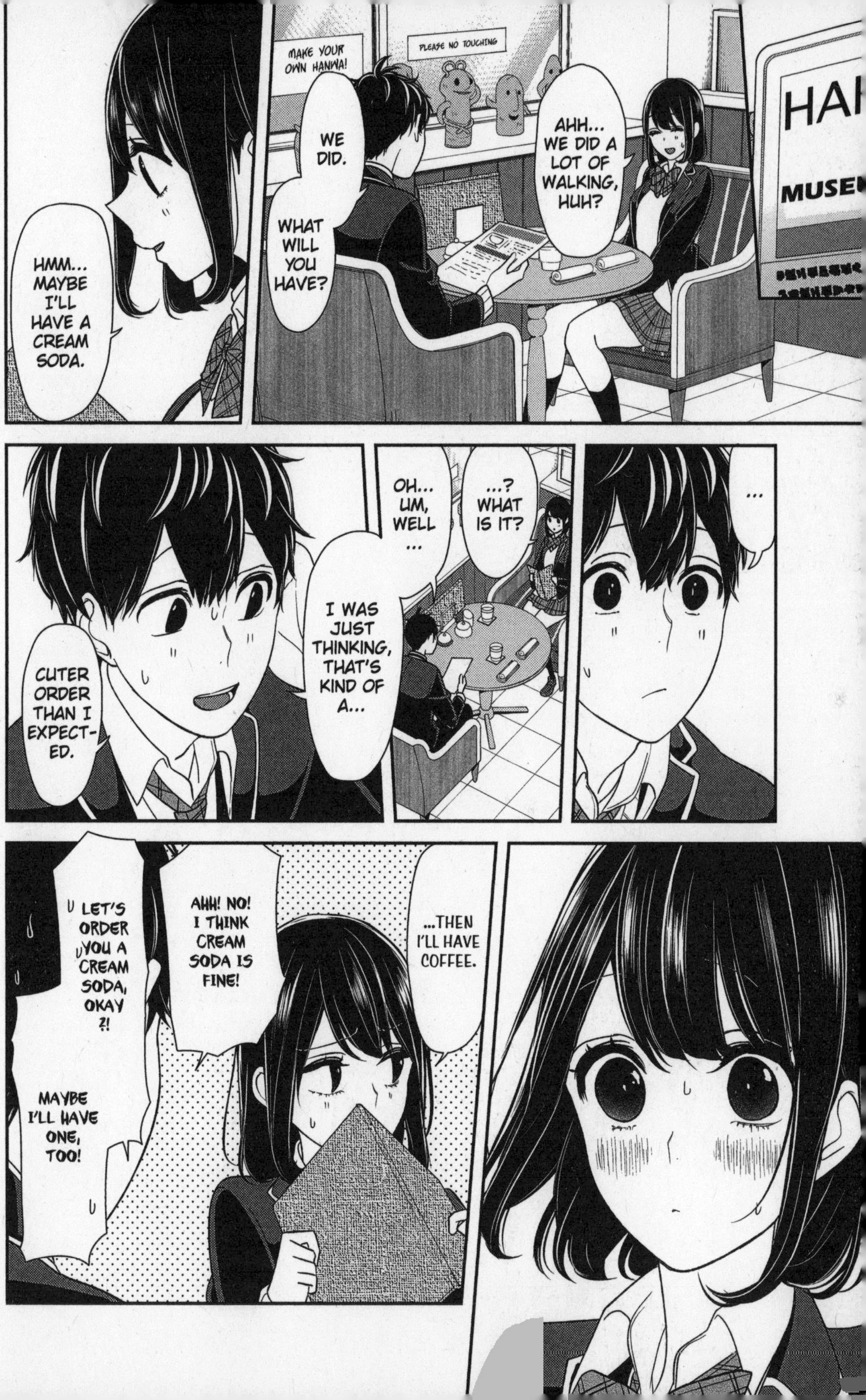

MAKE YOUR OWN HANWA!
PLEASE NO TOUCHING
AHH... WE DID A LOT OF WALKING, HUH?
WE DID.
WHAT WILL YOU HAVE?
HMM... MAYBE I'LL HAVE A CREAM SODA.
...
...? WHAT IS IT?
OH... UM, WELL...
I WAS JUST THINKING, THAT'S KIND OF A...
CUTER ORDER THAN I EXPECTED.
...THEN I'LL HAVE COFFEE.
AHH! NO! I THINK CREAM SODA IS FINE!
LET'S ORDER YOU A CREAM SODA, OKAY?!
MAYBE I'LL HAVE ONE, TOO!

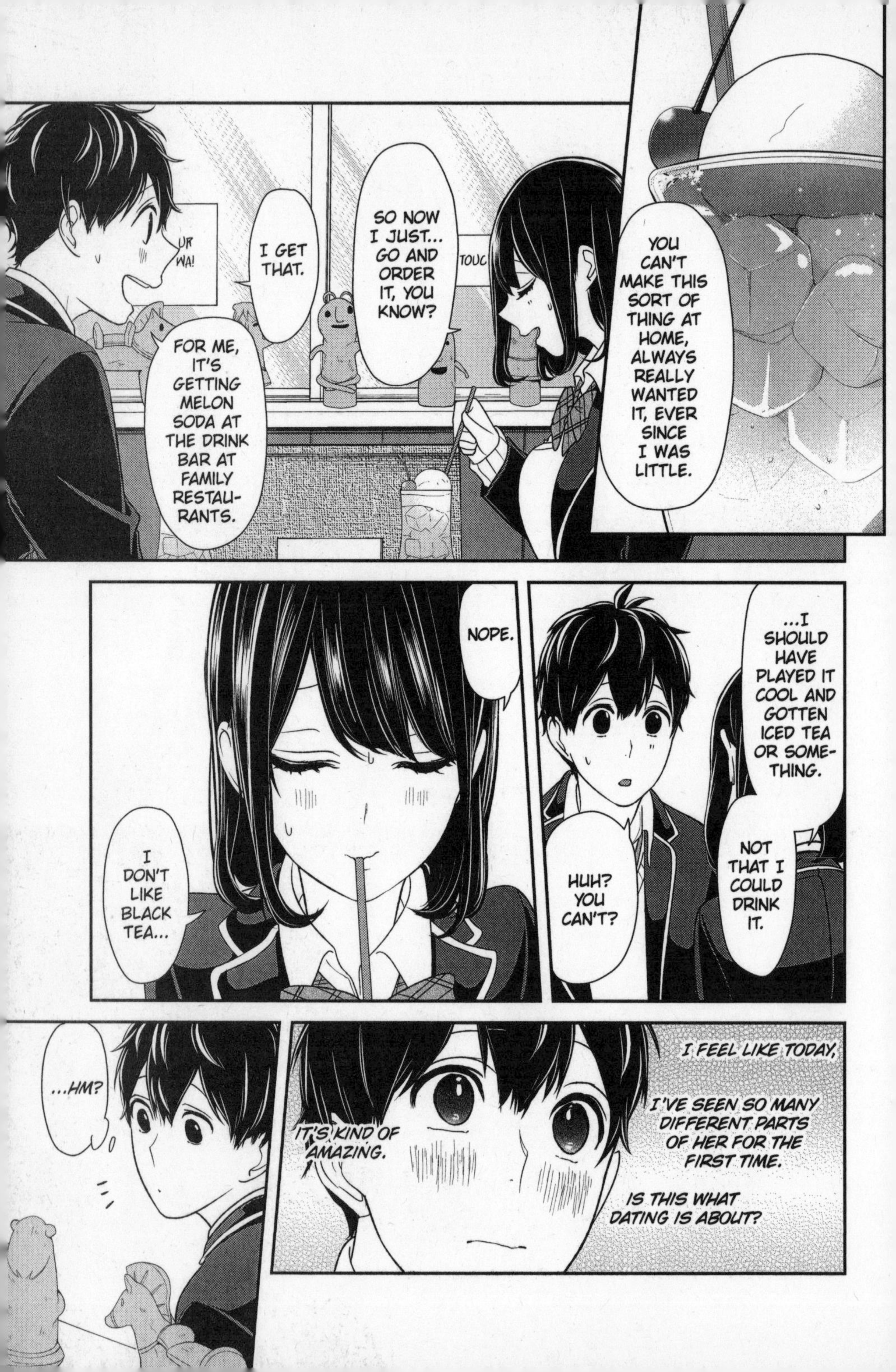
YOU CAN'T MAKE THIS SORT OF THING AT HOME, ALWAYS REALLY WANTED IT, EVER SINCE I WAS LITTLE.
TOUC
SO NOW I JUST... GO AND ORDER IT, YOU KNOW?
I GET THAT.
UR WA!
FOR ME, IT'S GETTING MELON SODA AT THE DRINK BAR AT FAMILY RESTAU-RANTS.
...I SHOULD HAVE PLAYED IT COOL AND GOTTEN ICED TEA OR SOME-THING.
NOT THAT I COULD DRINK IT.
HUH? YOU CAN'T?
NOPE.
I DON'T LIKE BLACK TEA...
I FEEL LIKE TODAY,
I'VE SEEN SO MANY DIFFERENT PARTS OF HER FOR THE FIRST TIME.
IS THIS WHAT DATING IS ABOUT?
IT'S KIND OF AMAZING.
...HM?

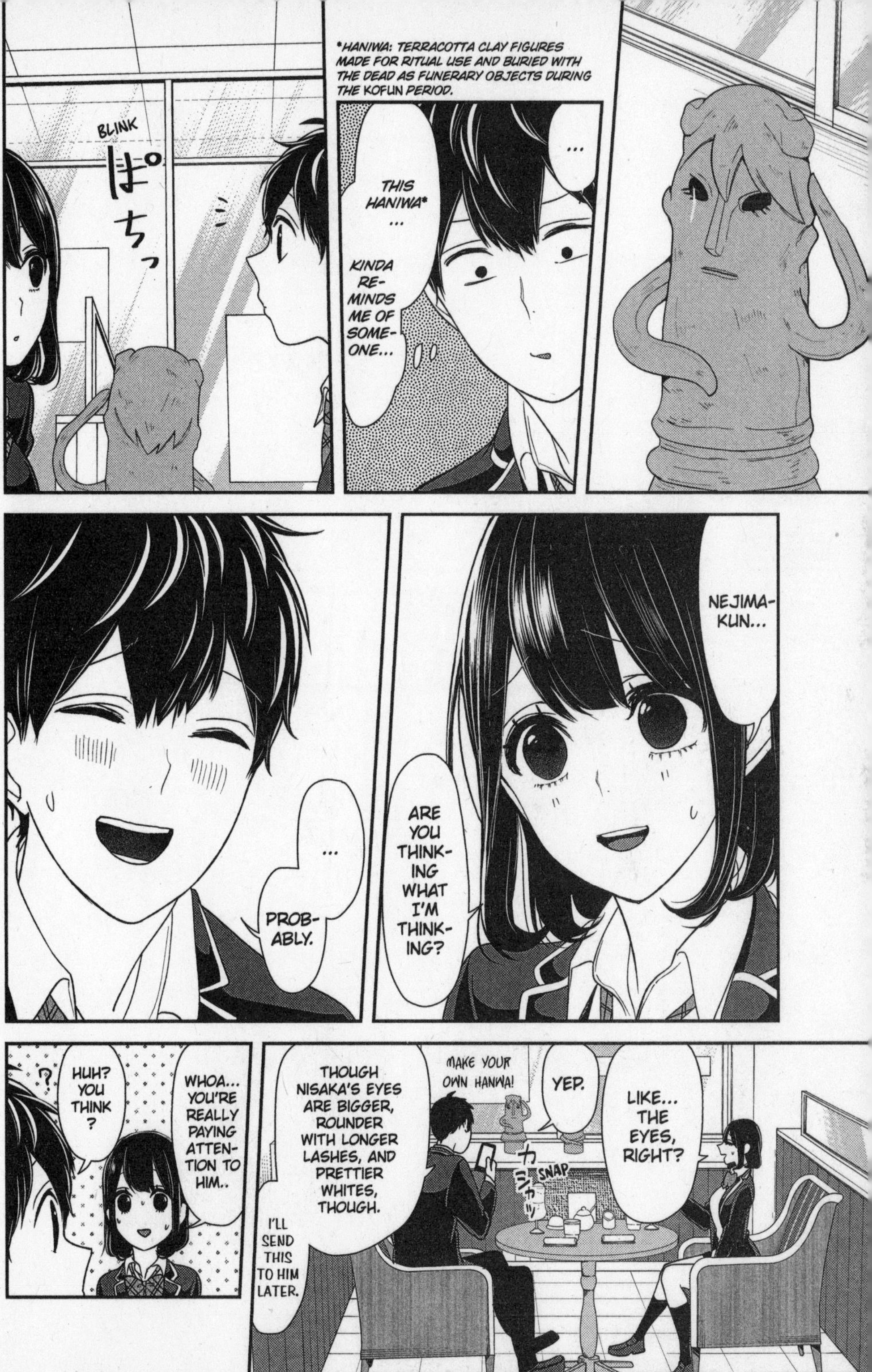
*HANIWA: TERRACOTTA CLAY FIGURES MADE FOR RITUAL USE AND BURIED WITH THE DEAD AS FUNERARY OBJECTS DURING THE KOFUN PERIOD.
...
THIS HANIWA* ... KINDA REMINDS ME OF SOMEONE...
BLINK
ぽちっ
NEJIMA-KUN...
ARE YOU THINKING WHAT I'M THINKING?
...
PROBABLY.
LIKE... THE EYES, RIGHT?
YEP.
MAKE YOUR OWN HANWA!
カシャッ
SNAP
THOUGH NISAKA'S EYES ARE BIGGER, ROUNDER WITH LONGER LASHES, AND PRETTIER WHITES, THOUGH.
I'LL SEND THIS TO HIM LATER.
WHOA... YOU'RE REALLY PAYING ATTENTION TO HIM..
HUH? YOU THINK?
?

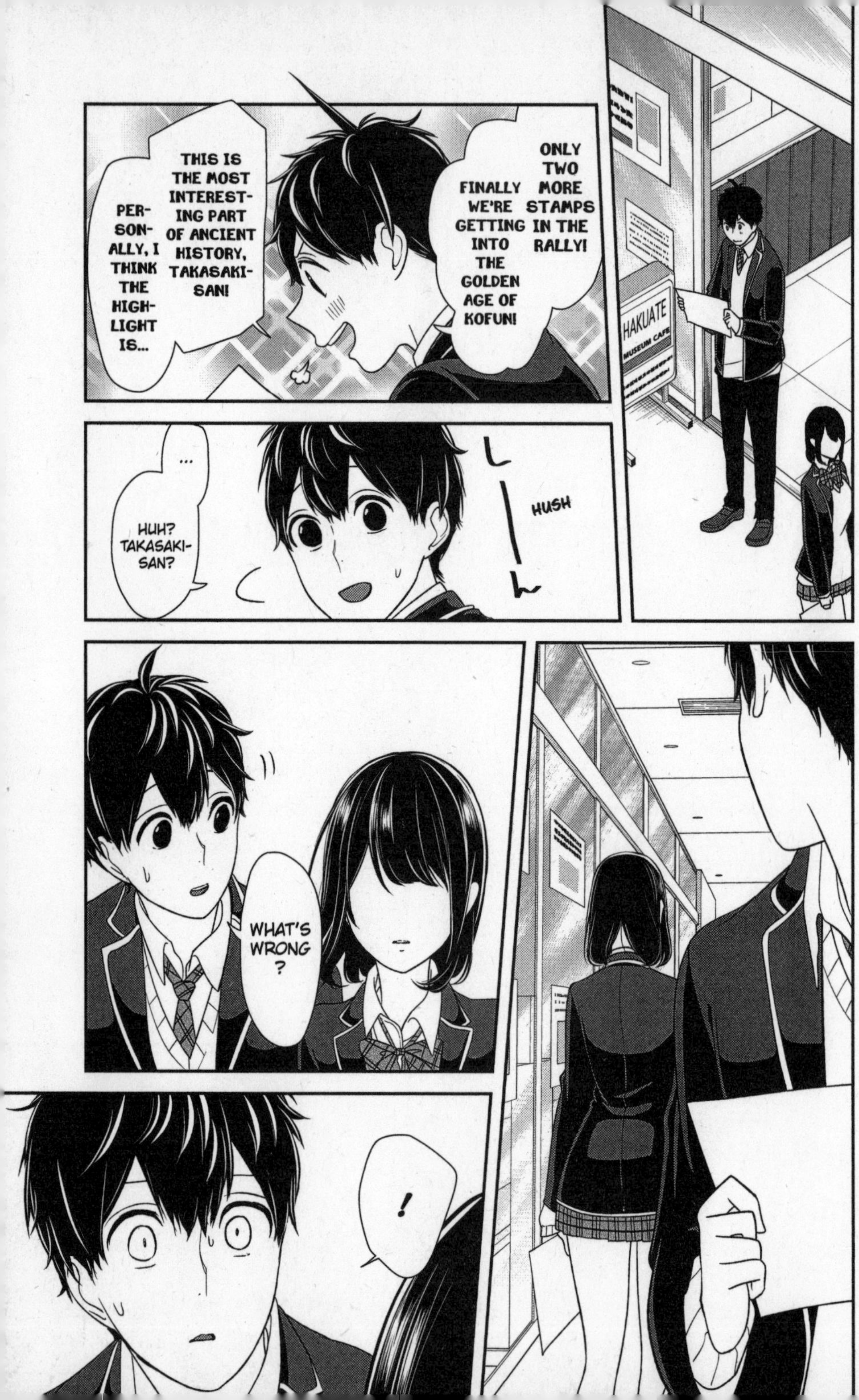
HAKUATE
MUSEUM CAFE
ONLY TWO MORE STAMPS IN THE RALLY!
FINALLY WE'RE GETTING INTO THE GOLDEN AGE OF KOFUN!
THIS IS THE MOST INTERESTING PART OF ANCIENT HISTORY, TAKASAKI-SAN!
PERSONALLY, I THINK THE HIGHLIGHT IS...
HUSH
...
HUH? TAKASAKI-SAN?
WHAT'S WRONG?
!

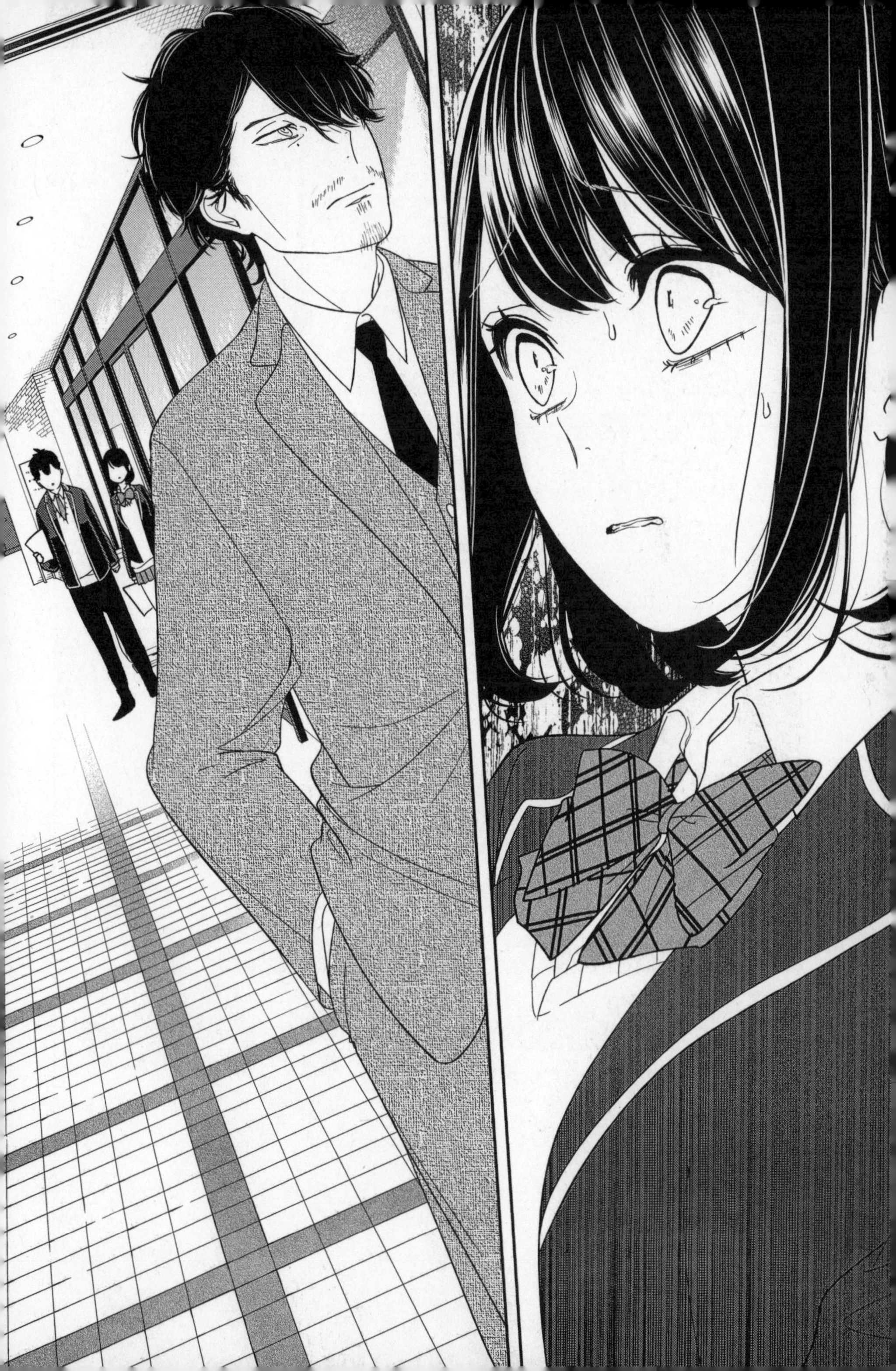

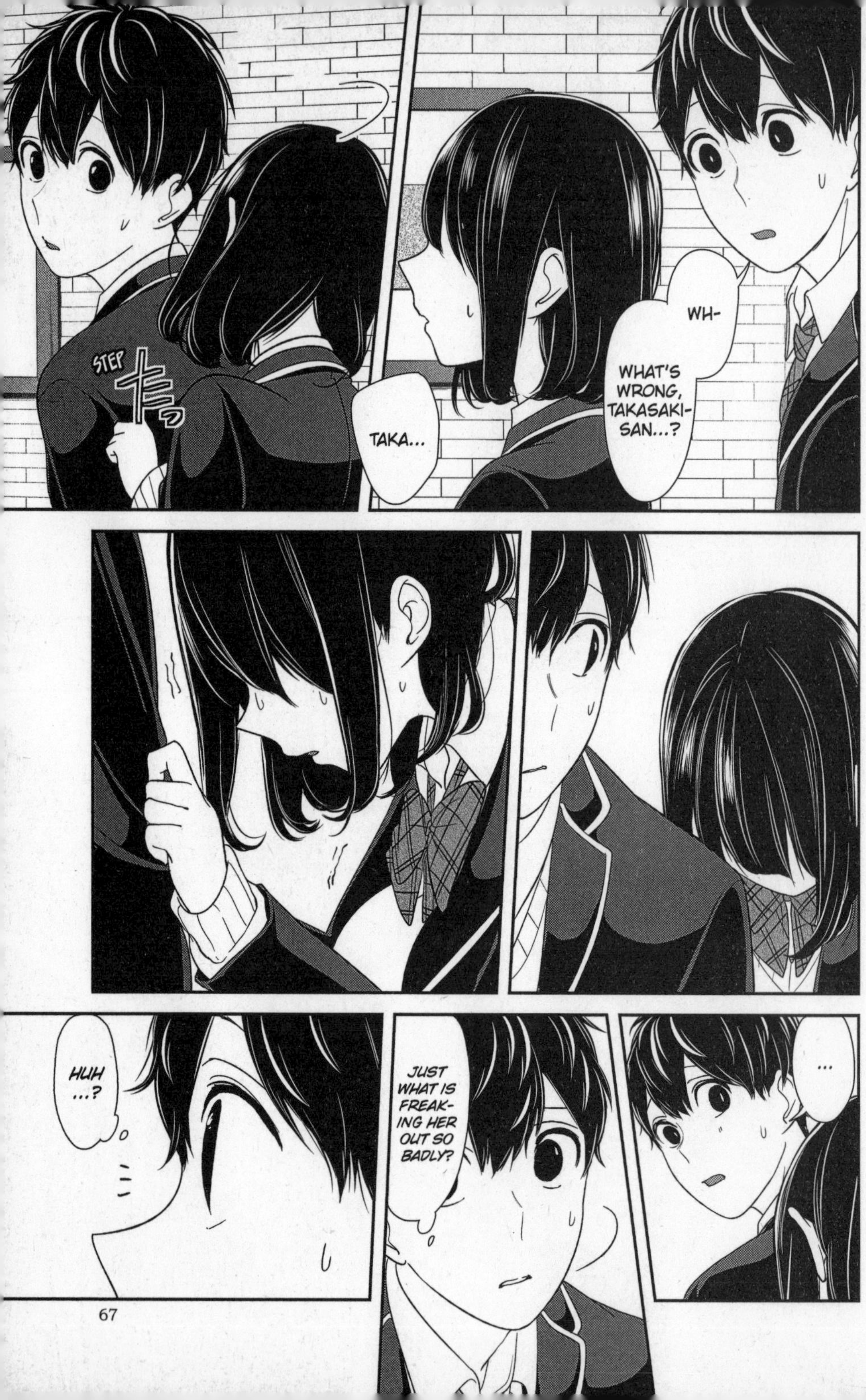
WH- WHAT'S WRONG, TAKASAKI-SAN...?
TAKA...
STEP
...
JUST WHAT IS FREAKING HER OUT SO BADLY?
HUH ...?

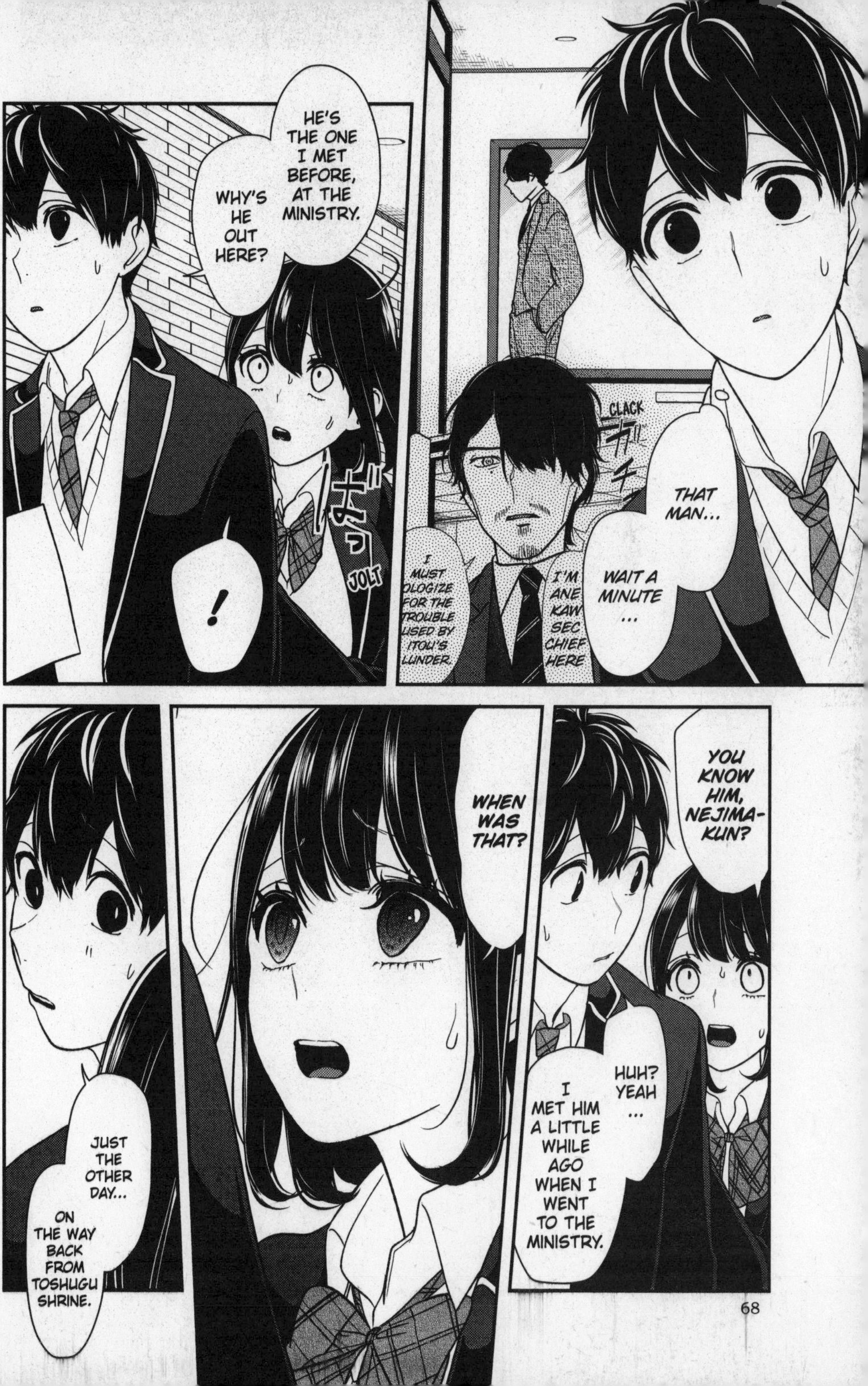
THAT MAN...
WAIT A MINUTE...
CLACK
I'M ANE KAW SEC CHIEF HERE
I MUST OLOGIZE FOR THE TROUBLE USED BY ITOU'S LUNDER.
HE'S THE ONE I MET BEFORE, AT THE MINISTRY.
WHY'S HE OUT HERE?
JOLT
!
YOU KNOW HIM, NEJIMA-KUN?
HUH? YEAH...
I MET HIM A LITTLE WHILE AGO WHEN I WENT TO THE MINISTRY.
WHEN WAS THAT?
JUST THE OTHER DAY...
ON THE WAY BACK FROM TOSHUGU SHRINE.

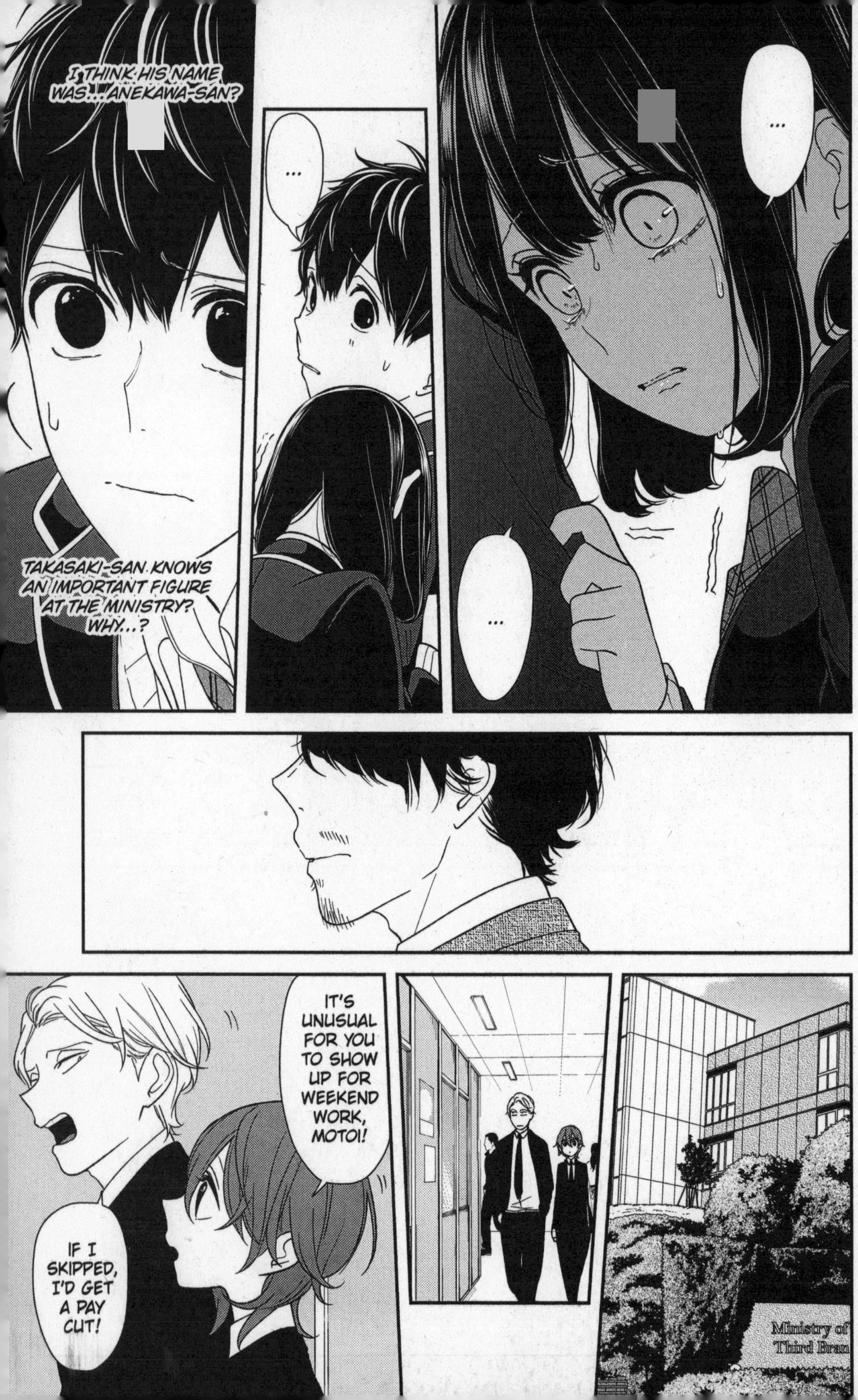
...
...
...
I THINK HIS NAME WAS... ANEKAWA-SAN?
TAKASAKI-SAN KNOWS AN IMPORTANT FIGURE AT THE MINISTRY? WHY...?
Ministry of
Third Bran
IT'S UNUSUAL FOR YOU TO SHOW UP FOR WEEKEND WORK, MOTOI!
IF I SKIPPED, I'D GET A PAY CUT!

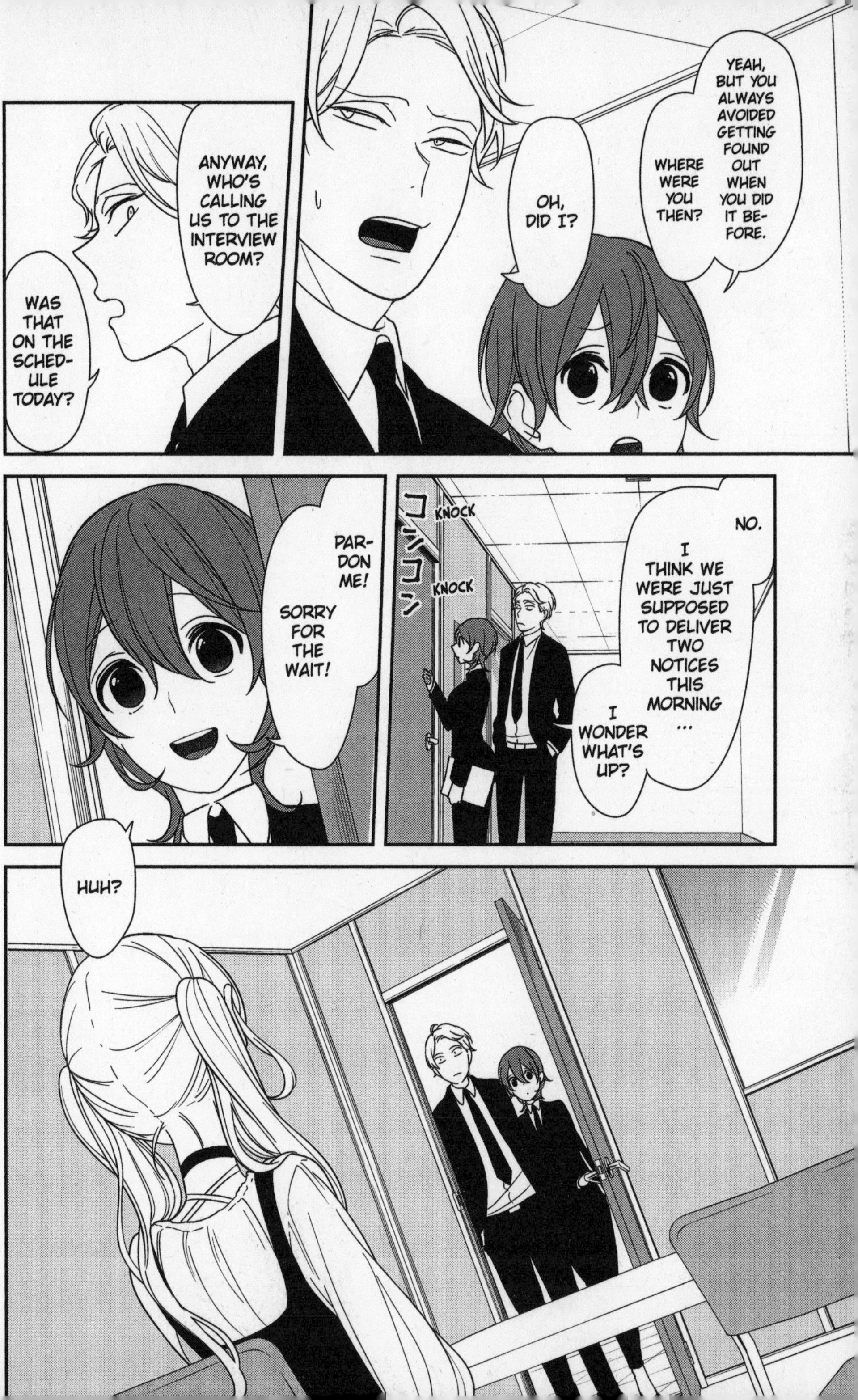
YEAH, BUT YOU ALWAYS AVOIDED GETTING FOUND OUT WHEN YOU DID IT BEFORE.
WHERE WERE YOU THEN?
OH, DID I?
ANYWAY, WHO'S CALLING US TO THE INTERVIEW ROOM?
WAS THAT ON THE SCHEDULE TODAY?
NO.
I THINK WE WERE JUST SUPPOSED TO DELIVER TWO NOTICES THIS MORNING...
I WONDER WHAT'S UP?
コンコン
KNOCK
KNOCK
PARDON ME!
SORRY FOR THE WAIT!
HUH?

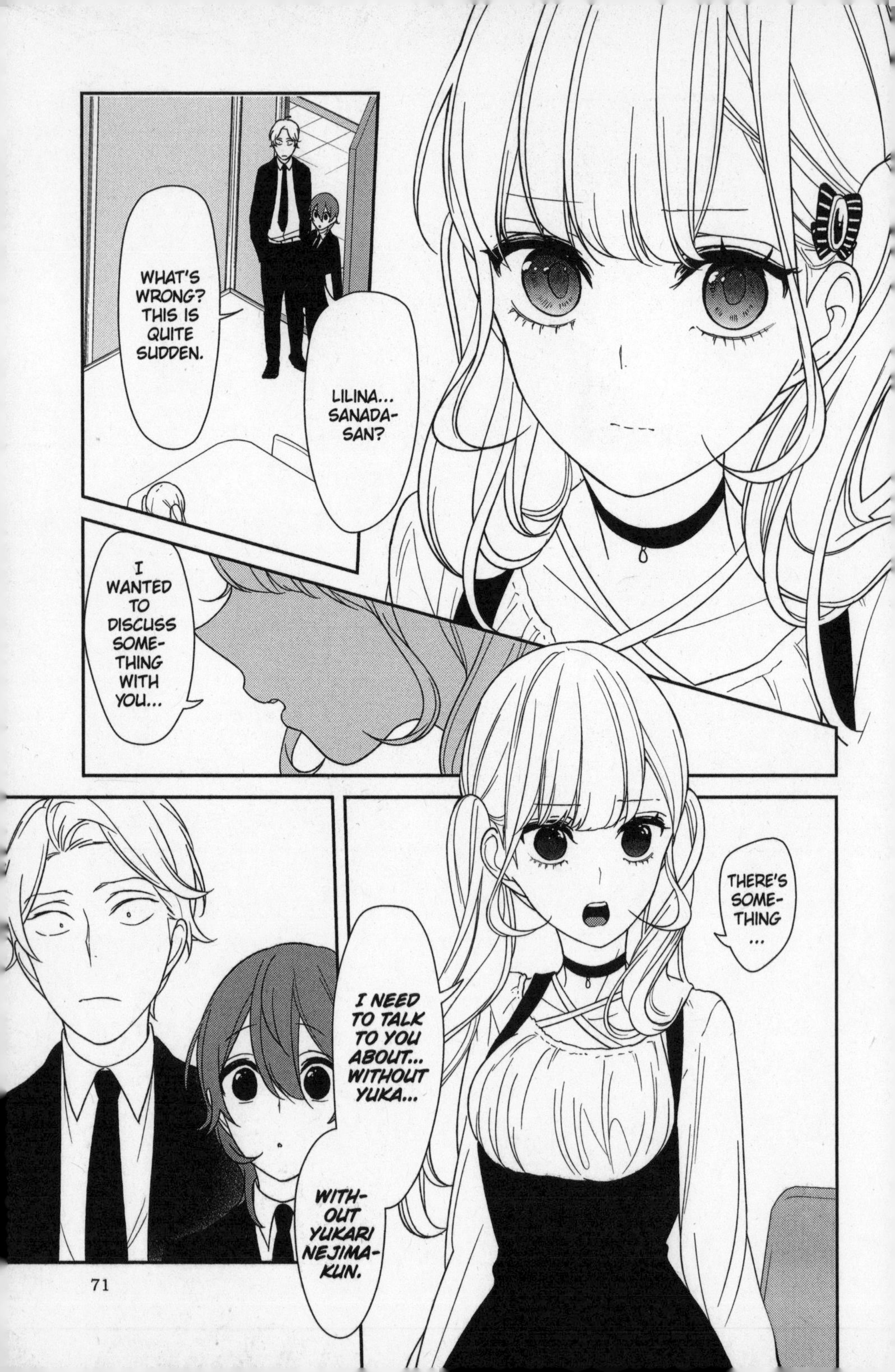
LILINA... SANADA-SAN?
WHAT'S WRONG? THIS IS QUITE SUDDEN.
I WANTED TO DISCUSS SOME-THING WITH YOU...
THERE'S SOME-THING...
I NEED TO TALK TO YOU ABOUT... WITHOUT YUKA...
WITH-OUT YUKARI NEJIMA-KUN.

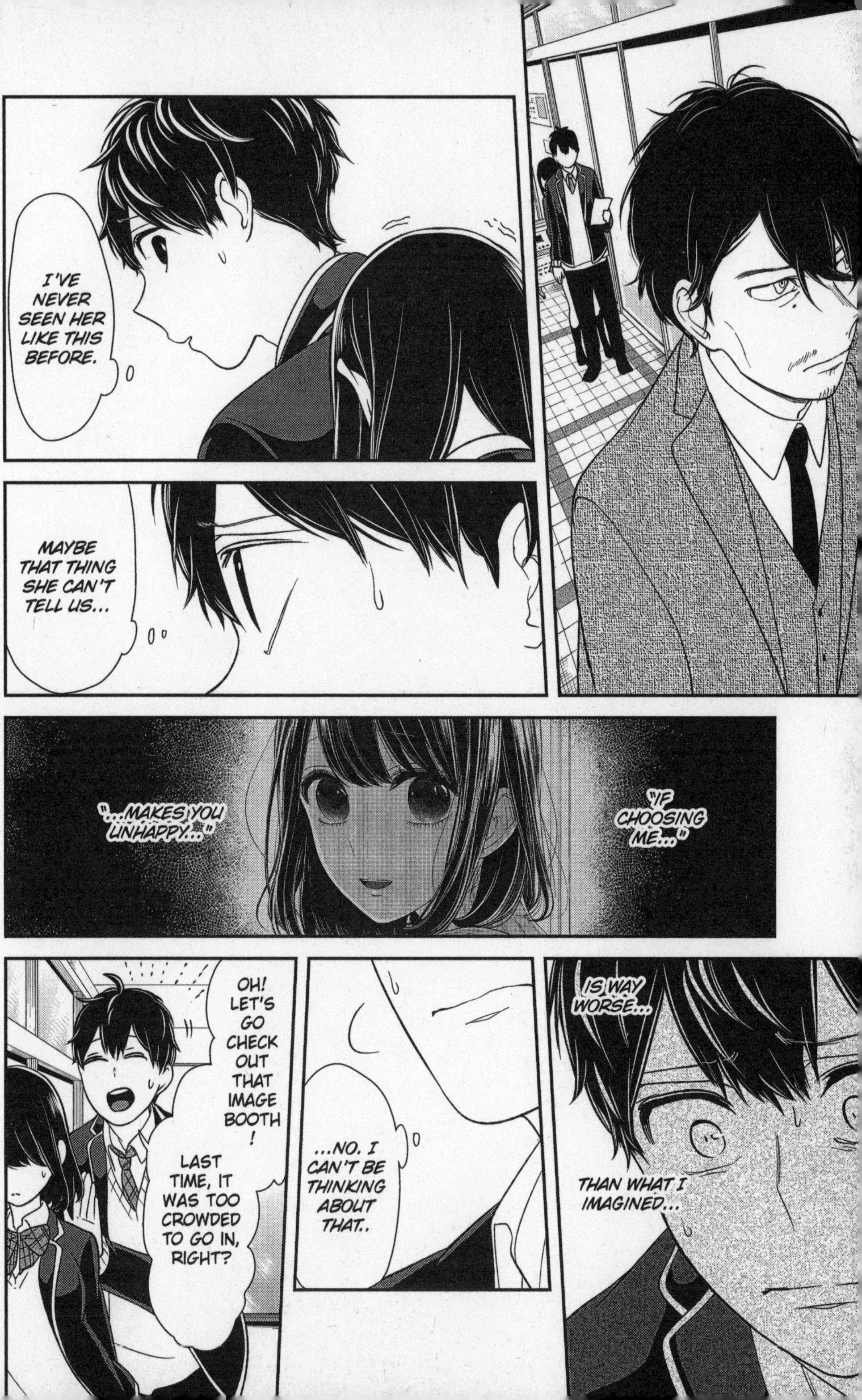
I'VE NEVER SEEN HER LIKE THIS BEFORE.
MAYBE THAT THING SHE CAN'T TELL US...
"IF CHOOSING ME..."
"...MAKES YOU UNHAPPY..."
IS WAY WORSE...
THAN WHAT I IMAGINED...
...NO. I CAN'T BE THINKING ABOUT THAT..
OH! LET'S GO CHECK OUT THAT IMAGE BOOTH!
LAST TIME, IT WAS TOO CROWDED TO GO IN, RIGHT?

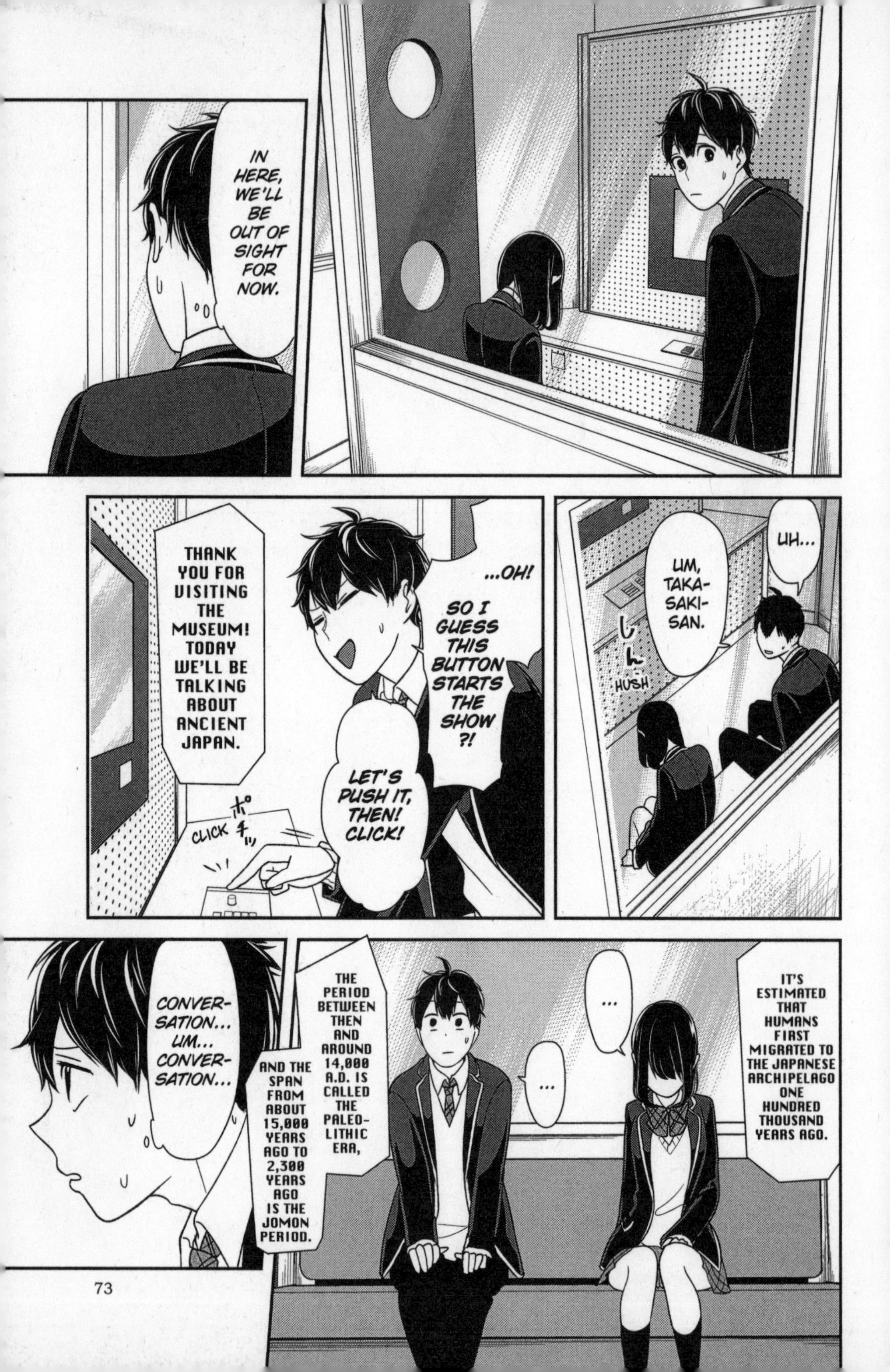
IN HERE, WE'LL BE OUT OF SIGHT FOR NOW.
UH...
UM, TAKASAKI-SAN.
しーん
HUSH
...OH!
SO I GUESS THIS BUTTON STARTS THE SHOW?!
LET'S PUSH IT, THEN! CLICK!
THANK YOU FOR VISITING THE MUSEUM! TODAY WE'LL BE TALKING ABOUT ANCIENT JAPAN.
ポチッ
CLICK
IT'S ESTIMATED THAT HUMANS FIRST MIGRATED TO THE JAPANESE ARCHIPELAGO ONE HUNDRED THOUSAND YEARS AGO.
...
...
THE PERIOD BETWEEN THEN AND AROUND 14,000 A.D. IS CALLED THE PALEO-LITHIC ERA,
AND THE SPAN FROM ABOUT 15,000 YEARS AGO TO 2,300 YEARS AGO IS THE JOMON PERIOD.
CONVER-SATION... UM... CONVER-SATION...

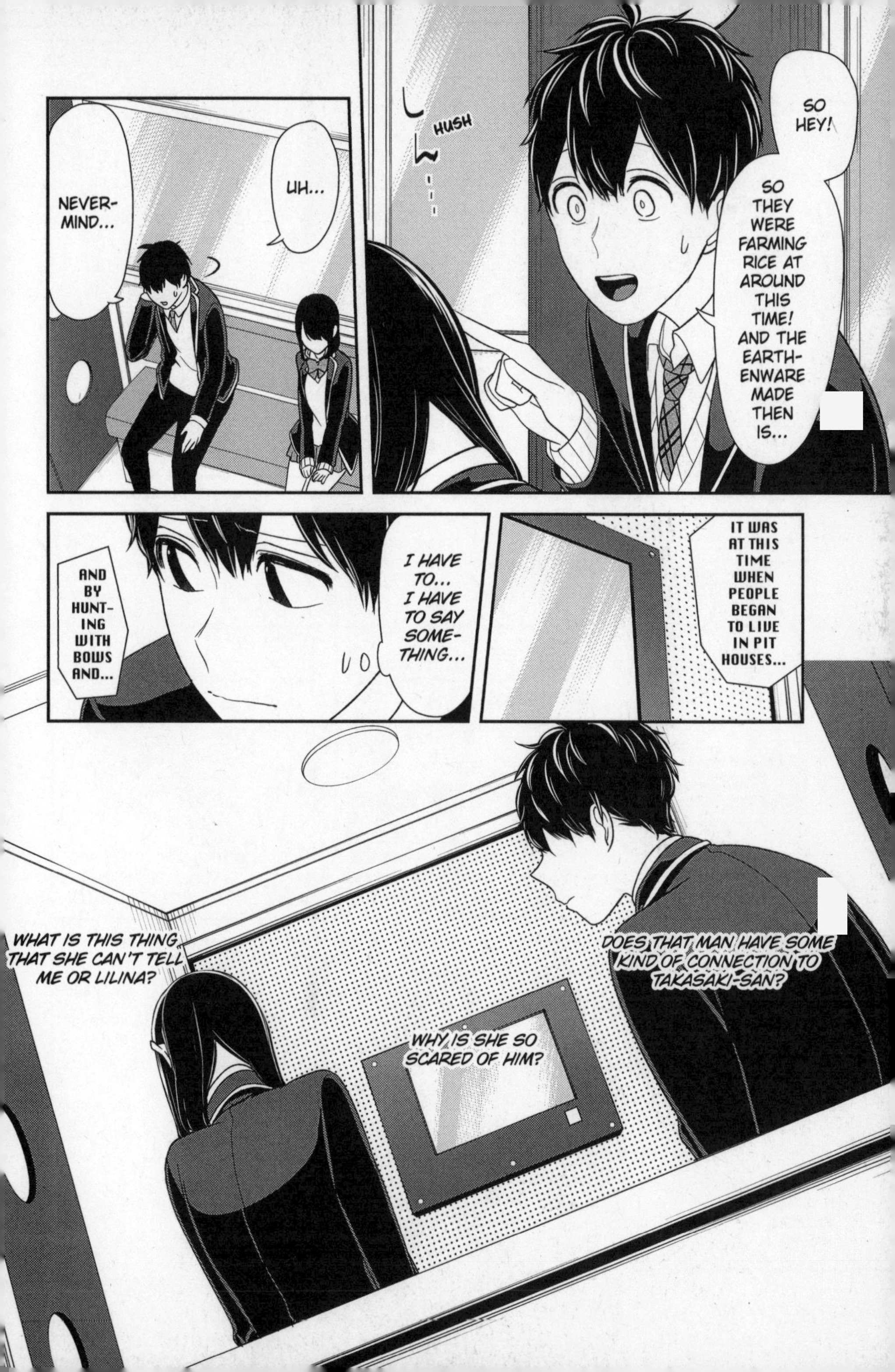
SO HEY!
SO THEY WERE FARMING RICE AT AROUND THIS TIME! AND THE EARTHENWARE MADE THEN IS...
HUSH
UH...
NEVER-MIND...
IT WAS AT THIS TIME WHEN PEOPLE BEGAN TO LIVE IN PIT HOUSES...
I HAVE TO... I HAVE TO SAY SOMETHING...
AND BY HUNTING WITH BOWS AND...
DOES THAT MAN HAVE SOME KIND OF CONNECTION TO TAKASAKI-SAN?
WHAT IS THIS THING THAT SHE CAN'T TELL ME OR LILINA?
WHY IS SHE SO SCARED OF HIM?

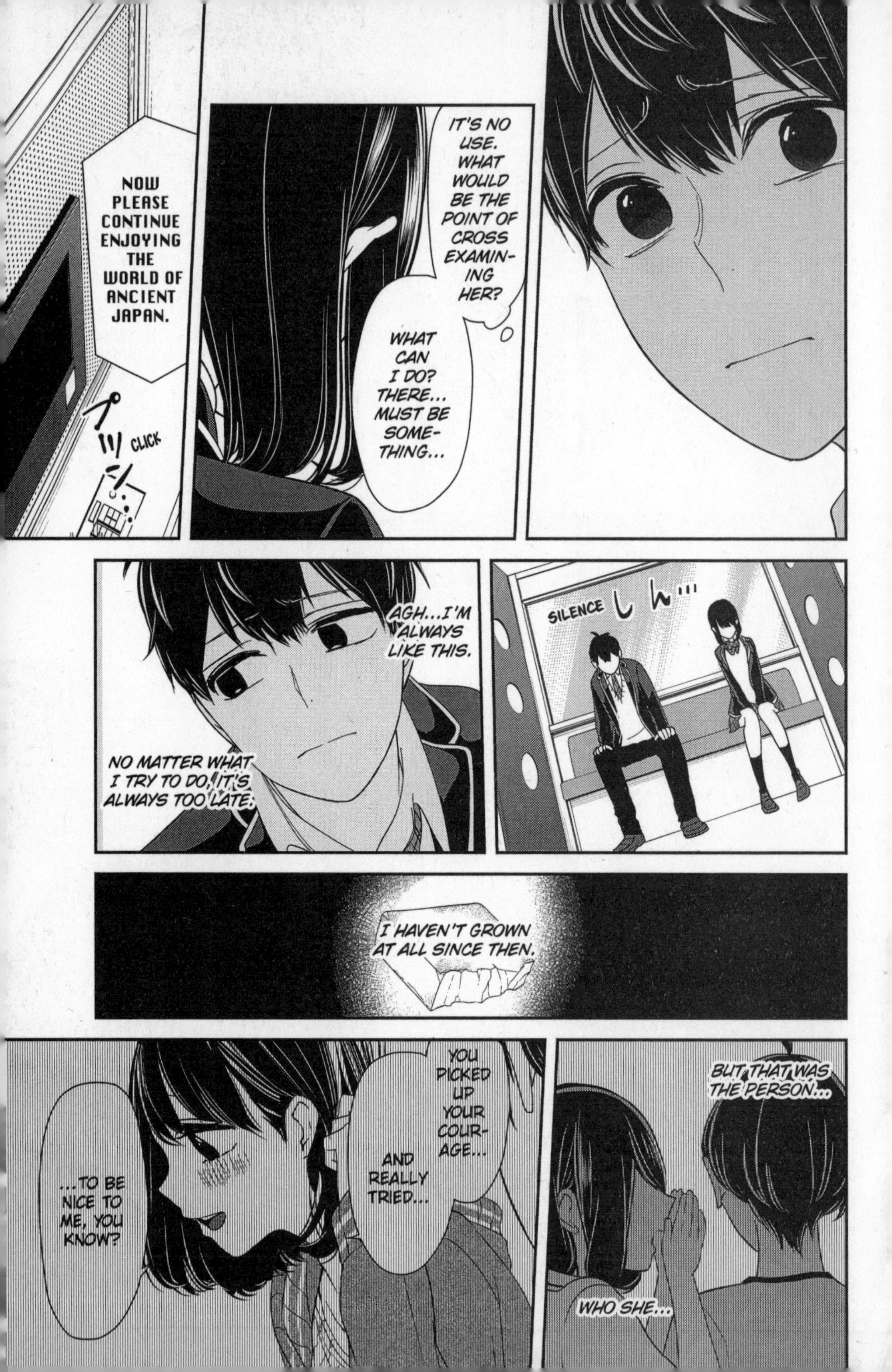
IT'S NO USE. WHAT WOULD BE THE POINT OF CROSS EXAMINING HER?
WHAT CAN I DO? THERE... MUST BE SOMETHING...
NOW PLEASE CONTINUE ENJOYING THE WORLD OF ANCIENT JAPAN.
CLICK
SILENCE しん…
AGH...I'M ALWAYS LIKE THIS.
NO MATTER WHAT I TRY TO DO, IT'S ALWAYS TOO LATE.
I HAVEN'T GROWN AT ALL SINCE THEN.
BUT THAT WAS THE PERSON...
WHO SHE...
YOU PICKED UP YOUR COURAGE...
AND REALLY TRIED...
...TO BE NICE TO ME, YOU KNOW?

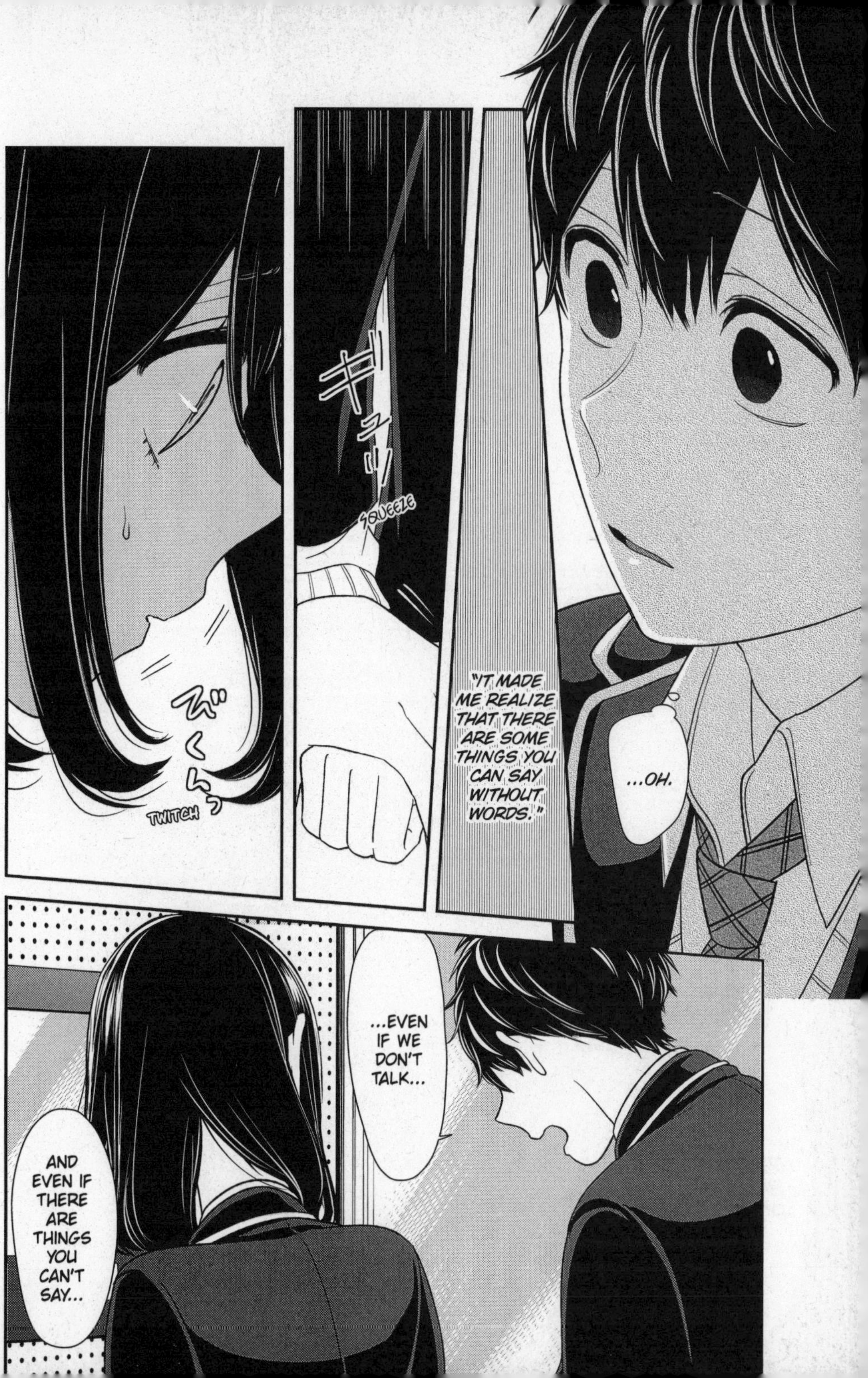
...OH.
"IT MADE ME REALIZE THAT THERE ARE SOME THINGS YOU CAN SAY WITHOUT WORDS."
SQUEEZE
TWITCH
...EVEN IF WE DON'T TALK...
AND EVEN IF THERE ARE THINGS YOU CAN'T SAY...

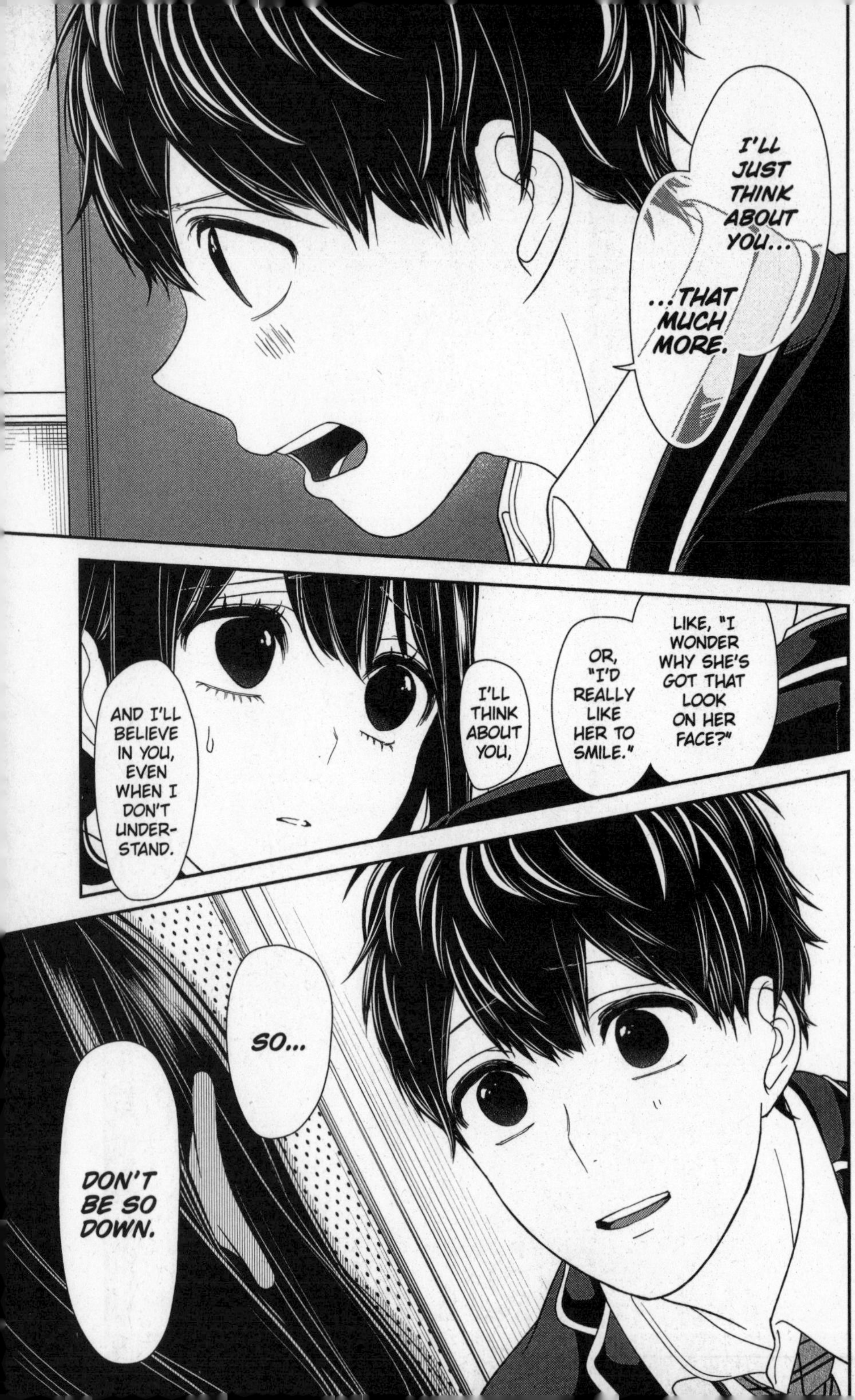
I'LL JUST THINK ABOUT YOU...
...THAT MUCH MORE.
LIKE, "I WONDER WHY SHE'S GOT THAT LOOK ON HER FACE?"
OR, "I'D REALLY LIKE HER TO SMILE."
I'LL THINK ABOUT YOU,
AND I'LL BELIEVE IN YOU, EVEN WHEN I DON'T UNDER-STAND.
SO...
DON'T BE SO DOWN.

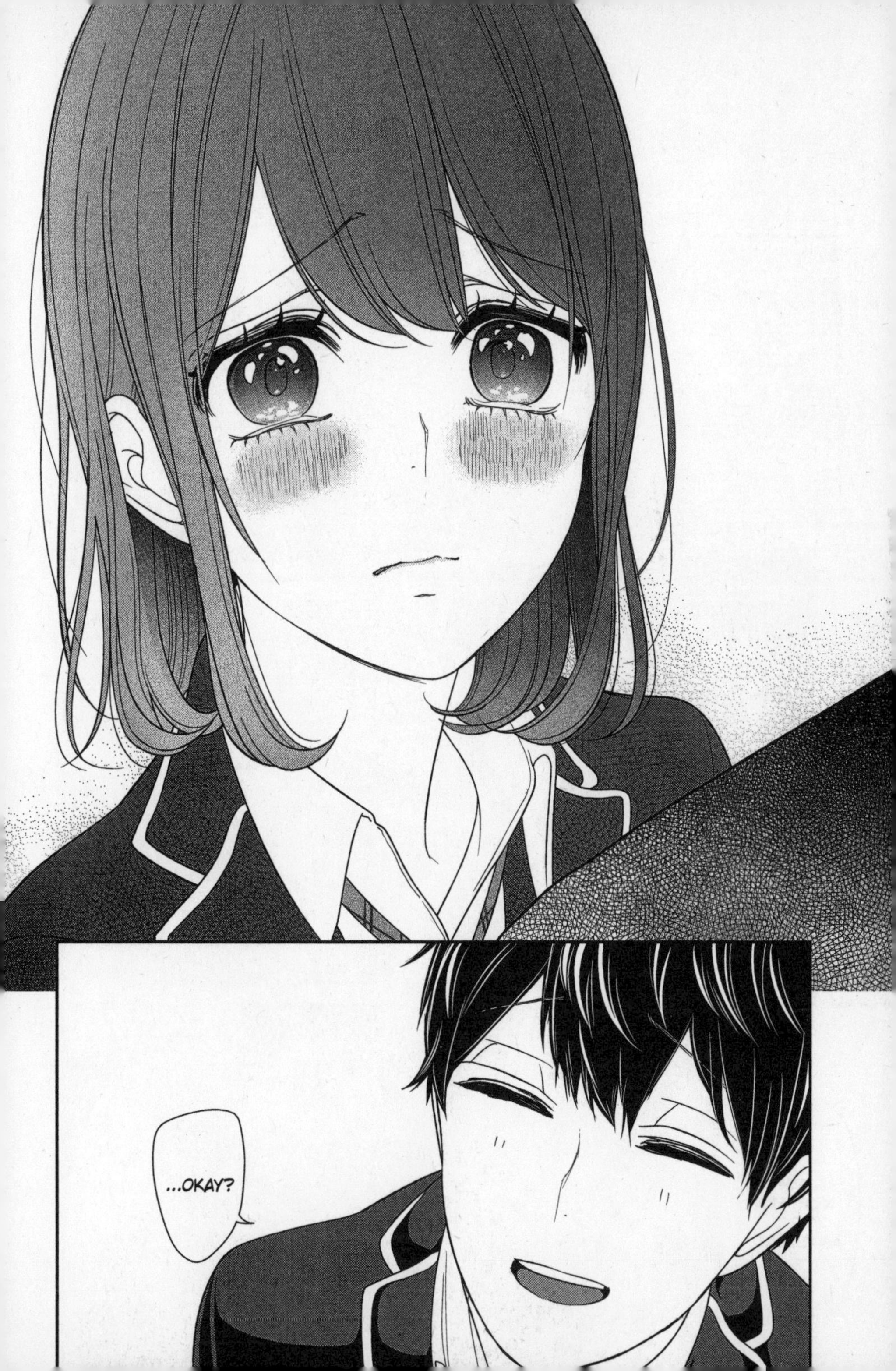
...OKAY?

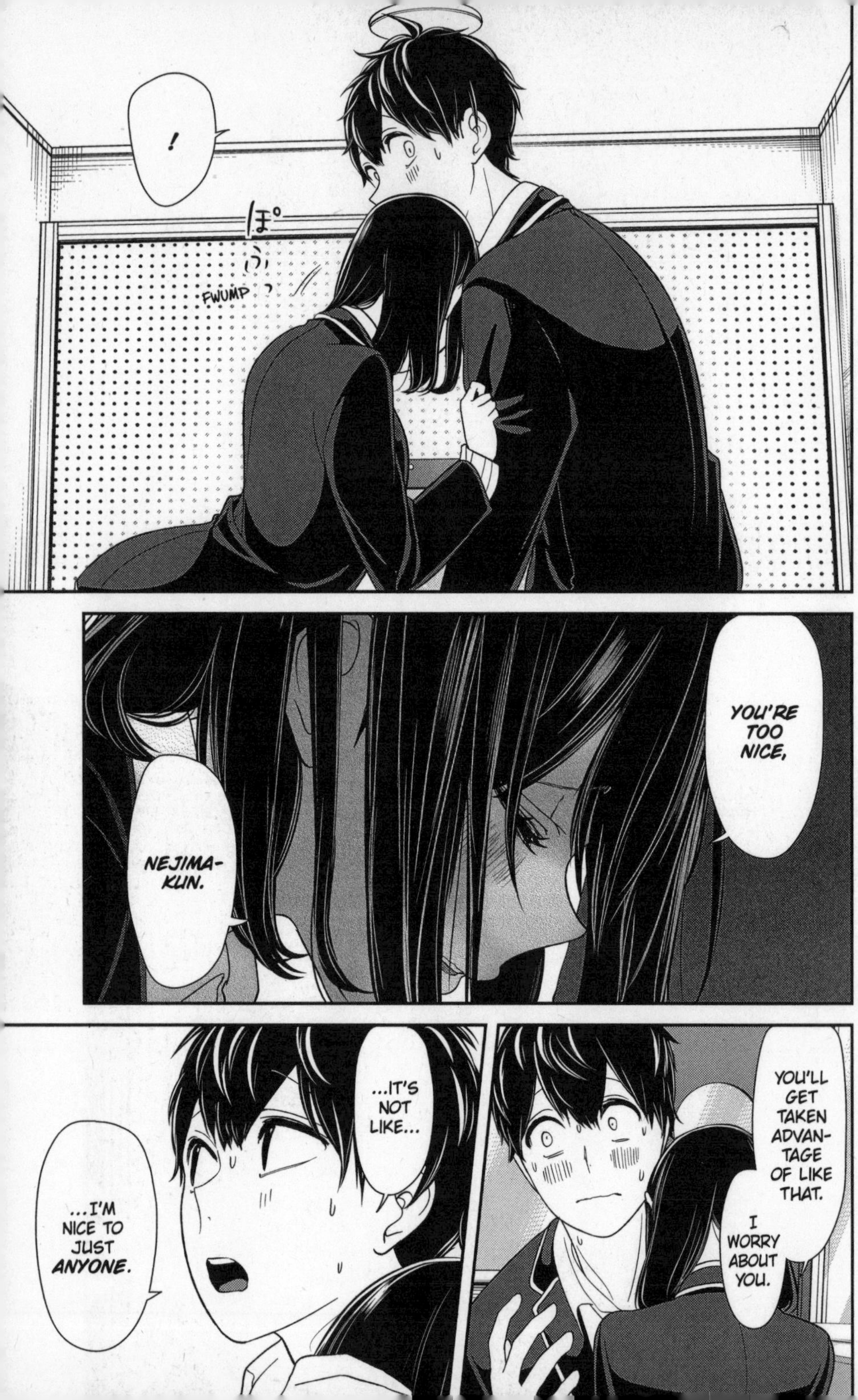
!
ぽふっ
FWUMP
YOU'RE TOO NICE,
NEJIMA-KUN.
YOU'LL GET TAKEN ADVANTAGE OF LIKE THAT.
I WORRY ABOUT YOU.
...IT'S NOT LIKE...
...I'M NICE TO JUST ANYONE.

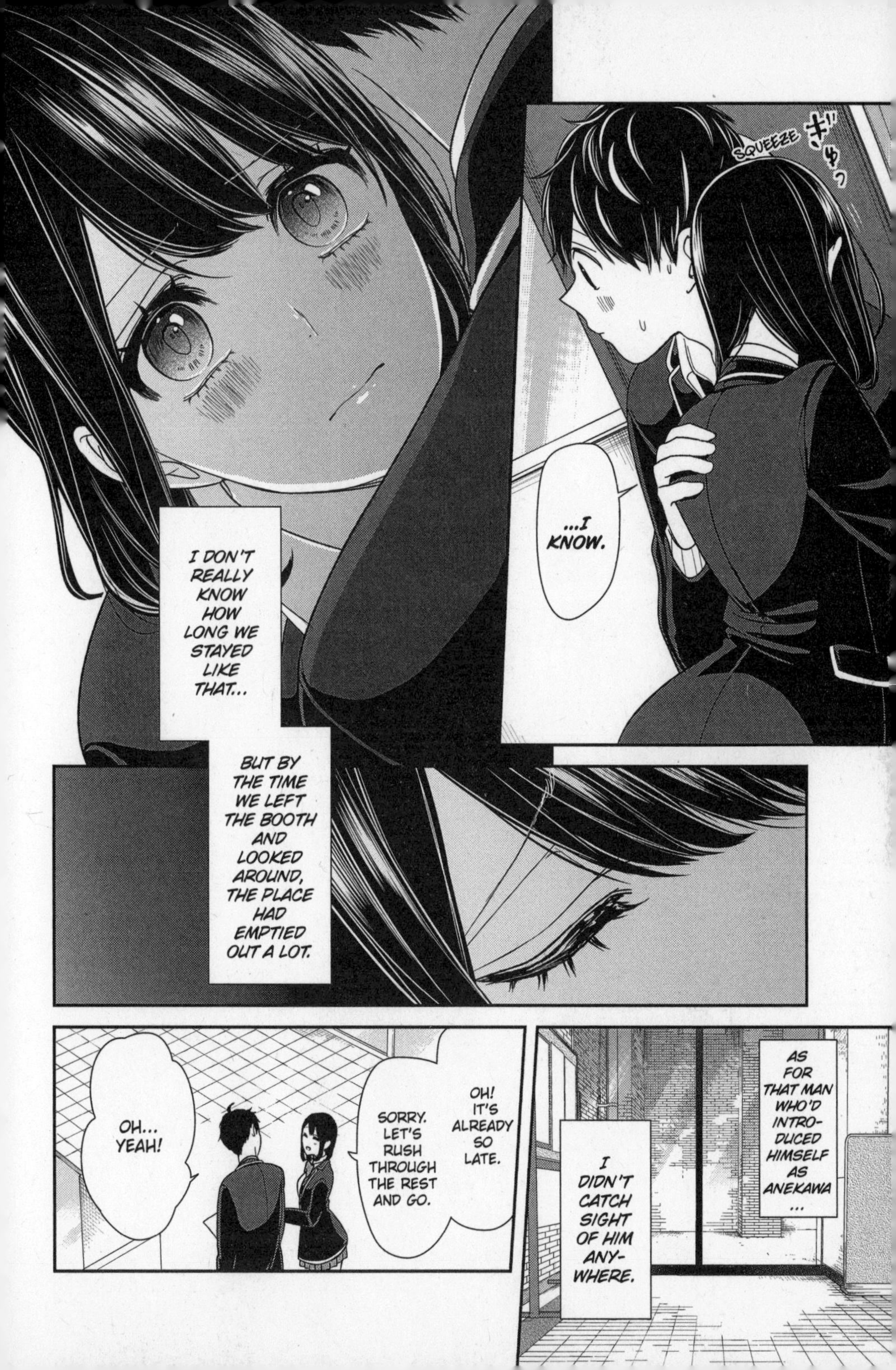

SQUEEZE
ぎゅっ
...I KNOW.
I DON'T REALLY KNOW HOW LONG WE STAYED LIKE THAT...
BUT BY THE TIME WE LEFT THE BOOTH AND LOOKED AROUND, THE PLACE HAD EMPTIED OUT A LOT.
AS FOR THAT MAN WHO'D INTRO-DUCED HIMSELF AS ANEKAWA ...
I DIDN'T CATCH SIGHT OF HIM ANY-WHERE.
OH! IT'S ALREADY SO LATE.
SORRY. LET'S RUSH THROUGH THE REST AND GO.
OH... YEAH!

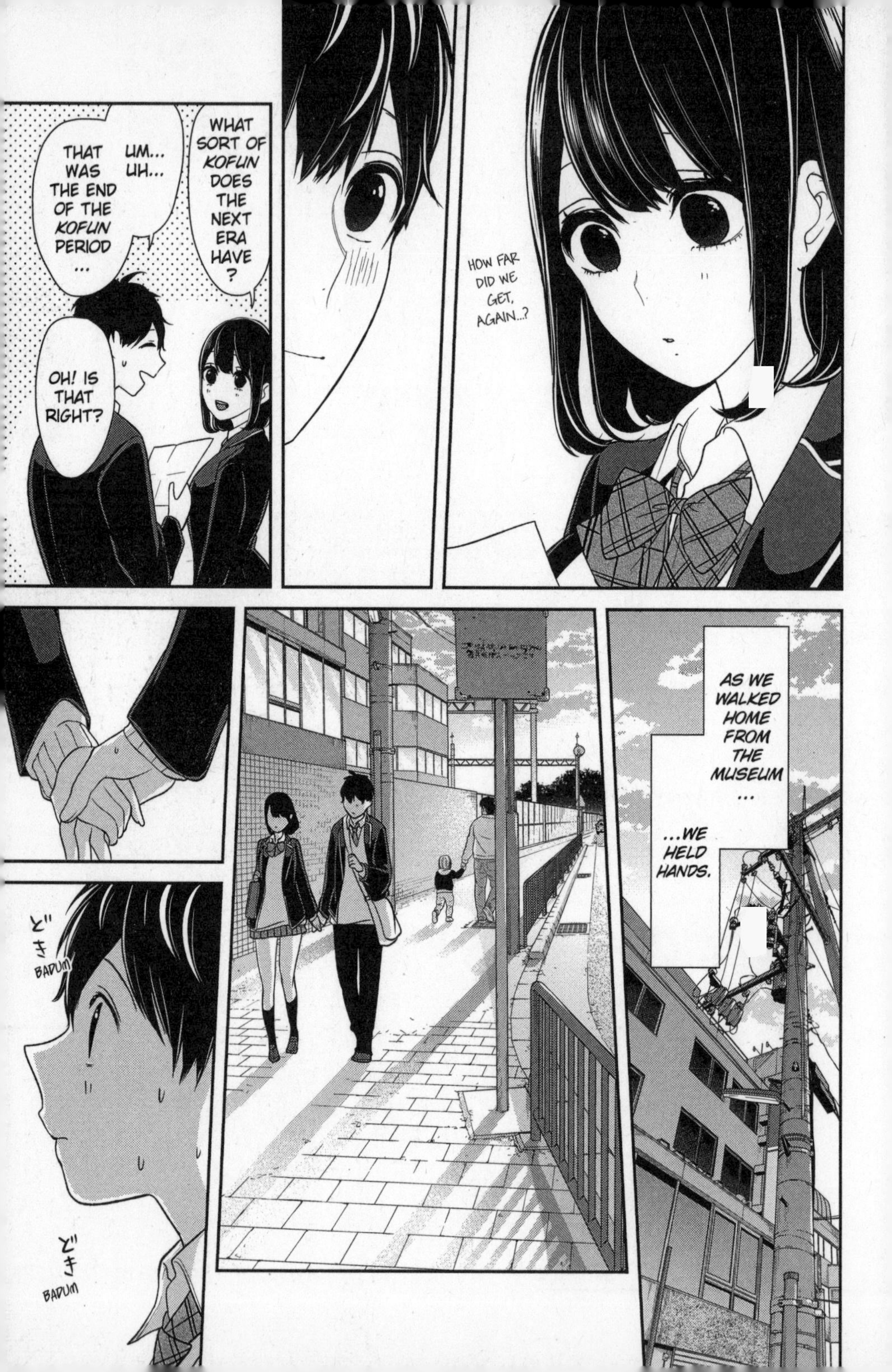
HOW FAR DID WE GET, AGAIN...?
WHAT SORT OF KOFUN DOES THE NEXT ERA HAVE?
UM... UH...
THAT WAS THE END OF THE KOFUN PERIOD...
OH! IS THAT RIGHT?
AS WE WALKED HOME FROM THE MUSEUM...
...WE HELD HANDS.
どき
BADUM
どき
BADUM

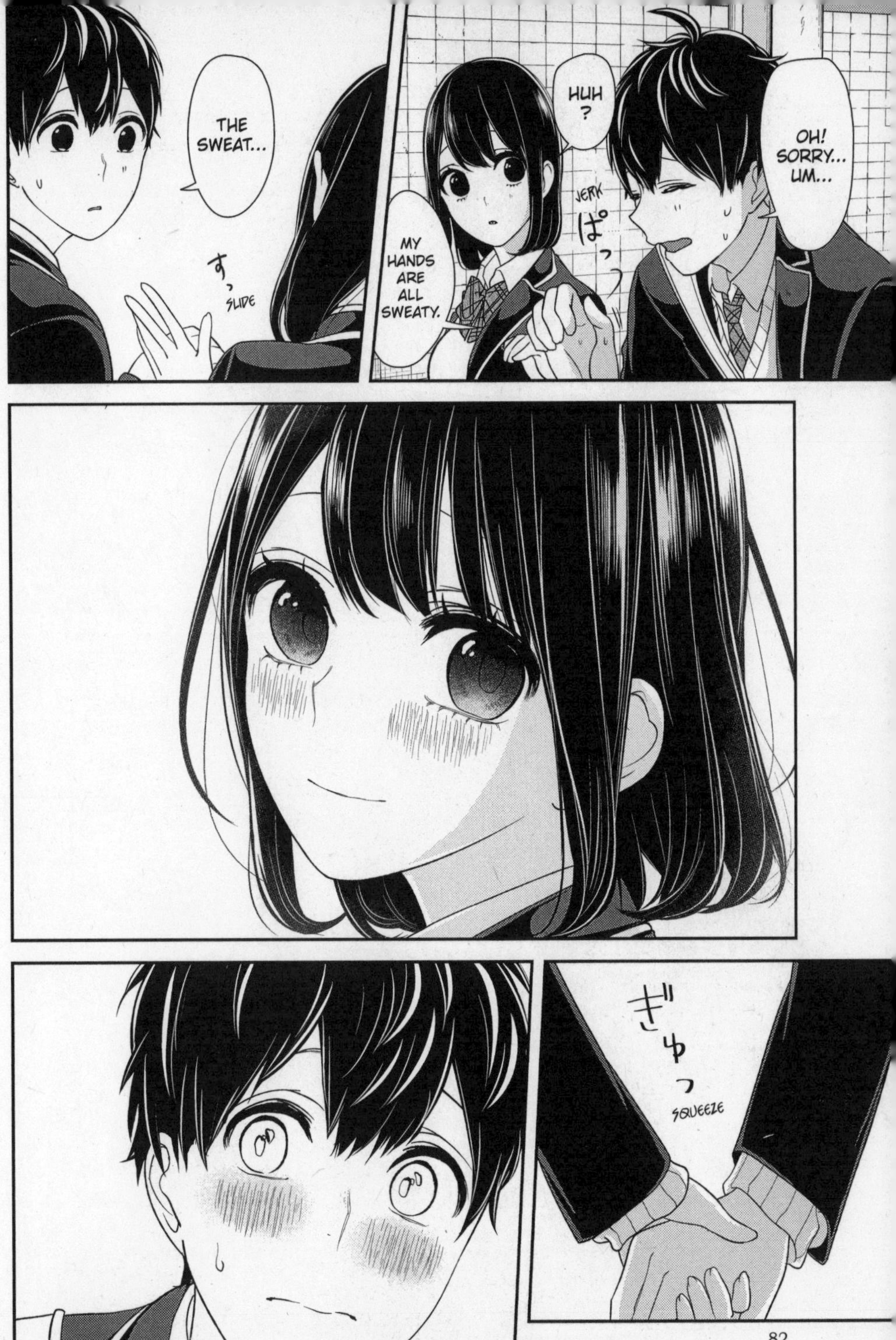
OH! SORRY... UM...
HUH?
ぱっ
JERK
MY HANDS ARE ALL SWEATY.
THE SWEAT...
すっ
SLIDE
ぎゅっ
SQUEEZE

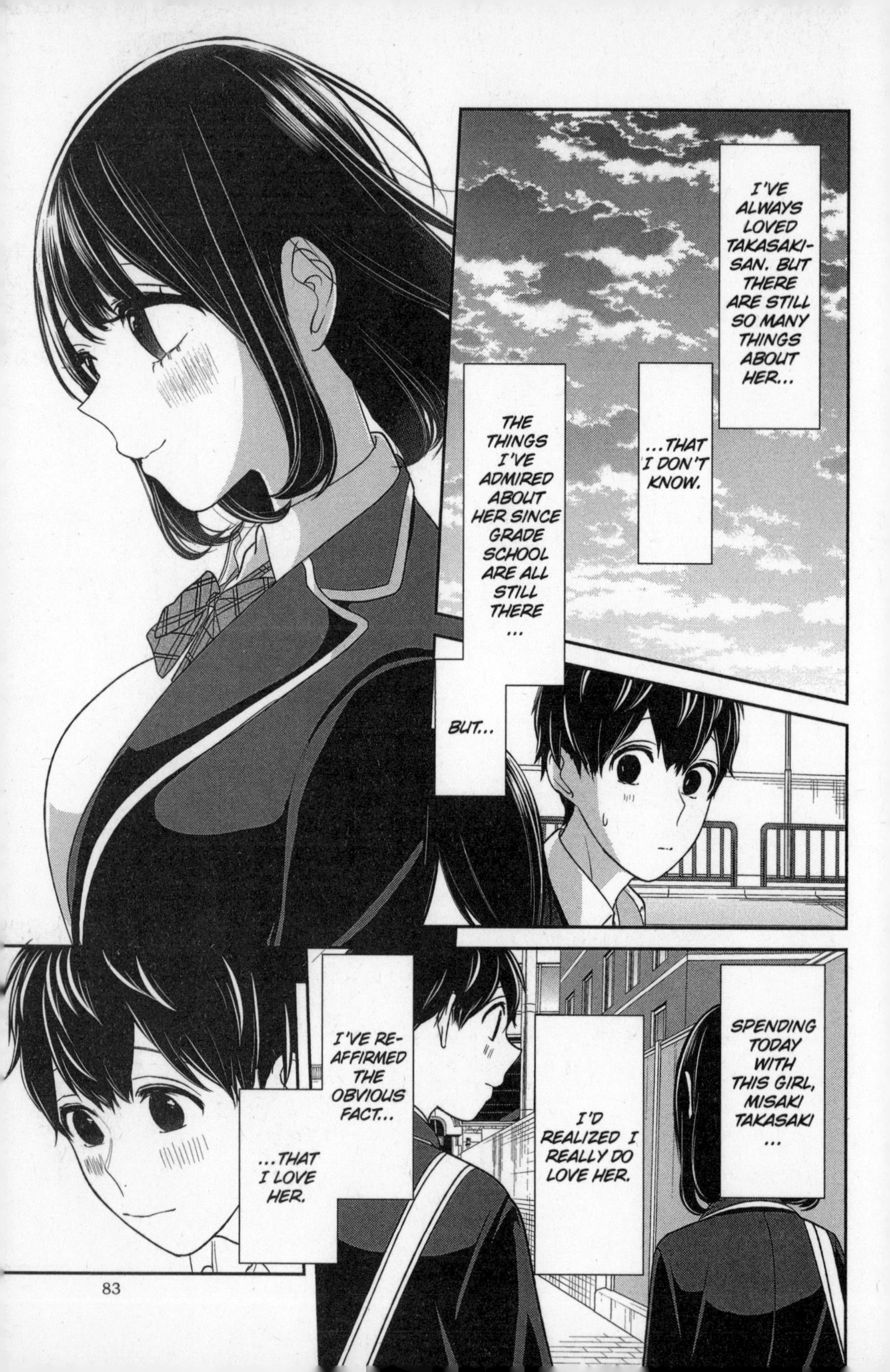
I'VE ALWAYS LOVED TAKASAKI-SAN. BUT THERE ARE STILL SO MANY THINGS ABOUT HER...
...THAT I DON'T KNOW.
THE THINGS I'VE ADMIRED ABOUT HER SINCE GRADE SCHOOL ARE ALL STILL THERE...
BUT...
SPENDING TODAY WITH THIS GIRL, MISAKI TAKASAKI...
I'D REALIZED I REALLY DO LOVE HER.
I'VE RE-AFFIRMED THE OBVIOUS FACT...
...THAT I LOVE HER.

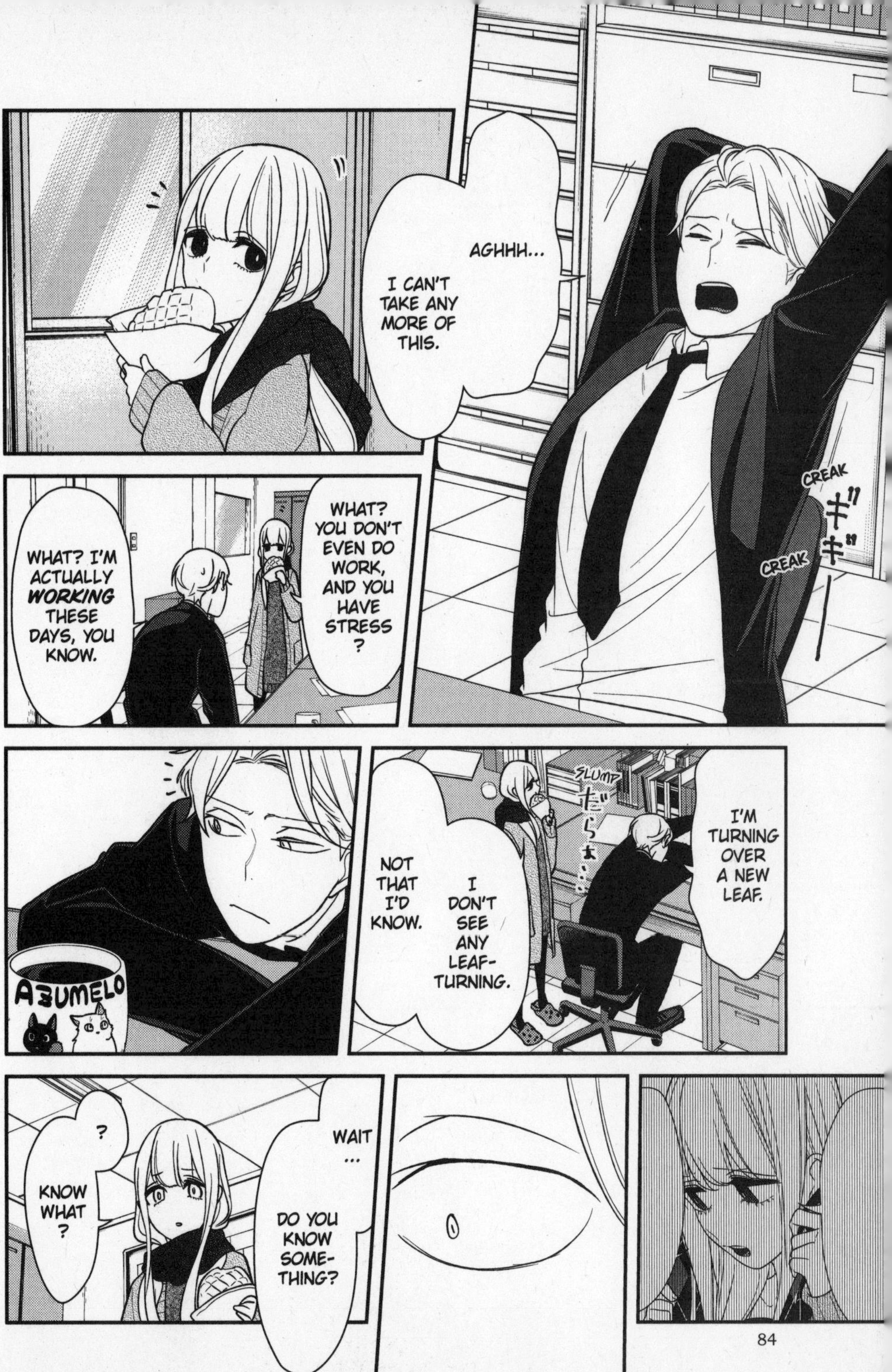
AGHHH...
I CAN'T TAKE ANY MORE OF THIS.
CREAK
CREAK
WHAT? YOU DON'T EVEN DO WORK, AND YOU HAVE STRESS?
WHAT? I'M ACTUALLY WORKING THESE DAYS, YOU KNOW.
I'M TURNING OVER A NEW LEAF.
SLUMP
I DON'T SEE ANY LEAF-TURNING.
NOT THAT I'D KNOW.
AZUMELO
WAIT...
DO YOU KNOW SOMETHING?
?
KNOW WHAT?

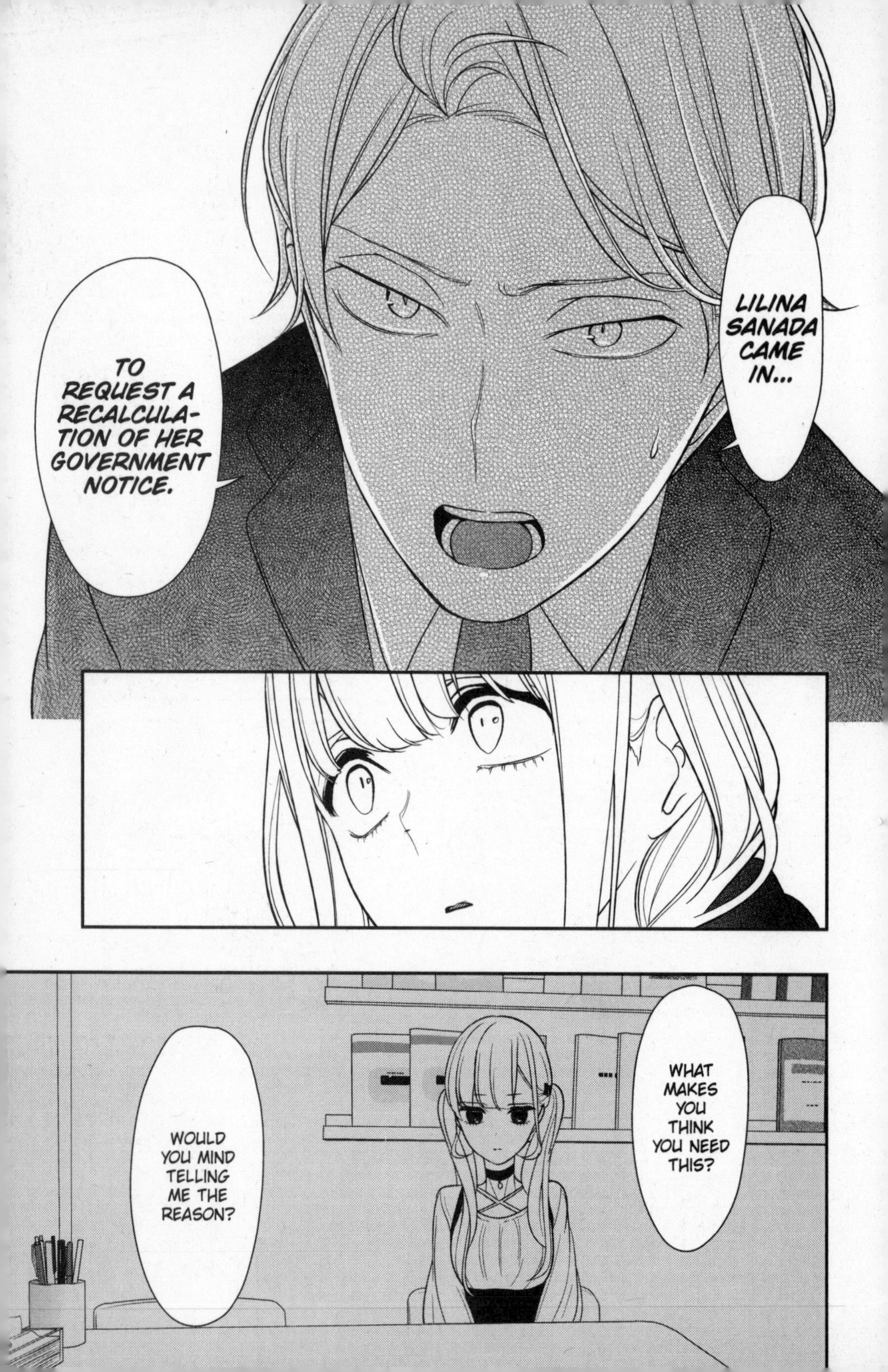
LILINA SANADA CAME IN...
TO REQUEST A RECALCULA-TION OF HER GOVERNMENT NOTICE.
WHAT MAKES YOU THINK YOU NEED THIS?
WOULD YOU MIND TELLING ME THE REASON?

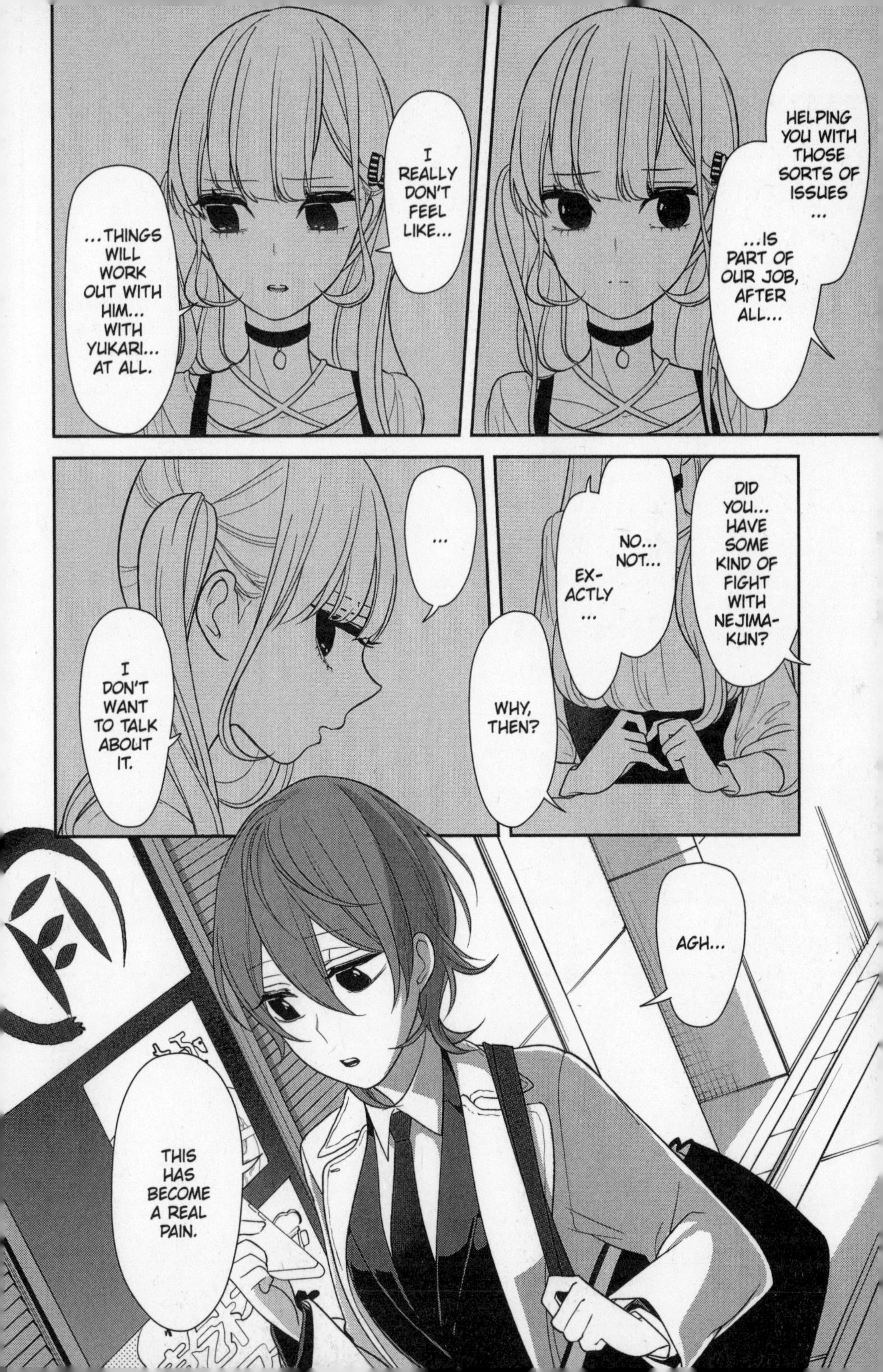
HELPING YOU WITH THOSE SORTS OF ISSUES...
...IS PART OF OUR JOB, AFTER ALL...
I REALLY DON'T FEEL LIKE...
...THINGS WILL WORK OUT WITH HIM... WITH YUKARI... AT ALL.
DID YOU... HAVE SOME KIND OF FIGHT WITH NEJIMA-KUN?
NO... NOT... EX-ACTLY...
WHY, THEN?
...
I DON'T WANT TO TALK ABOUT IT.
AGH...
THIS HAS BECOME A REAL PAIN.

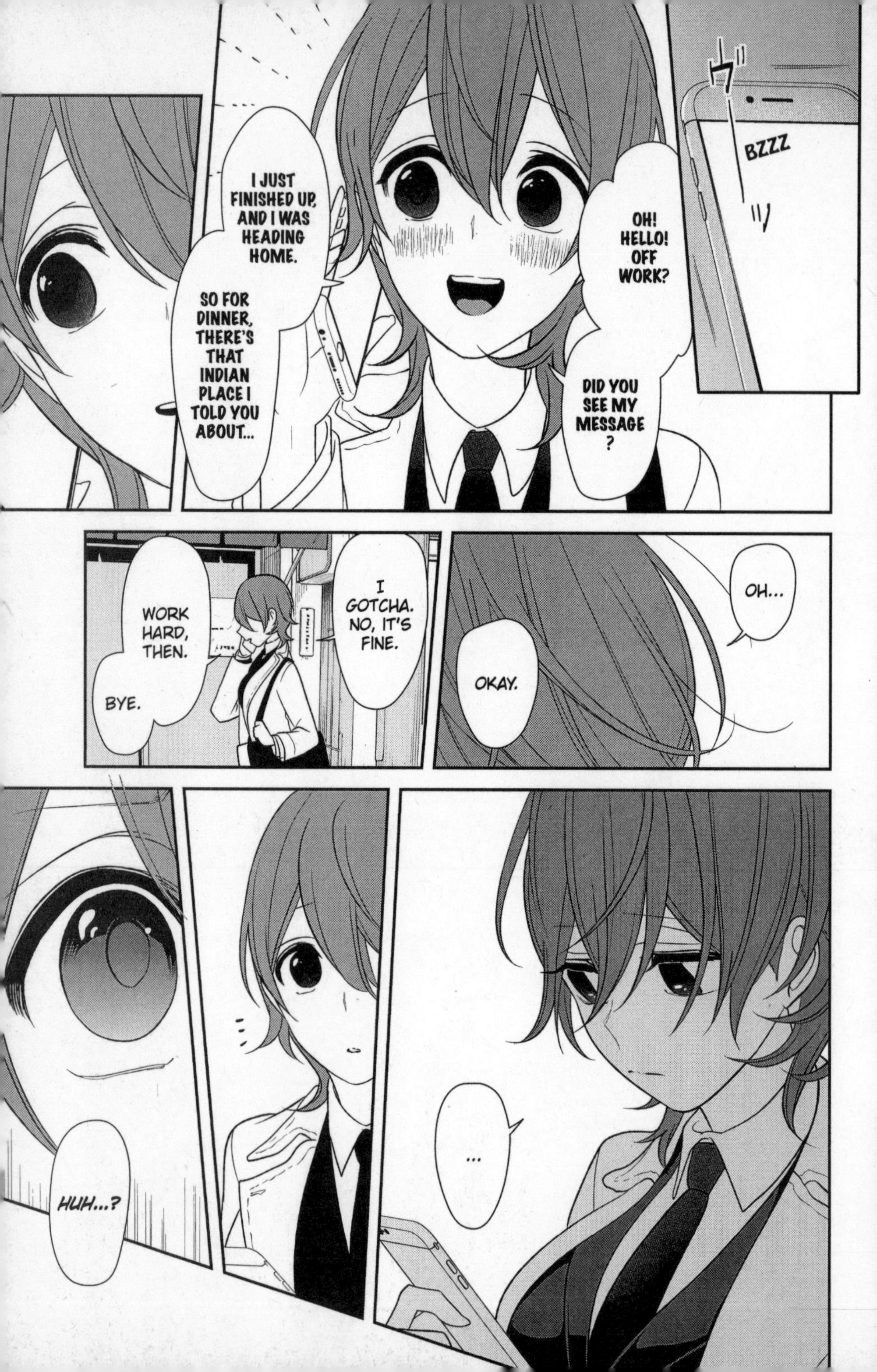

BZZZ
OH! HELLO! OFF WORK?
DID YOU SEE MY MESSAGE?
I JUST FINISHED UP, AND I WAS HEADING HOME.
SO FOR DINNER, THERE'S THAT INDIAN PLACE I TOLD YOU ABOUT...
OH...
OKAY.
I GOTCHA. NO, IT'S FINE.
WORK HARD, THEN.
BYE.
...
HUH...?

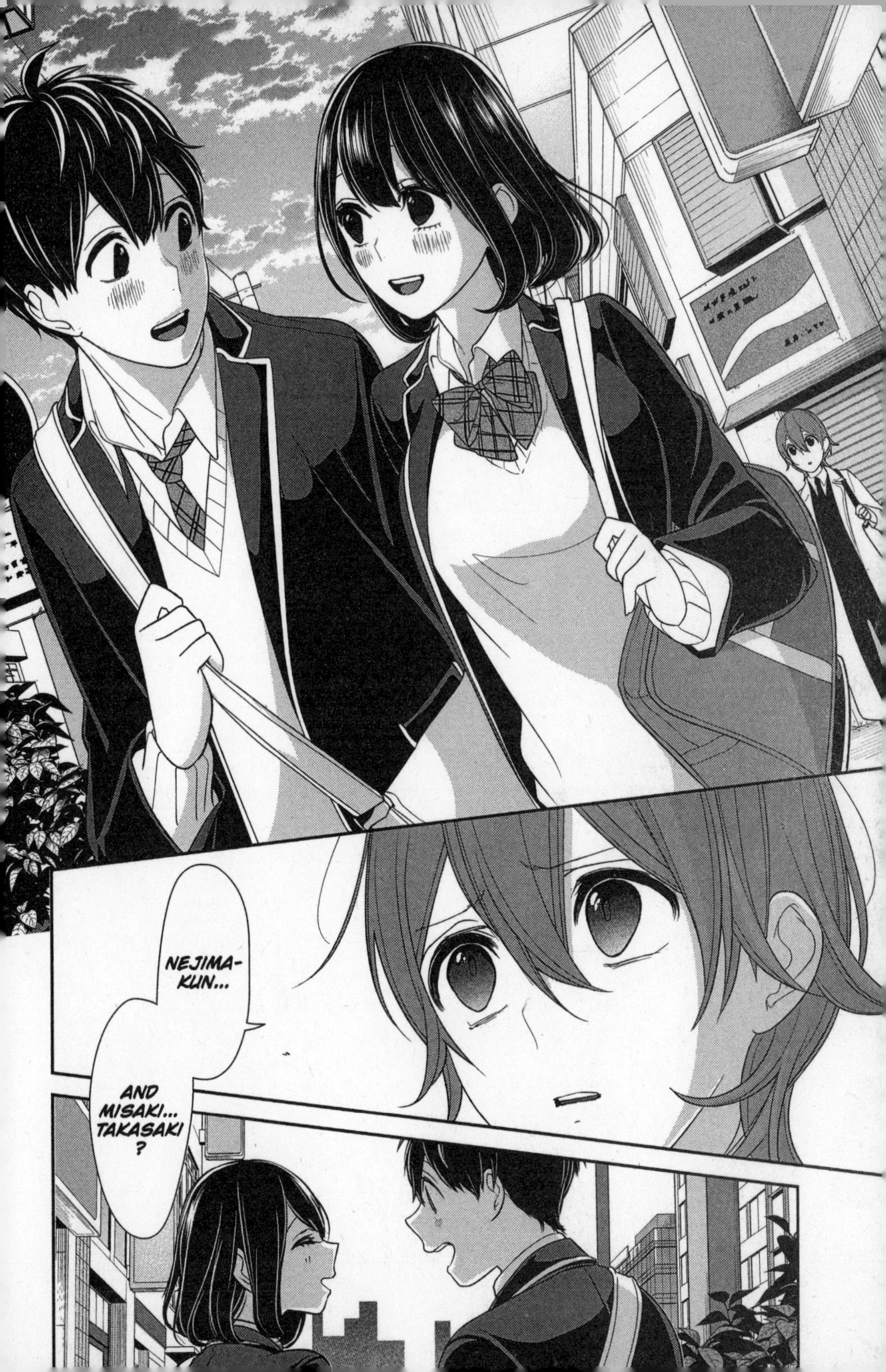
NEJIMA-KUN...
AND MISAKI... TAKASAKI?

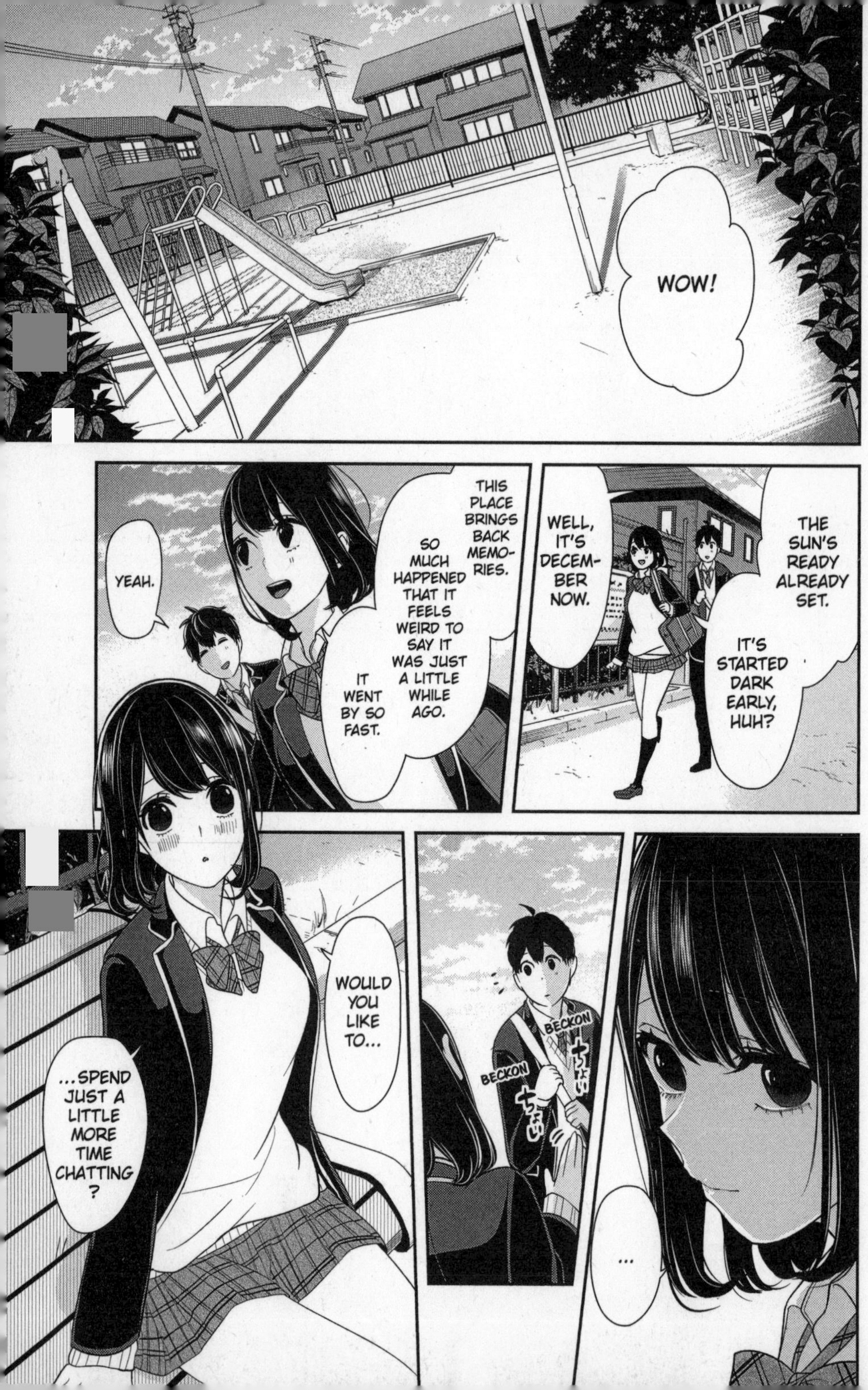
WOW!
THE SUN'S READY ALREADY SET.
IT'S STARTED DARK EARLY, HUH?
WELL, IT'S DECEMBER NOW.
THIS PLACE BRINGS BACK MEMORIES.
SO MUCH HAPPENED THAT IT FEELS WEIRD TO SAY IT WAS JUST A LITTLE WHILE AGO.
IT WENT BY SO FAST.
YEAH.
...
BECKON
ちょい
BECKON
ちょい
WOULD YOU LIKE TO...
...SPEND JUST A LITTLE MORE TIME CHATTING?

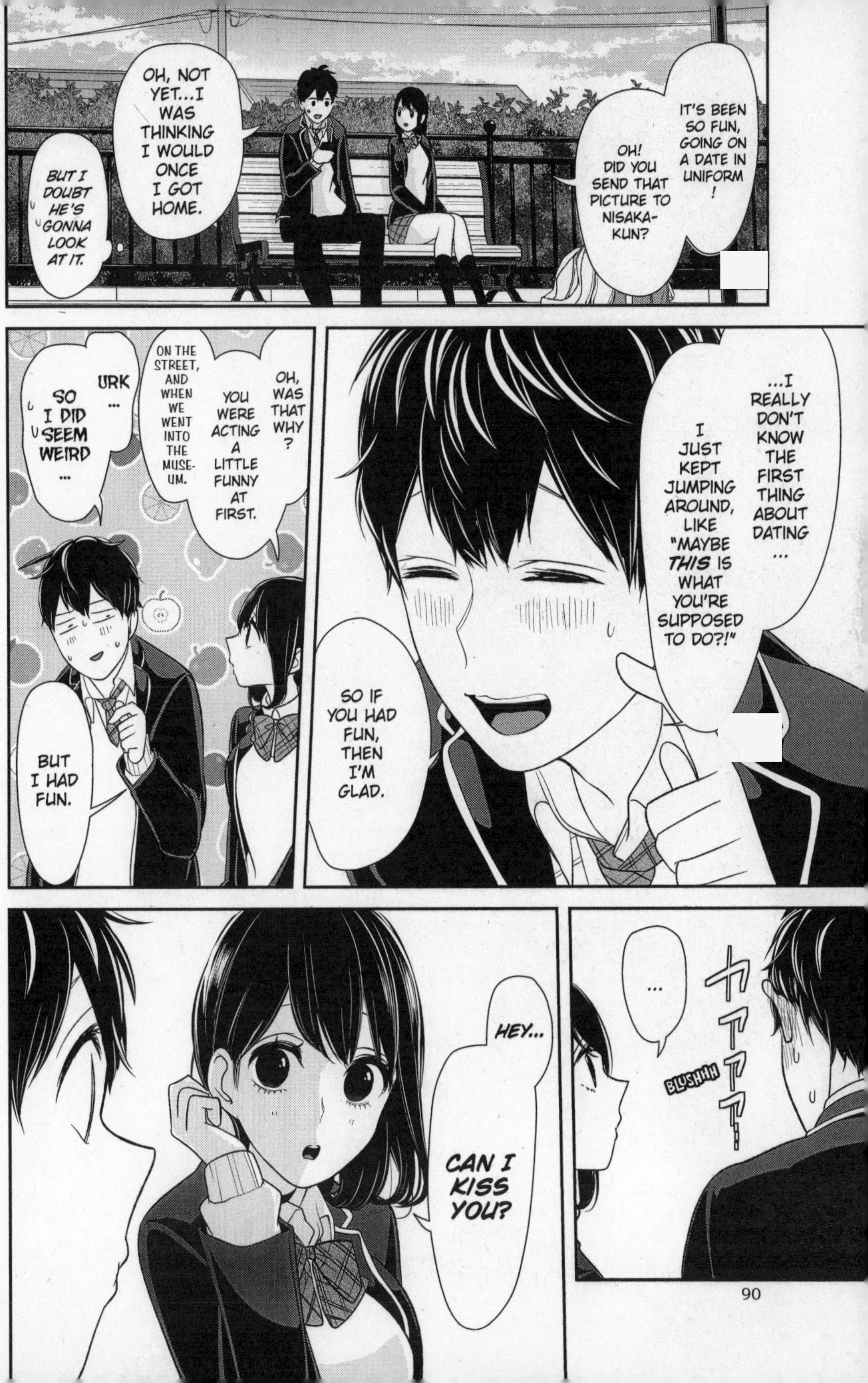

IT'S BEEN SO FUN, GOING ON A DATE IN UNIFORM!
OH! DID YOU SEND THAT PICTURE TO NISAKA-KUN?
OH, NOT YET...I WAS THINKING I WOULD ONCE I GOT HOME.
BUT I DOUBT HE'S GONNA LOOK AT IT.
...I REALLY DON'T KNOW THE FIRST THING ABOUT DATING...
I JUST KEPT JUMPING AROUND, LIKE "MAYBE THIS IS WHAT YOU'RE SUPPOSED TO DO?!"
SO IF YOU HAD FUN, THEN I'M GLAD.
OH, WAS THAT WHY?
YOU WERE ACTING A LITTLE FUNNY AT FIRST.
ON THE STREET, AND WHEN WE WENT INTO THE MUSE-UM.
URK...
SO I DID SEEM WEIRD...
BUT I HAD FUN.
...
BLUSHHH
HEY...
CAN I KISS YOU?

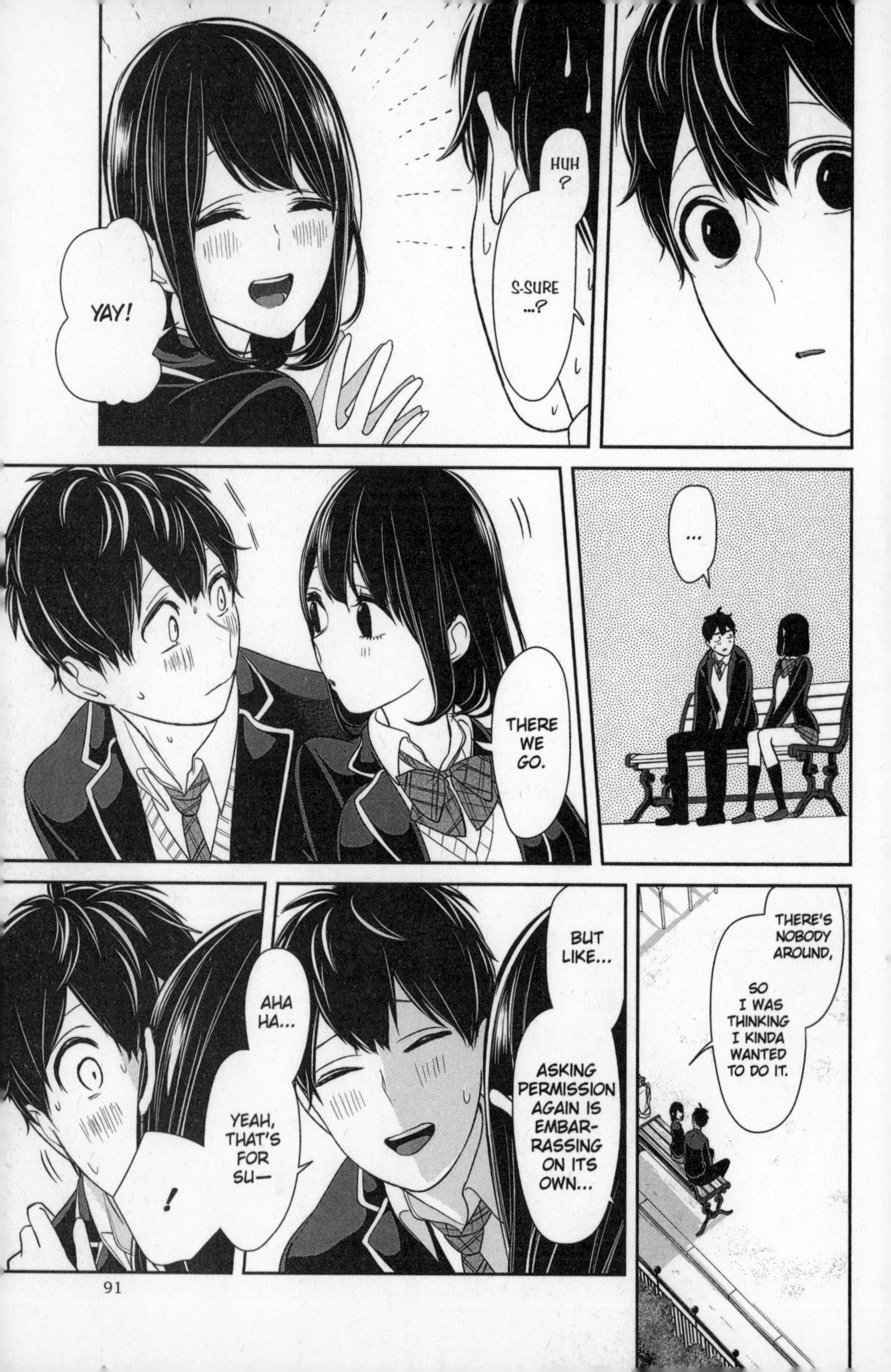
HUH?
S-SURE...?
YAY!
...
THERE WE GO.
THERE'S NOBODY AROUND,
SO I WAS THINKING I KINDA WANTED TO DO IT.
BUT LIKE...
ASKING PERMISSION AGAIN IS EMBARRASSING ON ITS OWN...
AHA HA...
YEAH, THAT'S FOR SU—
!

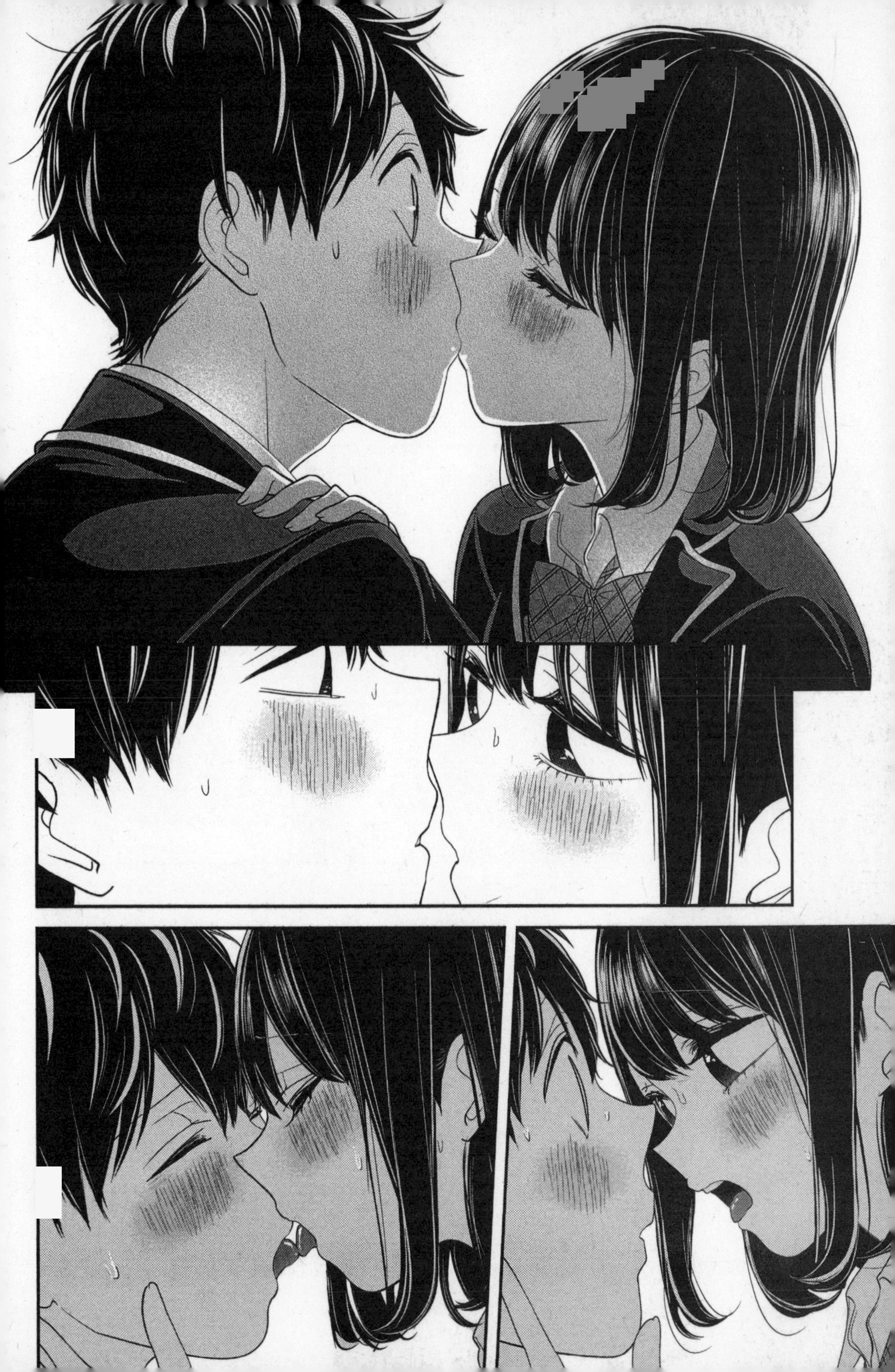

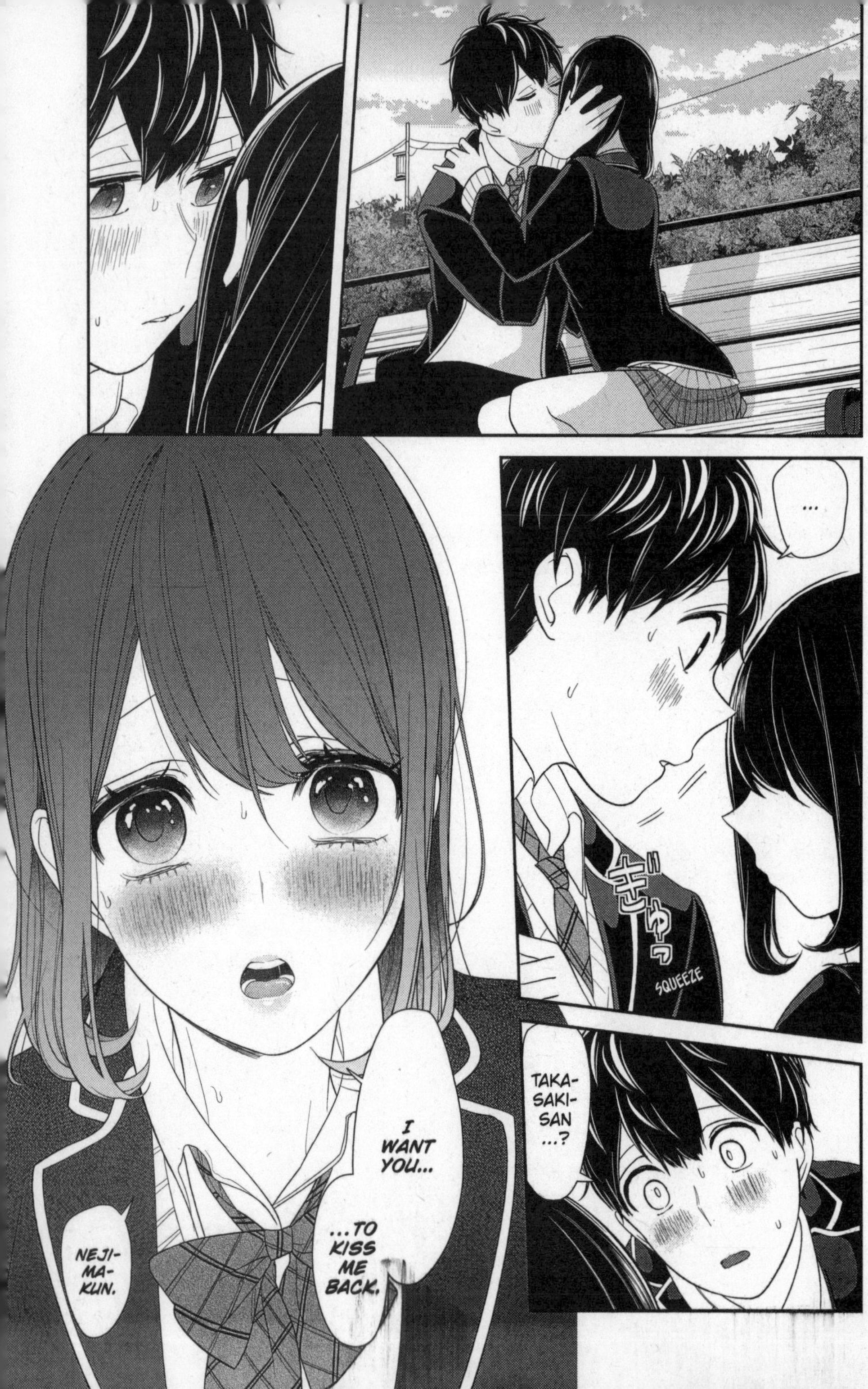
...
ぎゅっ
SQUEEZE
TAKA-SAKI-SAN ...?
I WANT YOU...
...TO KISS ME BACK.
NEJI-MA-KUN.

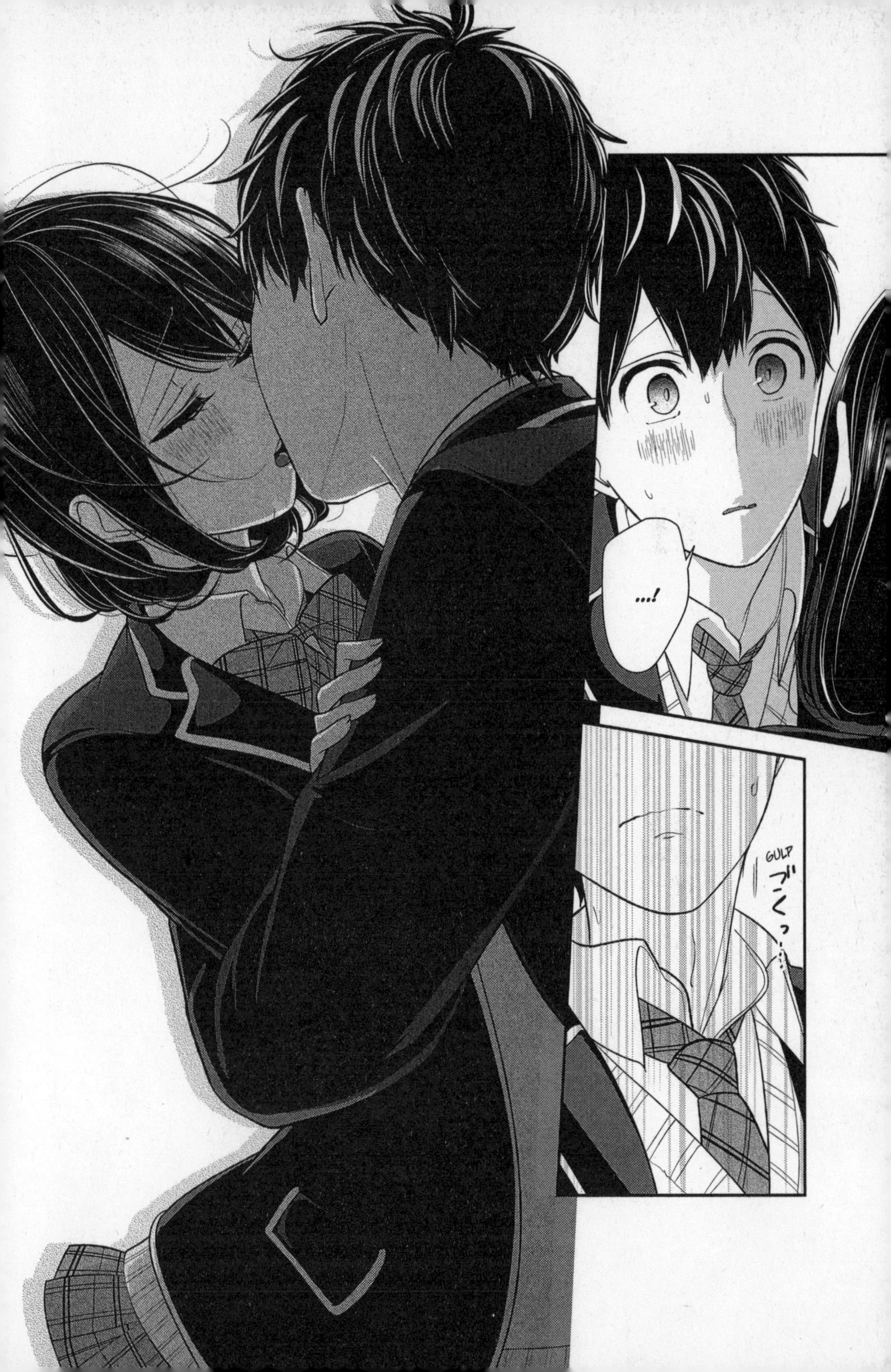
...!
GULP
ゴくっ…

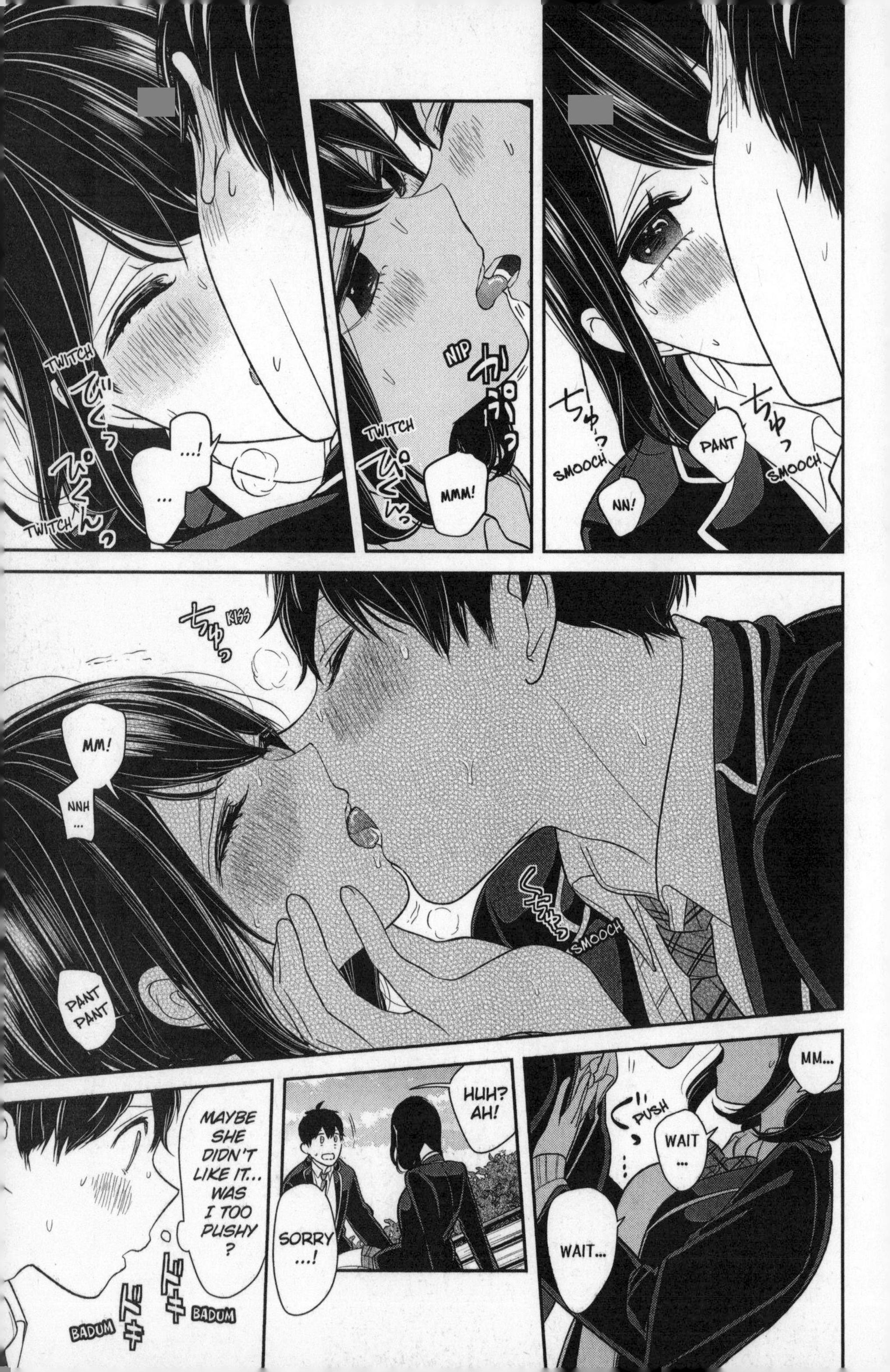
SMOOCH
PANT
SMOOCH
NN!
NIP
TWITCH
MMM!
TWITCH
...!
...
TWITCH
KISS
MM!
NNH ...
SMOOCH
PANT PANT
MM...
PUSH
WAIT ...
WAIT...
HUH? AH!
SORRY ...!
MAYBE SHE DIDN'T LIKE IT... WAS I TOO PUSHY?
BADUM
BADUM

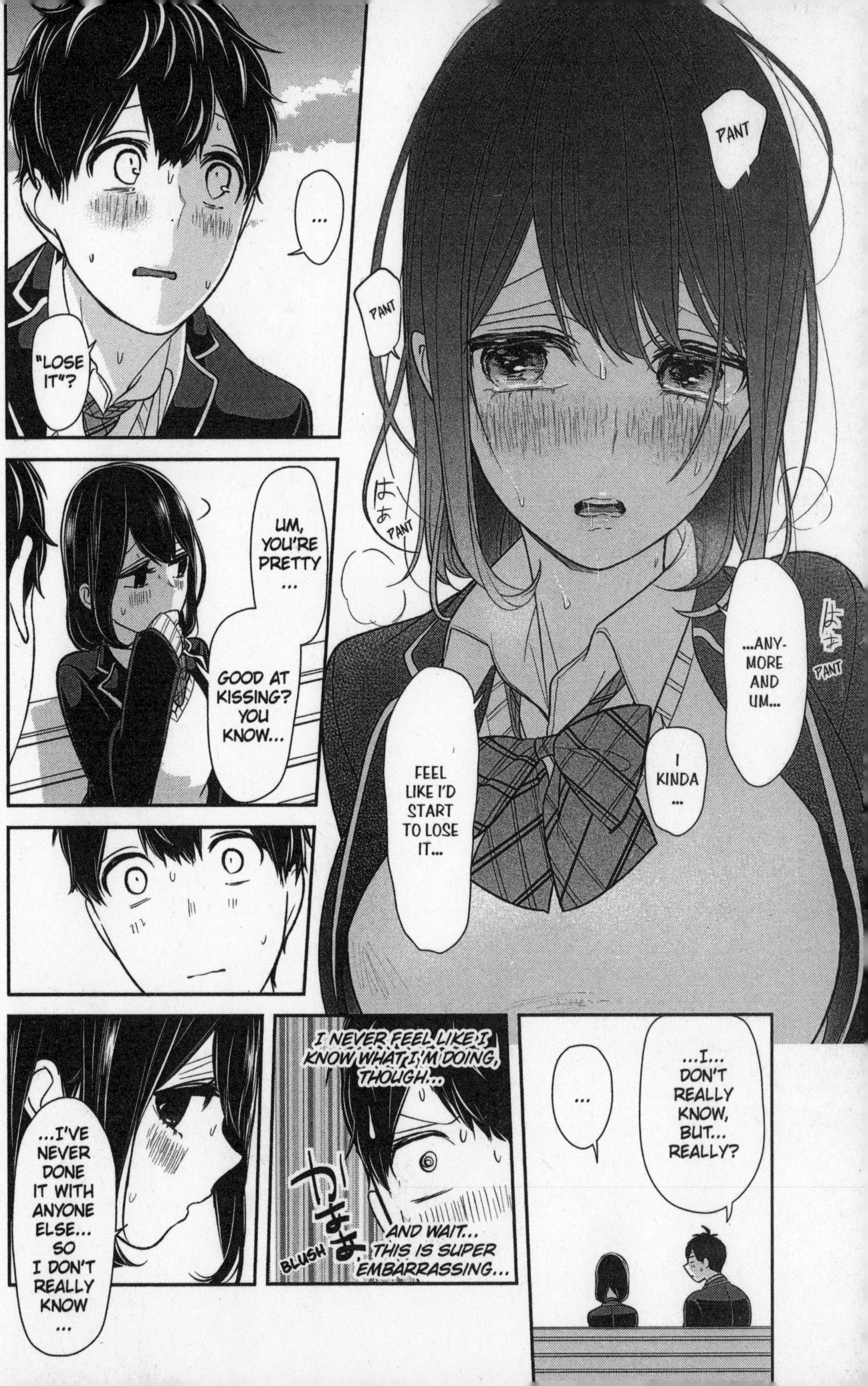
PANT
PANT
はぁ PANT
はぁ PANT
...ANY- MORE AND UM...
I KINDA ...
FEEL LIKE I'D START TO LOSE IT...
...
"LOSE IT"?
UM, YOU'RE PRETTY ...
GOOD AT KISSING? YOU KNOW...
...I... DON'T REALLY KNOW, BUT... REALLY?
...
I NEVER FEEL LIKE I KNOW WHAT I'M DOING, THOUGH...
BLUSH
AND WAIT... THIS IS SUPER EMBARRASSING...
...I'VE NEVER DONE IT WITH ANYONE ELSE... SO I DON'T REALLY KNOW ...

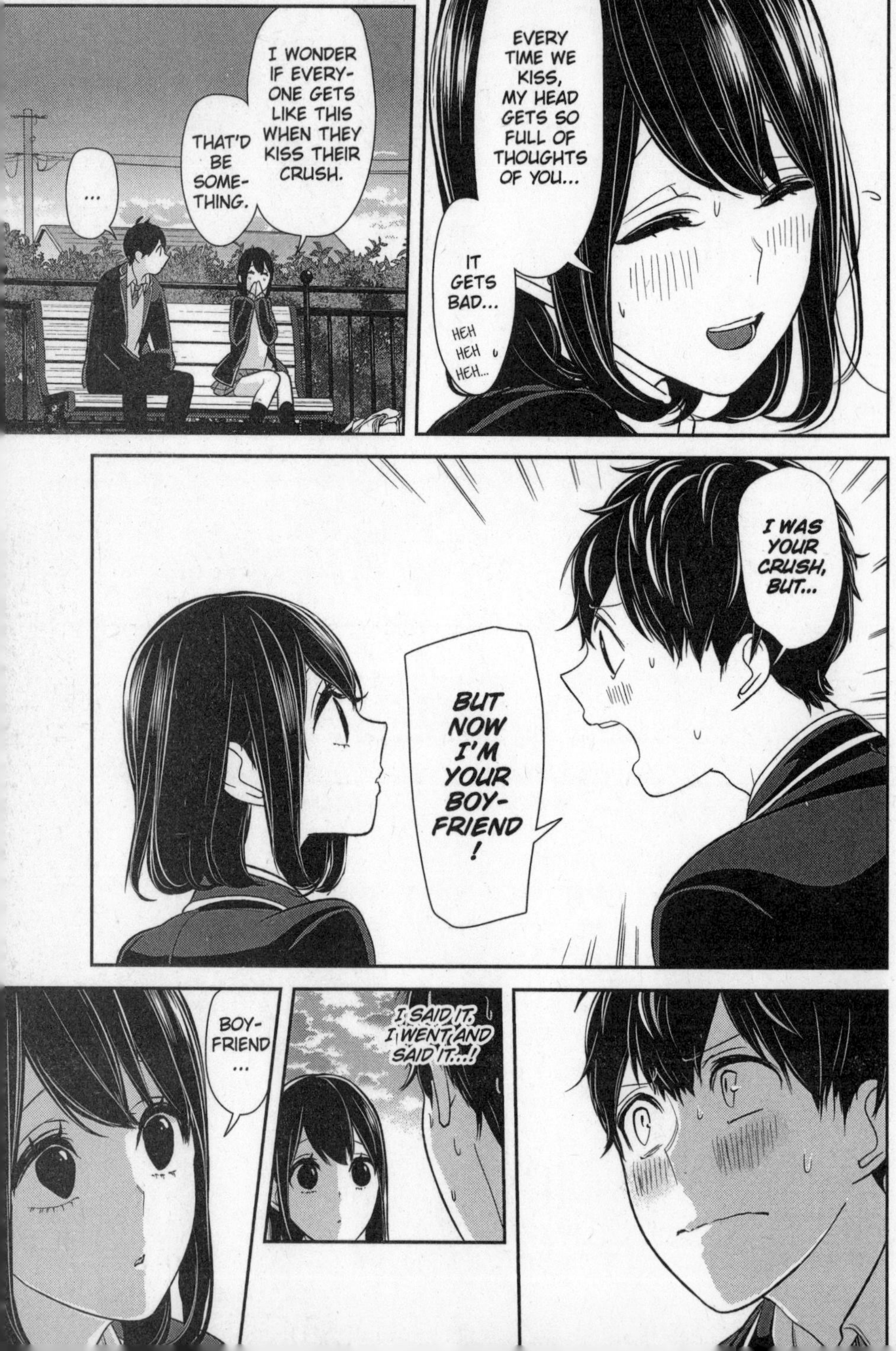

EVERY TIME WE KISS, MY HEAD GETS SO FULL OF THOUGHTS OF YOU...
IT GETS BAD...
HEH HEH HEH...
I WONDER IF EVERYONE GETS LIKE THIS WHEN THEY KISS THEIR CRUSH.
THAT'D BE SOMETHING.
...
I WAS YOUR CRUSH, BUT...
BUT NOW I'M YOUR BOYFRIEND!
I SAID IT. I WENT AND SAID IT...!
BOYFRIEND...

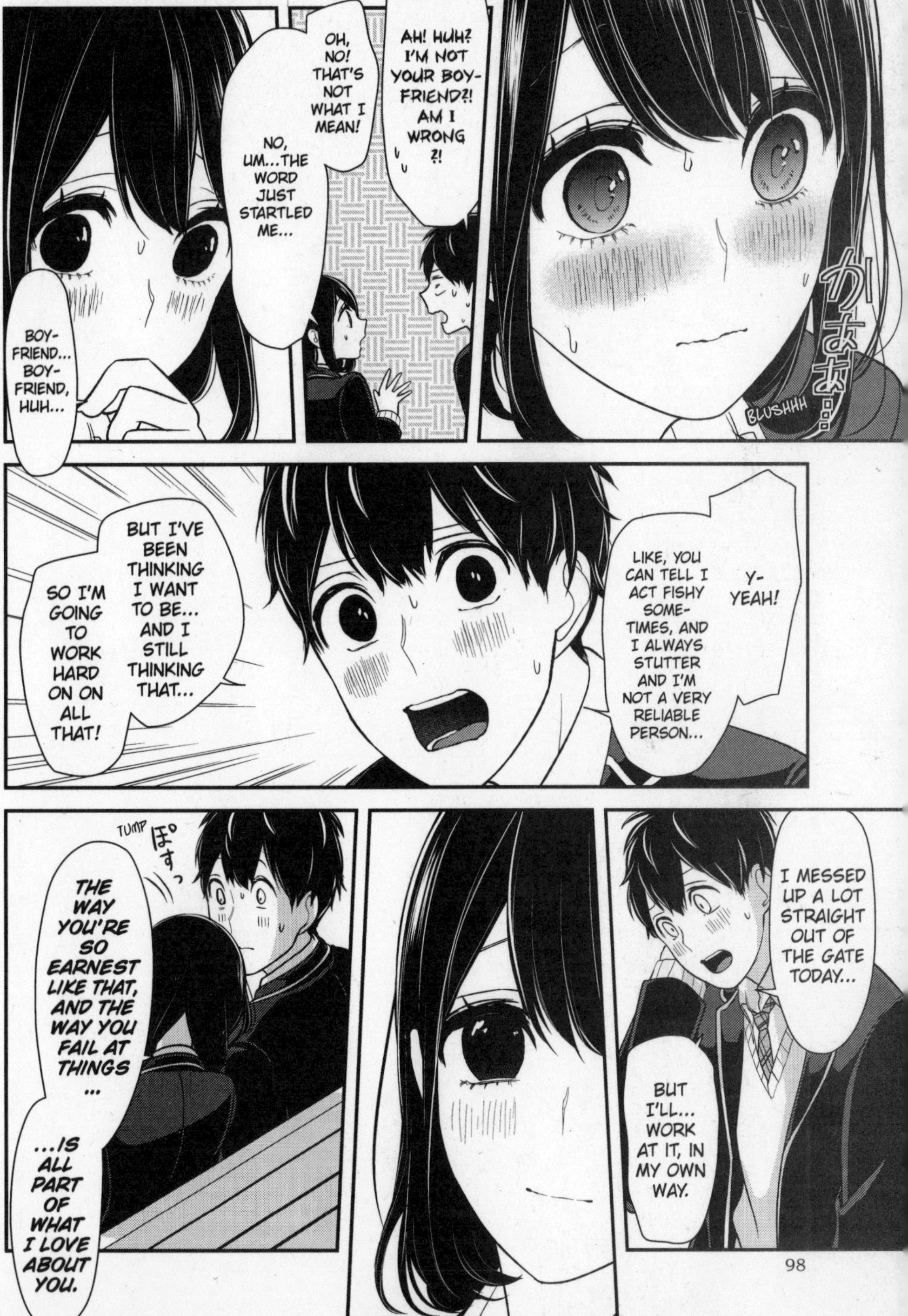
かぁぁ…
BLUSHHH
AH! HUH? I'M NOT YOUR BOY-FRIEND?! AM I WRONG?!
OH, NO! THAT'S NOT WHAT I MEAN!
NO, UM...THE WORD JUST STARTLED ME...
BOY-FRIEND... BOY-FRIEND, HUH...
Y-YEAH!
LIKE, YOU CAN TELL I ACT FISHY SOME-TIMES, AND I ALWAYS STUTTER AND I'M NOT A VERY RELIABLE PERSON...
BUT I'VE BEEN THINKING I WANT TO BE... AND I STILL THINKING THAT...
SO I'M GOING TO WORK HARD ON ON ALL THAT!
I MESSED UP A LOT STRAIGHT OUT OF THE GATE TODAY...
BUT I'LL... WORK AT IT, IN MY OWN WAY.
ぽすっ
TUMP
THE WAY YOU'RE SO EARNEST LIKE THAT, AND THE WAY YOU FAIL AT THINGS...
...IS ALL PART OF WHAT I LOVE ABOUT YOU.

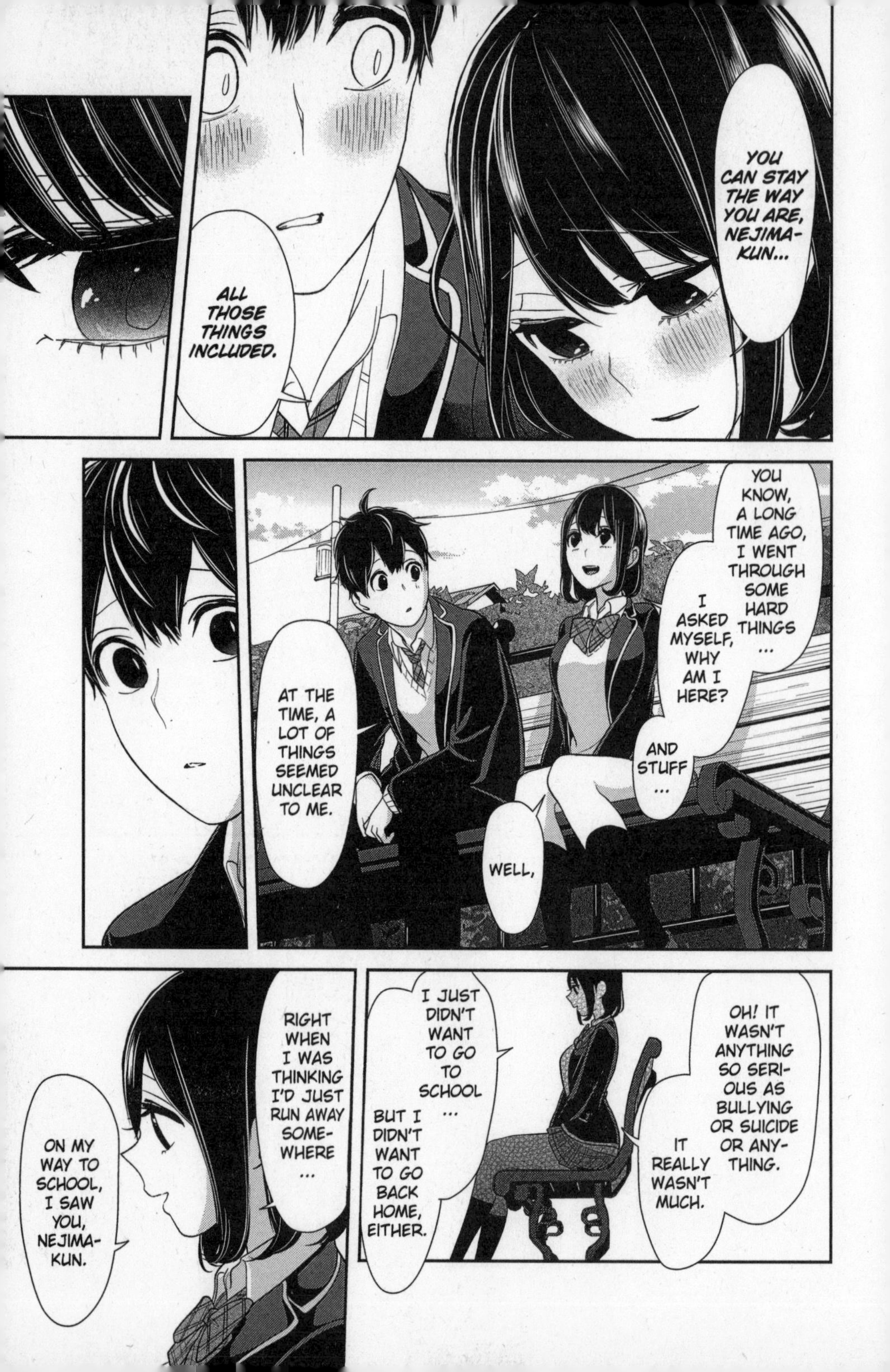
YOU CAN STAY THE WAY YOU ARE, NEJIMA-KUN...
ALL THOSE THINGS INCLUDED.
YOU KNOW, A LONG TIME AGO, I WENT THROUGH SOME HARD THINGS...
I ASKED MYSELF, WHY AM I HERE?
AND STUFF...
AT THE TIME, A LOT OF THINGS SEEMED UNCLEAR TO ME.
WELL,
OH! IT WASN'T ANYTHING SO SERIOUS AS BULLYING OR SUICIDE OR ANYTHING.
IT REALLY WASN'T MUCH.
I JUST DIDN'T WANT TO GO TO SCHOOL...
BUT I DIDN'T WANT TO GO BACK HOME, EITHER.
RIGHT WHEN I WAS THINKING I'D JUST RUN AWAY SOMEWHERE...
ON MY WAY TO SCHOOL, I SAW YOU, NEJIMA-KUN.

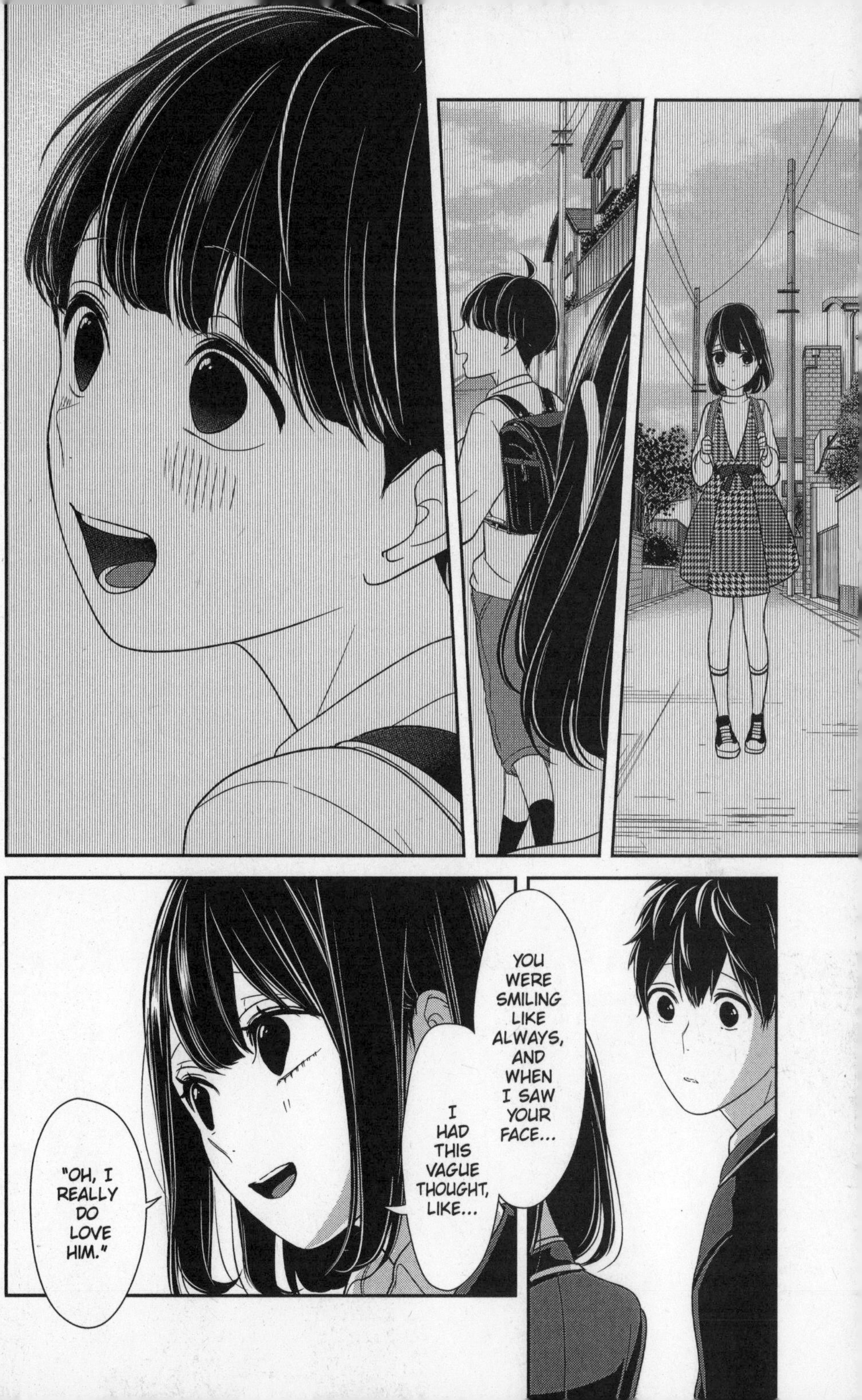
YOU WERE SMILING LIKE ALWAYS, AND WHEN I SAW YOUR FACE...
I HAD THIS VAGUE THOUGHT, LIKE...
"OH, I REALLY DO LOVE HIM."

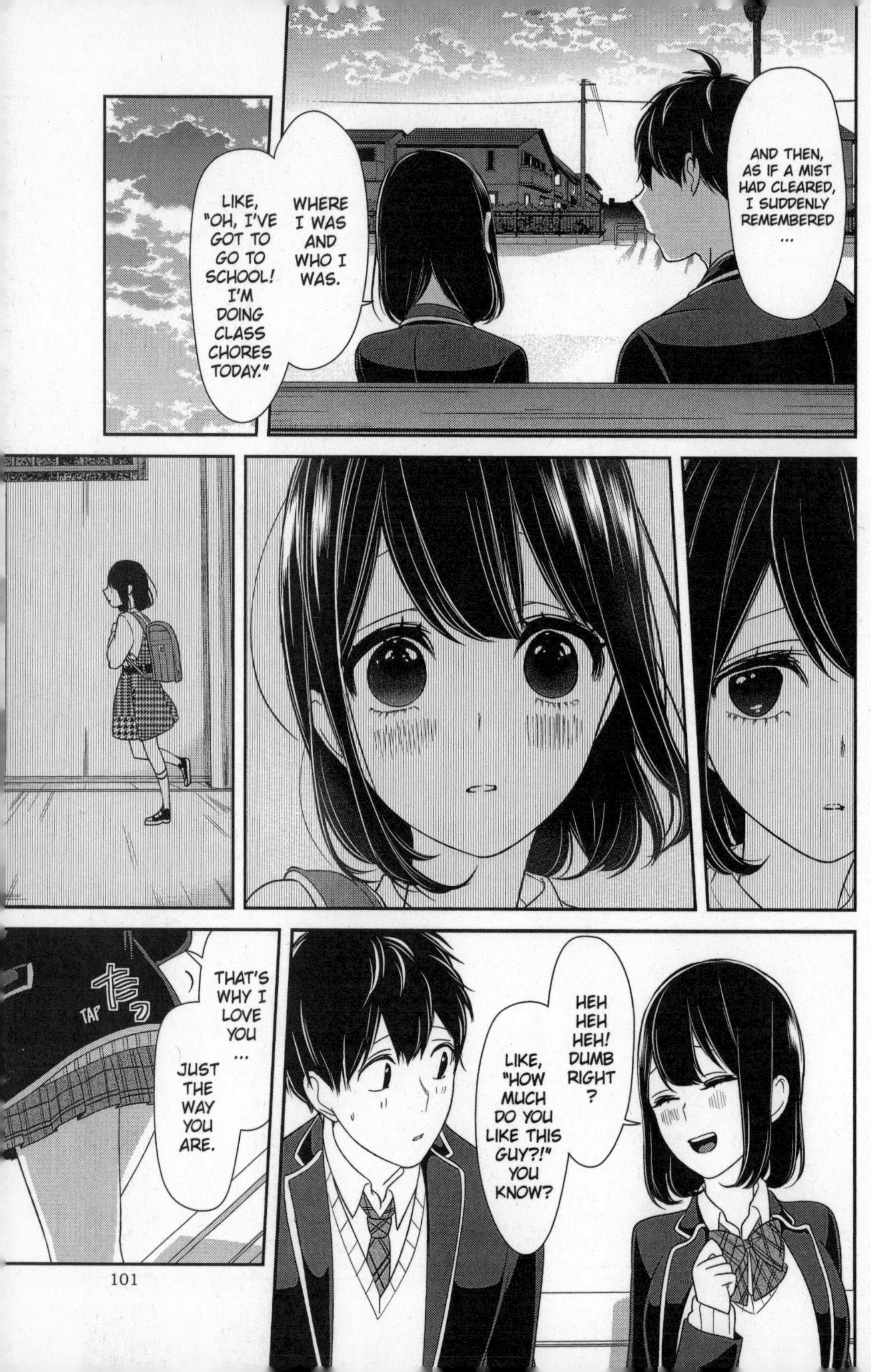
AND THEN, AS IF A MIST HAD CLEARED, I SUDDENLY REMEMBERED ...
WHERE I WAS AND WHO I WAS.
LIKE, "OH, I'VE GOT TO GO TO SCHOOL! I'M DOING CLASS CHORES TODAY."
HEH HEH HEH! DUMB RIGHT?
LIKE, "HOW MUCH DO YOU LIKE THIS GUY?!" YOU KNOW?
TAP
THAT'S WHY I LOVE YOU ... JUST THE WAY YOU ARE.

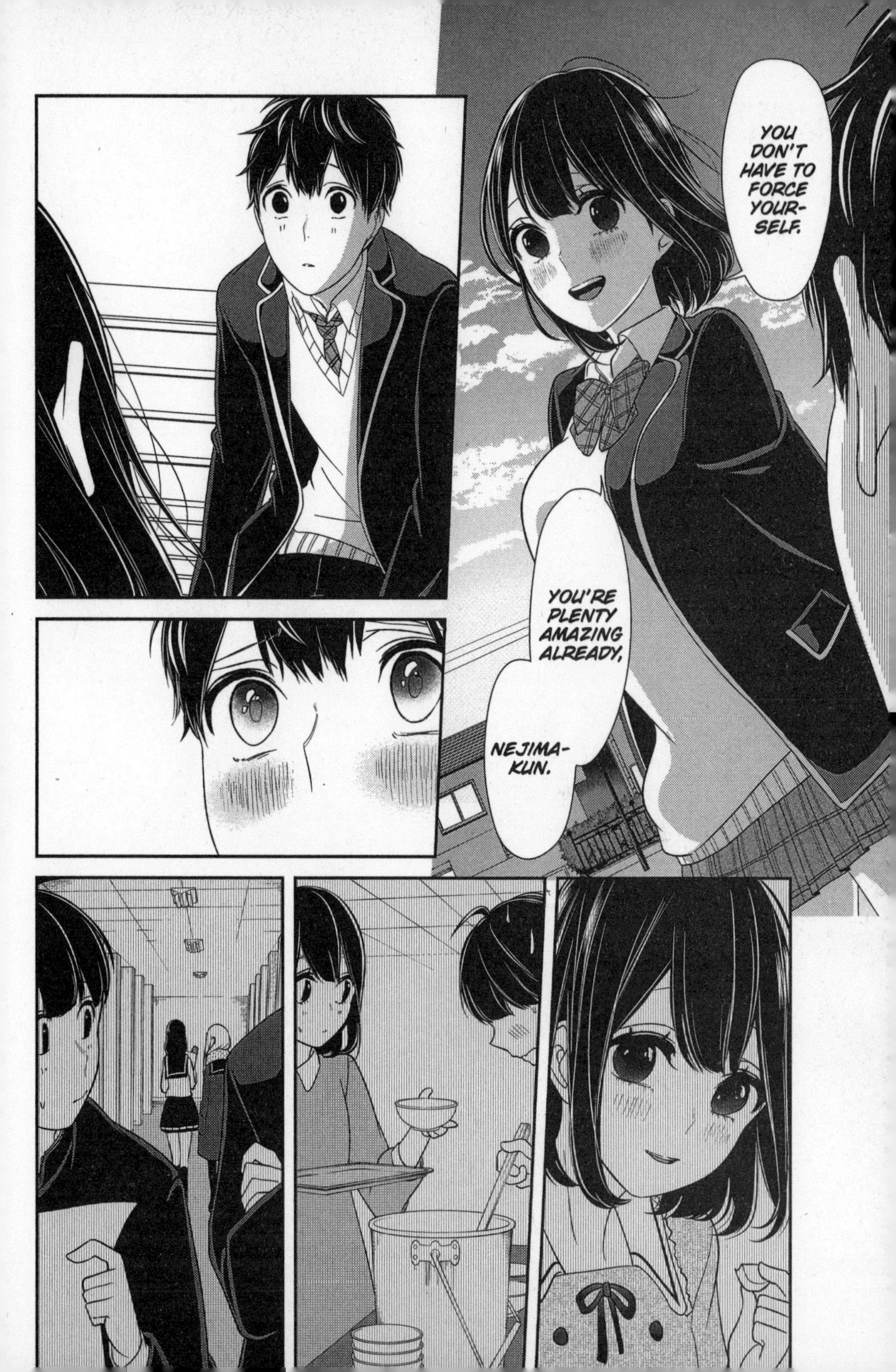
YOU DON'T HAVE TO FORCE YOUR-SELF.
YOU'RE PLENTY AMAZING ALREADY,
NEJIMA-KUN.

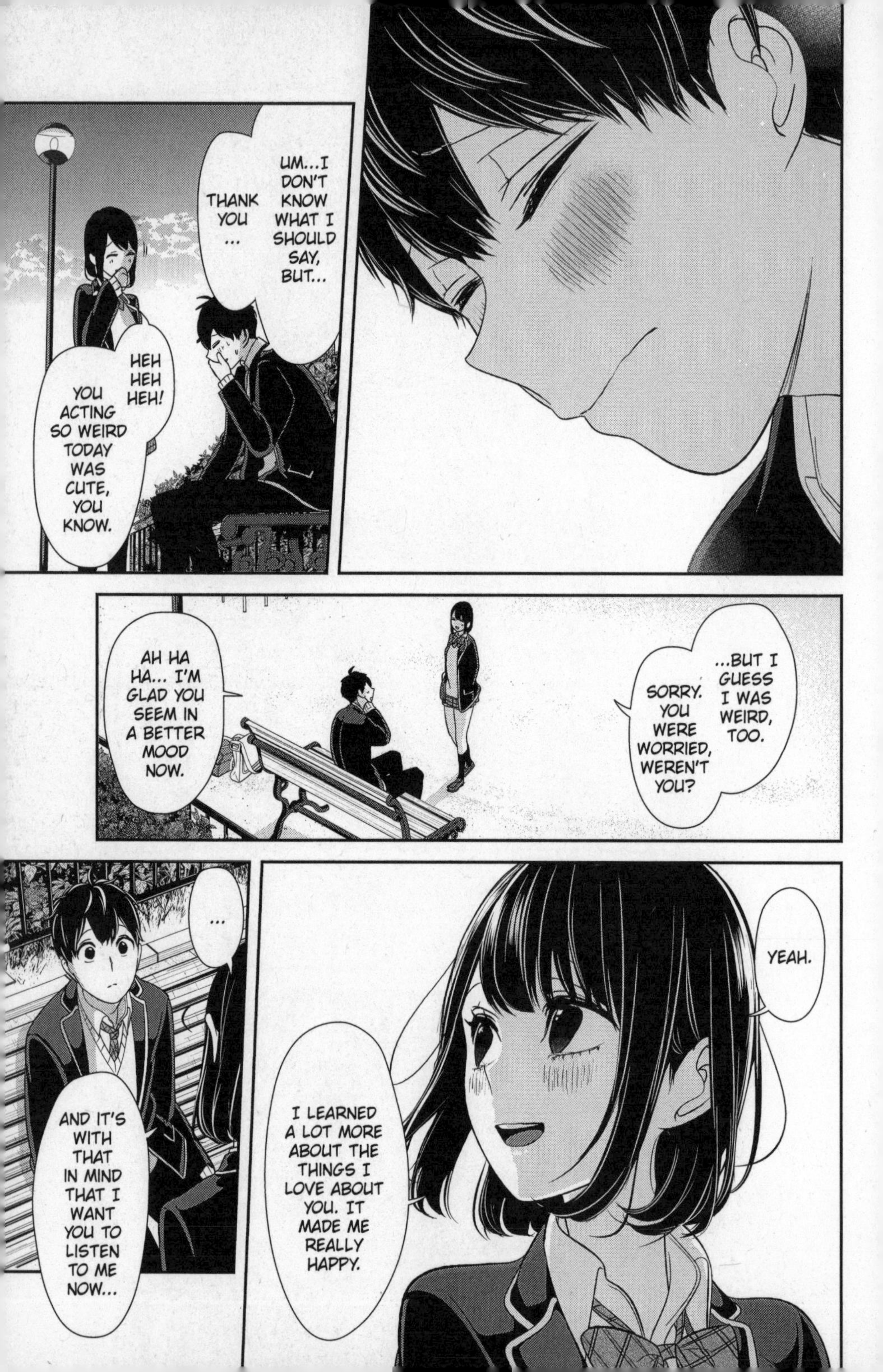
UM...I DON'T KNOW WHAT I SHOULD SAY, BUT...
THANK YOU...
HEH HEH HEH!
YOU ACTING SO WEIRD TODAY WAS CUTE, YOU KNOW.
...BUT I GUESS I WAS WEIRD, TOO.
SORRY. YOU WERE WORRIED, WEREN'T YOU?
AH HA HA... I'M GLAD YOU SEEM IN A BETTER MOOD NOW.
YEAH.
I LEARNED A LOT MORE ABOUT THE THINGS I LOVE ABOUT YOU. IT MADE ME REALLY HAPPY.
...
AND IT'S WITH THAT IN MIND THAT I WANT YOU TO LISTEN TO ME NOW...

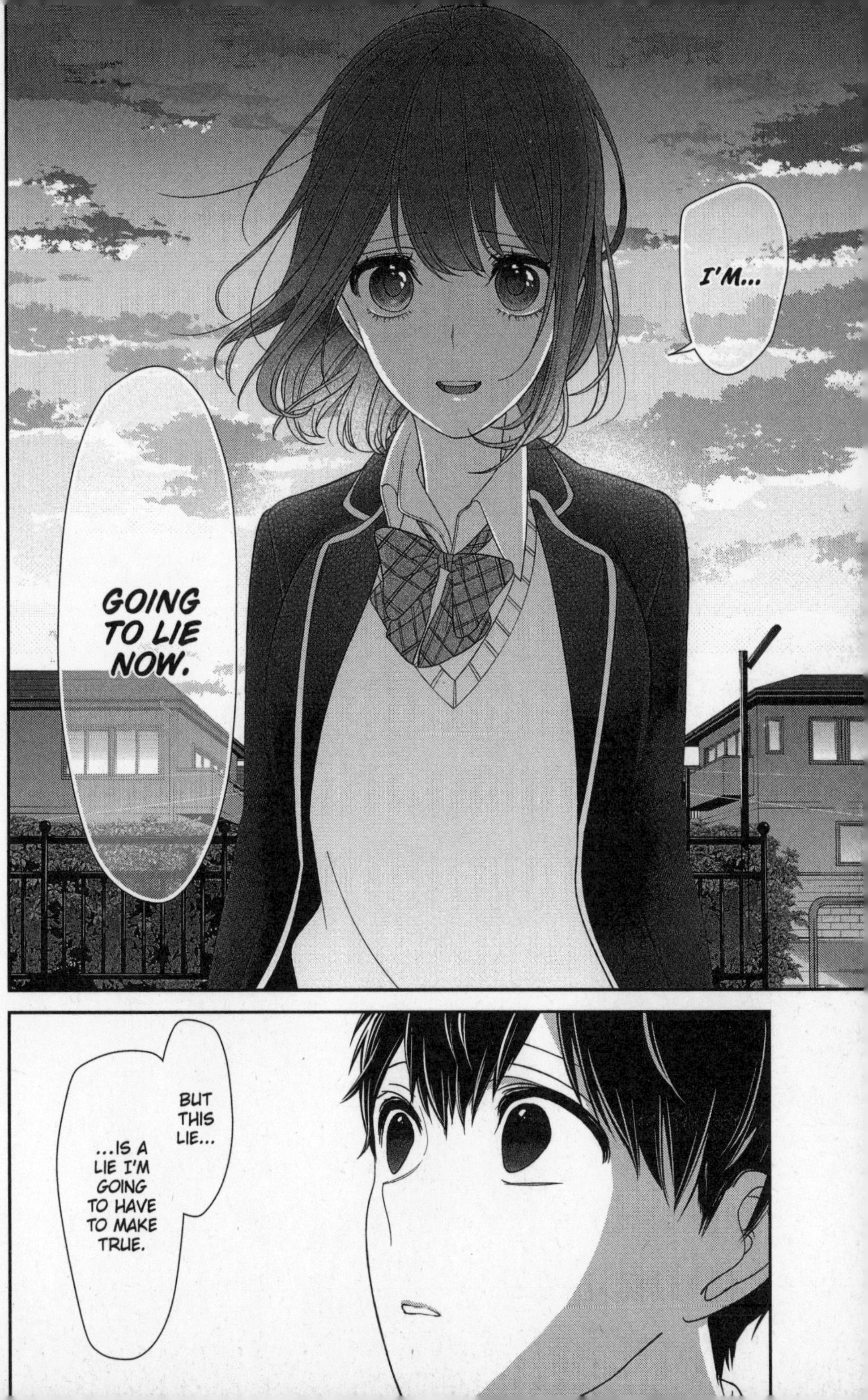
I'M...
GOING TO LIE NOW.
BUT THIS LIE...
...IS A LIE I'M GOING TO HAVE TO MAKE TRUE.

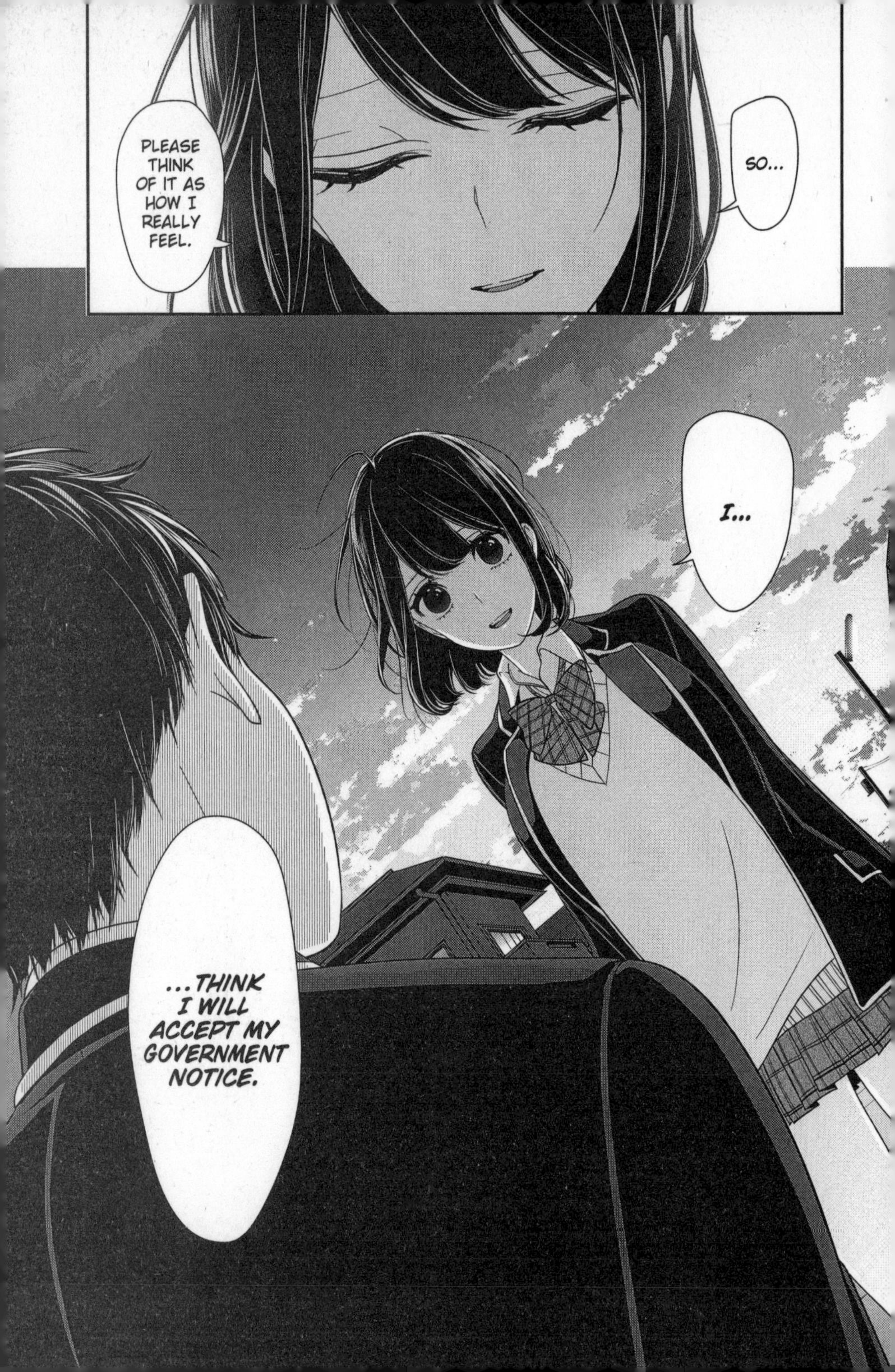
SO...
PLEASE THINK OF IT AS HOW I REALLY FEEL.
I...
...THINK I WILL ACCEPT MY GOVERNMENT NOTICE.

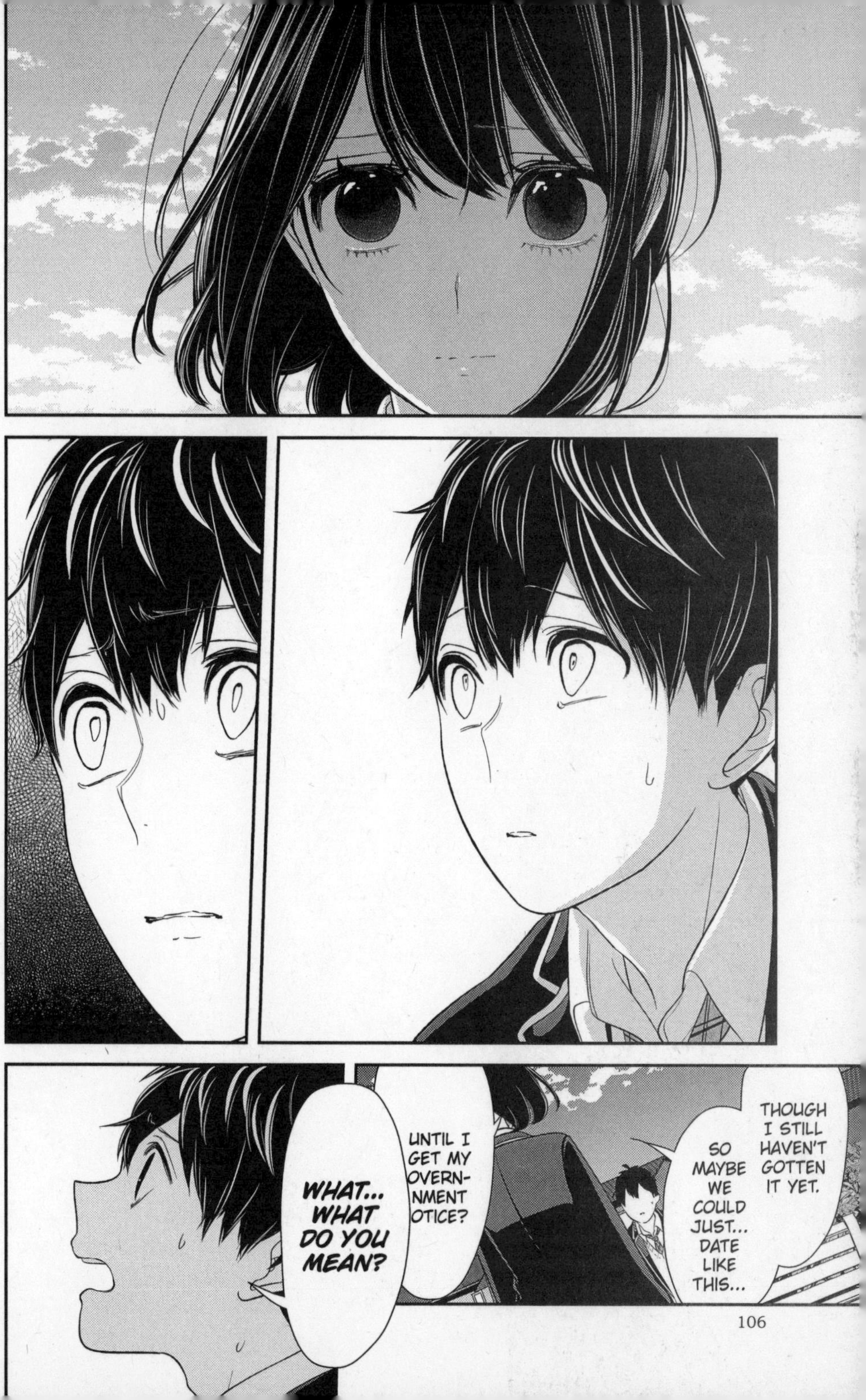
THOUGH I STILL HAVEN'T GOTTEN IT YET.
SO MAYBE WE COULD JUST... DATE LIKE THIS...
UNTIL I GET MY OVERN-NMENT OTICE?
WHAT... WHAT DO YOU MEAN?

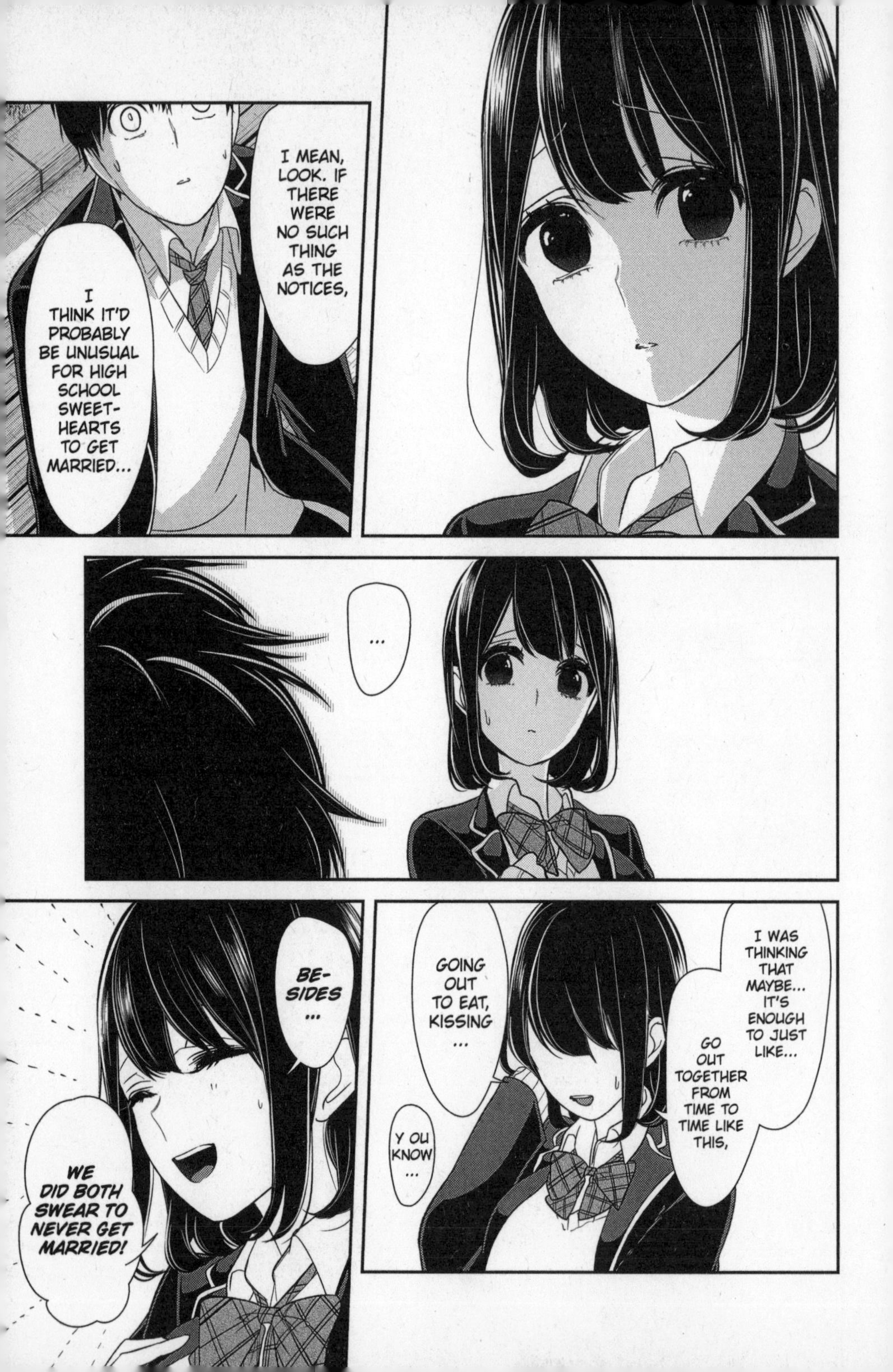
I MEAN, LOOK. IF THERE WERE NO SUCH THING AS THE NOTICES,
I THINK IT'D PROBABLY BE UNUSUAL FOR HIGH SCHOOL SWEET-HEARTS TO GET MARRIED...
...
I WAS THINKING THAT MAYBE... IT'S ENOUGH TO JUST LIKE...
GO OUT TOGETHER FROM TIME TO TIME LIKE THIS,
GOING OUT TO EAT, KISSING ...
Y OU KNOW ...
BE-SIDES ...
WE DID BOTH SWEAR TO NEVER GET MARRIED!

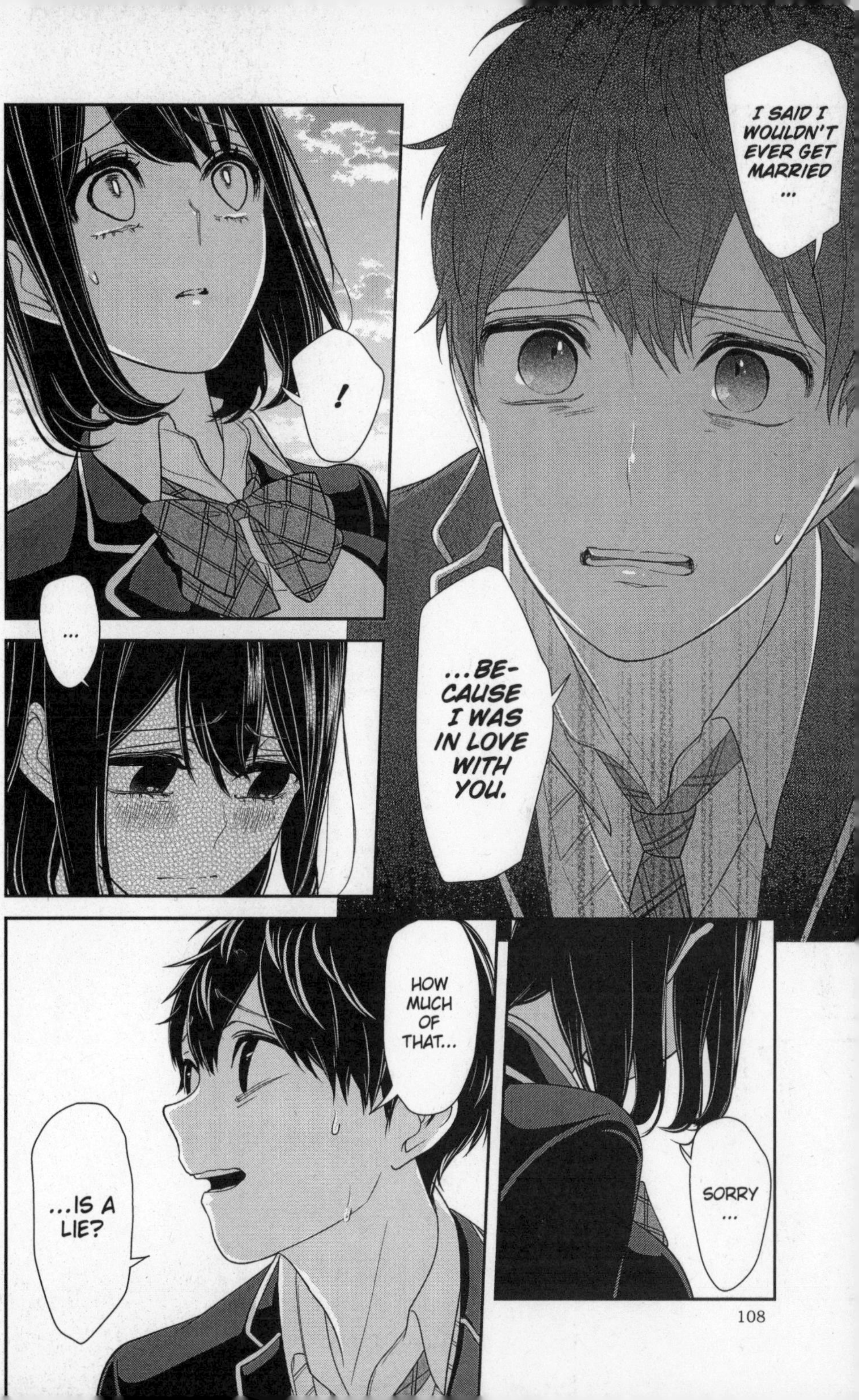
I SAID I WOULDN'T EVER GET MARRIED ...
...BE-CAUSE I WAS IN LOVE WITH YOU.
!
...
SORRY ...
HOW MUCH OF THAT...
...IS A LIE?

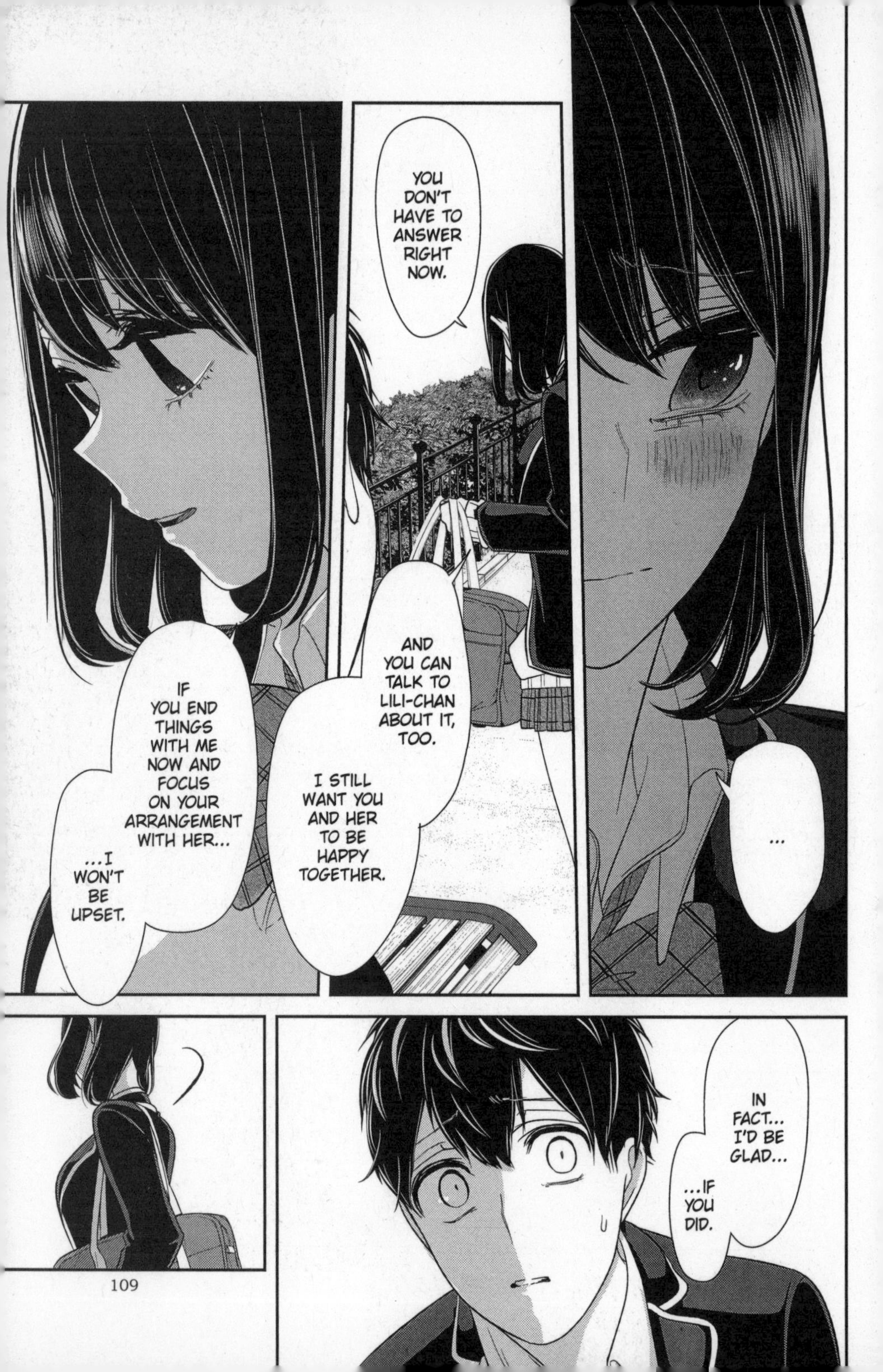
...
YOU DON'T HAVE TO ANSWER RIGHT NOW.
AND YOU CAN TALK TO LILI-CHAN ABOUT IT, TOO.
I STILL WANT YOU AND HER TO BE HAPPY TOGETHER.
IF YOU END THINGS WITH ME NOW AND FOCUS ON YOUR ARRANGEMENT WITH HER...
...I WON'T BE UPSET.
IN FACT... I'D BE GLAD...
...IF YOU DID.

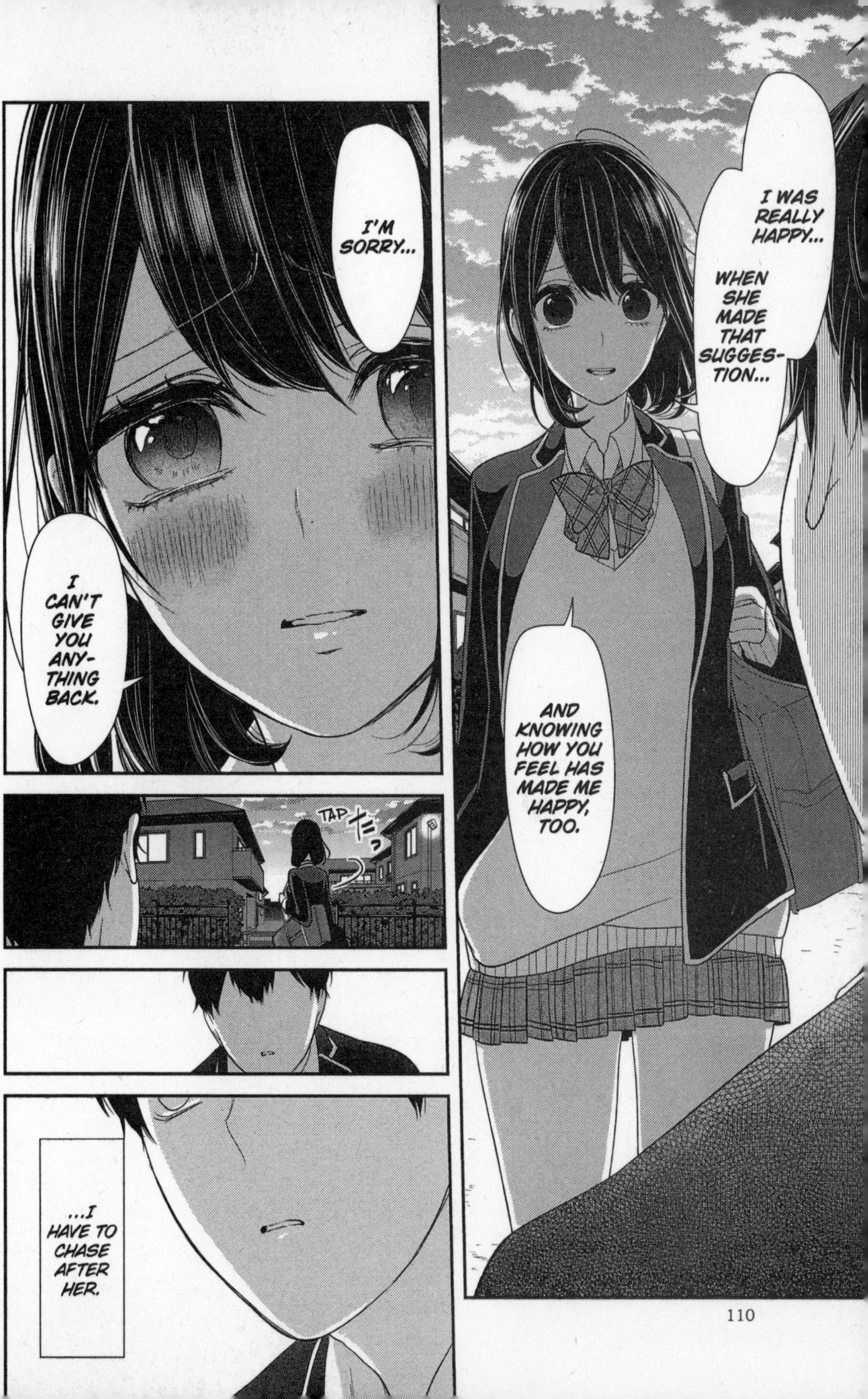
I WAS REALLY HAPPY...
WHEN SHE MADE THAT SUGGESTION...
AND KNOWING HOW YOU FEEL HAS MADE ME HAPPY, TOO.
I'M SORRY...
I CAN'T GIVE YOU ANYTHING BACK.
TAP
...I HAVE TO CHASE AFTER HER.

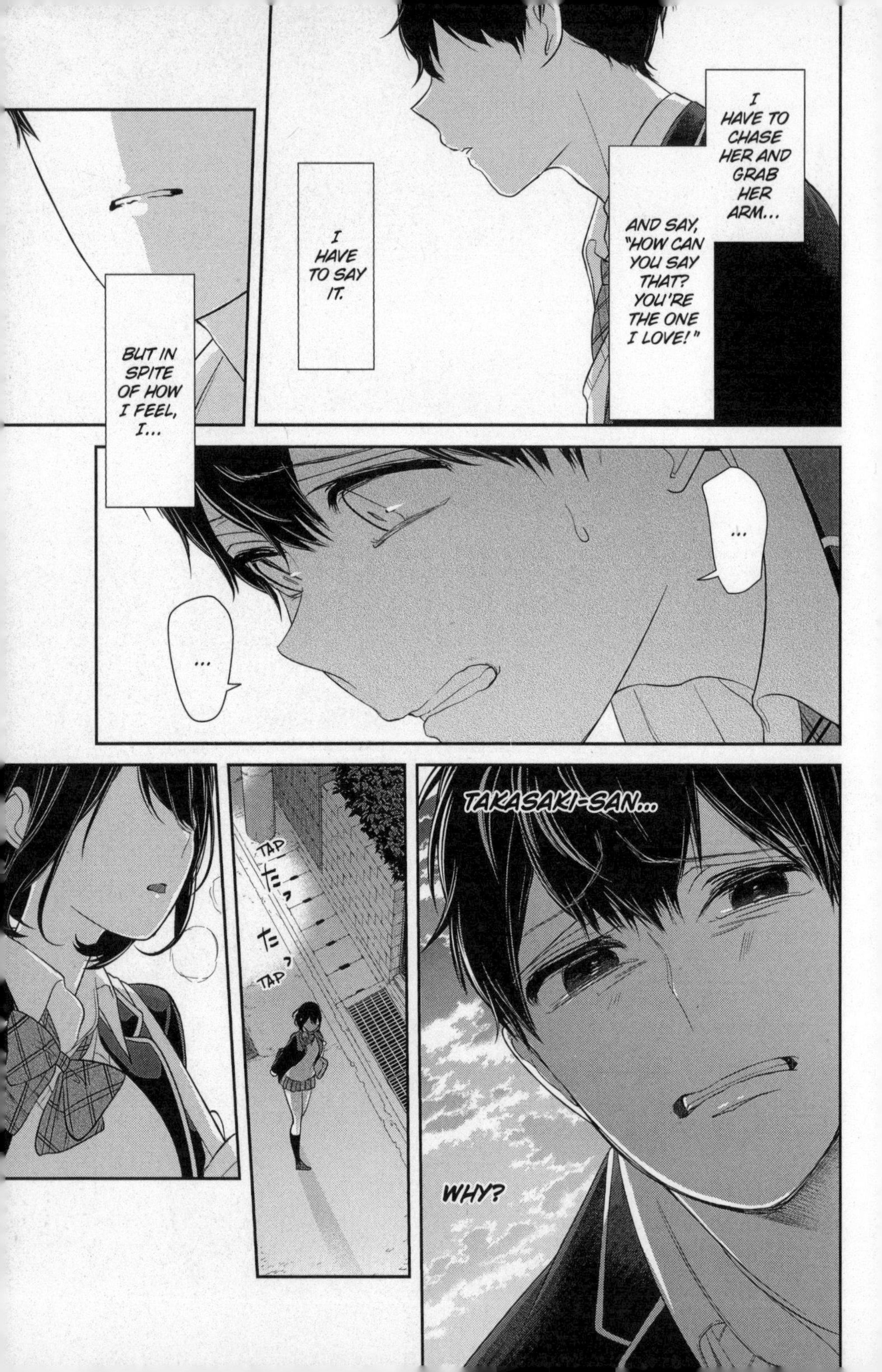
I HAVE TO CHASE HER AND GRAB HER ARM...
AND SAY, "HOW CAN YOU SAY THAT? YOU'RE THE ONE I LOVE!"
I HAVE TO SAY IT.
BUT IN SPITE OF HOW I FEEL, I...
...
...
TAKASAKI-SAN...
WHY?
TAP
たっ
たっ
TAP

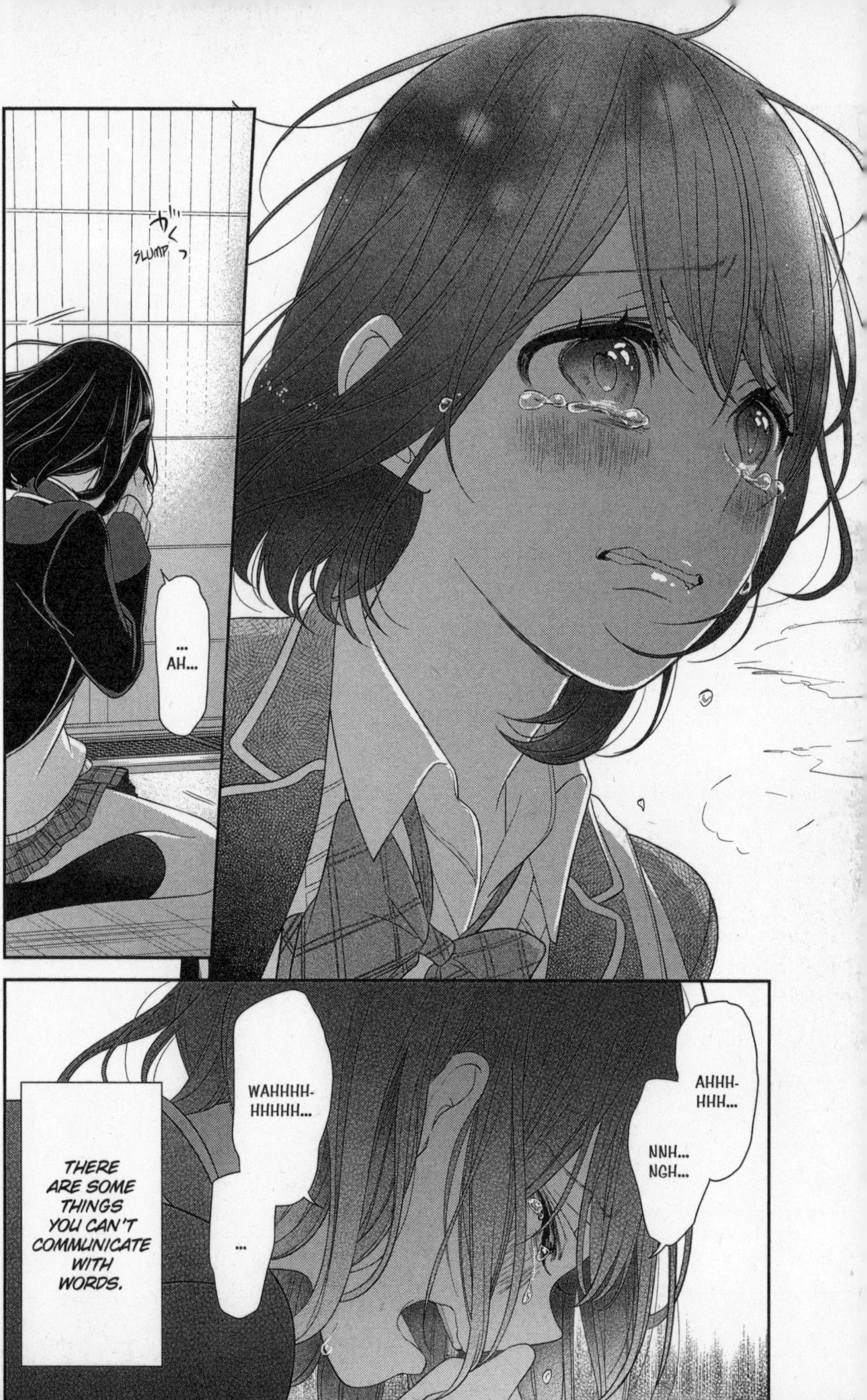
がく
SLUMP
... AH...
AHHH-HHH...
NNH... NGH...
WAHHHH-HHHHH...
...
THERE ARE SOME THINGS YOU CAN'T COMMUNICATE WITH WORDS.

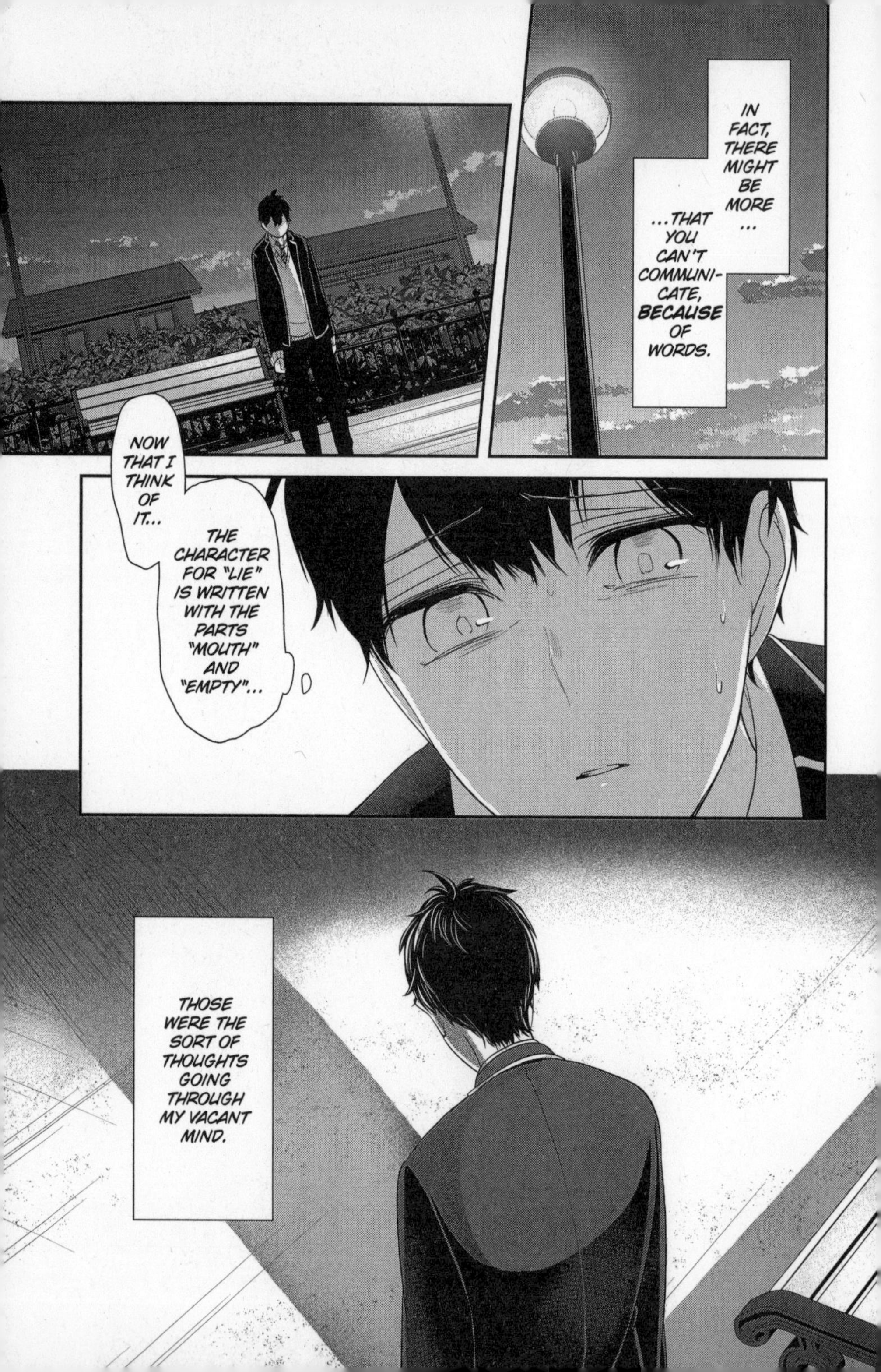
IN FACT, THERE MIGHT BE MORE ...
...THAT YOU CAN'T COMMUNICATE, **BECAUSE** OF WORDS.
NOW THAT I THINK OF IT...
THE CHARACTER FOR "LIE" IS WRITTEN WITH THE PARTS "MOUTH" AND "EMPTY"...
THOSE WERE THE SORT OF THOUGHTS GOING THROUGH MY VACANT MIND.

Love&Lies

Chapter 29: Love's Responsibility

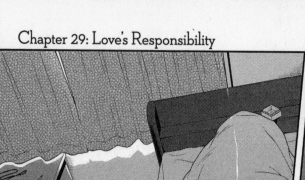

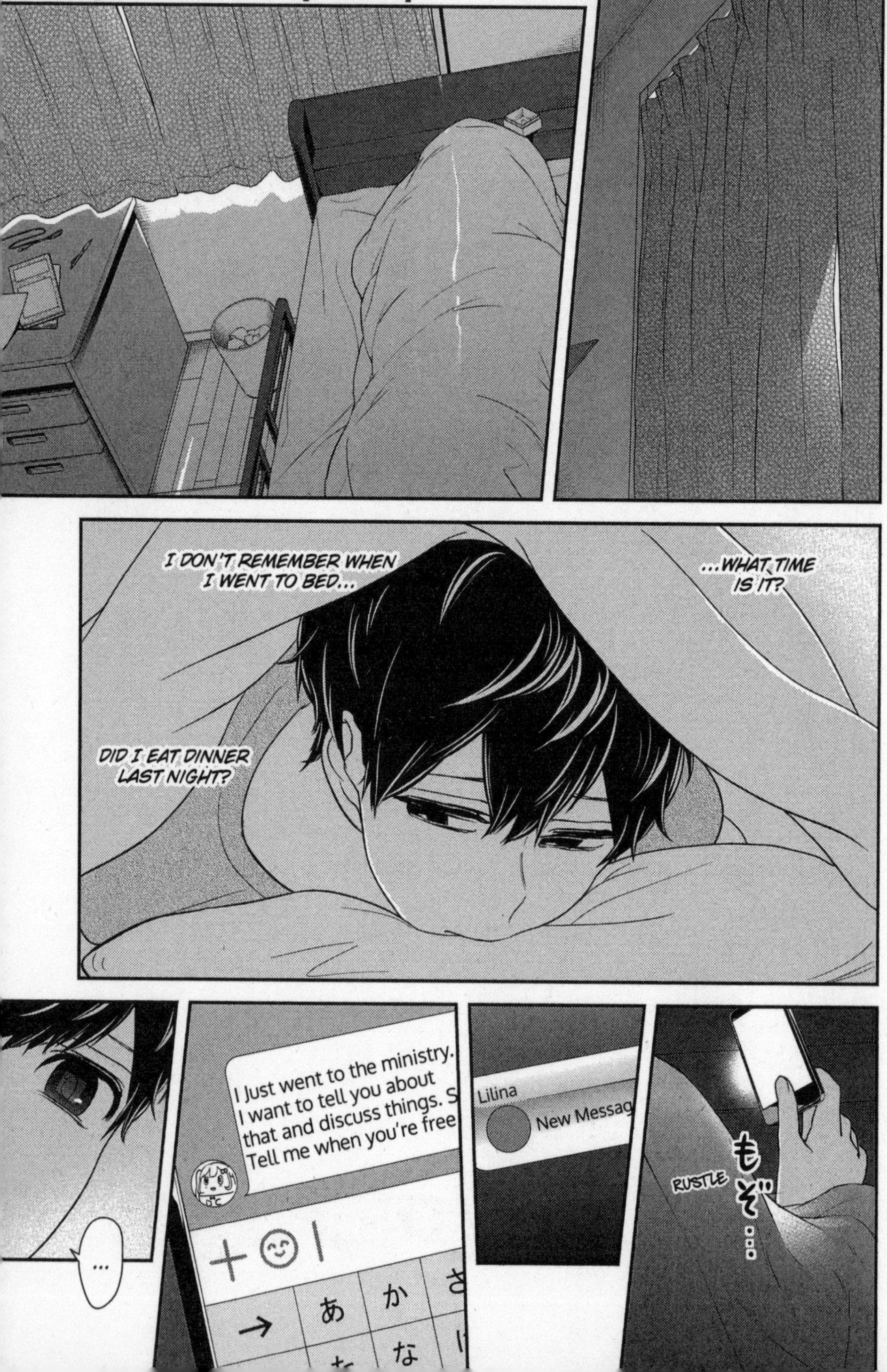
...WHAT TIME IS IT?
I DON'T REMEMBER WHEN I WENT TO BED...
DID I EAT DINNER LAST NIGHT?
もぞ…
RUSTLE
Lilina
New Messag
I Just went to the ministry. I want to tell you about that and discuss things. S Tell me when you're free
あ か さ
な
...

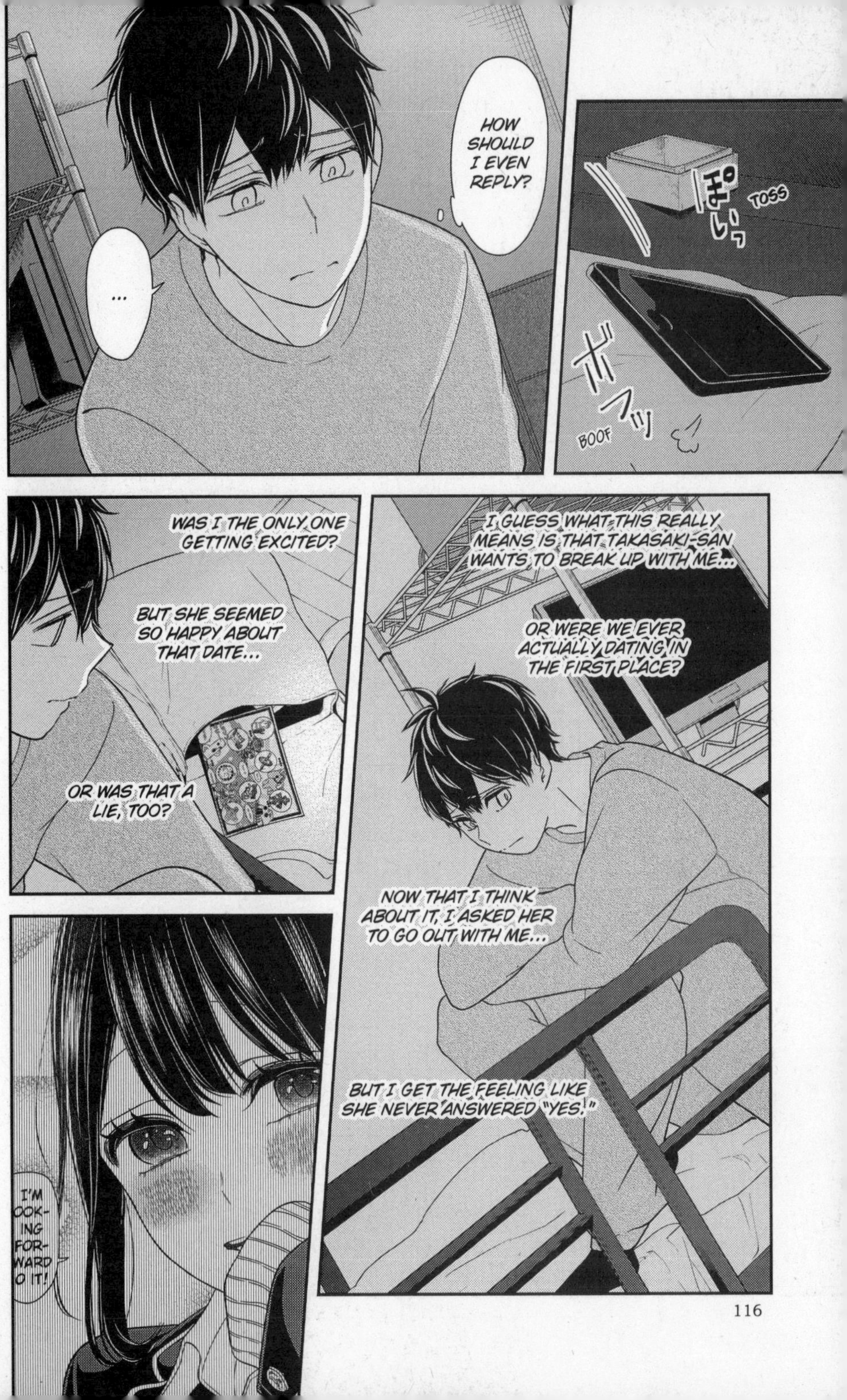
ぽいっ
TOSS
ボフッ
BOOF
HOW SHOULD I EVEN REPLY?
...
I GUESS WHAT THIS REALLY MEANS IS THAT TAKASAKI-SAN WANTS TO BREAK UP WITH ME...
OR WERE WE EVER ACTUALLY DATING IN THE FIRST PLACE?
NOW THAT I THINK ABOUT IT, I ASKED HER TO GO OUT WITH ME...
BUT I GET THE FEELING LIKE SHE NEVER ANSWERED "YES."
WAS I THE ONLY ONE GETTING EXCITED?
BUT SHE SEEMED SO HAPPY ABOUT THAT DATE...
OR WAS THAT A LIE, TOO?
I'M OOK-ING FOR-WARD O IT!

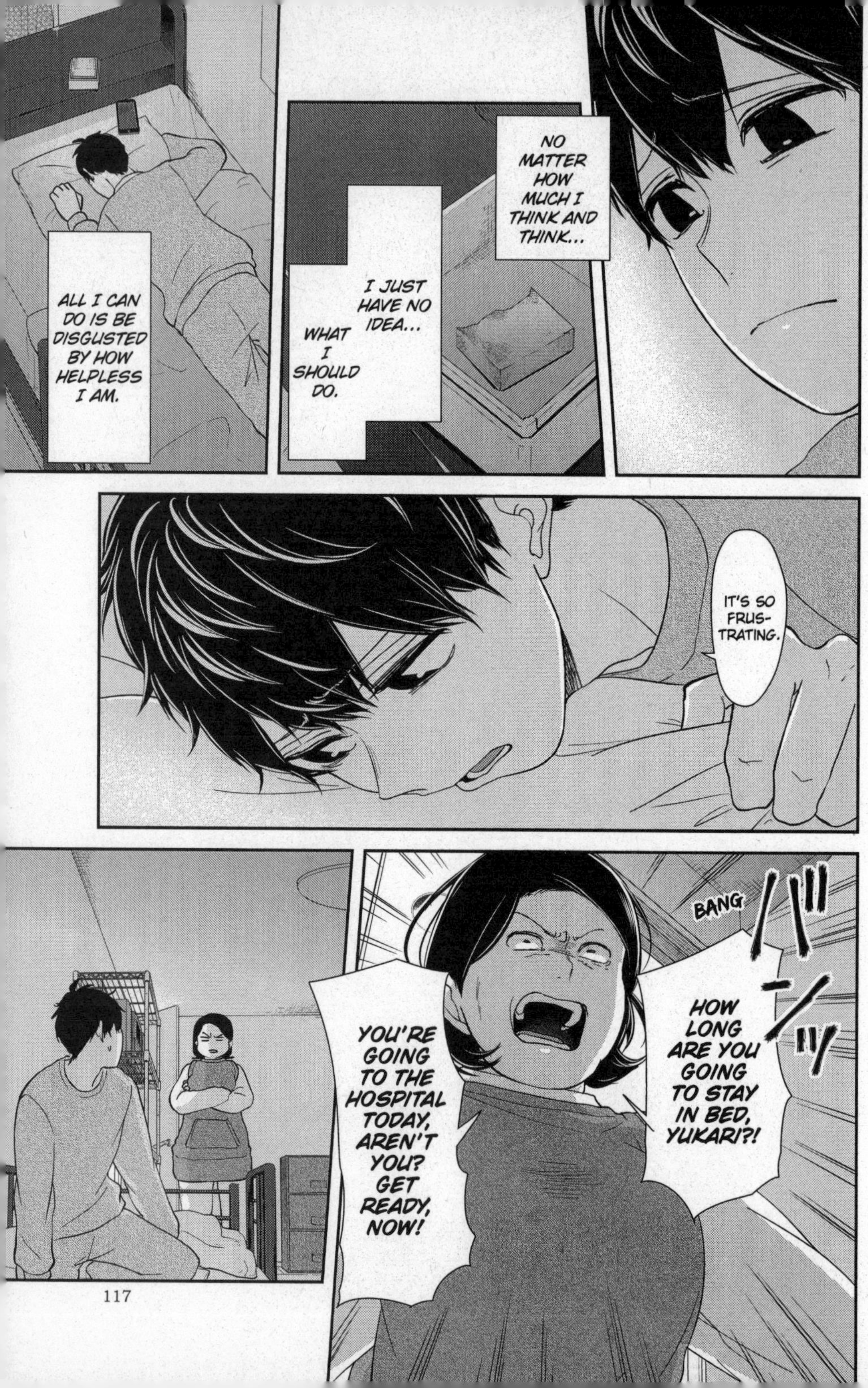
NO MATTER HOW MUCH I THINK AND THINK...
I JUST HAVE NO IDEA...
WHAT I SHOULD DO.
ALL I CAN DO IS BE DISGUSTED BY HOW HELPLESS I AM.
IT'S SO FRUS-TRATING.
BANG
HOW LONG ARE YOU GOING TO STAY IN BED, YUKARI?!
YOU'RE GOING TO THE HOSPITAL TODAY, AREN'T YOU? GET READY, NOW!

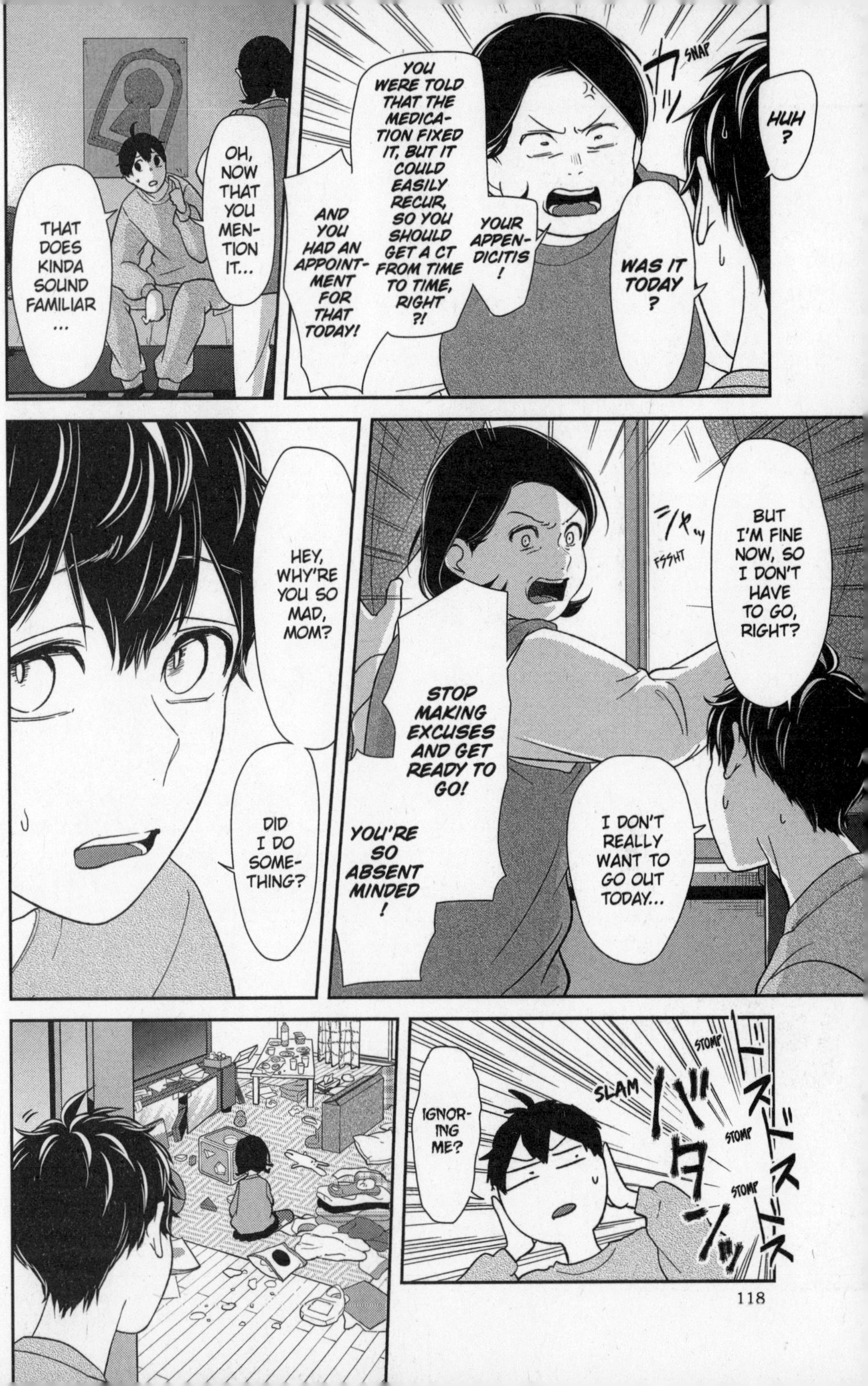
SNAP
HUH?
WAS IT TODAY?
YOUR APPENDICITIS!
YOU WERE TOLD THAT THE MEDICATION FIXED IT, BUT IT COULD EASILY RECUR, SO YOU SHOULD GET A CT FROM TIME TO TIME, RIGHT?!
AND YOU HAD AN APPOINTMENT FOR THAT TODAY!
OH, NOW THAT YOU MENTION IT...
THAT DOES KINDA SOUND FAMILIAR...
BUT I'M FINE NOW, SO I DON'T HAVE TO GO, RIGHT?
FSSHT
I DON'T REALLY WANT TO GO OUT TODAY...
STOP MAKING EXCUSES AND GET READY TO GO!
YOU'RE SO ABSENT MINDED!
HEY, WHY'RE YOU SO MAD, MOM?
DID I DO SOMETHING?
STOMP
STOMP
STOMP
SLAM
IGNORING ME?

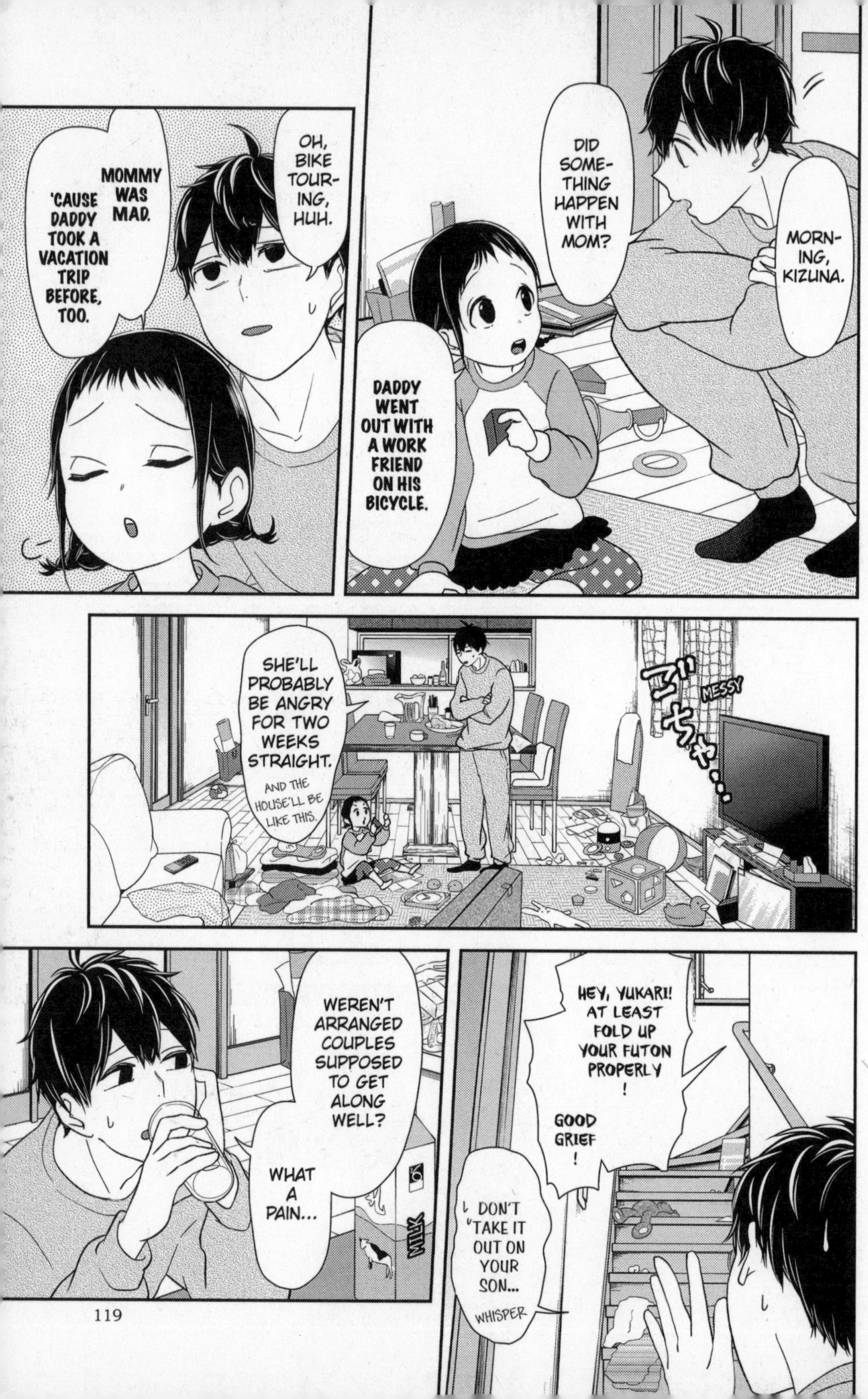
MORNING, KIZUNA.
DID SOMETHING HAPPEN WITH MOM?
DADDY WENT OUT WITH A WORK FRIEND ON HIS BICYCLE.
OH, BIKE TOURING, HUH.
MOMMY WAS MAD.
'CAUSE DADDY TOOK A VACATION TRIP BEFORE, TOO.
MESSY
SHE'LL PROBABLY BE ANGRY FOR TWO WEEKS STRAIGHT.
AND THE HOUSE'LL BE LIKE THIS.
HEY, YUKARI! AT LEAST FOLD UP YOUR FUTON PROPERLY!
GOOD GRIEF!
DON'T TAKE IT OUT ON YOUR SON...
WHISPER
WEREN'T ARRANGED COUPLES SUPPOSED TO GET ALONG WELL?
WHAT A PAIN...
MILK

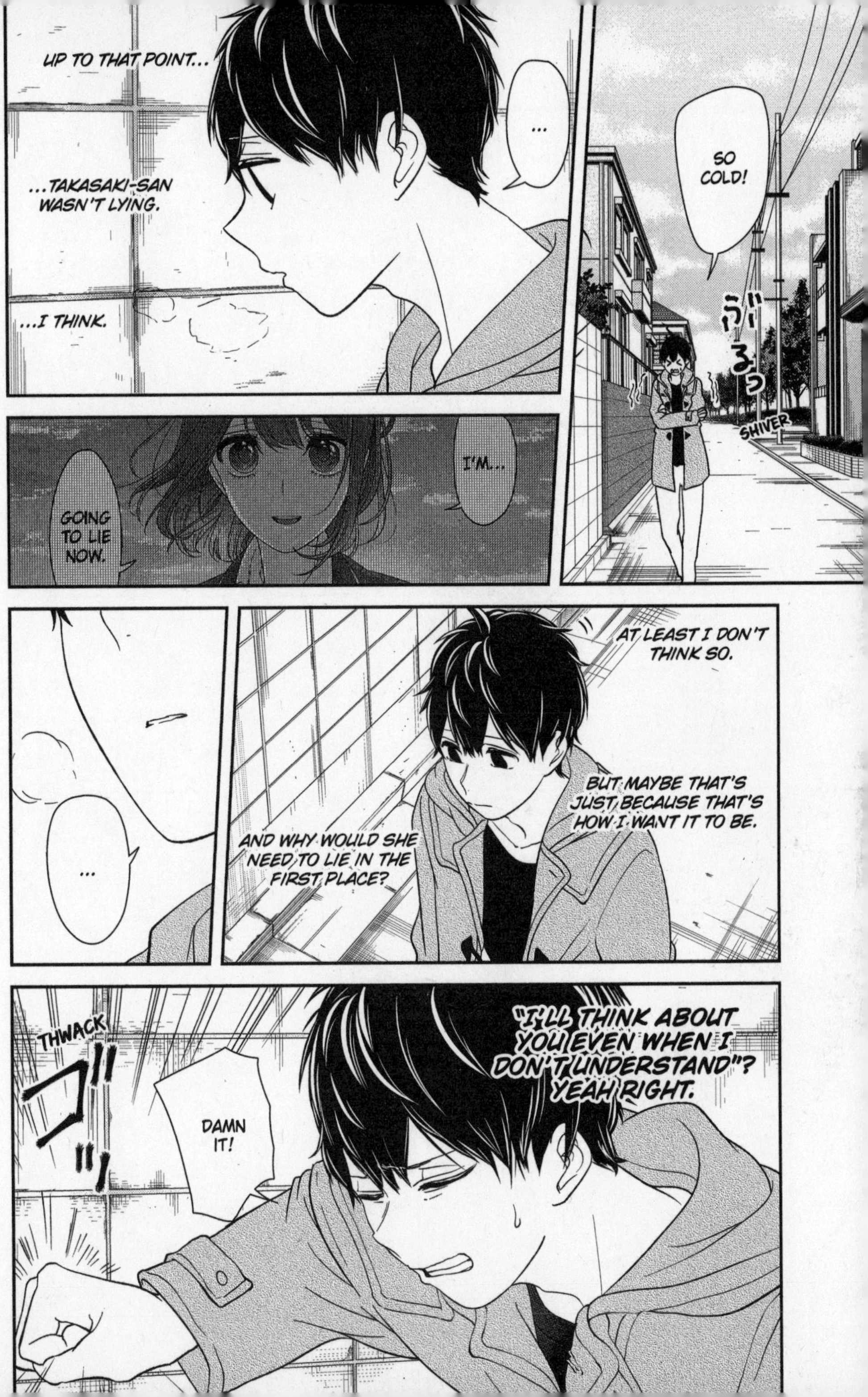
SO COLD!
ぶるっ
SHIVER
...
UP TO THAT POINT...
...TAKASAKI-SAN WASN'T LYING.
...I THINK.
I'M...
GOING TO LIE NOW.
AT LEAST I DON'T THINK SO.
BUT MAYBE THAT'S JUST BECAUSE THAT'S HOW I WANT IT TO BE.
AND WHY WOULD SHE NEED TO LIE IN THE FIRST PLACE?
...
"I'LL THINK ABOUT YOU EVEN WHEN I DON'T UNDERSTAND"? YEAH RIGHT.
DAMN IT!
THWACK
ゴッ

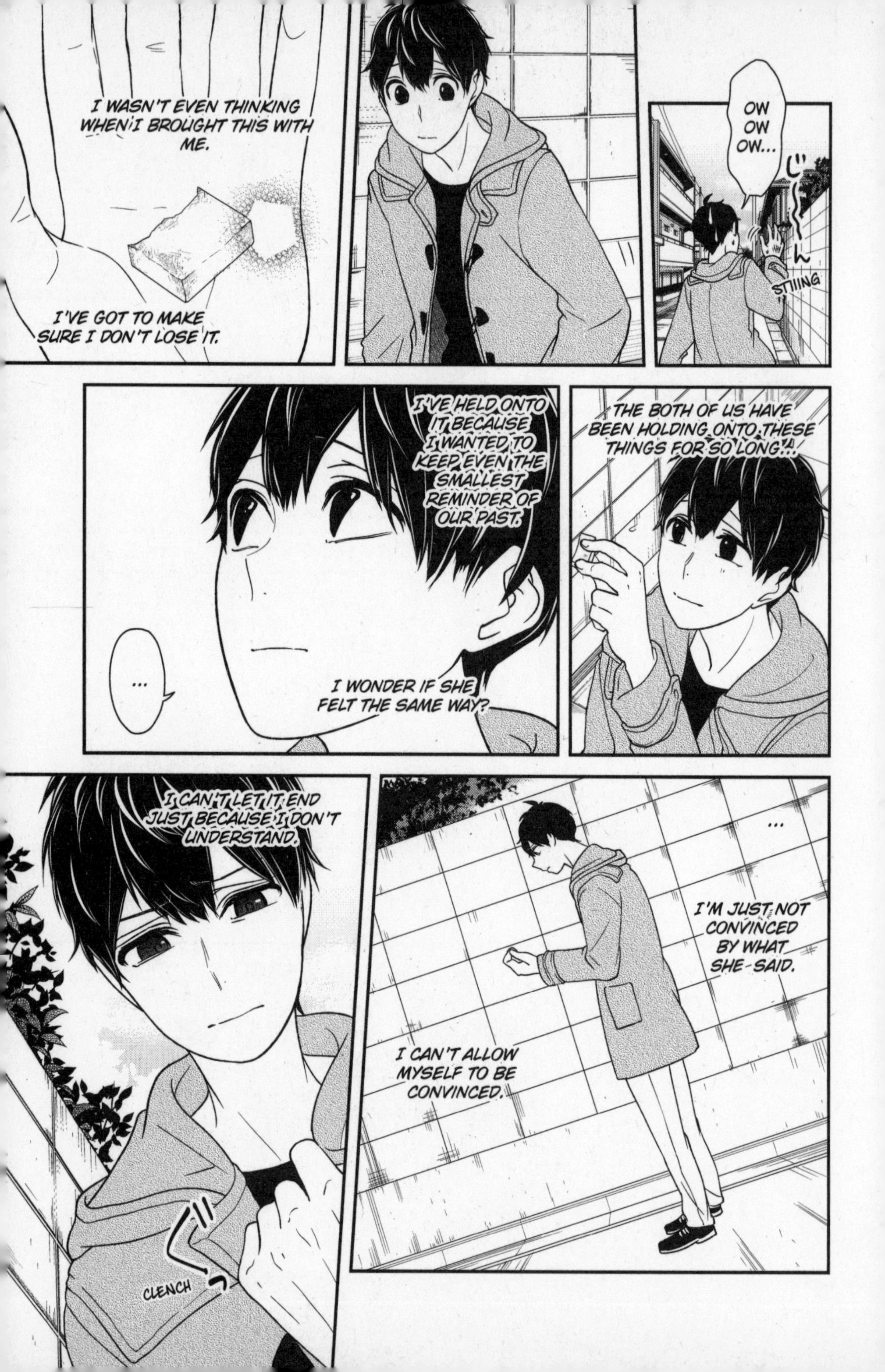
OW OW OW...
じ～ん
STIING
I WASN'T EVEN THINKING WHEN I BROUGHT THIS WITH ME.
I'VE GOT TO MAKE SURE I DON'T LOSE IT.
THE BOTH OF US HAVE BEEN HOLDING ONTO THESE THINGS FOR SO LONG...
I'VE HELD ONTO IT BECAUSE I WANTED TO KEEP EVEN THE SMALLEST REMINDER OF OUR PAST.
...
I WONDER IF SHE FELT THE SAME WAY?
...
I'M JUST NOT CONVINCED BY WHAT SHE SAID.
I CAN'T ALLOW MYSELF TO BE CONVINCED.
I CAN'T LET IT END JUST BECAUSE I DON'T UNDERSTAND.
CLENCH

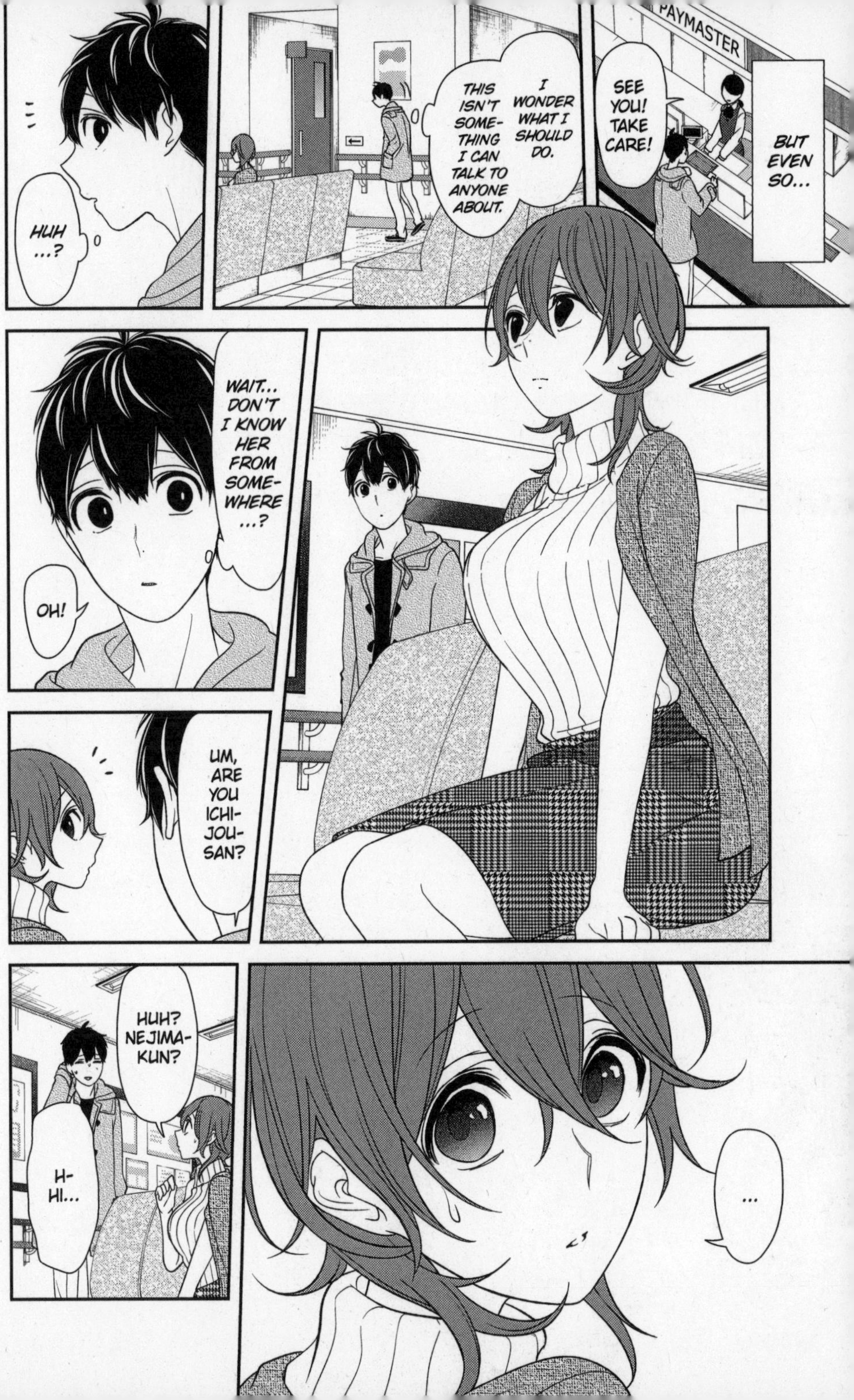
BUT EVEN SO...
SEE YOU! TAKE CARE!
PAYMASTER
I WONDER WHAT I SHOULD DO.
THIS ISN'T SOME-THING I CAN TALK TO ANYONE ABOUT.
HUH ...?
WAIT... DON'T I KNOW HER FROM SOME-WHERE ...?
OH!
UM, ARE YOU ICHI-JOU-SAN?
...
HUH? NEJIMA-KUN?
H-HI...

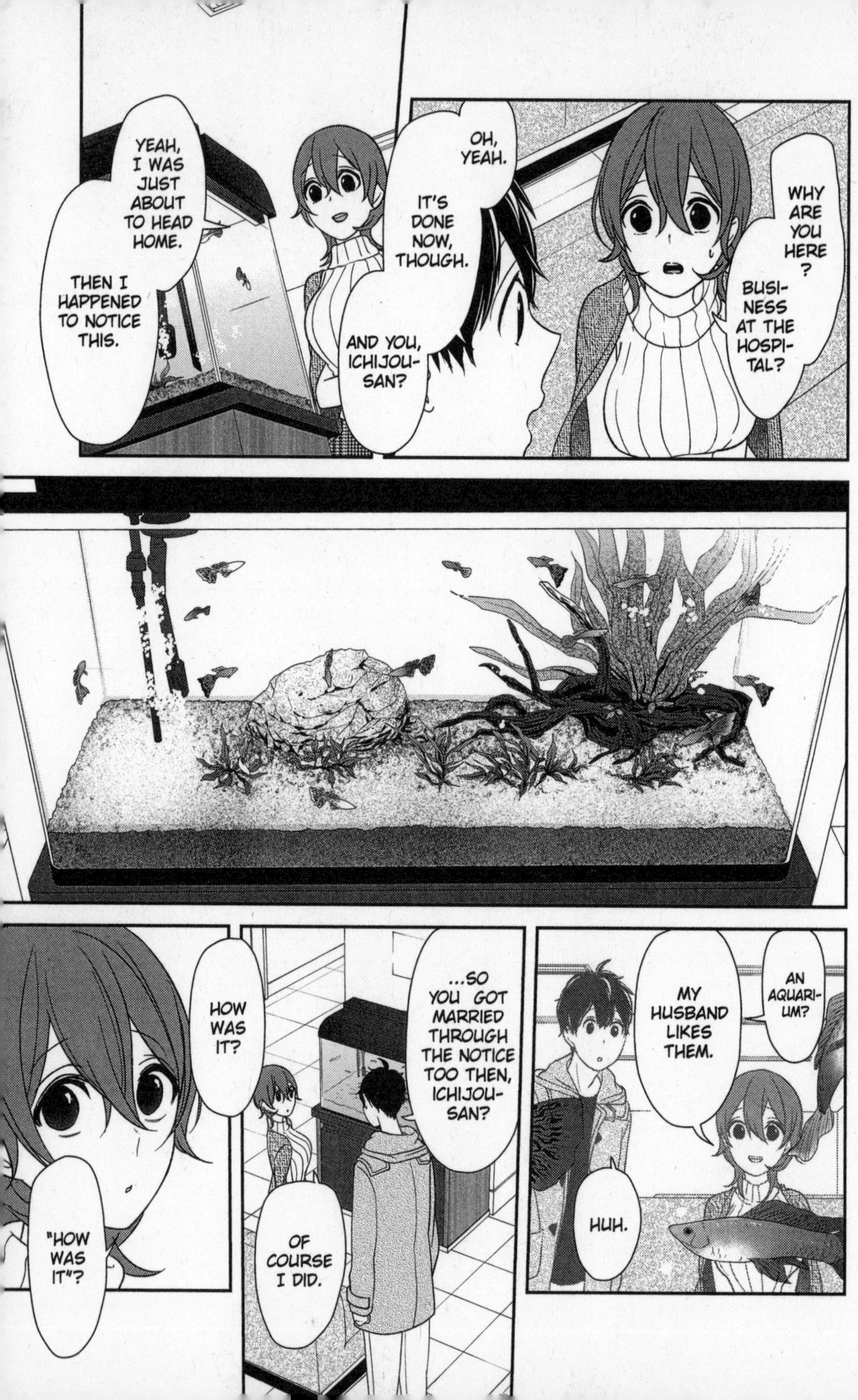
WHY ARE YOU HERE? BUSINESS AT THE HOSPITAL?
OH, YEAH. IT'S DONE NOW, THOUGH.
AND YOU, ICHIJOU-SAN?
YEAH, I WAS JUST ABOUT TO HEAD HOME.
THEN I HAPPENED TO NOTICE THIS.
AN AQUARIUM?
MY HUSBAND LIKES THEM.
HUH.
...SO YOU GOT MARRIED THROUGH THE NOTICE TOO THEN, ICHIJOU-SAN?
OF COURSE I DID.
HOW WAS IT?
"HOW WAS IT"?

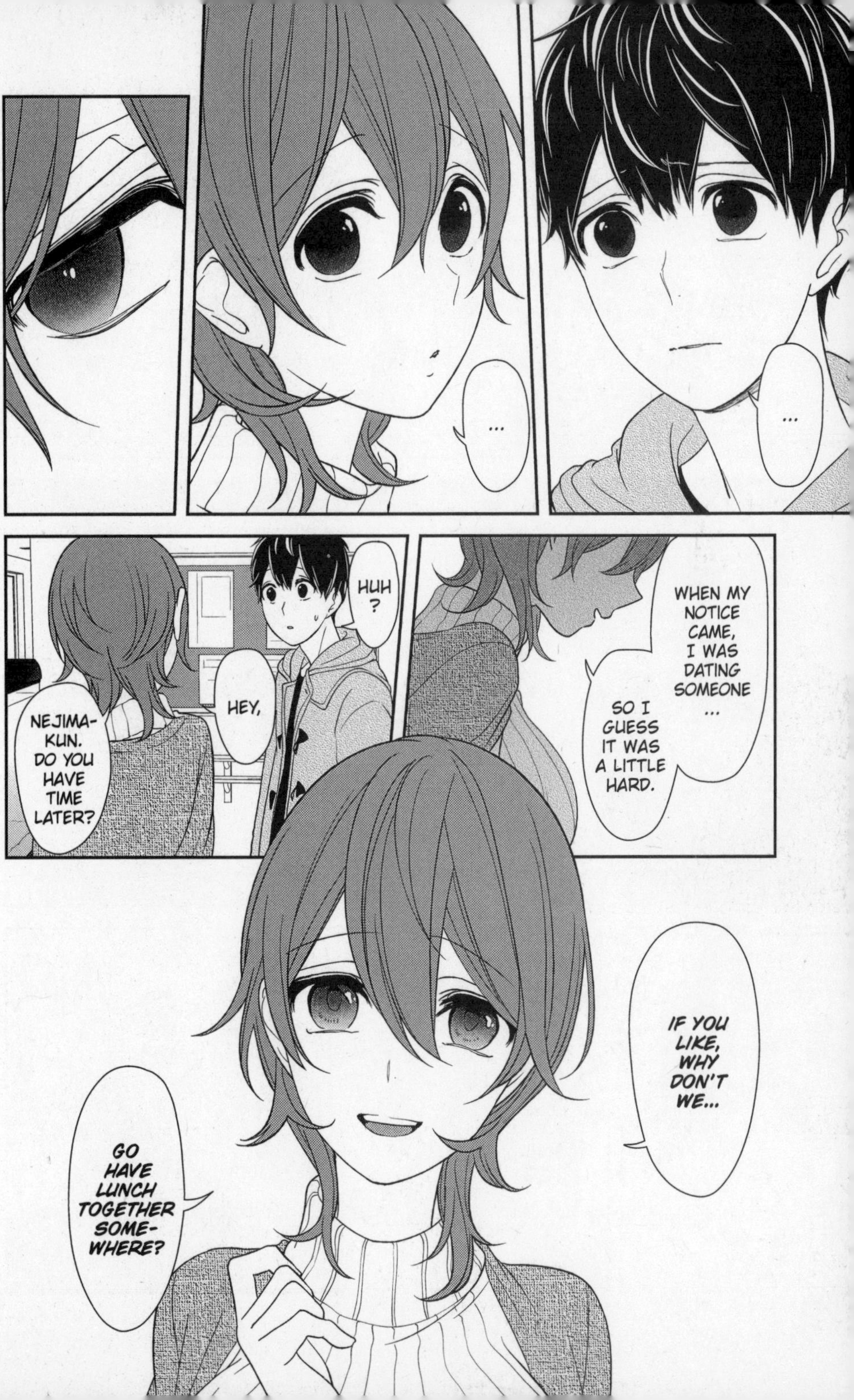
...
...
WHEN MY NOTICE CAME, I WAS DATING SOMEONE ...
SO I GUESS IT WAS A LITTLE HARD.
HUH ?
HEY,
NEJIMA-KUN. DO YOU HAVE TIME LATER?
IF YOU LIKE, WHY DON'T WE...
GO HAVE LUNCH TOGETHER SOME-WHERE?

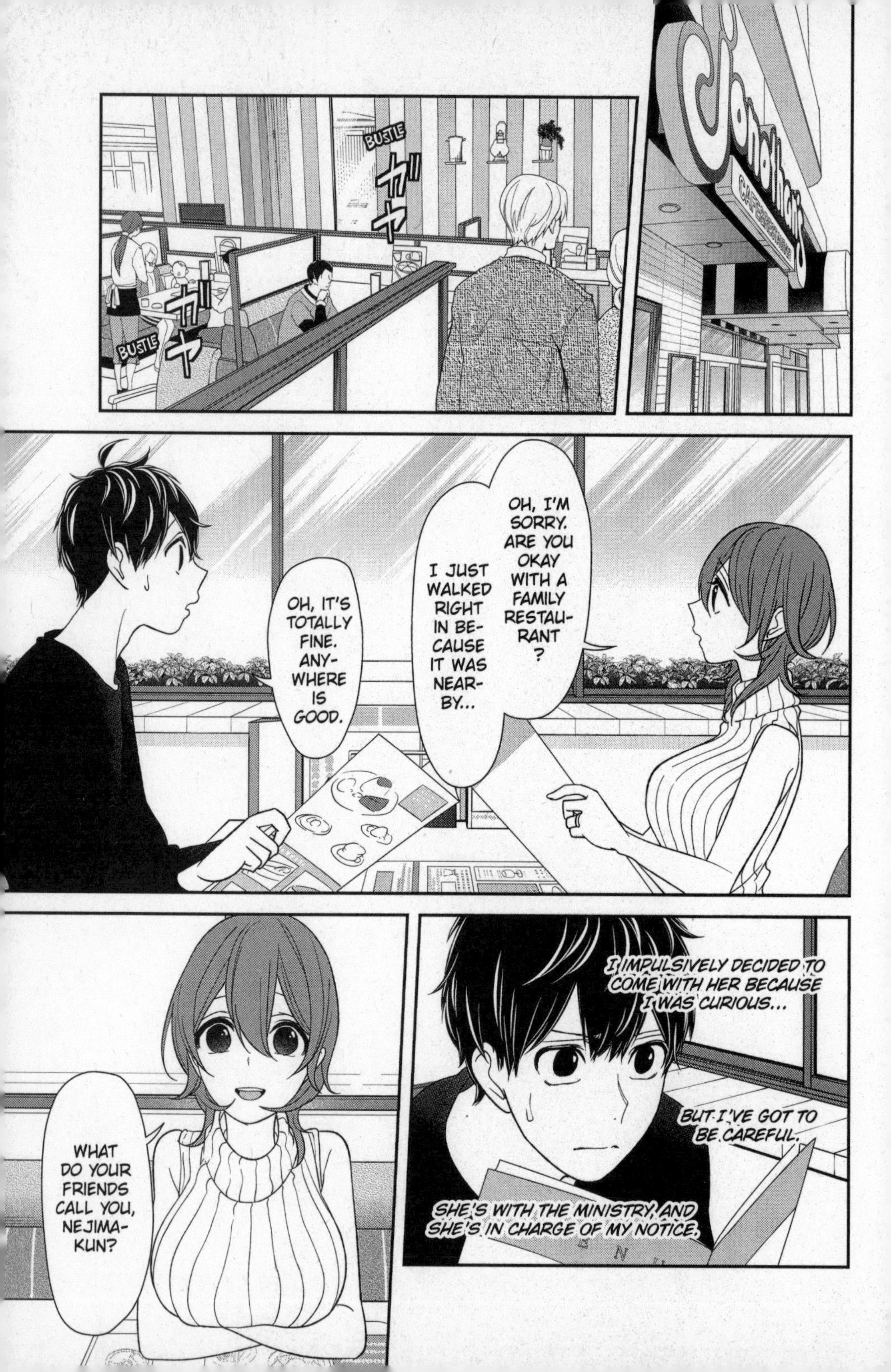
BUSTLE
BUSTLE
OH, I'M SORRY. ARE YOU OKAY WITH A FAMILY RESTAURANT?
I JUST WALKED RIGHT IN BECAUSE IT WAS NEARBY...
OH, IT'S TOTALLY FINE. ANYWHERE IS GOOD.
I IMPULSIVELY DECIDED TO COME WITH HER BECAUSE I WAS CURIOUS...
BUT I'VE GOT TO BE CAREFUL.
SHE'S WITH THE MINISTRY, AND SHE'S IN CHARGE OF MY NOTICE.
WHAT DO YOUR FRIENDS CALL YOU, NEJIMA-KUN?

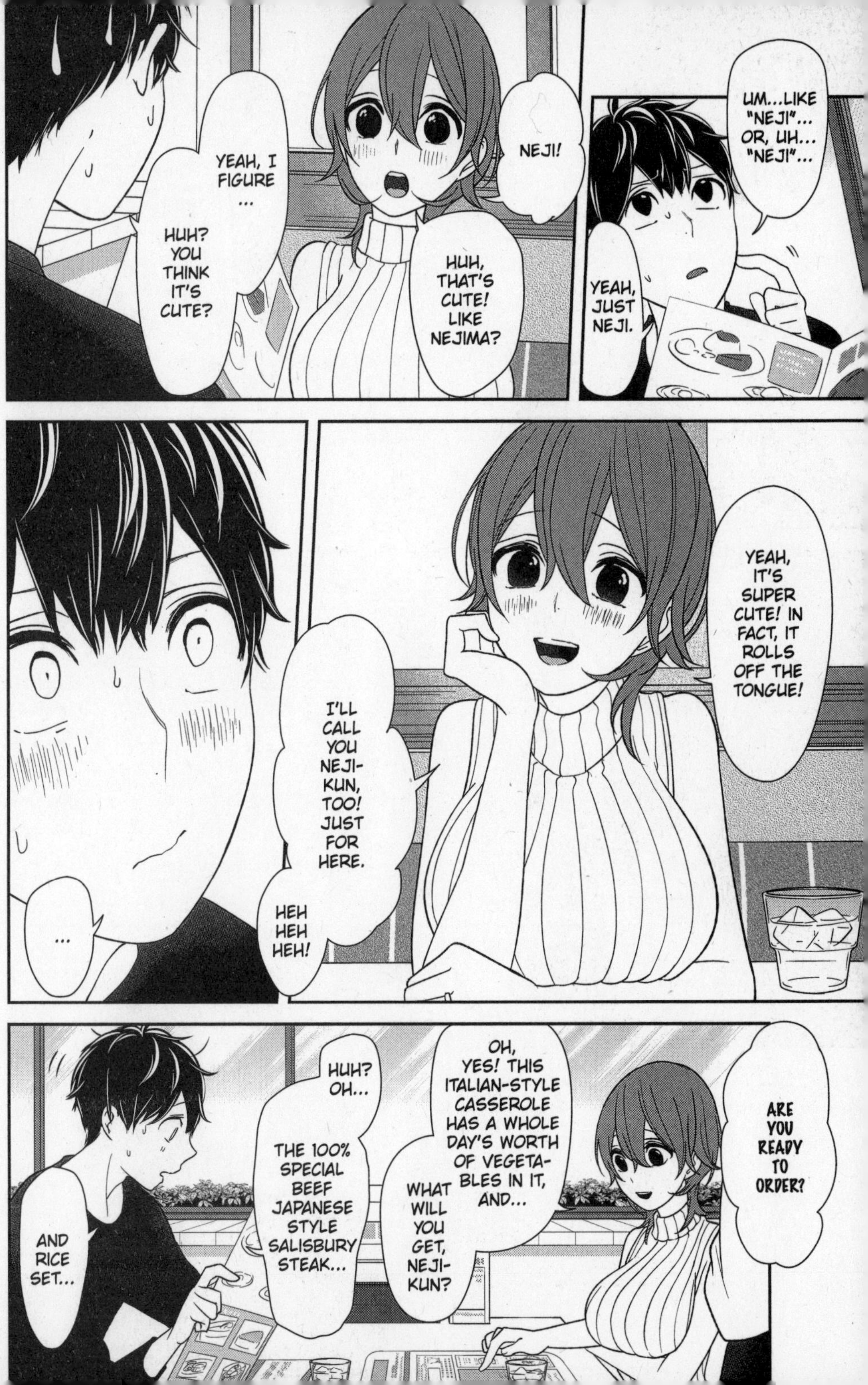
UM...LIKE "NEJI"... OR, UH... "NEJI"...
YEAH, JUST NEJI.
NEJI!
HUH, THAT'S CUTE! LIKE NEJIMA?
YEAH, I FIGURE ...
HUH? YOU THINK IT'S CUTE?
YEAH, IT'S SUPER CUTE! IN FACT, IT ROLLS OFF THE TONGUE!
I'LL CALL YOU NEJI-KUN, TOO! JUST FOR HERE.
HEH HEH HEH!
...
ARE YOU READY TO ORDER?
OH, YES! THIS ITALIAN-STYLE CASSEROLE HAS A WHOLE DAY'S WORTH OF VEGETA-BLES IN IT, AND...
WHAT WILL YOU GET, NEJI-KUN?
HUH? OH...
THE 100% SPECIAL BEEF JAPANESE STYLE SALISBURY STEAK...
AND RICE SET...

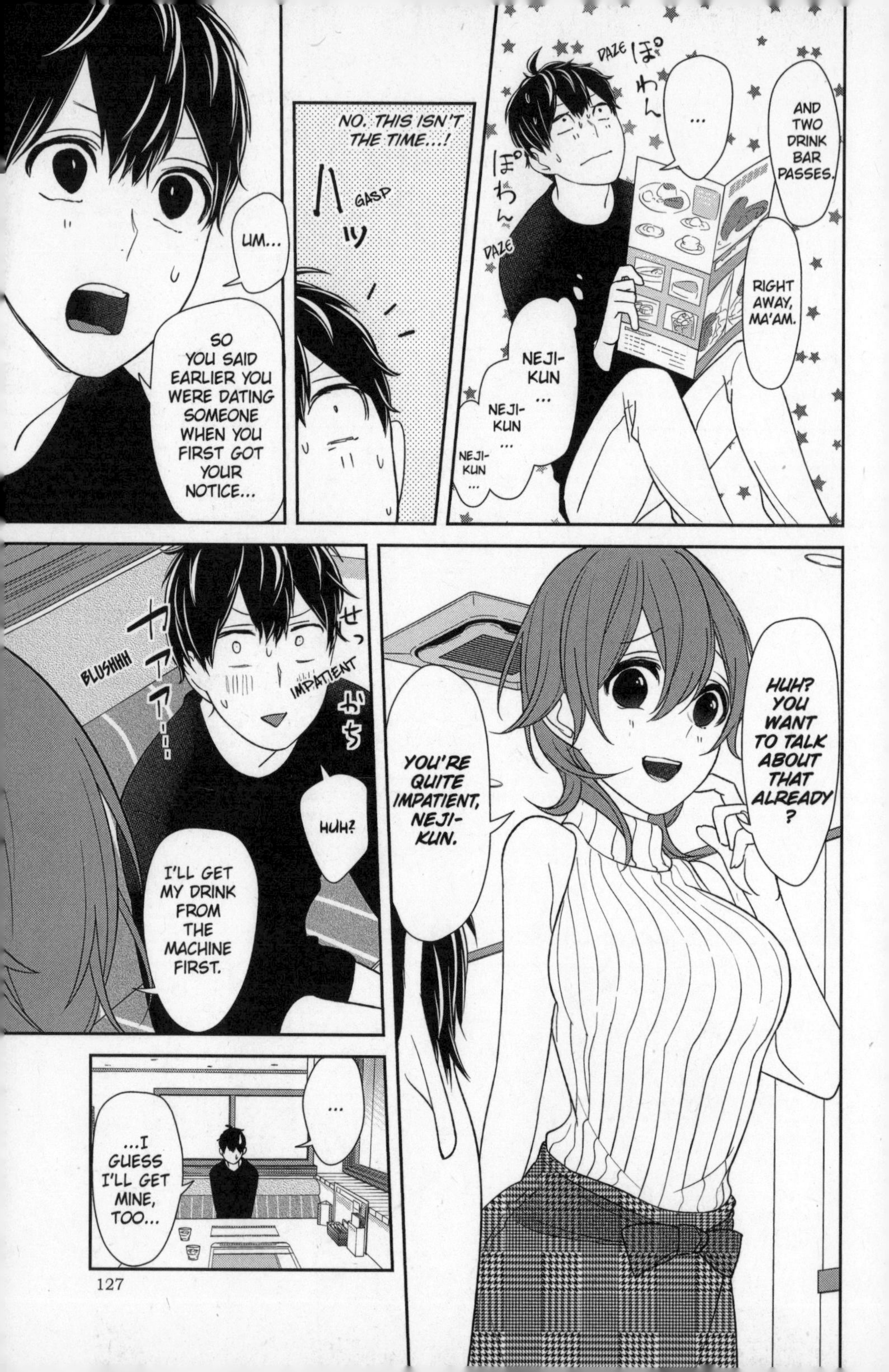
AND TWO DRINK BAR PASSES.
...
DAZE
RIGHT AWAY, MA'AM.
DAZE
NEJI-KUN...
NEJI-KUN...
NEJI-KUN...
NO. THIS ISN'T THE TIME...!
GASP
UM...
SO YOU SAID EARLIER YOU WERE DATING SOMEONE WHEN YOU FIRST GOT YOUR NOTICE...
HUH? YOU WANT TO TALK ABOUT THAT ALREADY?
YOU'RE QUITE IMPATIENT, NEJI-KUN.
IMPATIENT
BLUSHHH
HUH?
I'LL GET MY DRINK FROM THE MACHINE FIRST.
...
...I GUESS I'LL GET MINE, TOO...

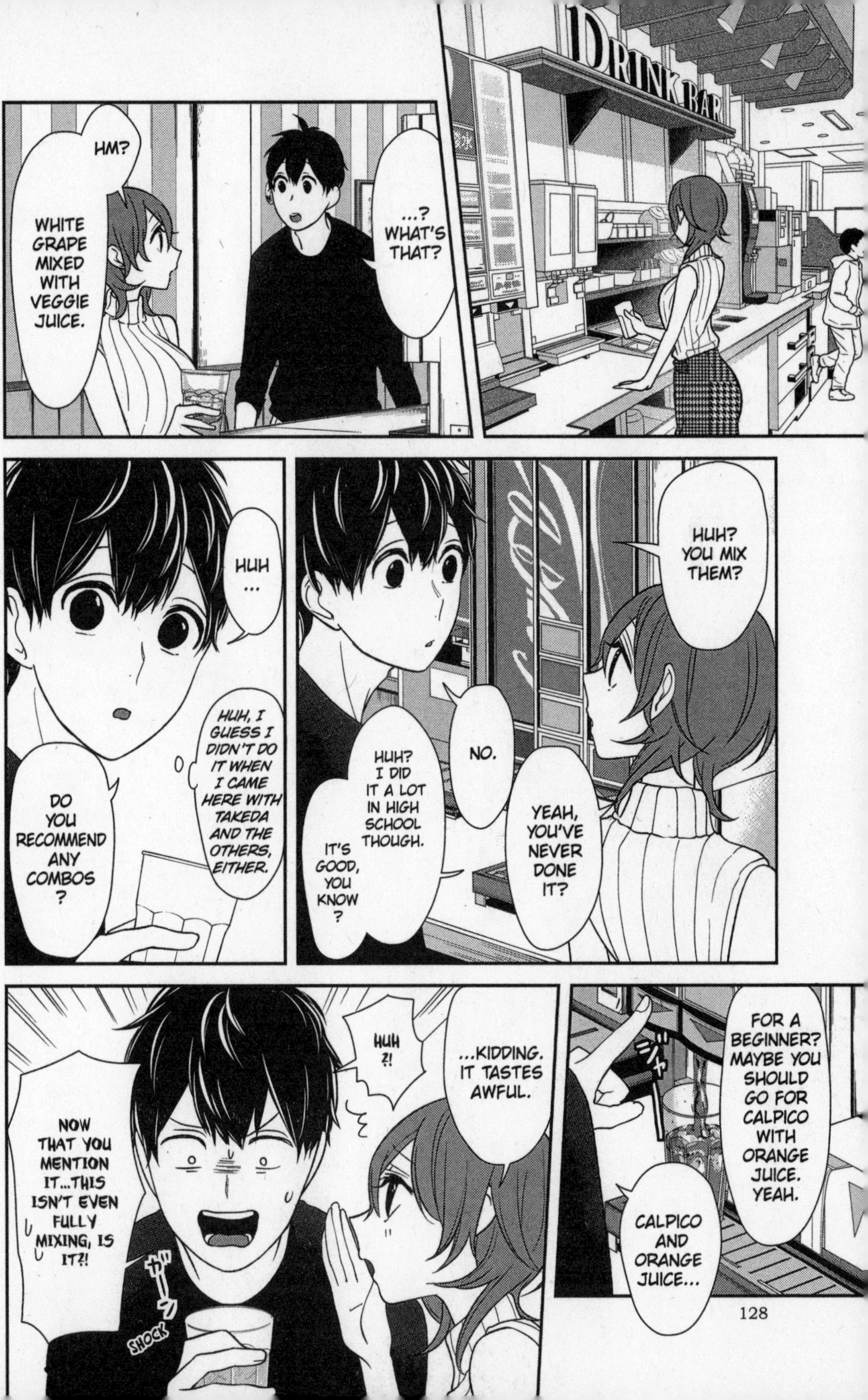
DRINK BAR
...? WHAT'S THAT?
HM?
WHITE GRAPE MIXED WITH VEGGIE JUICE.
HUH? YOU MIX THEM?
HUH? I DID IT A LOT IN HIGH SCHOOL THOUGH.
IT'S GOOD, YOU KNOW?
YEAH, YOU'VE NEVER DONE IT?
NO.
HUH ...
HUH, I GUESS I DIDN'T DO IT WHEN I CAME HERE WITH TAKEDA AND THE OTHERS, EITHER.
DO YOU RECOMMEND ANY COMBOS?
FOR A BEGINNER? MAYBE YOU SHOULD GO FOR CALPICO WITH ORANGE JUICE. YEAH.
CALPICO AND ORANGE JUICE...
...KIDDING. IT TASTES AWFUL.
HUH?!
NOW THAT YOU MENTION IT...THIS ISN'T EVEN FULLY MIXING, IS IT?!
SHOCK

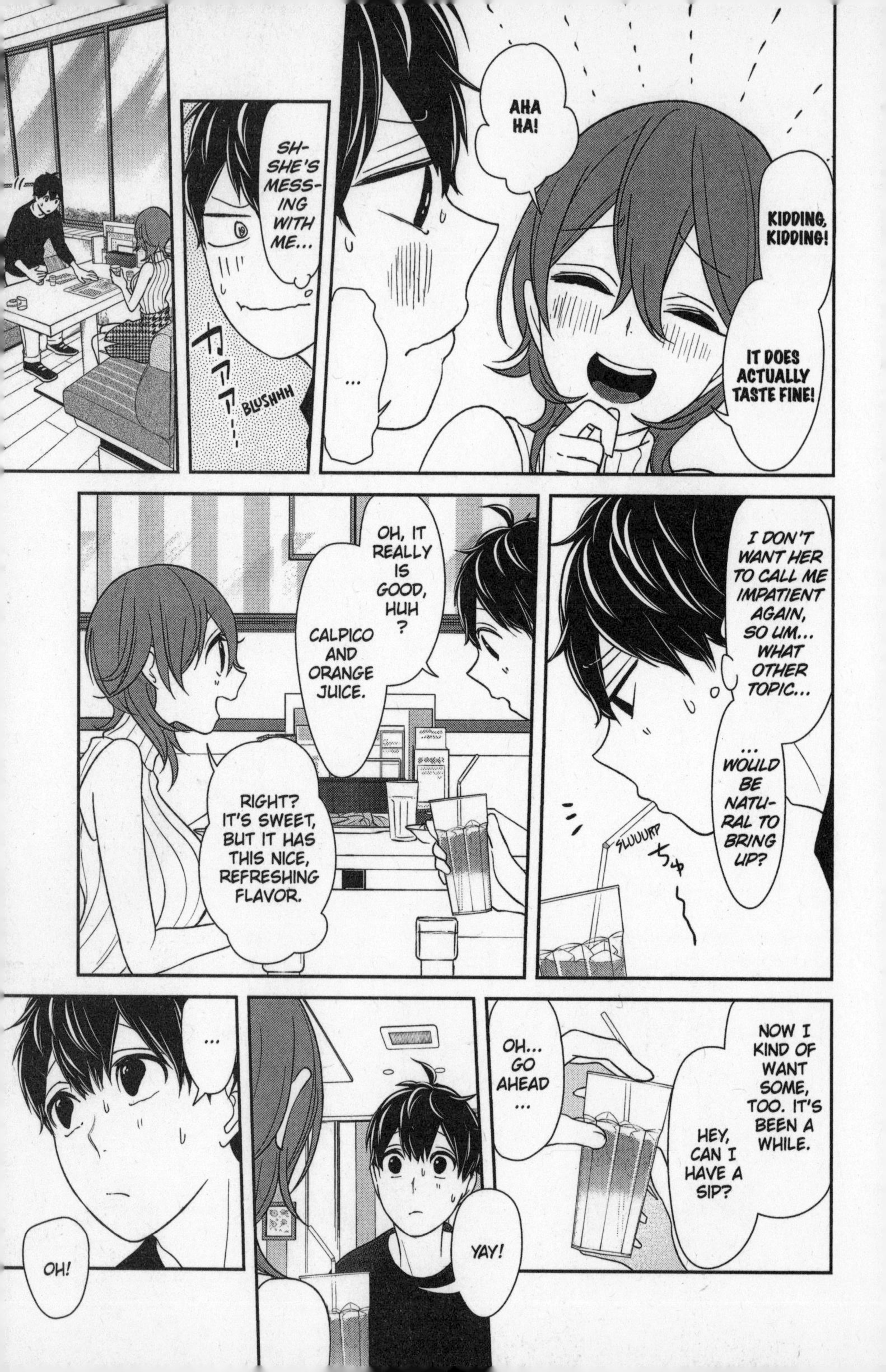
AHA HA!
KIDDING, KIDDING!
IT DOES ACTUALLY TASTE FINE!
...
SH-SHE'S MESSING WITH ME...
BLUSHHH
I DON'T WANT HER TO CALL ME IMPATIENT AGAIN, SO UM... WHAT OTHER TOPIC...
...WOULD BE NATURAL TO BRING UP?
SLUUURP
OH, IT REALLY IS GOOD, HUH?
CALPICO AND ORANGE JUICE.
RIGHT? IT'S SWEET, BUT IT HAS THIS NICE, REFRESHING FLAVOR.
NOW I KIND OF WANT SOME, TOO. IT'S BEEN A WHILE.
HEY, CAN I HAVE A SIP?
OH... GO AHEAD...
YAY!
...
OH!

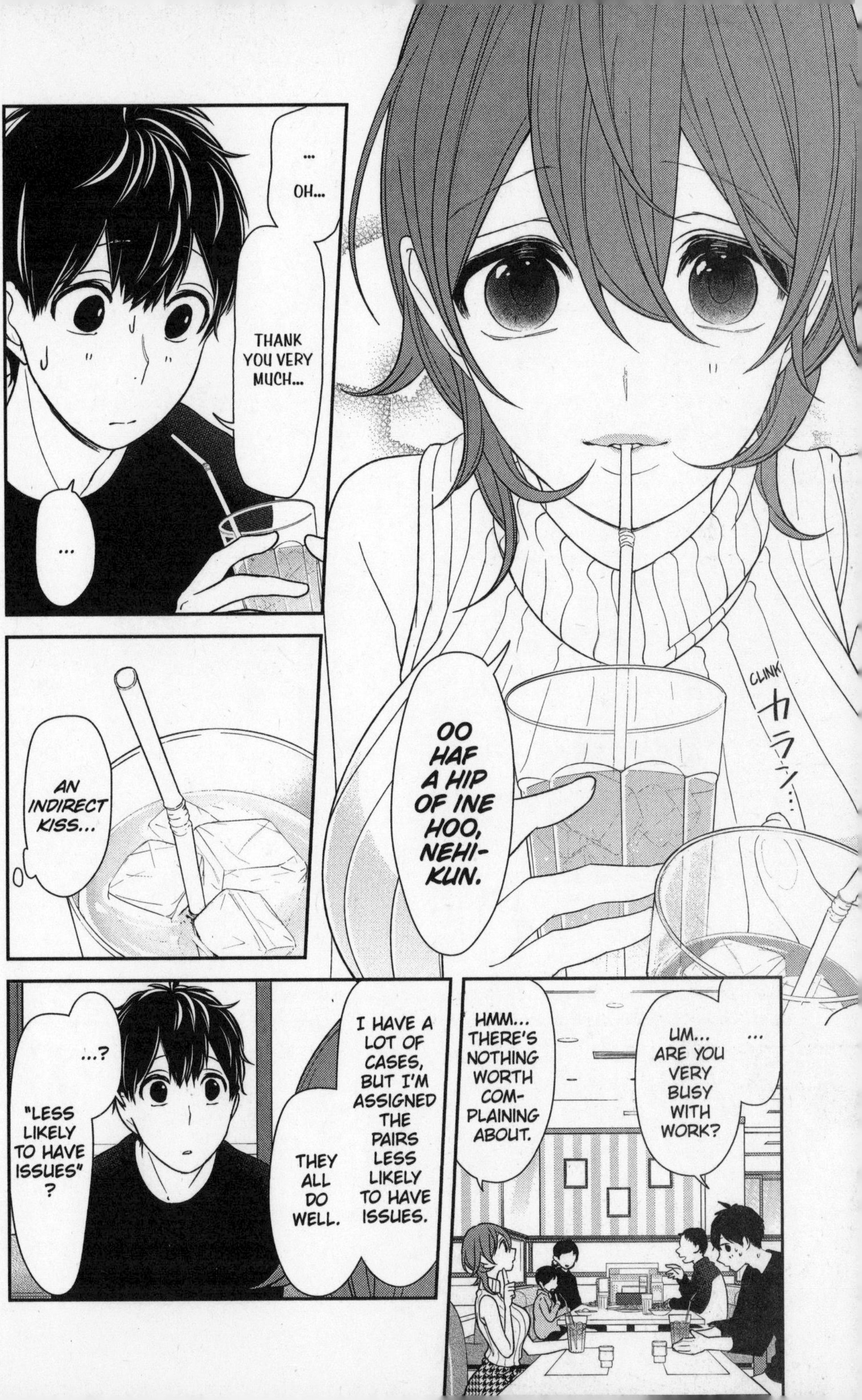
CLINK
カラン…
OO HAF A HIP OF INE HOO, NEHI-KUN.
... OH... THANK YOU VERY MUCH...
...
AN INDIRECT KISS...
...
UM... ARE YOU VERY BUSY WITH WORK?
HMM... THERE'S NOTHING WORTH COM-PLAINING ABOUT.
I HAVE A LOT OF CASES, BUT I'M ASSIGNED THE PAIRS LESS LIKELY TO HAVE ISSUES.
THEY ALL DO WELL.
...?
"LESS LIKELY TO HAVE ISSUES"?

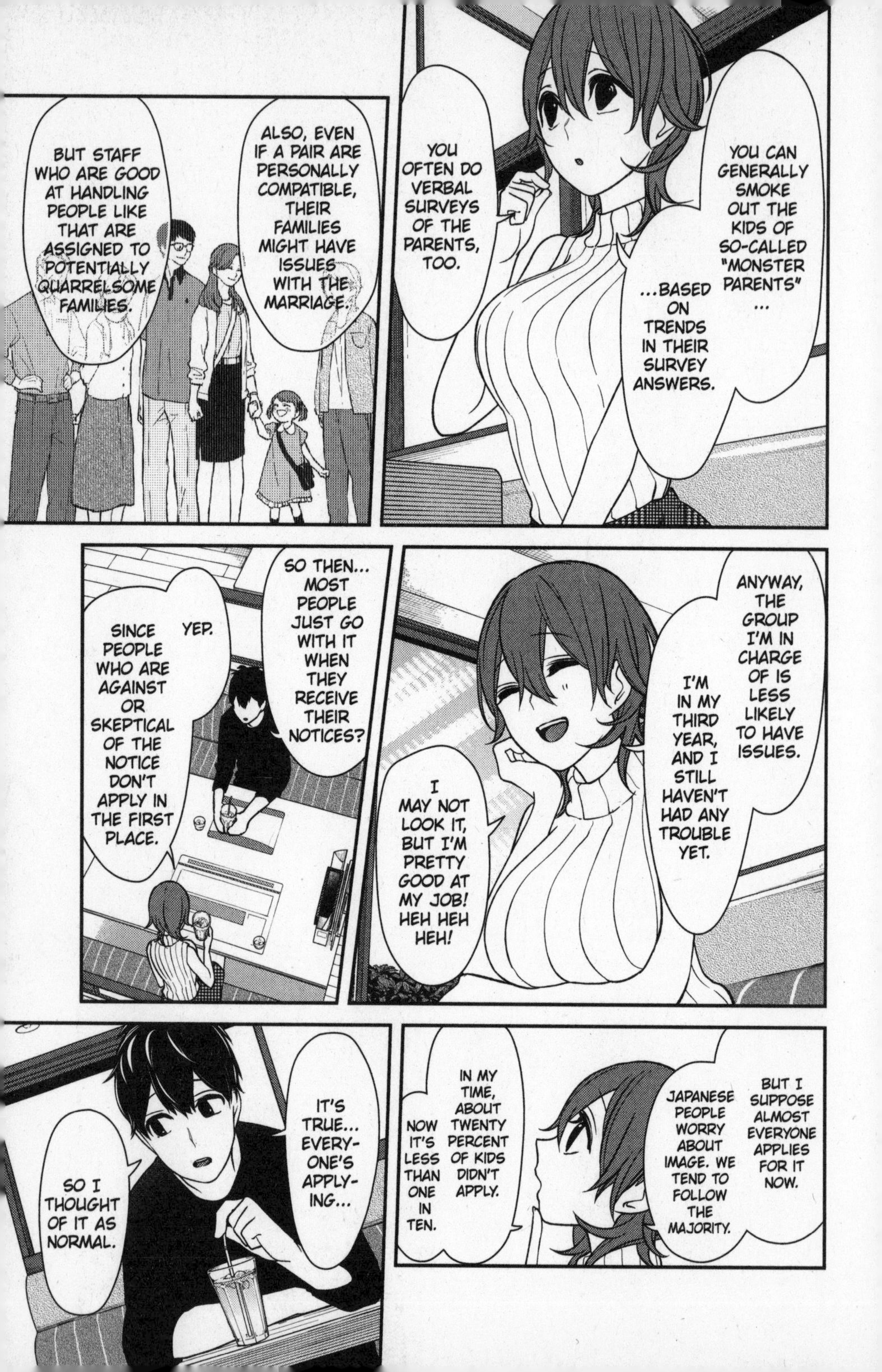
YOU CAN GENERALLY SMOKE OUT THE KIDS OF SO-CALLED "MONSTER PARENTS"...
...BASED ON TRENDS IN THEIR SURVEY ANSWERS.
YOU OFTEN DO VERBAL SURVEYS OF THE PARENTS, TOO.
ALSO, EVEN IF A PAIR ARE PERSONALLY COMPATIBLE, THEIR FAMILIES MIGHT HAVE ISSUES WITH THE MARRIAGE.
BUT STAFF WHO ARE GOOD AT HANDLING PEOPLE LIKE THAT ARE ASSIGNED TO POTENTIALLY QUARRELSOME FAMILIES.
ANYWAY, THE GROUP I'M IN CHARGE OF IS LESS LIKELY TO HAVE ISSUES.
I'M IN MY THIRD YEAR, AND I STILL HAVEN'T HAD ANY TROUBLE YET.
I MAY NOT LOOK IT, BUT I'M PRETTY GOOD AT MY JOB! HEH HEH HEH!
SO THEN... MOST PEOPLE JUST GO WITH IT WHEN THEY RECEIVE THEIR NOTICES?
YEP.
SINCE PEOPLE WHO ARE AGAINST OR SKEPTICAL OF THE NOTICE DON'T APPLY IN THE FIRST PLACE.
BUT I SUPPOSE ALMOST EVERYONE APPLIES FOR IT NOW.
JAPANESE PEOPLE WORRY ABOUT IMAGE. WE TEND TO FOLLOW THE MAJORITY.
IN MY TIME, ABOUT TWENTY PERCENT OF KIDS DIDN'T APPLY.
NOW IT'S LESS THAN ONE IN TEN.
IT'S TRUE... EVERY-ONE'S APPLY-ING...
SO I THOUGHT OF IT AS NORMAL.

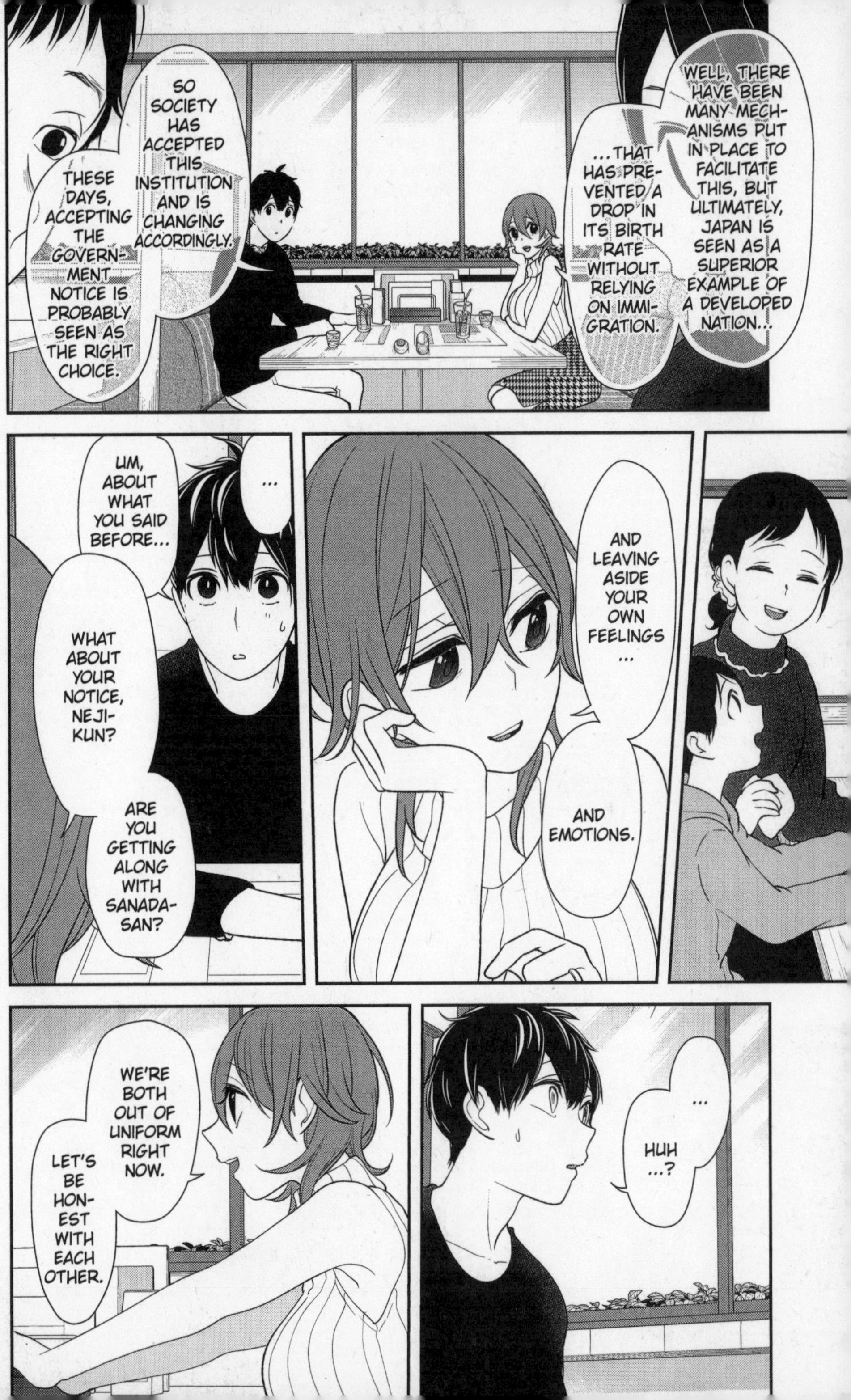
WELL, THERE HAVE BEEN MANY MECHANISMS PUT IN PLACE TO FACILITATE THIS, BUT ULTIMATELY, JAPAN IS SEEN AS A SUPERIOR EXAMPLE OF A DEVELOPED NATION...
...THAT HAS PREVENTED A DROP IN ITS BIRTH RATE WITHOUT RELYING ON IMMIGRATION.
SO SOCIETY HAS ACCEPTED THIS INSTITUTION AND IS CHANGING ACCORDINGLY.
THESE DAYS, ACCEPTING THE GOVERNMENT NOTICE IS PROBABLY SEEN AS THE RIGHT CHOICE.
AND LEAVING ASIDE YOUR OWN FEELINGS...
AND EMOTIONS.
...
UM, ABOUT WHAT YOU SAID BEFORE...
WHAT ABOUT YOUR NOTICE, NEJI-KUN?
ARE YOU GETTING ALONG WITH SANADA-SAN?
...
HUH...?
WE'RE BOTH OUT OF UNIFORM RIGHT NOW.
LET'S BE HONEST WITH EACH OTHER.

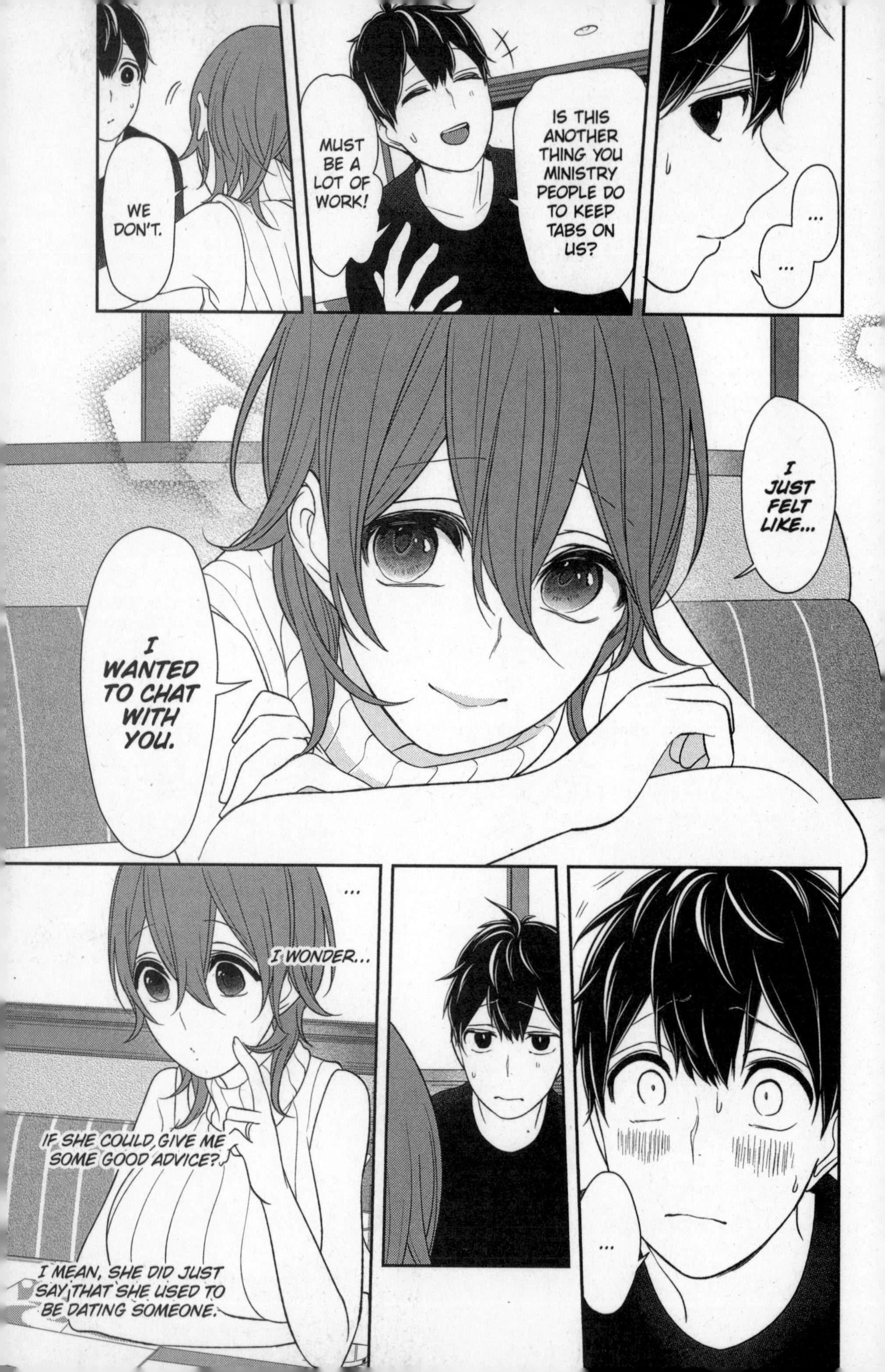
...
...
IS THIS ANOTHER THING YOU MINISTRY PEOPLE DO TO KEEP TABS ON US?
MUST BE A LOT OF WORK!
WE DON'T.
I JUST FELT LIKE...
I WANTED TO CHAT WITH YOU.
...
...
I WONDER...
IF SHE COULD GIVE ME SOME GOOD ADVICE?
I MEAN, SHE DID JUST SAY THAT SHE USED TO BE DATING SOMEONE.

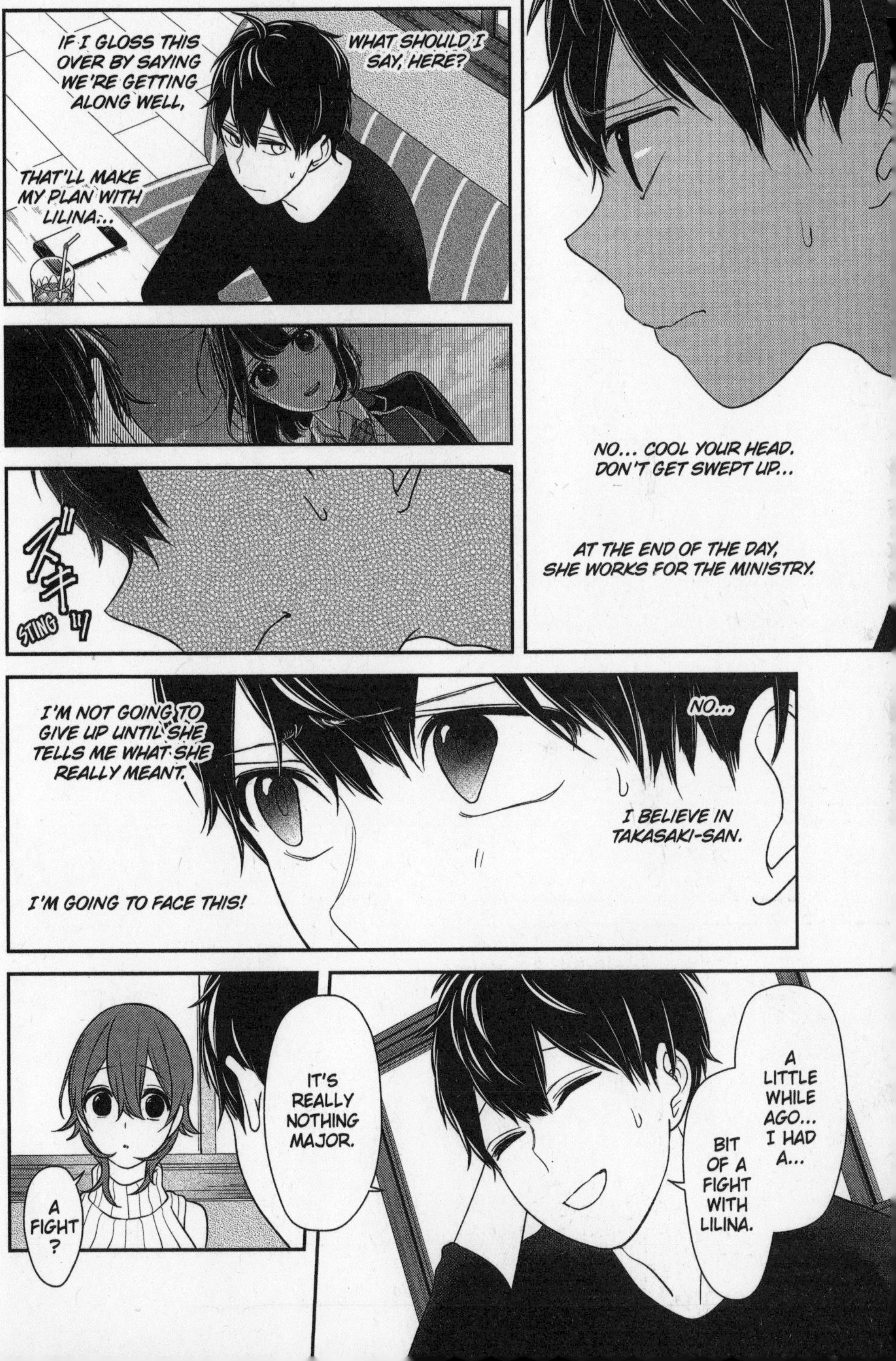
NO... COOL YOUR HEAD. DON'T GET SWEPT UP...
AT THE END OF THE DAY, SHE WORKS FOR THE MINISTRY.
WHAT SHOULD I SAY, HERE?
IF I GLOSS THIS OVER BY SAYING WE'RE GETTING ALONG WELL,
THAT'LL MAKE MY PLAN WITH LILINA...
ズキッ
STING
NO...
I BELIEVE IN TAKASAKI-SAN.
I'M NOT GOING TO GIVE UP UNTIL SHE TELLS ME WHAT SHE REALLY MEANT.
I'M GOING TO FACE THIS!
A LITTLE WHILE AGO... I HAD A...
BIT OF A FIGHT WITH LILINA.
IT'S REALLY NOTHING MAJOR.
A FIGHT?

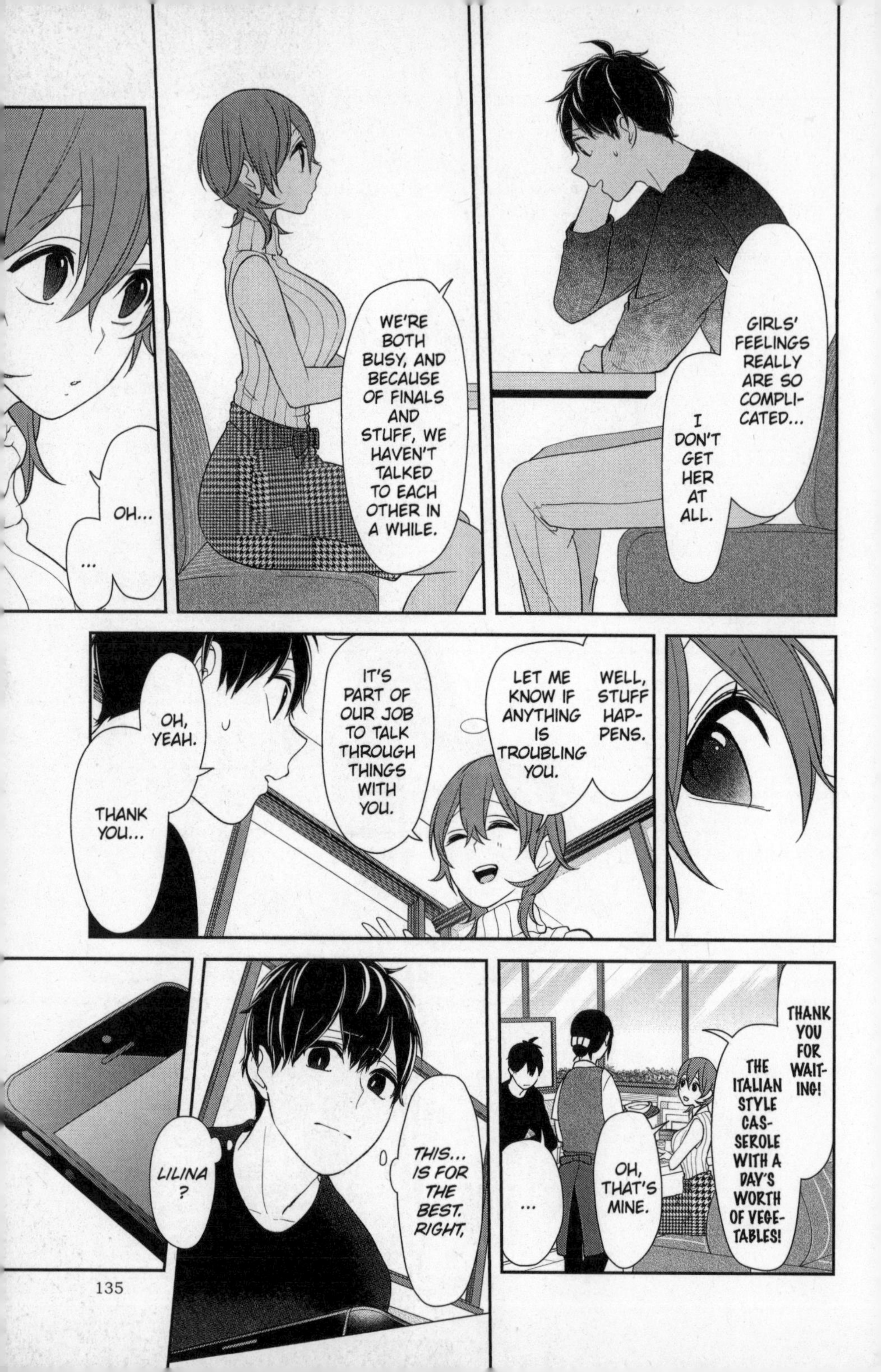
GIRLS' FEELINGS REALLY ARE SO COMPLICATED...
I DON'T GET HER AT ALL.
WE'RE BOTH BUSY, AND BECAUSE OF FINALS AND STUFF, WE HAVEN'T TALKED TO EACH OTHER IN A WHILE.
OH...
...
WELL, STUFF HAPPENS.
LET ME KNOW IF ANYTHING IS TROUBLING YOU.
IT'S PART OF OUR JOB TO TALK THROUGH THINGS WITH YOU.
OH, YEAH.
THANK YOU...
THANK YOU FOR WAITING!
THE ITALIAN STYLE CASSEROLE WITH A DAY'S WORTH OF VEGETABLES!
OH, THAT'S MINE.
...
THIS... IS FOR THE BEST. RIGHT,
LILINA?

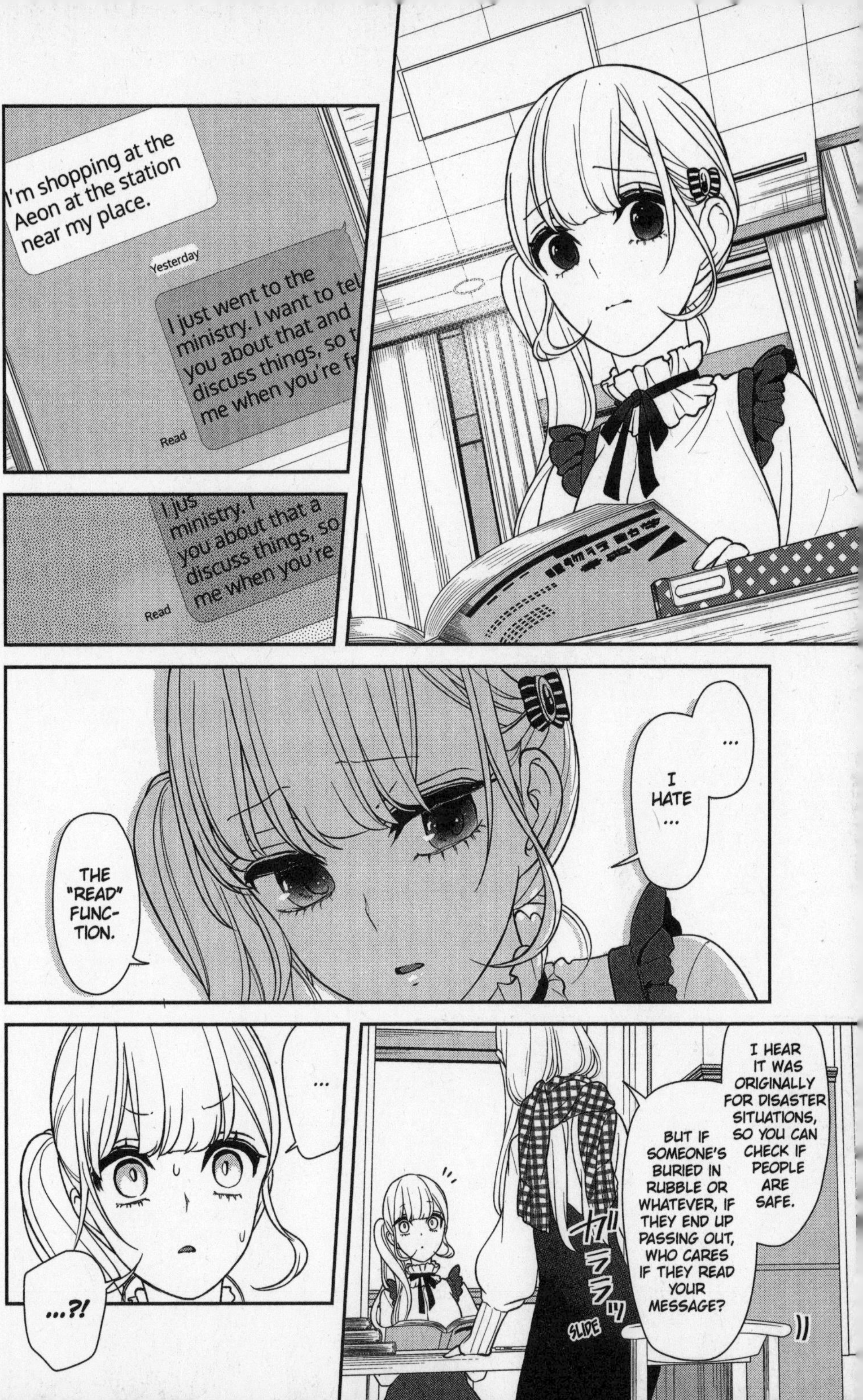
I'm shopping at the Aeon at the station near my place.
Yesterday
I just went to the ministry. I want to tel you about that and discuss things, so t me when you're f
Read
I jus ministry. I you about that a discuss things, so me when you're
Read
... I HATE ...
THE "READ" FUNCTION.
I HEAR IT WAS ORIGINALLY FOR DISASTER SITUATIONS, SO YOU CAN CHECK IF PEOPLE ARE SAFE.
BUT IF SOMEONE'S BURIED IN RUBBLE OR WHATEVER, IF THEY END UP PASSING OUT, WHO CARES IF THEY READ YOUR MESSAGE?
SLIDE
...
...?!

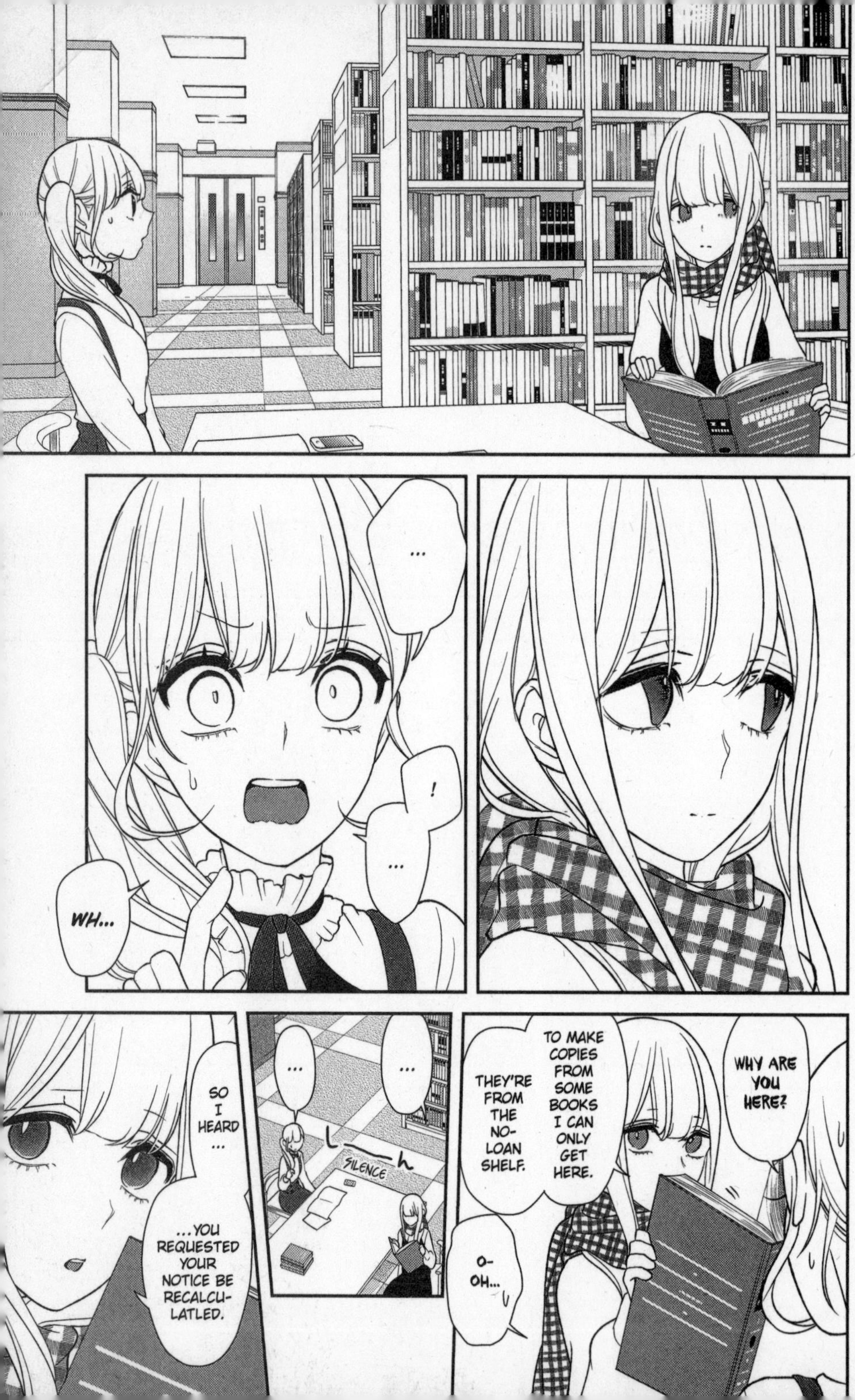
...
!
...
WH...
WHY ARE YOU HERE?
TO MAKE COPIES FROM SOME BOOKS I CAN ONLY GET HERE.
THEY'RE FROM THE NO-LOAN SHELF.
O-OH...
...
...
SILENCE
SO I HEARD...
...YOU REQUESTED YOUR NOTICE BE RECALCULATLED.

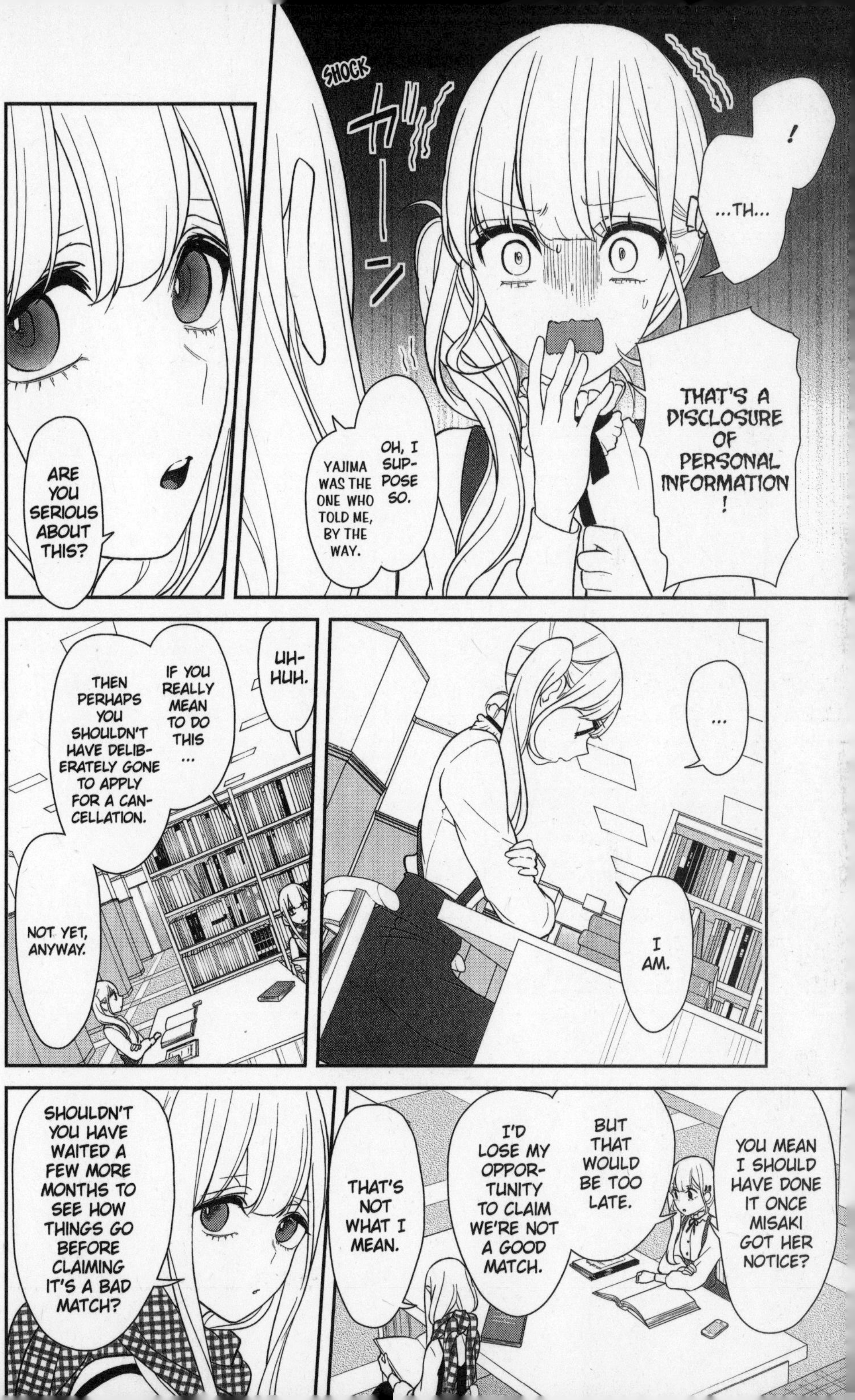
SHOCK
ガーン
!
...TH...
THAT'S A DISCLOSURE OF PERSONAL INFORMATION!
OH, I SUPPOSE SO.
YAJIMA WAS THE ONE WHO TOLD ME, BY THE WAY.
ARE YOU SERIOUS ABOUT THIS?
...
I AM.
UH-HUH.
IF YOU REALLY MEAN TO DO THIS ...
THEN PERHAPS YOU SHOULDN'T HAVE DELIBERATELY GONE TO APPLY FOR A CANCELLATION.
NOT YET, ANYWAY.
YOU MEAN I SHOULD HAVE DONE IT ONCE MISAKI GOT HER NOTICE?
BUT THAT WOULD BE TOO LATE.
I'D LOSE MY OPPORTUNITY TO CLAIM WE'RE NOT A GOOD MATCH.
THAT'S NOT WHAT I MEAN.
SHOULDN'T YOU HAVE WAITED A FEW MORE MONTHS TO SEE HOW THINGS GO BEFORE CLAIMING IT'S A BAD MATCH?

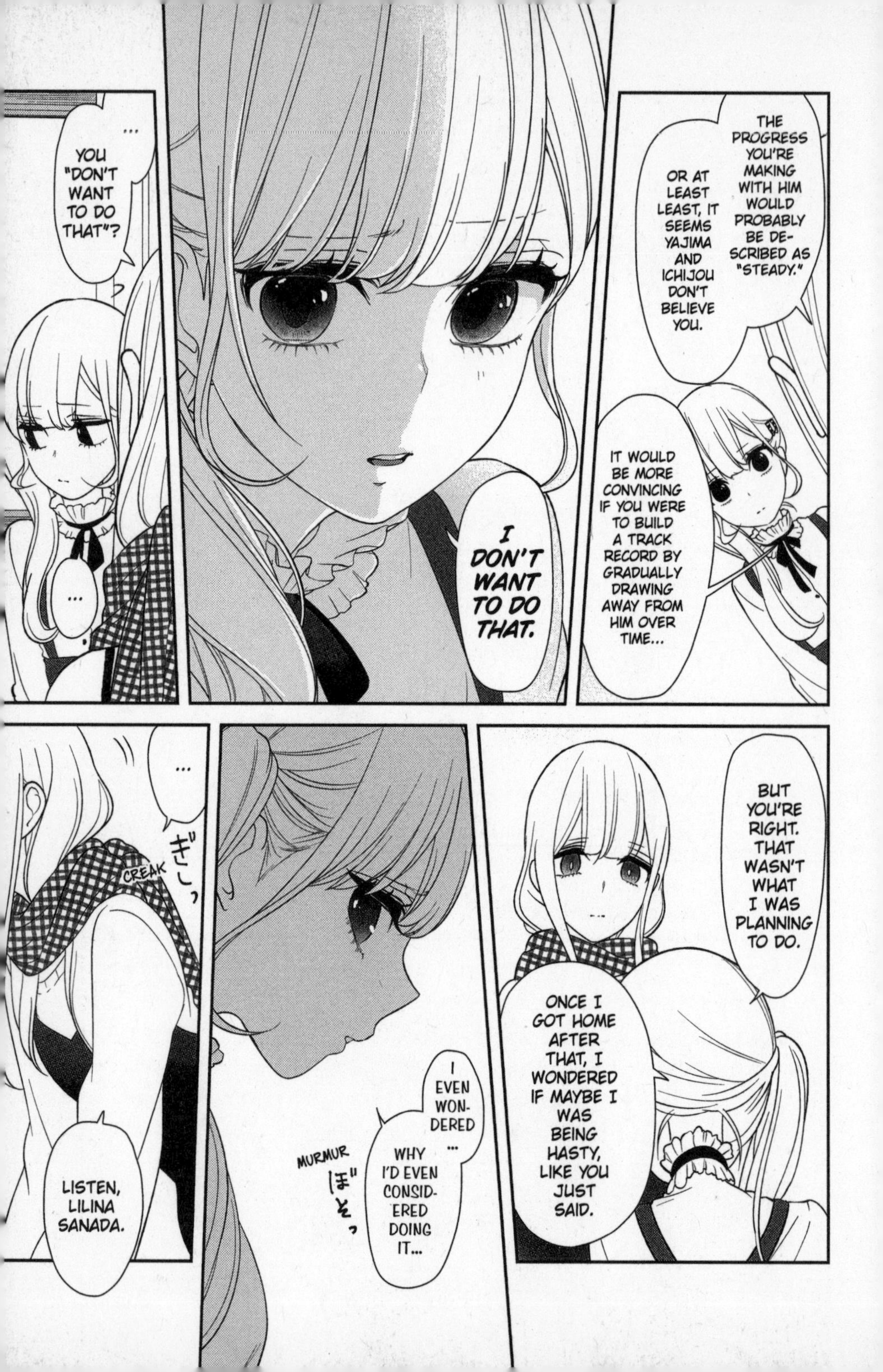
THE PROGRESS YOU'RE MAKING WITH HIM WOULD PROBABLY BE DESCRIBED AS "STEADY."
OR AT LEAST LEAST, IT SEEMS YAJIMA AND ICHIJOU DON'T BELIEVE YOU.
IT WOULD BE MORE CONVINCING IF YOU WERE TO BUILD A TRACK RECORD BY GRADUALLY DRAWING AWAY FROM HIM OVER TIME...
I DON'T WANT TO DO THAT.
...
YOU "DON'T WANT TO DO THAT"?
...
BUT YOU'RE RIGHT. THAT WASN'T WHAT I WAS PLANNING TO DO.
...
ONCE I GOT HOME AFTER THAT, I WONDERED IF MAYBE I WAS BEING HASTY, LIKE YOU JUST SAID.
I EVEN WONDERED...
WHY I'D EVEN CONSIDERED DOING IT...
ぼそっ
MURMUR
...
ぎしっ
CREAK
LISTEN, LILINA SANADA.

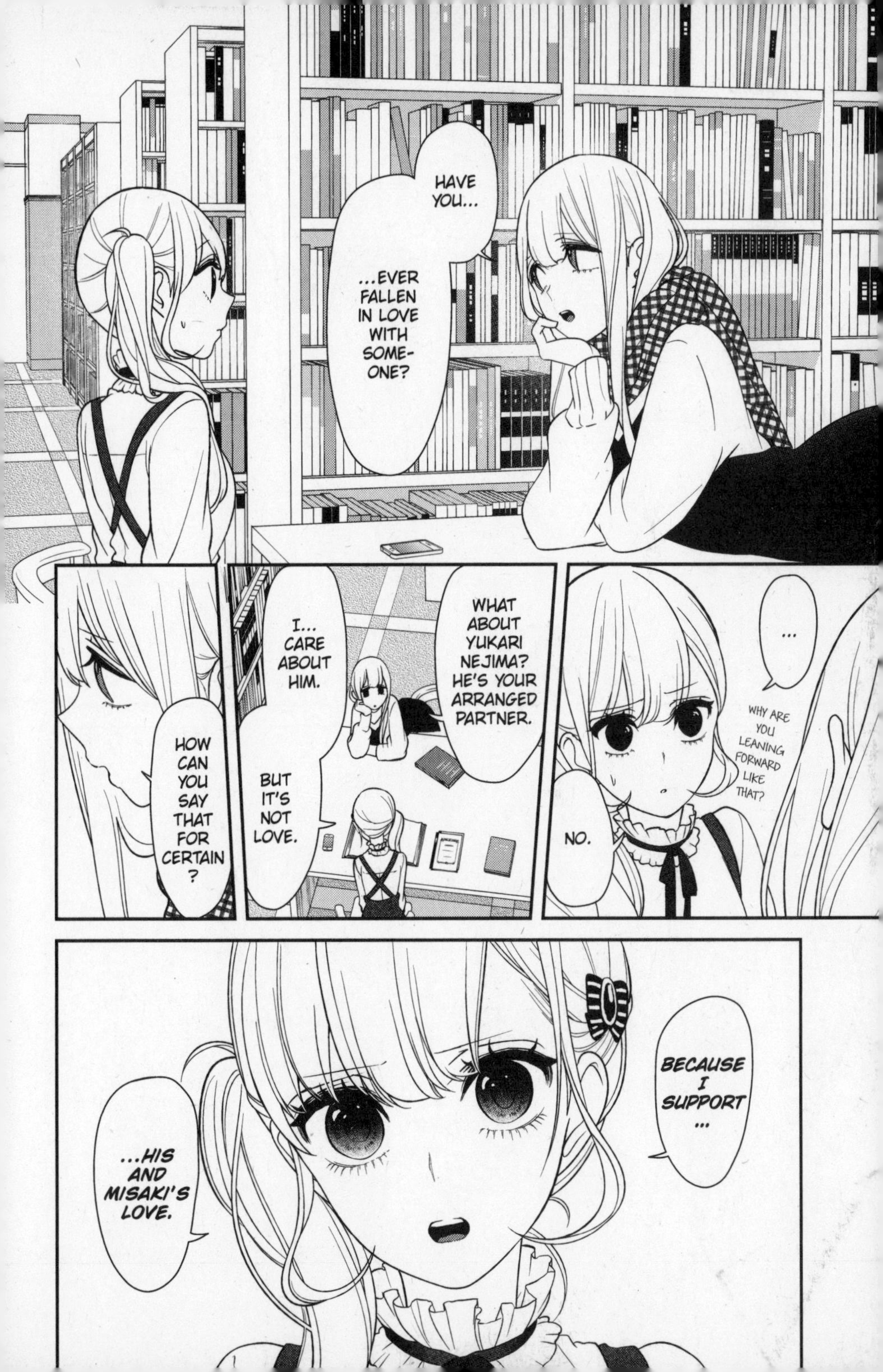
HAVE YOU...
...EVER FALLEN IN LOVE WITH SOME-ONE?
...
WHY ARE YOU LEANING FORWARD LIKE THAT?
NO.
WHAT ABOUT YUKARI NEJIMA? HE'S YOUR ARRANGED PARTNER.
I... CARE ABOUT HIM.
BUT IT'S NOT LOVE.
HOW CAN YOU SAY THAT FOR CERTAIN?
BECAUSE I SUPPORT...
...HIS AND MISAKI'S LOVE.

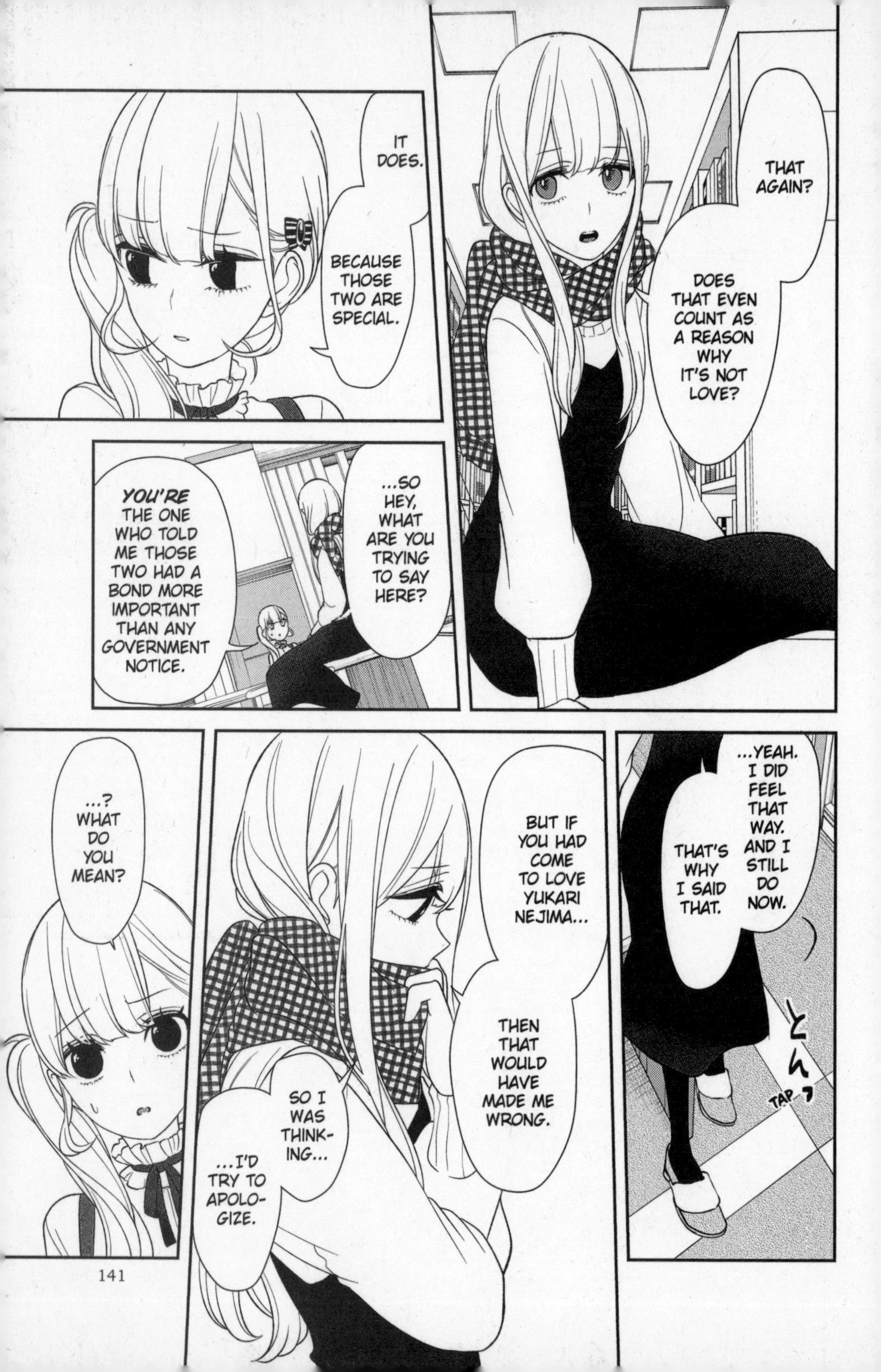
THAT AGAIN?
DOES THAT EVEN COUNT AS A REASON WHY IT'S NOT LOVE?
IT DOES.
BECAUSE THOSE TWO ARE SPECIAL.
...SO HEY, WHAT ARE YOU TRYING TO SAY HERE?
YOU'RE THE ONE WHO TOLD ME THOSE TWO HAD A BOND MORE IMPORTANT THAN ANY GOVERNMENT NOTICE.
...YEAH. I DID FEEL THAT WAY. AND I STILL DO NOW.
THAT'S WHY I SAID THAT.
とん
TAP
BUT IF YOU HAD COME TO LOVE YUKARI NEJIMA...
THEN THAT WOULD HAVE MADE ME WRONG.
SO I WAS THINKING-ING...
...I'D TRY TO APOLOGIZE.
...? WHAT DO YOU MEAN?

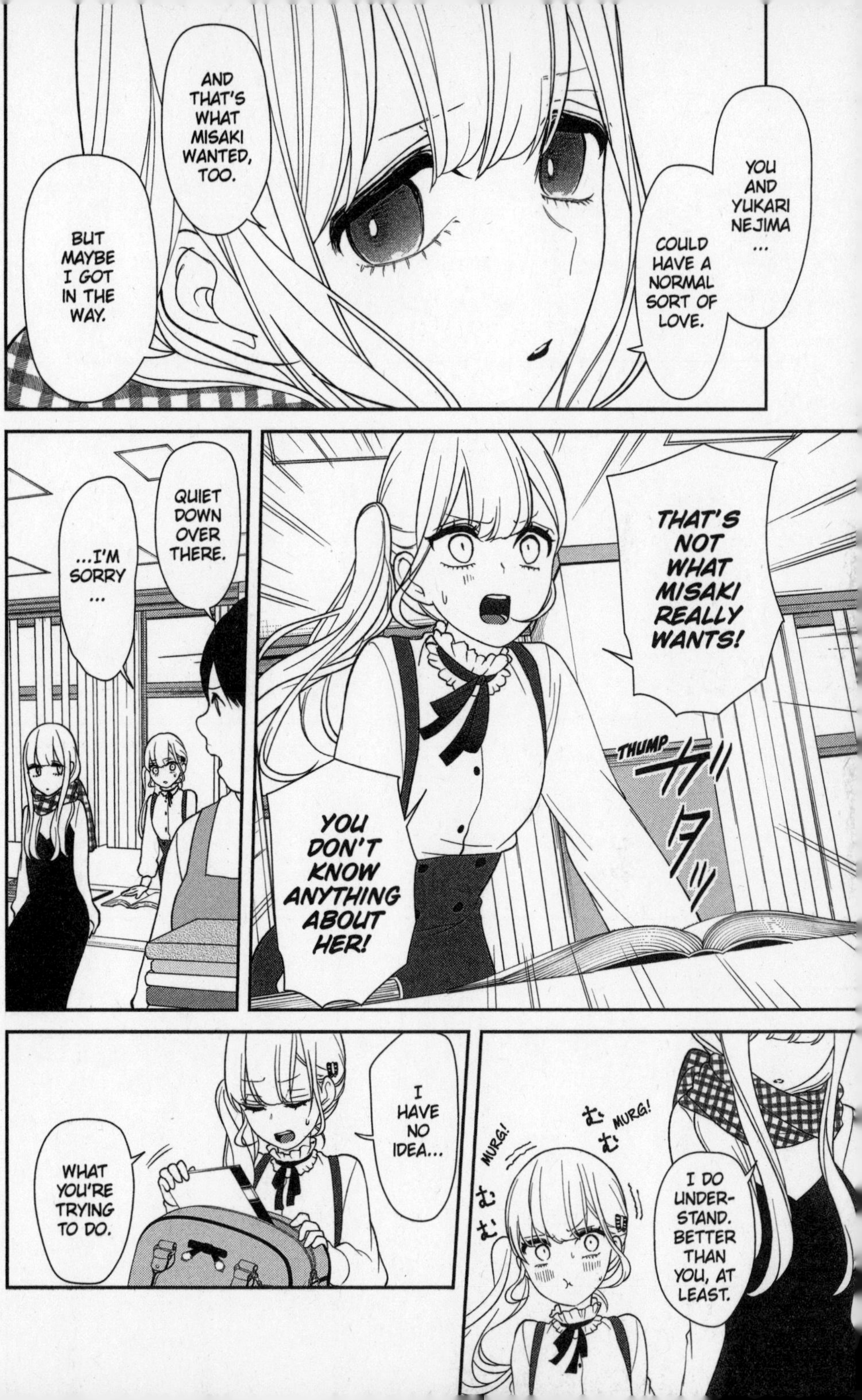
YOU AND YUKARI NEJIMA...
COULD HAVE A NORMAL SORT OF LOVE.
AND THAT'S WHAT MISAKI WANTED, TOO.
BUT MAYBE I GOT IN THE WAY.
THAT'S NOT WHAT MISAKI REALLY WANTS!
THUMP
ガタッ
YOU DON'T KNOW ANYTHING ABOUT HER!
QUIET DOWN OVER THERE.
...I'M SORRY...
MURG!
むむ
MURG!
むむ
I DO UNDER-STAND. BETTER THAN YOU, AT LEAST.
I HAVE NO IDEA...
WHAT YOU'RE TRYING TO DO.

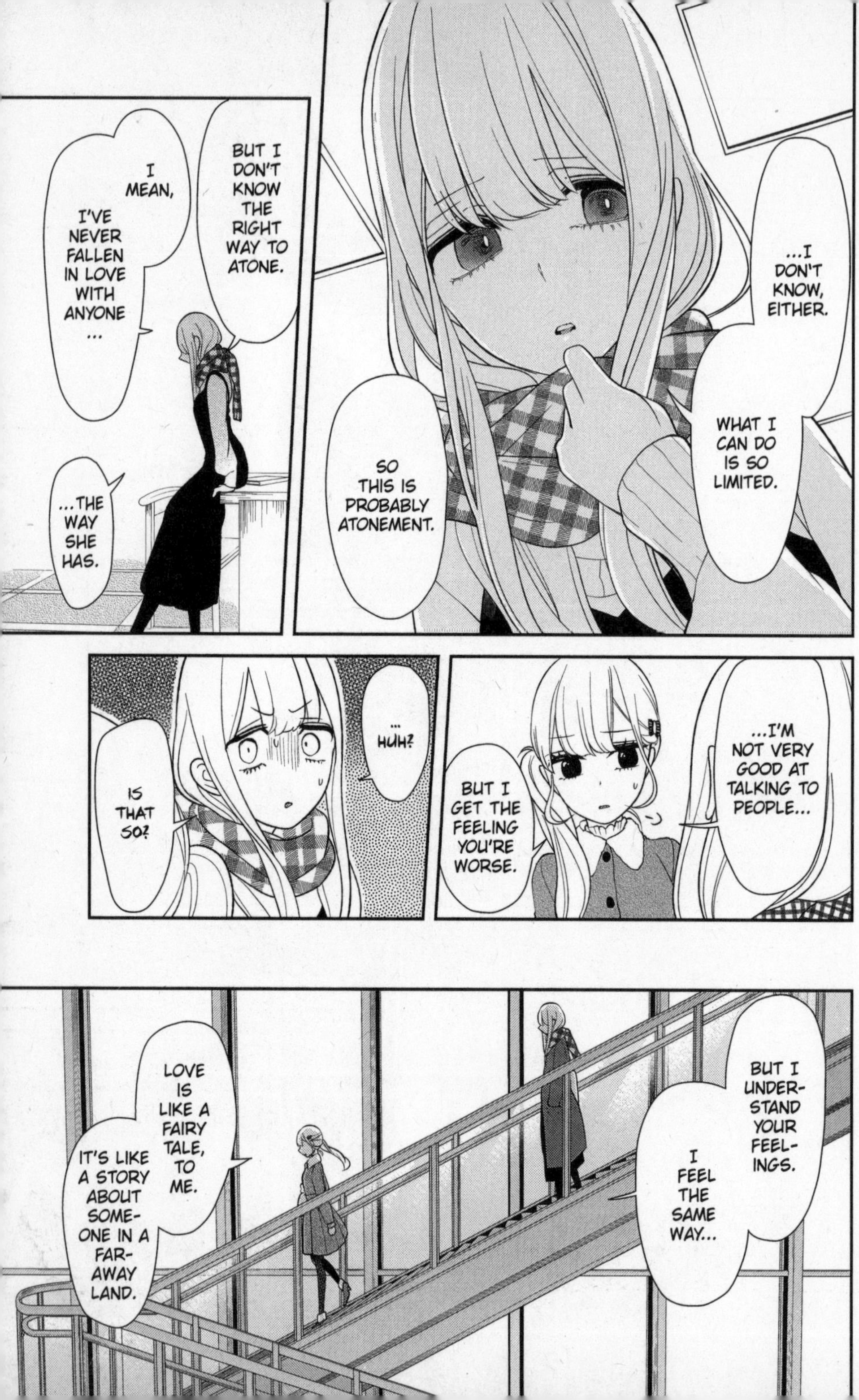
...I DON'T KNOW, EITHER.
WHAT I CAN DO IS SO LIMITED.
SO THIS IS PROBABLY ATONEMENT.
BUT I DON'T KNOW THE RIGHT WAY TO ATONE.
I MEAN,
I'VE NEVER FALLEN IN LOVE WITH ANYONE ...
...THE WAY SHE HAS.
...I'M NOT VERY GOOD AT TALKING TO PEOPLE...
BUT I GET THE FEELING YOU'RE WORSE.
... HUH?
IS THAT SO?
BUT I UNDER-STAND YOUR FEEL-INGS.
I FEEL THE SAME WAY...
LOVE IS LIKE A FAIRY TALE, TO ME.
IT'S LIKE A STORY ABOUT SOME-ONE IN A FAR-AWAY LAND.

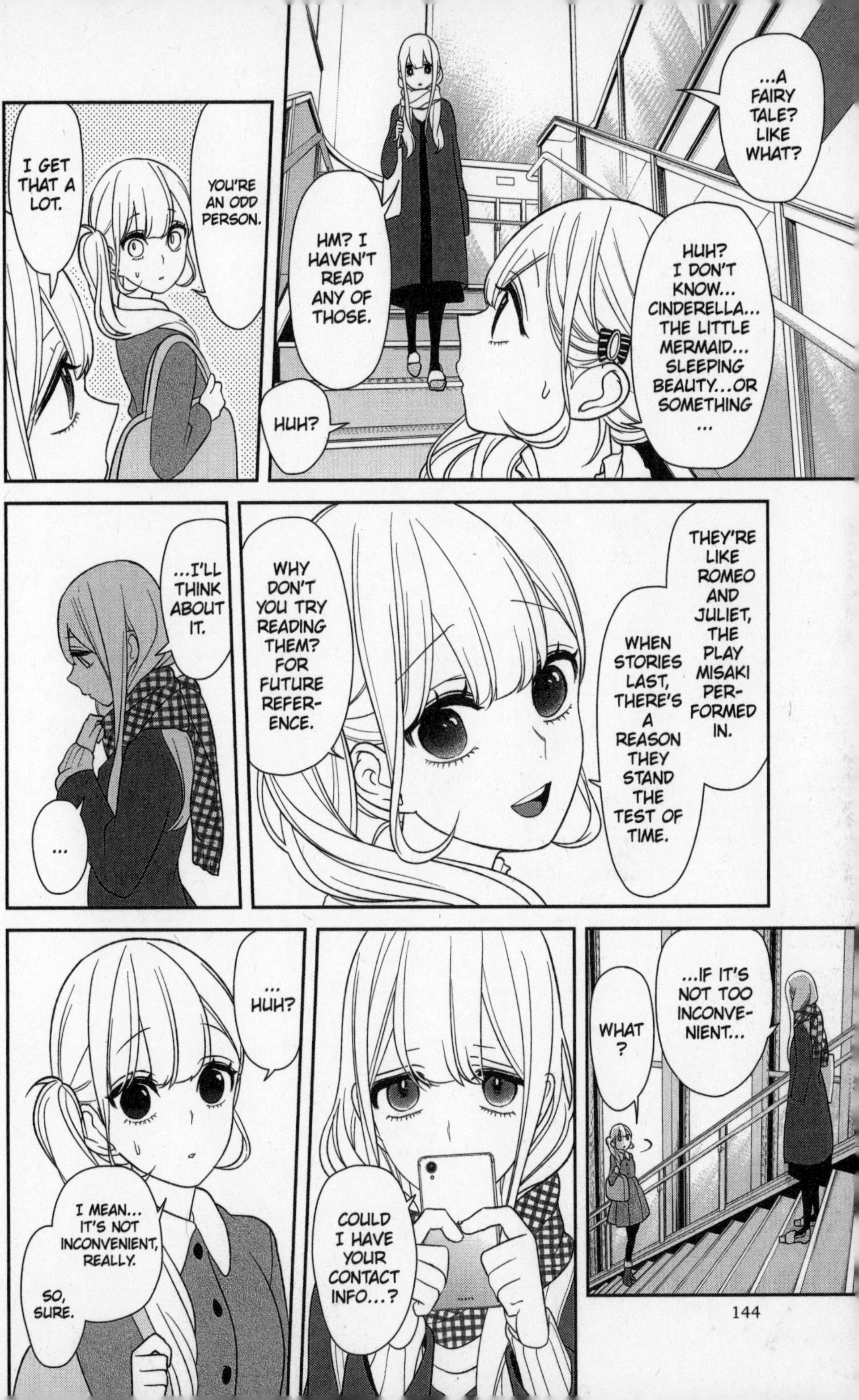
...A FAIRY TALE? LIKE WHAT?
HUH? I DON'T KNOW... CINDERELLA... THE LITTLE MERMAID... SLEEPING BEAUTY...OR SOMETHING ...
HM? I HAVEN'T READ ANY OF THOSE.
HUH?
YOU'RE AN ODD PERSON.
I GET THAT A LOT.
THEY'RE LIKE ROMEO AND JULIET, THE PLAY MISAKI PER-FORMED IN.
WHEN STORIES LAST, THERE'S A REASON THEY STAND THE TEST OF TIME.
WHY DON'T YOU TRY READING THEM? FOR FUTURE REFER-ENCE.
...I'LL THINK ABOUT IT.
...
...IF IT'S NOT TOO INCONVE-NIENT...
WHAT ?
COULD I HAVE YOUR CONTACT INFO...?
... HUH?
I MEAN... IT'S NOT INCONVENIENT, REALLY.
SO, SURE.

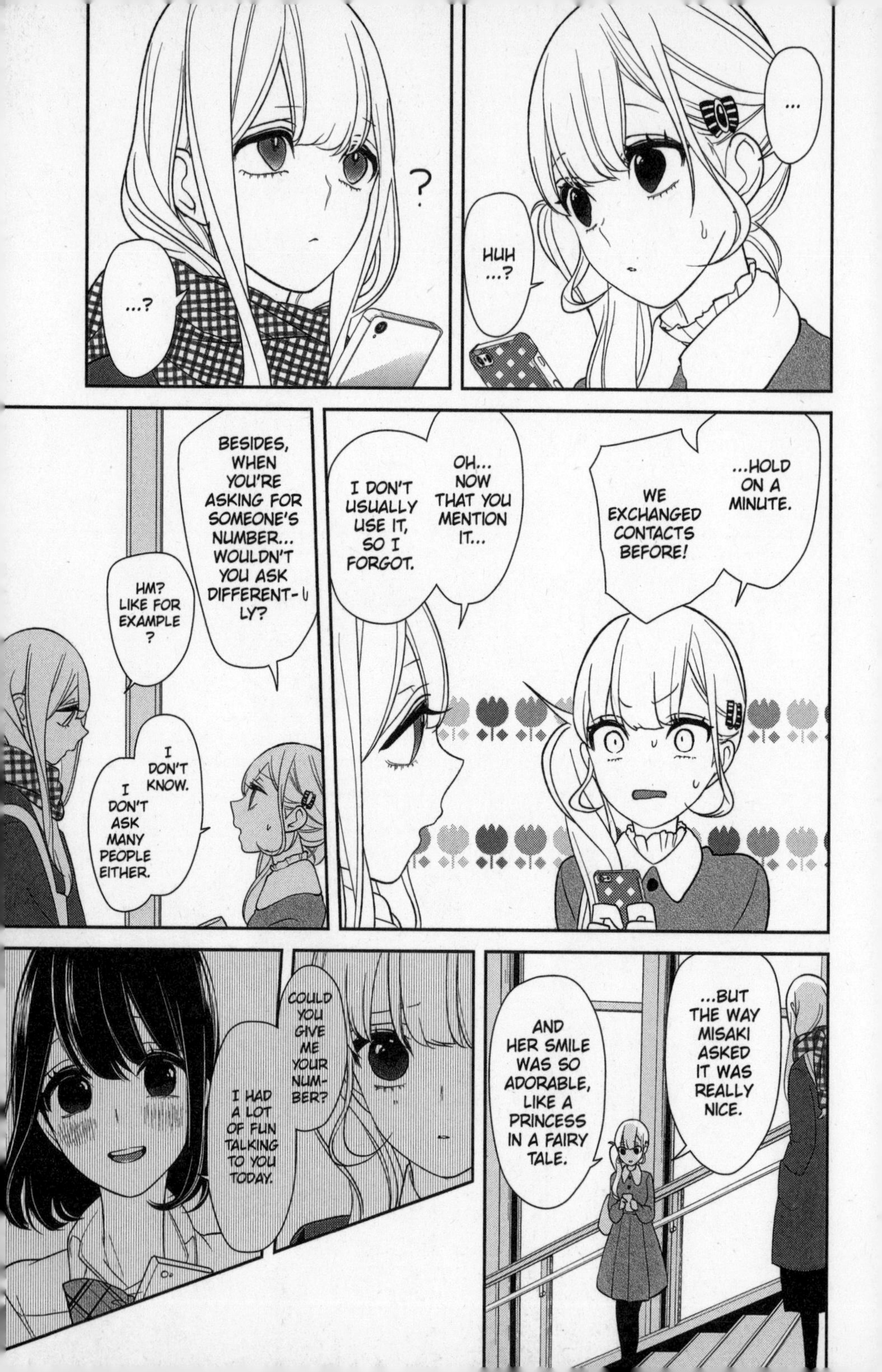
...
HUH ...?
?
...?
...HOLD ON A MINUTE.
WE EXCHANGED CONTACTS BEFORE!
OH... NOW THAT YOU MENTION IT...
I DON'T USUALLY USE IT, SO I FORGOT.
BESIDES, WHEN YOU'RE ASKING FOR SOMEONE'S NUMBER... WOULDN'T YOU ASK DIFFERENT-LY?
HM? LIKE FOR EXAMPLE?
I DON'T KNOW.
I DON'T ASK MANY PEOPLE EITHER.
...BUT THE WAY MISAKI ASKED IT WAS REALLY NICE.
AND HER SMILE WAS SO ADORABLE, LIKE A PRINCESS IN A FAIRY TALE.
COULD YOU GIVE ME YOUR NUMBER?
I HAD A LOT OF FUN TALKING TO YOU TODAY.

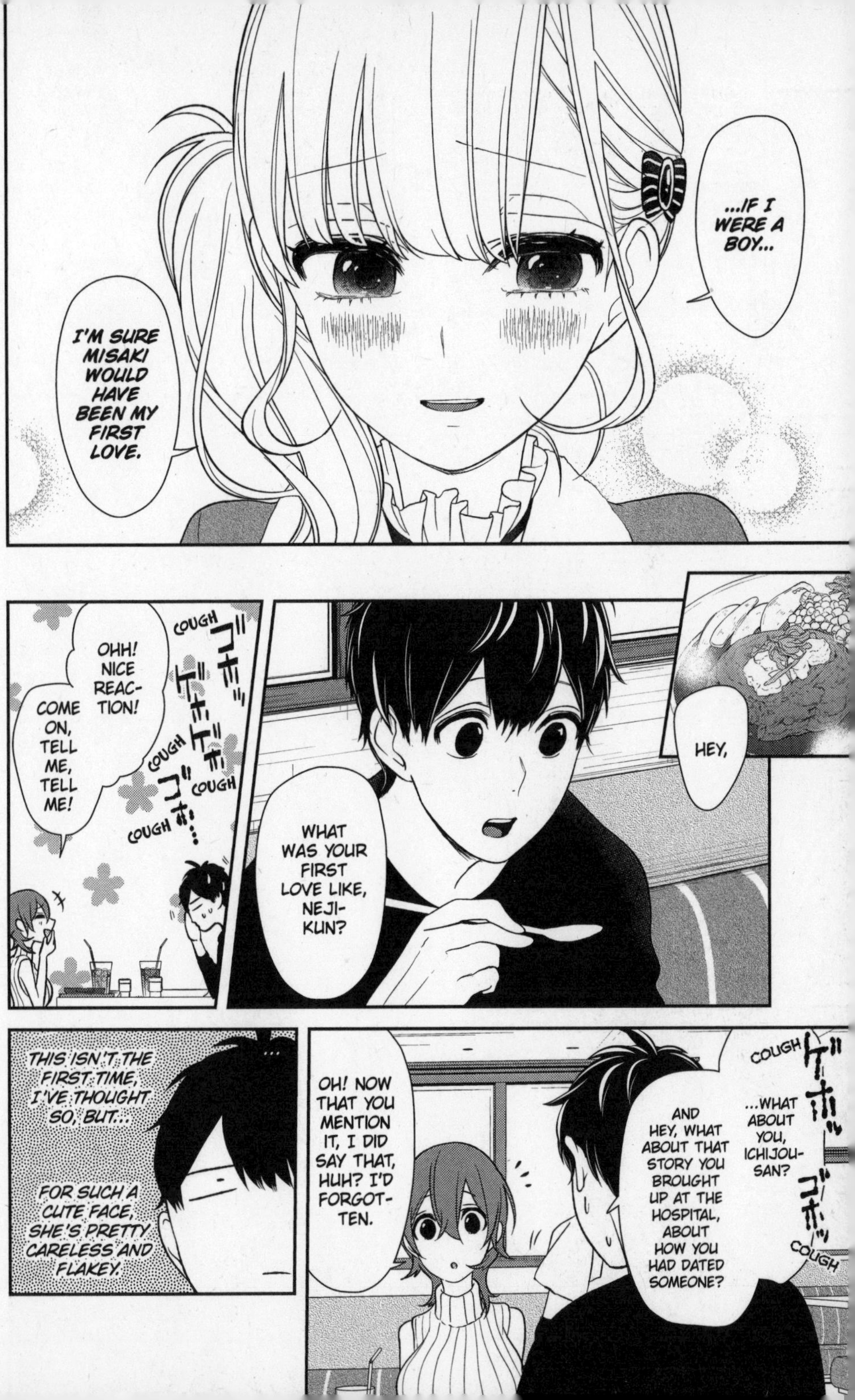
...IF I WERE A BOY...
I'M SURE MISAKI WOULD HAVE BEEN MY FIRST LOVE.
HEY,
WHAT WAS YOUR FIRST LOVE LIKE, NEJI-KUN?
COUGH
COUGH
COUGH
COUGH
OHH! NICE REAC-TION!
COME ON, TELL ME, TELL ME!
COUGH
...WHAT ABOUT YOU, ICHIJOU-SAN?
COUGH
AND HEY, WHAT ABOUT THAT STORY YOU BROUGHT UP AT THE HOSPITAL, ABOUT HOW YOU HAD DATED SOMEONE?
OH! NOW THAT YOU MENTION IT, I DID SAY THAT, HUH? I'D FORGOT-TEN.
THIS ISN'T THE FIRST TIME I'VE THOUGHT SO, BUT...
FOR SUCH A CUTE FACE, SHE'S PRETTY CARELESS AND FLAKEY.

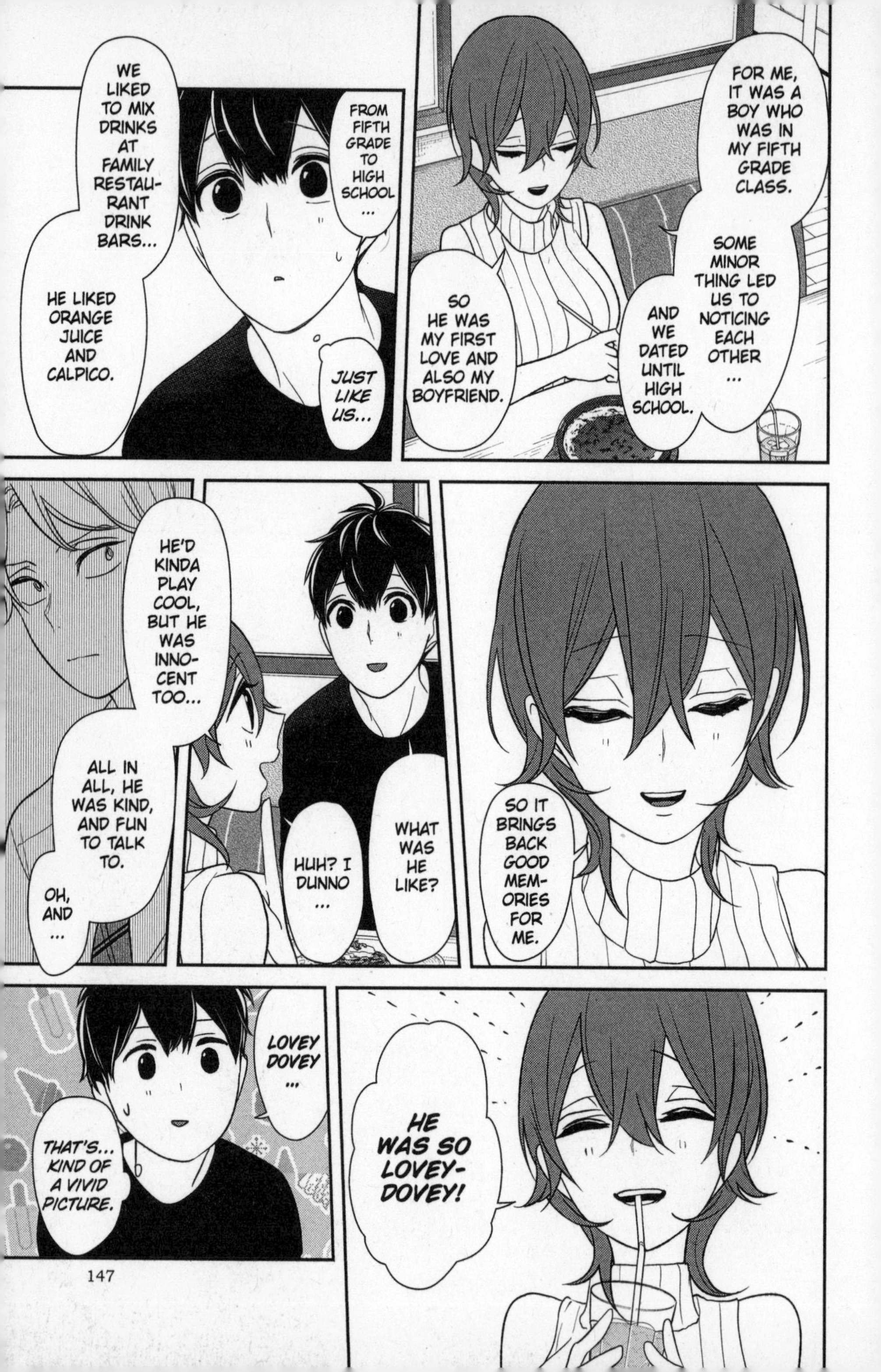
FOR ME, IT WAS A BOY WHO WAS IN MY FIFTH GRADE CLASS.
SOME MINOR THING LED US TO NOTICING EACH OTHER ...
AND WE DATED UNTIL HIGH SCHOOL.
SO HE WAS MY FIRST LOVE AND ALSO MY BOYFRIEND.
FROM FIFTH GRADE TO HIGH SCHOOL ...
JUST LIKE US...
WE LIKED TO MIX DRINKS AT FAMILY RESTAURANT DRINK BARS...
HE LIKED ORANGE JUICE AND CALPICO.
SO IT BRINGS BACK GOOD MEMORIES FOR ME.
WHAT WAS HE LIKE?
HUH? I DUNNO ...
HE'D KINDA PLAY COOL, BUT HE WAS INNOCENT TOO...
ALL IN ALL, HE WAS KIND, AND FUN TO TALK TO.
OH, AND ...
HE WAS SO LOVEY-DOVEY!
LOVEY DOVEY ...
THAT'S... KIND OF A VIVID PICTURE.

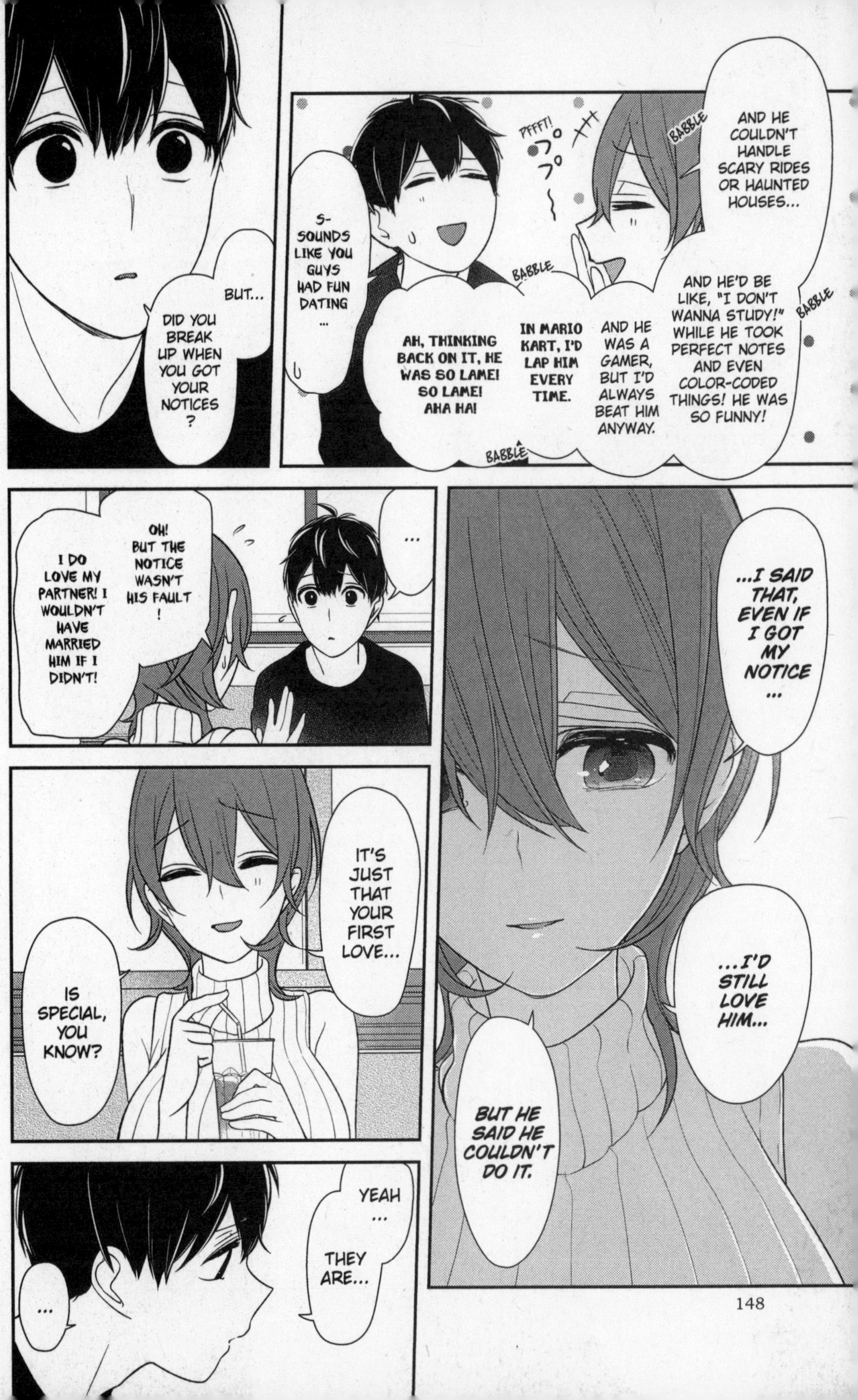
PFFFT!
BABBLE
AND HE COULDN'T HANDLE SCARY RIDES OR HAUNTED HOUSES...
BABBLE
AND HE'D BE LIKE, "I DON'T WANNA STUDY!" WHILE HE TOOK PERFECT NOTES AND EVEN COLOR-CODED THINGS! HE WAS SO FUNNY!
BABBLE
AND HE WAS A GAMER, BUT I'D ALWAYS BEAT HIM ANYWAY.
IN MARIO KART, I'D LAP HIM EVERY TIME.
AH, THINKING BACK ON IT, HE WAS SO LAME! SO LAME! AHA HA!
BABBLE
S-SOUNDS LIKE YOU GUYS HAD FUN DATING ...
BUT...
DID YOU BREAK UP WHEN YOU GOT YOUR NOTICES ?
...I SAID THAT, EVEN IF I GOT MY NOTICE ...
...I'D STILL LOVE HIM...
BUT HE SAID HE COULDN'T DO IT.
...
OH! BUT THE NOTICE WASN'T HIS FAULT !
I DO LOVE MY PARTNER! I WOULDN'T HAVE MARRIED HIM IF I DIDN'T!
IT'S JUST THAT YOUR FIRST LOVE...
IS SPECIAL, YOU KNOW?
YEAH ...
THEY ARE...
...

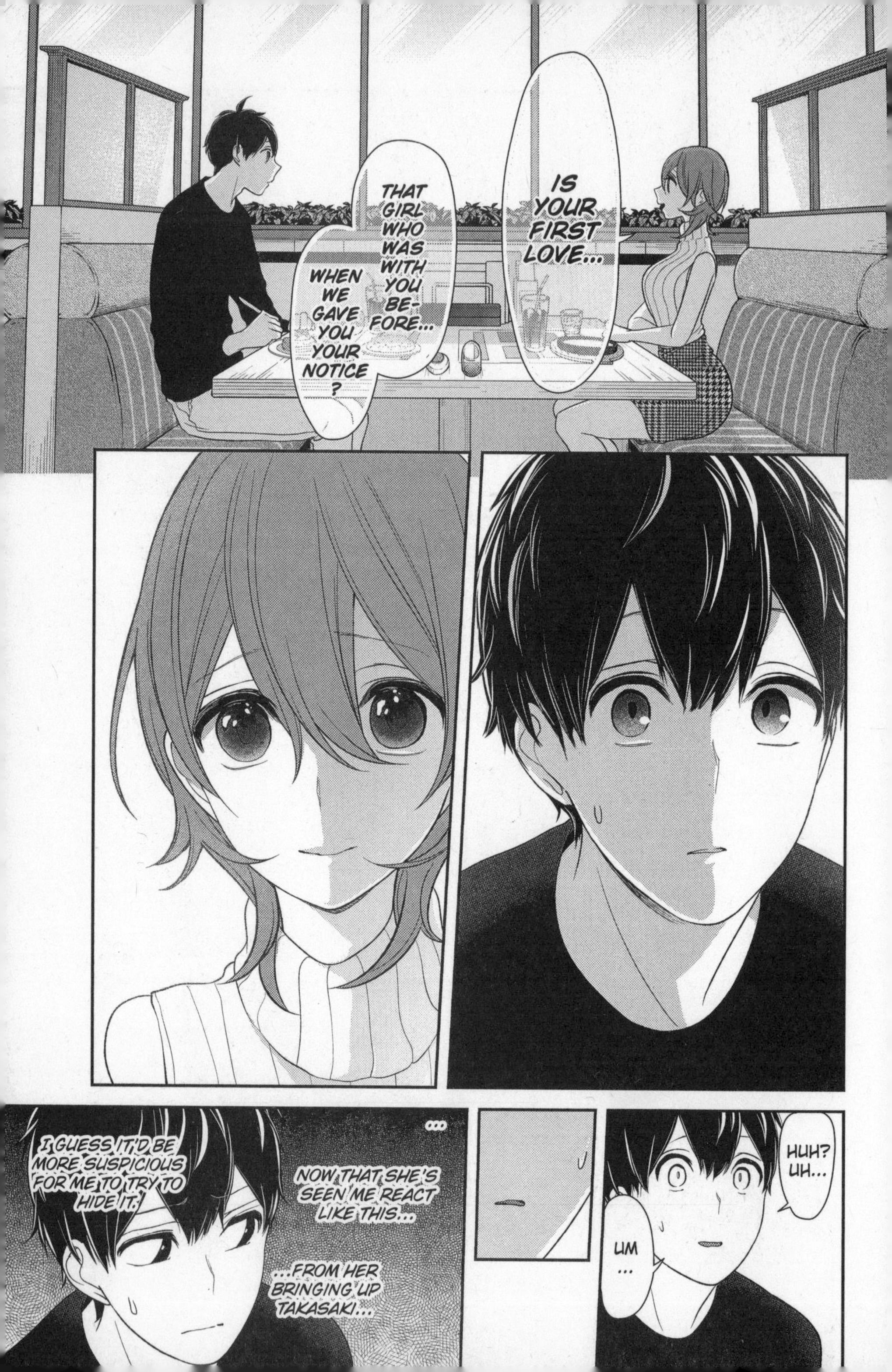
IS YOUR FIRST LOVE...
THAT GIRL WHO WAS WITH YOU BE-FORE...
WHEN WE GAVE YOU YOUR NOTICE ?
HUH? UH...
UM ...
...
NOW THAT SHE'S SEEN ME REACT LIKE THIS...
...FROM HER BRINGING UP TAKASAKI...
I GUESS IT'D BE MORE SUSPICIOUS FOR ME TO TRY TO HIDE IT.

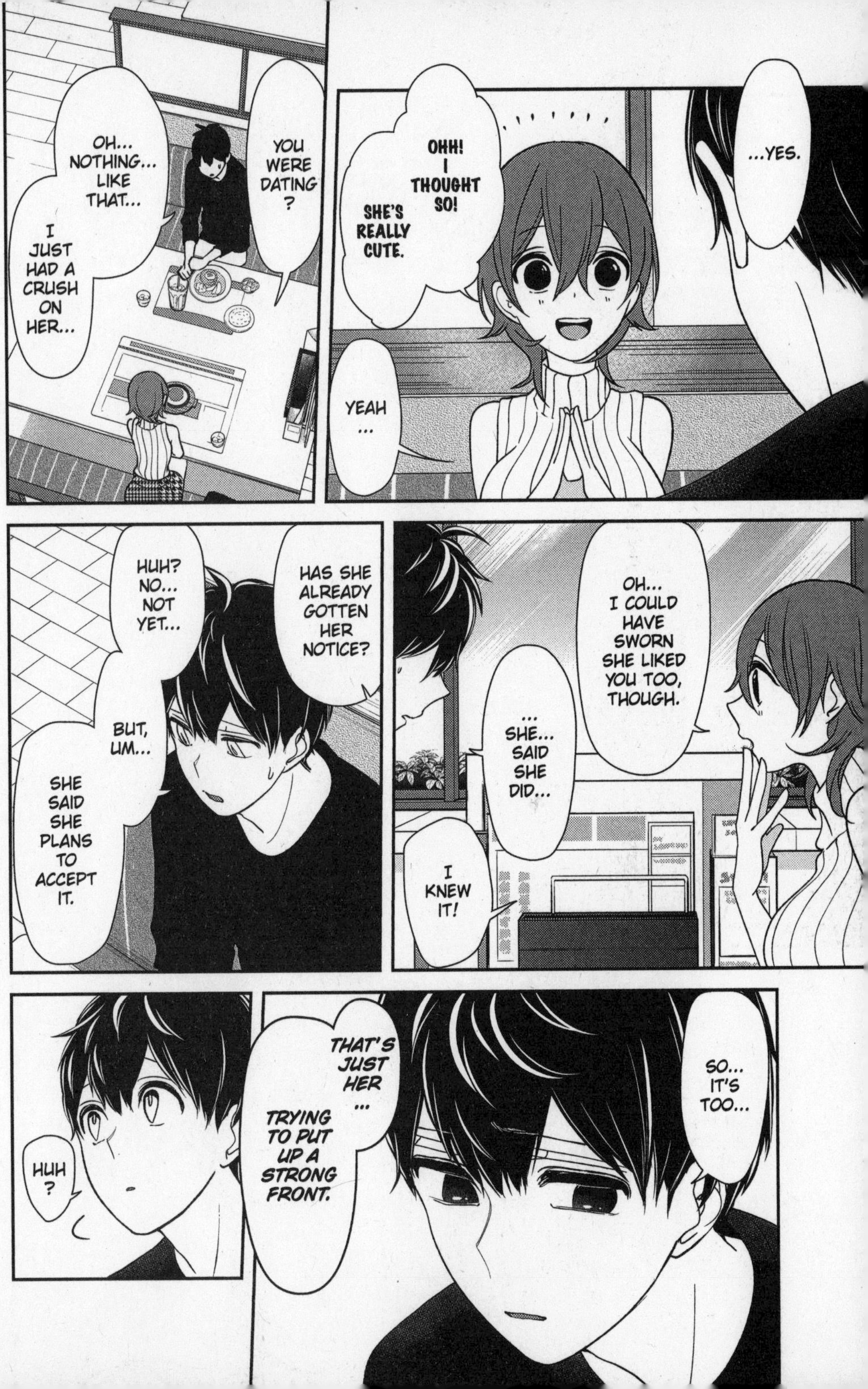
...YES.
OHH! I THOUGHT SO!
SHE'S REALLY CUTE.
YEAH ...
YOU WERE DATING ?
OH... NOTHING... LIKE THAT...
I JUST HAD A CRUSH ON HER...
OH... I COULD HAVE SWORN SHE LIKED YOU TOO, THOUGH.
... SHE... SAID SHE DID...
I KNEW IT!
HAS SHE ALREADY GOTTEN HER NOTICE?
HUH? NO... NOT YET...
BUT, UM...
SHE SAID SHE PLANS TO ACCEPT IT.
SO... IT'S TOO...
THAT'S JUST HER ...
TRYING TO PUT UP A STRONG FRONT.
HUH ?

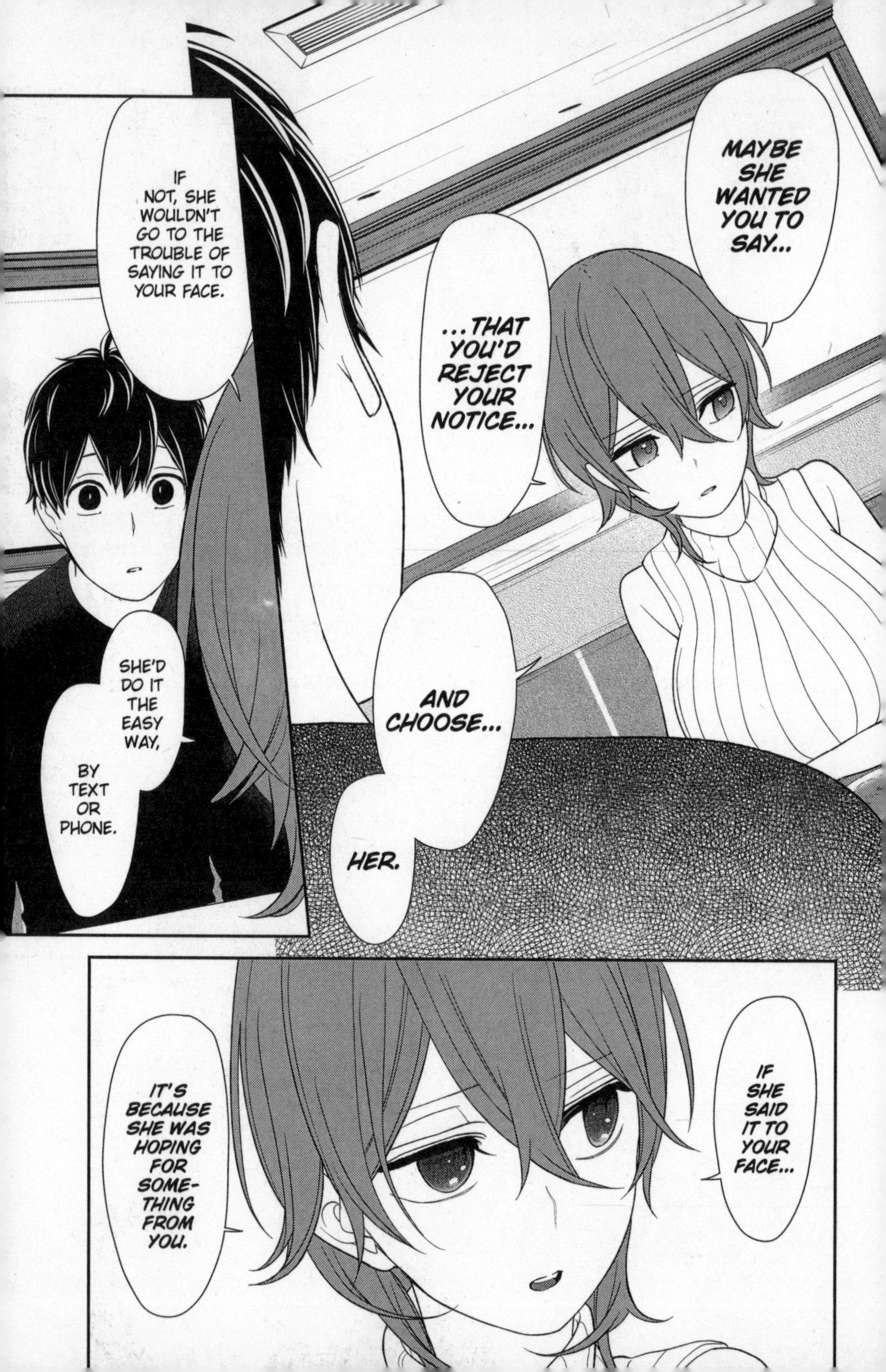
MAYBE SHE WANTED YOU TO SAY...
...THAT YOU'D REJECT YOUR NOTICE...
AND CHOOSE...
HER.
IF NOT, SHE WOULDN'T GO TO THE TROUBLE OF SAYING IT TO YOUR FACE.
SHE'D DO IT THE EASY WAY,
BY TEXT OR PHONE.
IF SHE SAID IT TO YOUR FACE...
IT'S BECAUSE SHE WAS HOPING FOR SOME-THING FROM YOU.

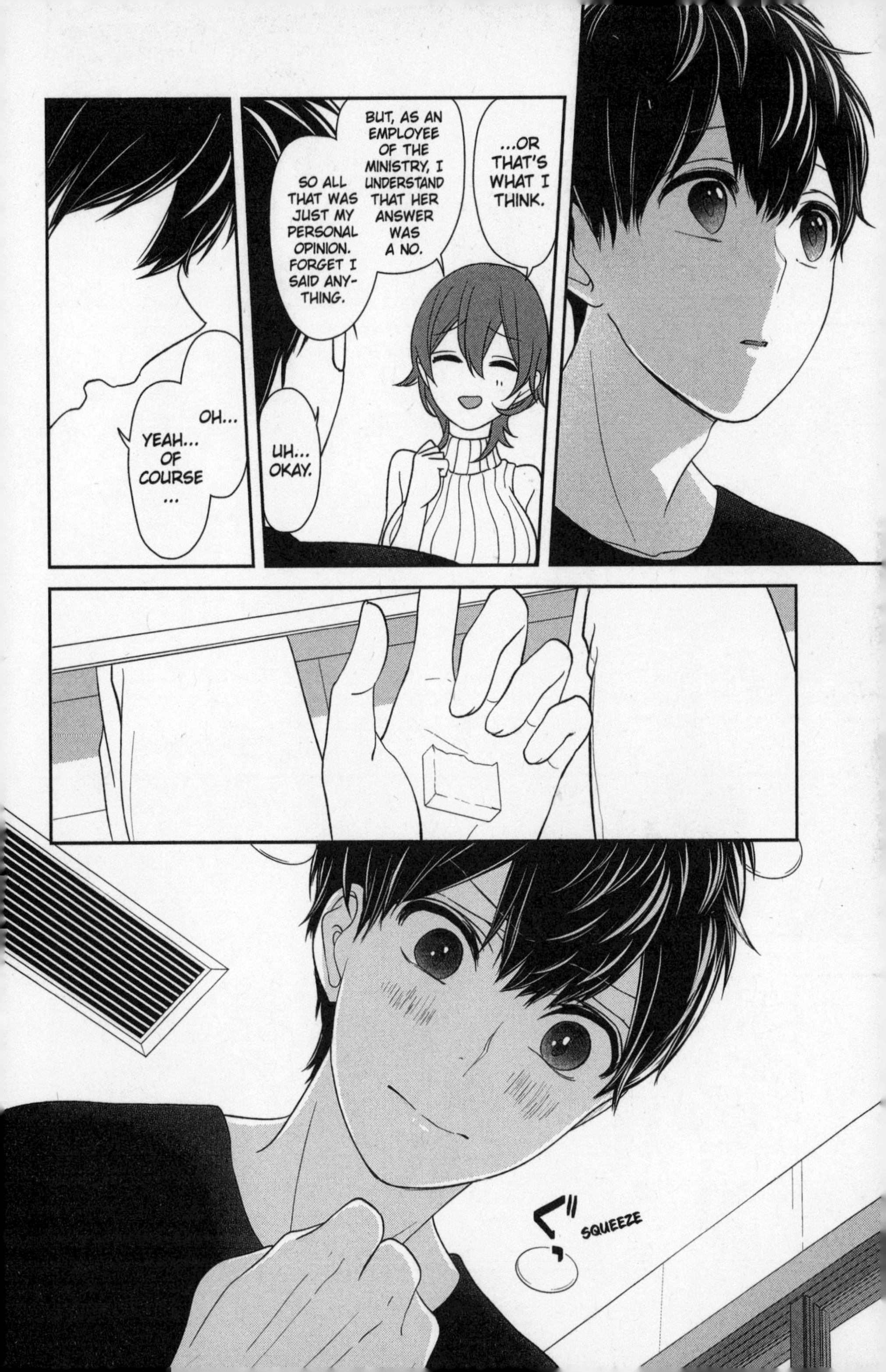
...OR THAT'S WHAT I THINK.
BUT, AS AN EMPLOYEE OF THE MINISTRY, I UNDERSTAND THAT HER ANSWER WAS A NO.
SO ALL THAT WAS JUST MY PERSONAL OPINION. FORGET I SAID ANY-THING.
UH... OKAY.
OH... YEAH... OF COURSE ...
SQUEEZE

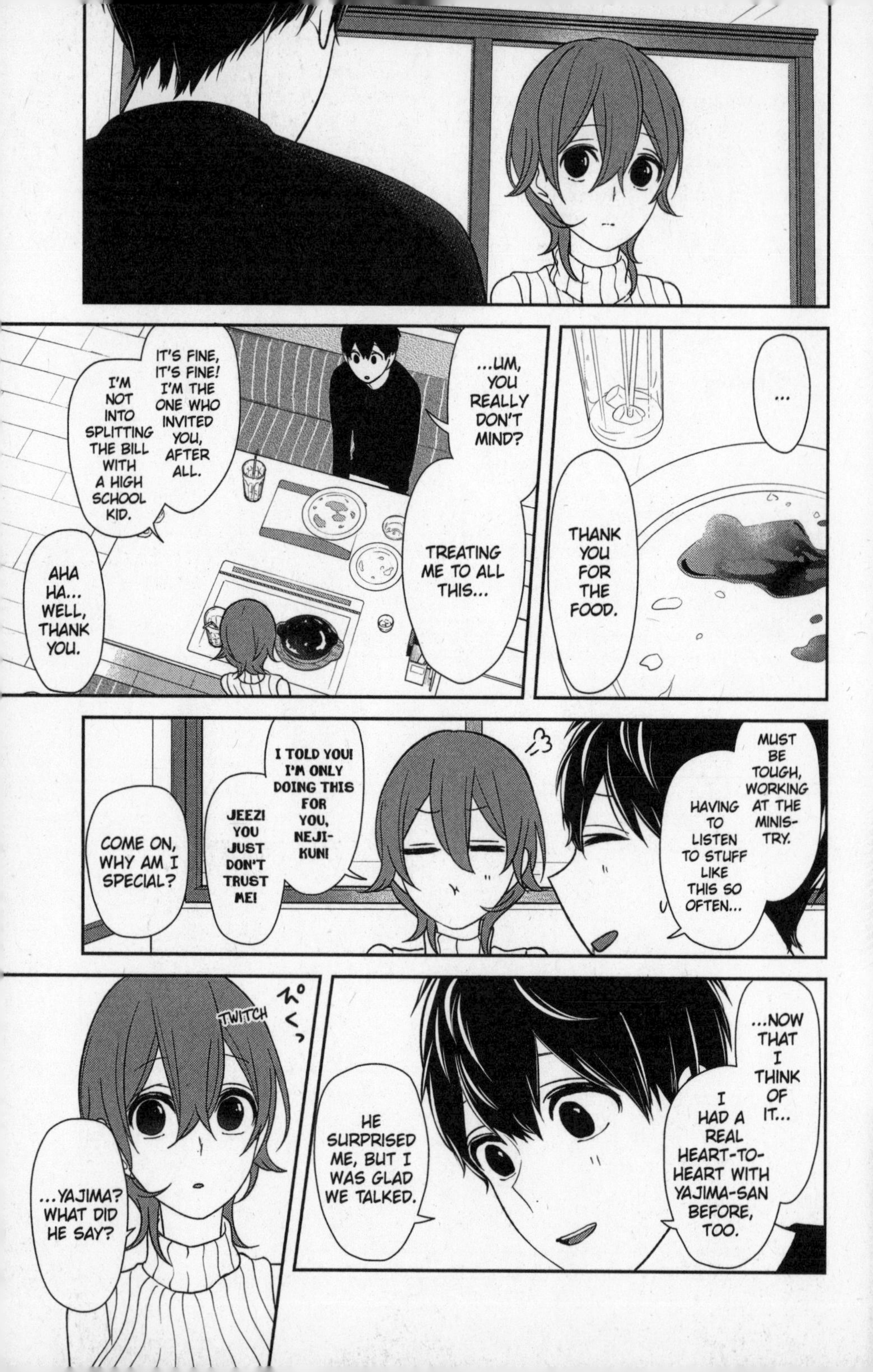
...
THANK YOU FOR THE FOOD.
...UM, YOU REALLY DON'T MIND?
TREATING ME TO ALL THIS...
IT'S FINE, IT'S FINE! I'M THE ONE WHO INVITED YOU, AFTER ALL.
I'M NOT INTO SPLITTING THE BILL WITH A HIGH SCHOOL KID.
AHA HA... WELL, THANK YOU.
MUST BE TOUGH, WORKING AT THE MINISTRY.
HAVING TO LISTEN TO STUFF LIKE THIS SO OFTEN...
I TOLD YOU! I'M ONLY DOING THIS FOR YOU, NEJI-KUN!
JEEZ! YOU JUST DON'T TRUST ME!
COME ON, WHY AM I SPECIAL?
...NOW THAT I THINK OF IT...
I HAD A REAL HEART-TO-HEART WITH YAJIMA-SAN BEFORE, TOO.
HE SURPRISED ME, BUT I WAS GLAD WE TALKED.
ぴくっ
TWITCH
...YAJIMA? WHAT DID HE SAY?

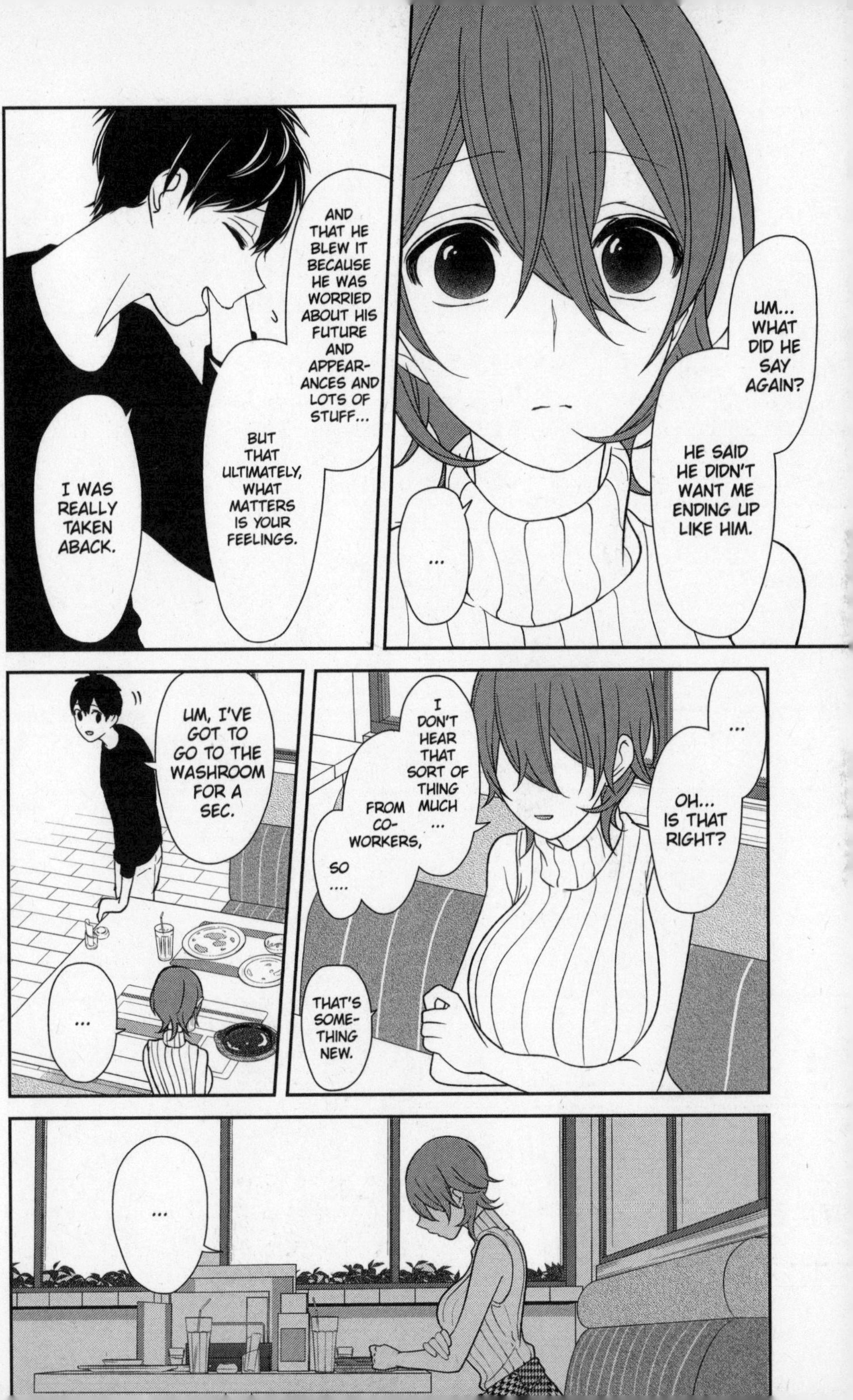
UM... WHAT DID HE SAY AGAIN?
HE SAID HE DIDN'T WANT ME ENDING UP LIKE HIM.
...
AND THAT HE BLEW IT BECAUSE HE WAS WORRIED ABOUT HIS FUTURE AND APPEAR-ANCES AND LOTS OF STUFF...
BUT THAT ULTIMATELY, WHAT MATTERS IS YOUR FEELINGS.
I WAS REALLY TAKEN ABACK.
...
OH... IS THAT RIGHT?
I DON'T HEAR THAT SORT OF THING MUCH...
FROM CO-WORKERS,
SO ....
THAT'S SOME-THING NEW.
UM, I'VE GOT TO GO TO THE WASHROOM FOR A SEC.
...
...

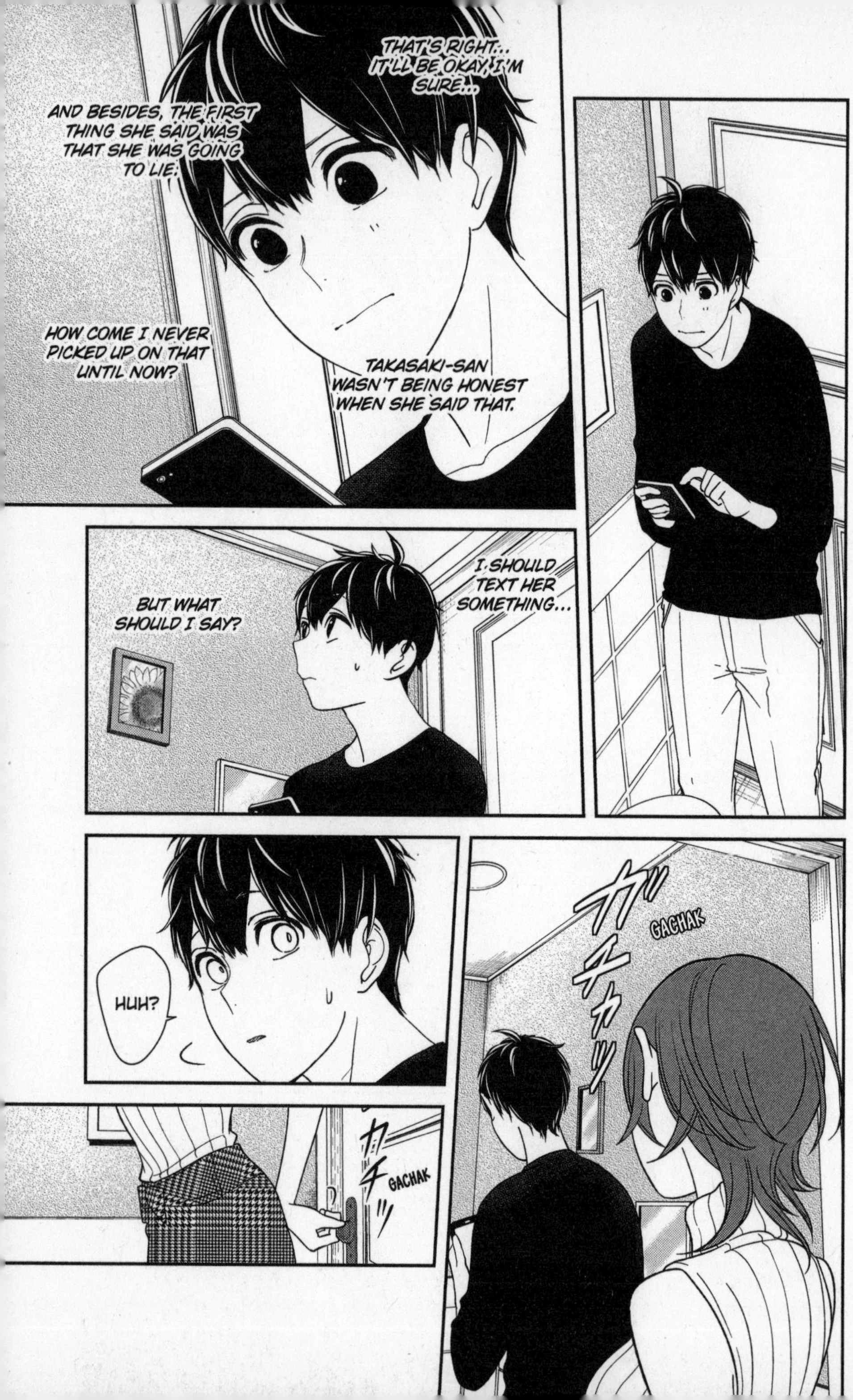
THAT'S RIGHT... IT'LL BE OKAY, I'M SURE...
AND BESIDES, THE FIRST THING SHE SAID WAS THAT SHE WAS GOING TO LIE.
TAKASAKI-SAN WASN'T BEING HONEST WHEN SHE SAID THAT.
HOW COME I NEVER PICKED UP ON THAT UNTIL NOW?
I SHOULD TEXT HER SOMETHING...
BUT WHAT SHOULD I SAY?
GACHAK
HUH?
GACHAK

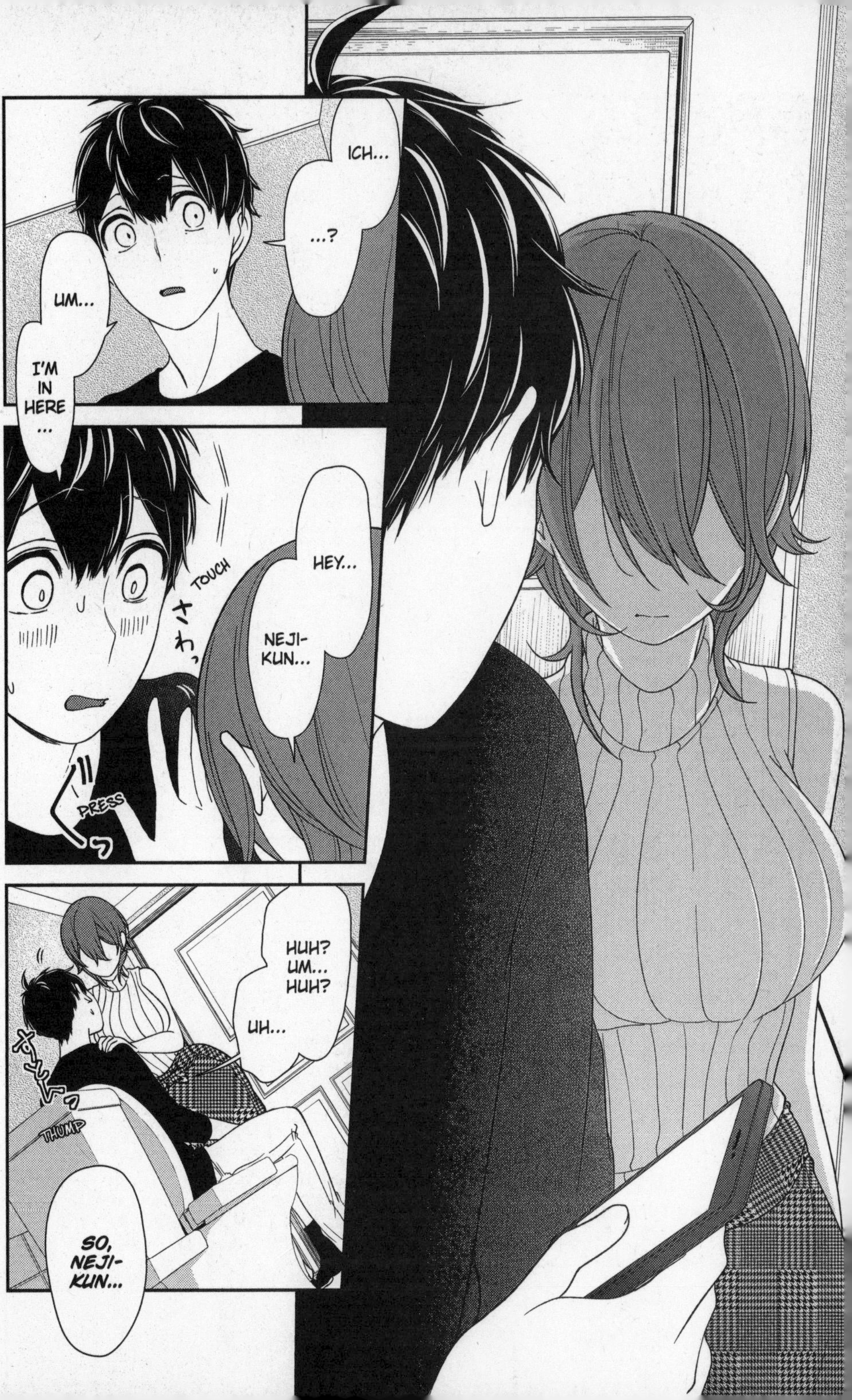
ICH... ...?
UM...
I'M IN HERE ...
HEY... NEJI-KUN...
TOUCH
さわっ
PRESS
HUH? UM... HUH?
UH...
THUMP
SO, NEJI-KUN...

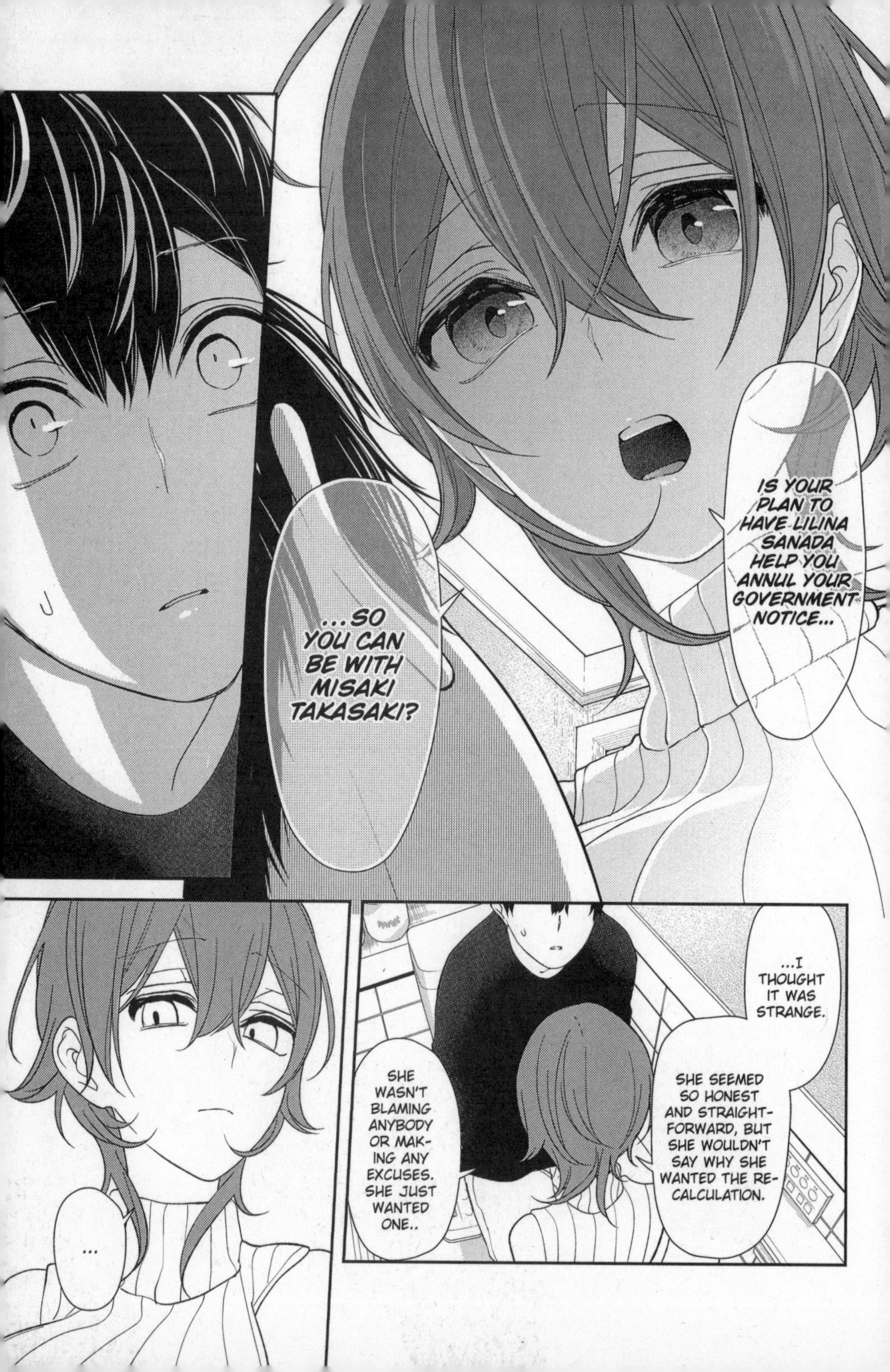
IS YOUR PLAN TO HAVE LILINA SANADA HELP YOU ANNUL YOUR GOVERNMENT NOTICE...
...SO YOU CAN BE WITH MISAKI TAKASAKI?
...I THOUGHT IT WAS STRANGE.
SHE SEEMED SO HONEST AND STRAIGHT-FORWARD, BUT SHE WOULDN'T SAY WHY SHE WANTED THE RE-CALCULATION.
SHE WASN'T BLAMING ANYBODY OR MAK-ING ANY EXCUSES. SHE JUST WANTED ONE..
...

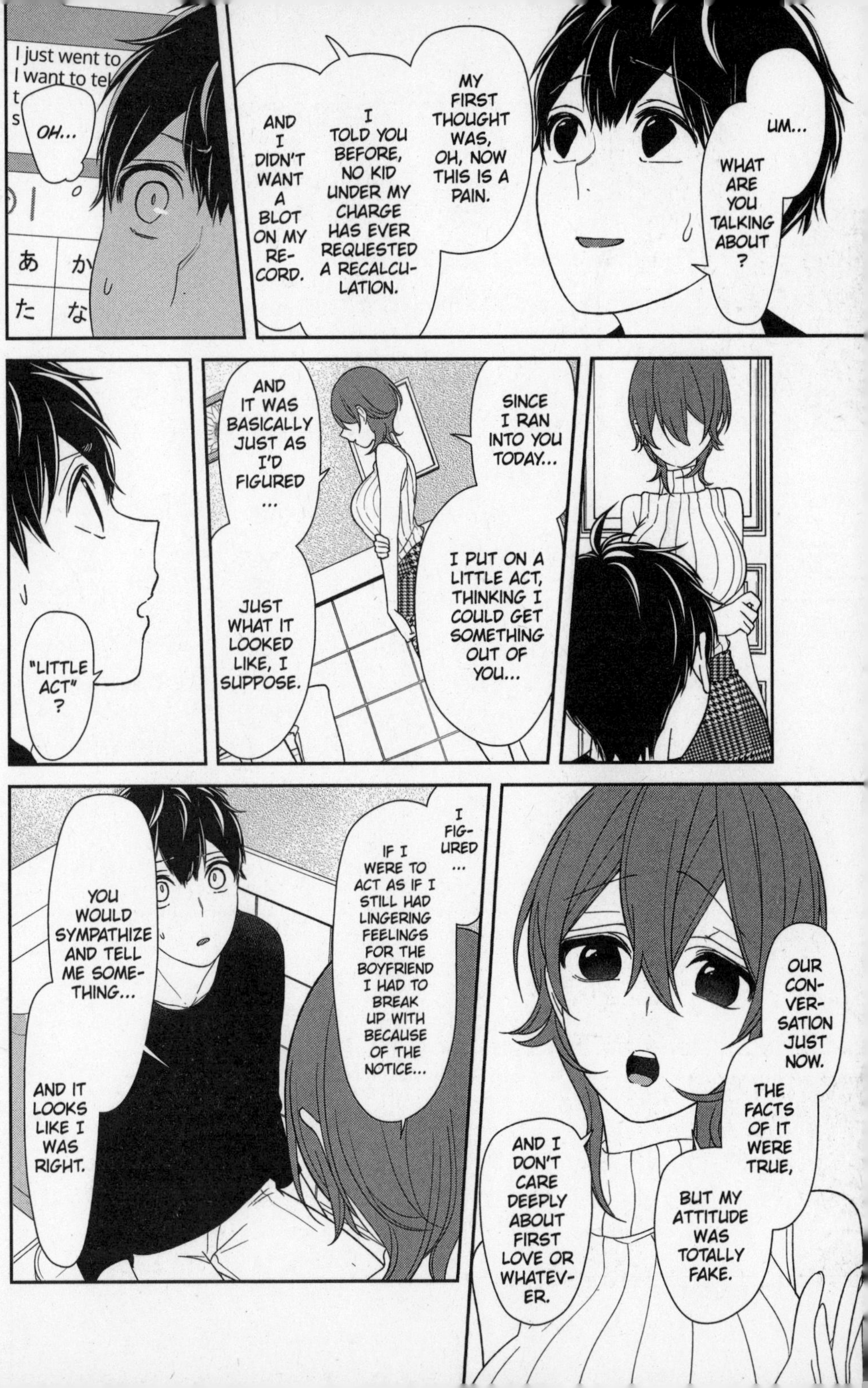
UM...
WHAT ARE YOU TALKING ABOUT?
MY FIRST THOUGHT WAS, OH, NOW THIS IS A PAIN.
I TOLD YOU BEFORE, NO KID UNDER MY CHARGE HAS EVER REQUESTED A RECALCULATION.
AND I DIDN'T WANT A BLOT ON MY RECORD.
I just went to
OH...
SINCE I RAN INTO YOU TODAY...
I PUT ON A LITTLE ACT, THINKING I COULD GET SOMETHING OUT OF YOU...
AND IT WAS BASICALLY JUST AS I'D FIGURED...
JUST WHAT IT LOOKED LIKE, I SUPPOSE.
"LITTLE ACT"?
OUR CONVERSATION JUST NOW.
THE FACTS OF IT WERE TRUE,
BUT MY ATTITUDE WAS TOTALLY FAKE.
AND I DON'T CARE DEEPLY ABOUT FIRST LOVE OR WHATEVER.
I FIGURED...
IF I WERE TO ACT AS IF I STILL HAD LINGERING FEELINGS FOR THE BOYFRIEND I HAD TO BREAK UP WITH BECAUSE OF THE NOTICE...
YOU WOULD SYMPATHIZE AND TELL ME SOMETHING...
AND IT LOOKS LIKE I WAS RIGHT.

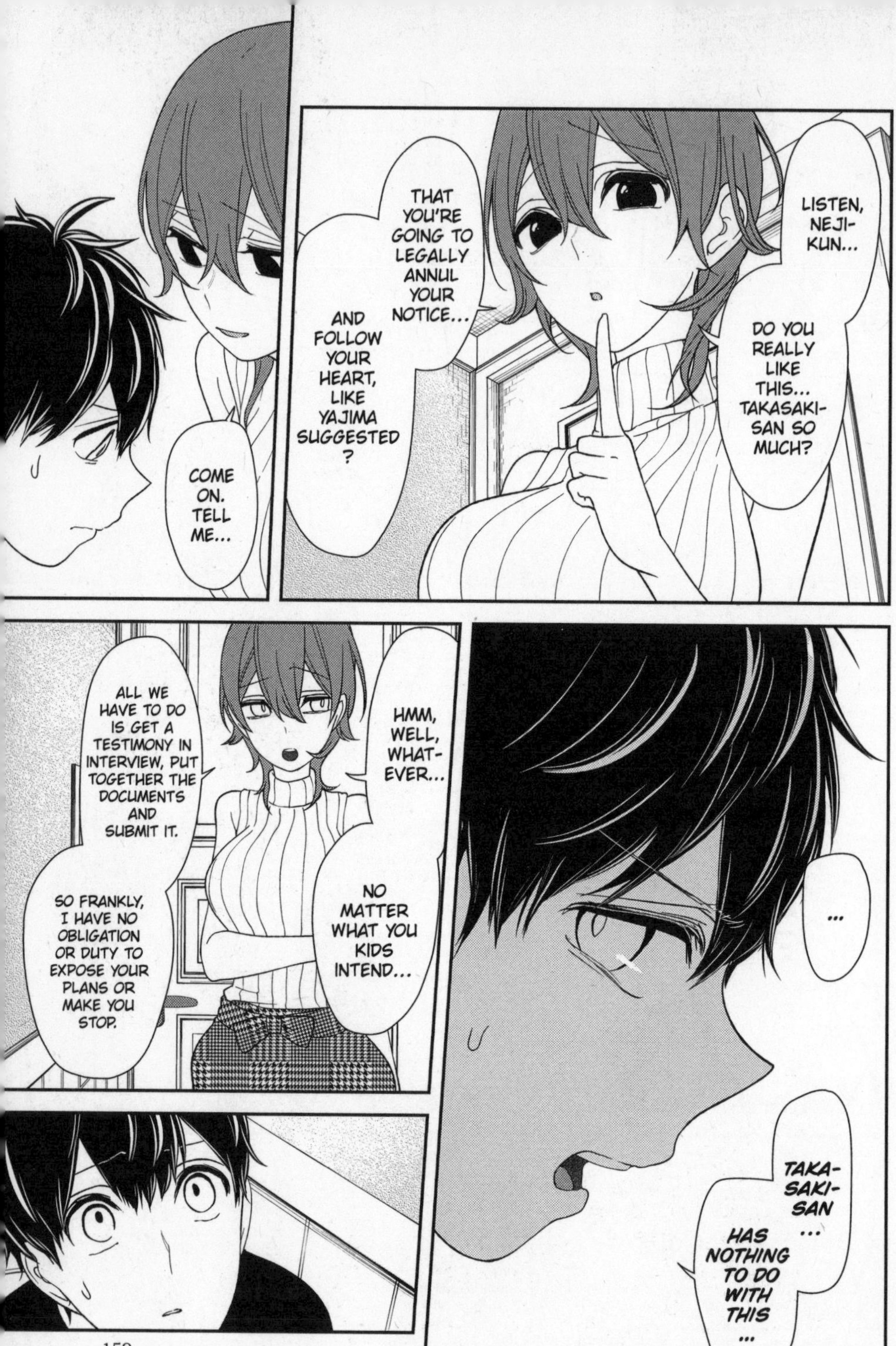
LISTEN, NEJI-KUN...
DO YOU REALLY LIKE THIS... TAKASAKI-SAN SO MUCH?
THAT YOU'RE GOING TO LEGALLY ANNUL YOUR NOTICE...
AND FOLLOW YOUR HEART, LIKE YAJIMA SUGGESTED?
COME ON. TELL ME...
...
TAKA-SAKI-SAN...
HAS NOTHING TO DO WITH THIS...
HMM, WELL, WHAT-EVER...
ALL WE HAVE TO DO IS GET A TESTIMONY IN INTERVIEW, PUT TOGETHER THE DOCUMENTS AND SUBMIT IT.
NO MATTER WHAT YOU KIDS INTEND...
SO FRANKLY, I HAVE NO OBLIGATION OR DUTY TO EXPOSE YOUR PLANS OR MAKE YOU STOP.

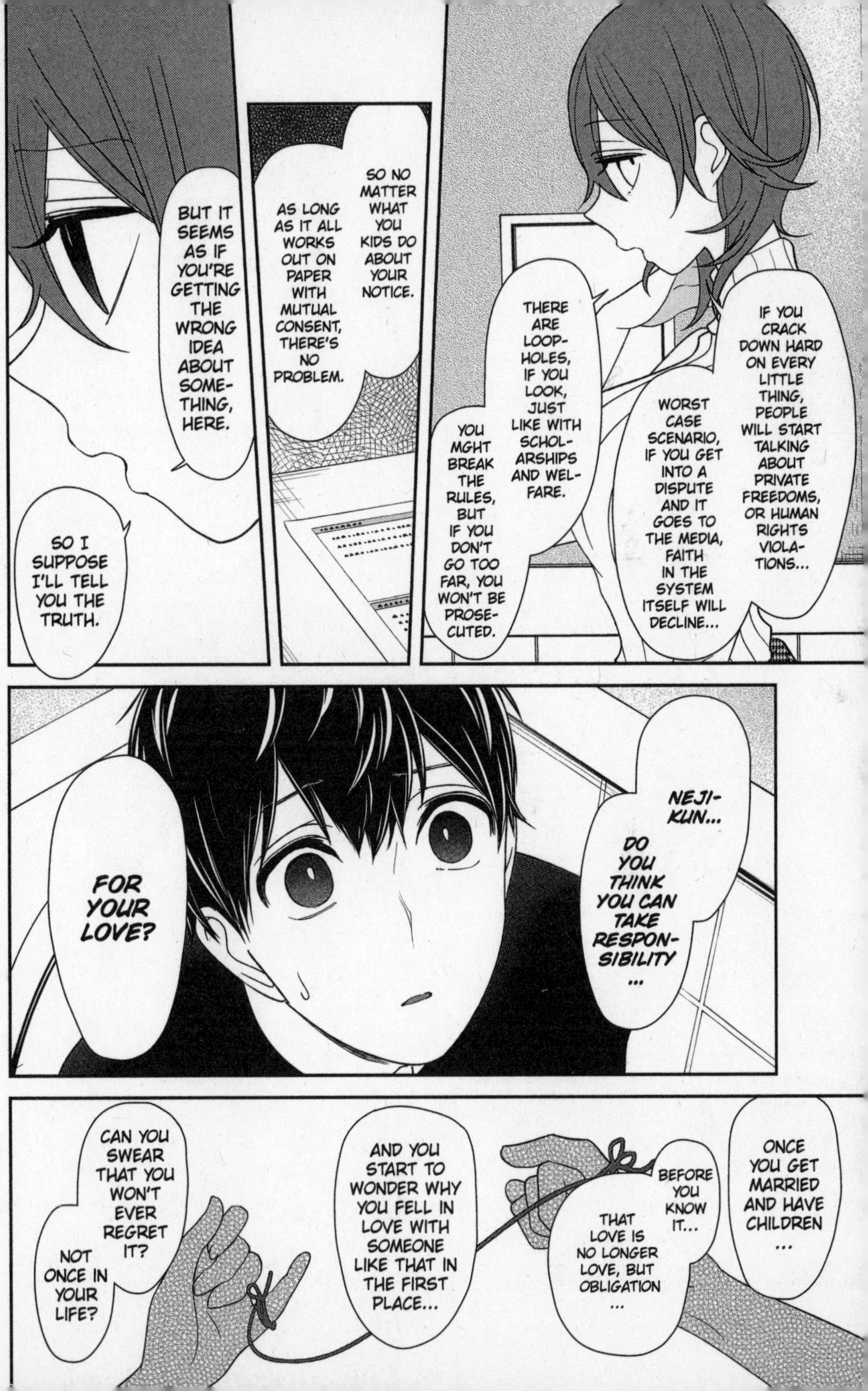
IF YOU CRACK DOWN HARD ON EVERY LITTLE THING, PEOPLE WILL START TALKING ABOUT PRIVATE FREEDOMS, OR HUMAN RIGHTS VIOLATIONS...
WORST CASE SCENARIO, IF YOU GET INTO A DISPUTE AND IT GOES TO THE MEDIA, FAITH IN THE SYSTEM ITSELF WILL DECLINE...
THERE ARE LOOPHOLES, IF YOU LOOK, JUST LIKE WITH SCHOLARSHIPS AND WELFARE.
YOU MGHT BREAK THE RULES, BUT IF YOU DON'T GO TOO FAR, YOU WON'T BE PROSECUTED.
SO NO MATTER WHAT YOU KIDS DO ABOUT YOUR NOTICE.
AS LONG AS IT ALL WORKS OUT ON PAPER WITH MUTUAL CONSENT, THERE'S NO PROBLEM.
BUT IT SEEMS AS IF YOU'RE GETTING THE WRONG IDEA ABOUT SOMETHING, HERE.
SO I SUPPOSE I'LL TELL YOU THE TRUTH.
NEJI-KUN... DO YOU THINK YOU CAN TAKE RESPONSIBILITY...
FOR YOUR LOVE?
ONCE YOU GET MARRIED AND HAVE CHILDREN...
BEFORE YOU KNOW IT...
THAT LOVE IS NO LONGER LOVE, BUT OBLIGATION...
AND YOU START TO WONDER WHY YOU FELL IN LOVE WITH SOMEONE LIKE THAT IN THE FIRST PLACE...
CAN YOU SWEAR THAT YOU WON'T EVER REGRET IT?
NOT ONCE IN YOUR LIFE?

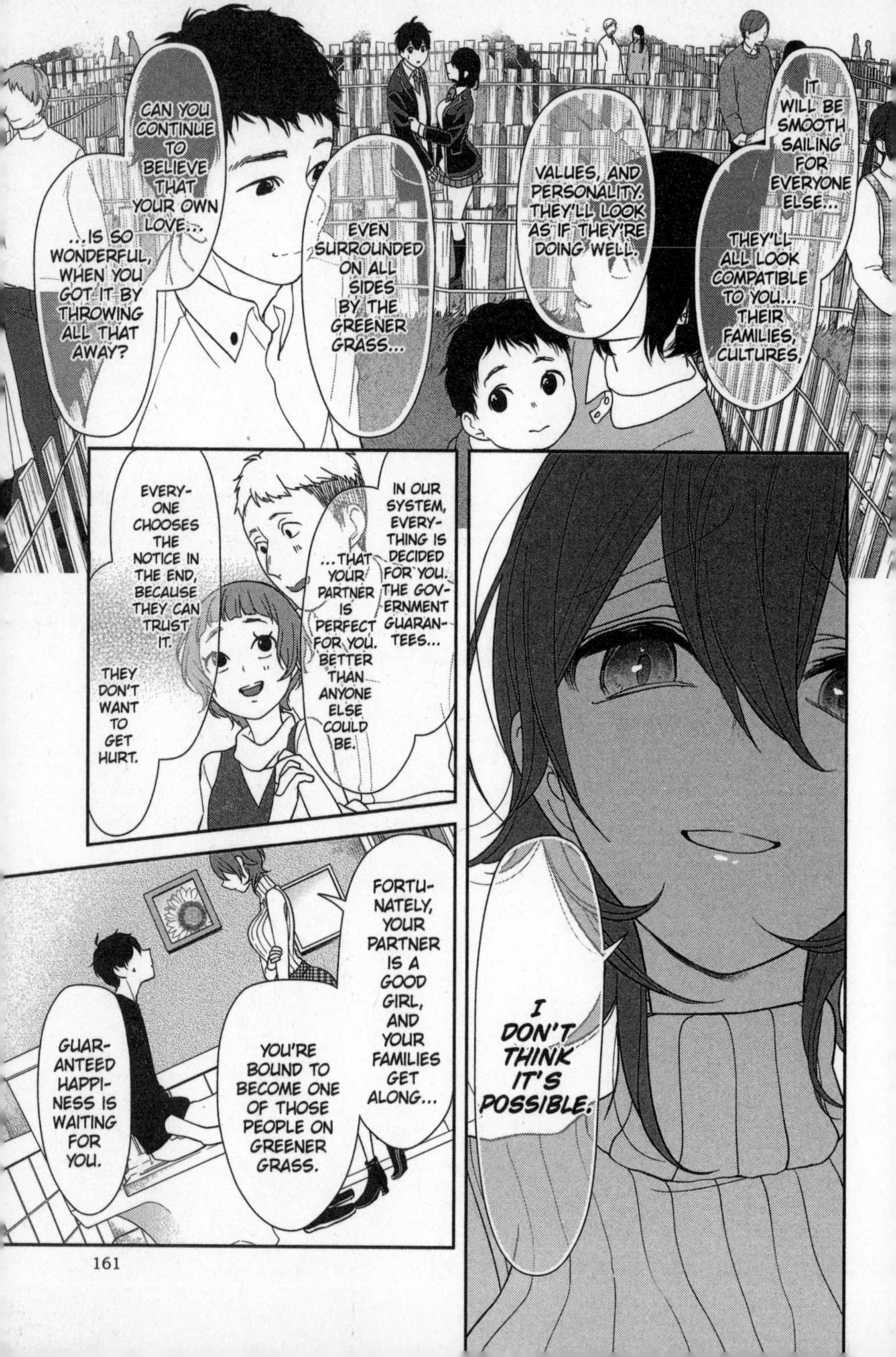
IT WILL BE SMOOTH SAILING FOR EVERYONE ELSE...
THEY'LL ALL LOOK COMPATIBLE TO YOU... THEIR FAMILIES, CULTURES,
VALUES, AND PERSONALITY. THEY'LL LOOK AS IF THEY'RE DOING WELL.
EVEN SURROUNDED ON ALL SIDES BY THE GREENER GRASS...
CAN YOU CONTINUE TO BELIEVE THAT YOUR OWN LOVE...
...IS SO WONDERFUL, WHEN YOU GOT IT BY THROWING ALL THAT AWAY?
I DON'T THINK IT'S POSSIBLE.
IN OUR SYSTEM, EVERYTHING IS DECIDED FOR YOU. THE GOVERNMENT GUARANTEES...
...THAT YOUR PARTNER IS PERFECT FOR YOU. BETTER THAN ANYONE ELSE COULD BE.
EVERYONE CHOOSES THE NOTICE IN THE END, BECAUSE THEY CAN TRUST IT.
THEY DON'T WANT TO GET HURT.
FORTUNATELY, YOUR PARTNER IS A GOOD GIRL, AND YOUR FAMILIES GET ALONG...
YOU'RE BOUND TO BECOME ONE OF THOSE PEOPLE ON GREENER GRASS.
GUARANTEED HAPPINESS IS WAITING FOR YOU.

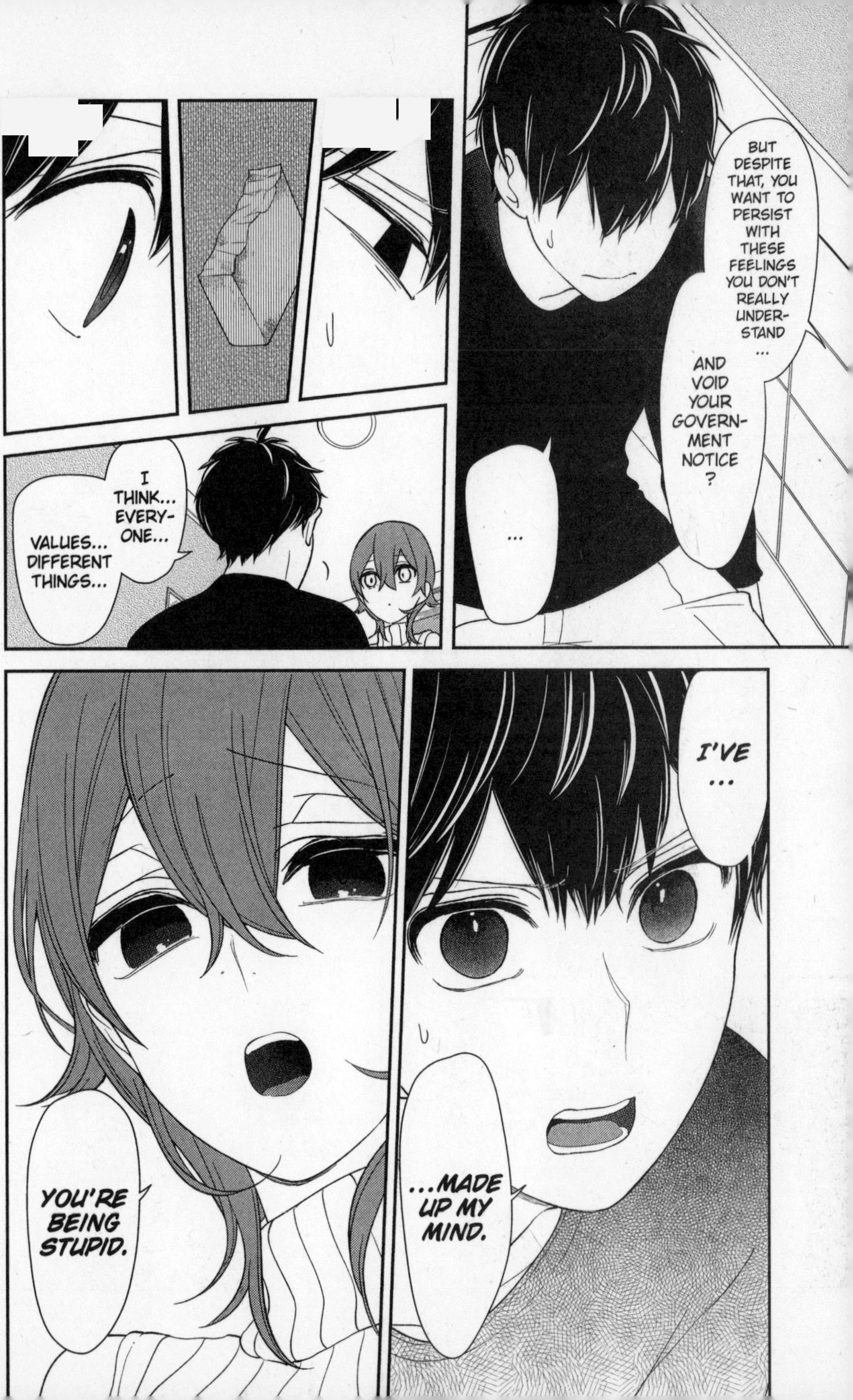
BUT DESPITE THAT, YOU WANT TO PERSIST WITH THESE FEELINGS YOU DON'T REALLY UNDER-STAND ...
AND VOID YOUR GOVERN-MENT NOTICE ?
...
I THINK... EVERY-ONE...
VALUES... DIFFERENT THINGS...
I'VE ...
...MADE UP MY MIND.
YOU'RE BEING STUPID.

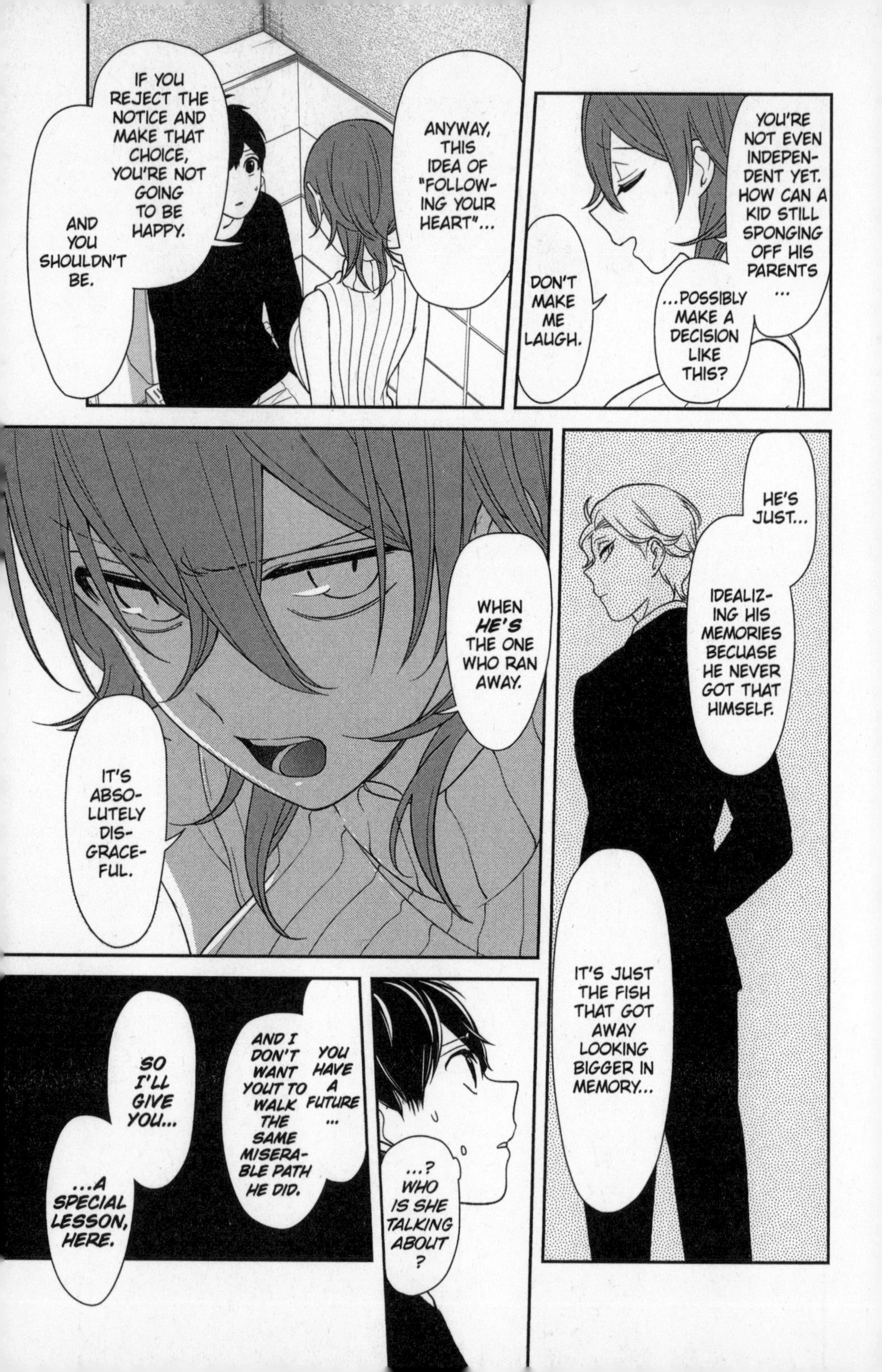
YOU'RE NOT EVEN INDEPENDENT YET. HOW CAN A KID STILL SPONGING OFF HIS PARENTS...
...POSSIBLY MAKE A DECISION LIKE THIS?
DON'T MAKE ME LAUGH.
ANYWAY, THIS IDEA OF "FOLLOWING YOUR HEART"...
IF YOU REJECT THE NOTICE AND MAKE THAT CHOICE, YOU'RE NOT GOING TO BE HAPPY.
AND YOU SHOULDN'T BE.
HE'S JUST...
IDEALIZING HIS MEMORIES BECUASE HE NEVER GOT THAT HIMSELF.
IT'S JUST THE FISH THAT GOT AWAY LOOKING BIGGER IN MEMORY...
WHEN *HE'S* THE ONE WHO RAN AWAY.
IT'S ABSOLUTELY DISGRACEFUL.
YOU HAVE A FUTURE...
AND I DON'T WANT YOUT TO WALK THE SAME MISERABLE PATH HE DID.
...? WHO IS SHE TALKING ABOUT?
SO I'LL GIVE YOU...
...A SPECIAL LESSON, HERE.

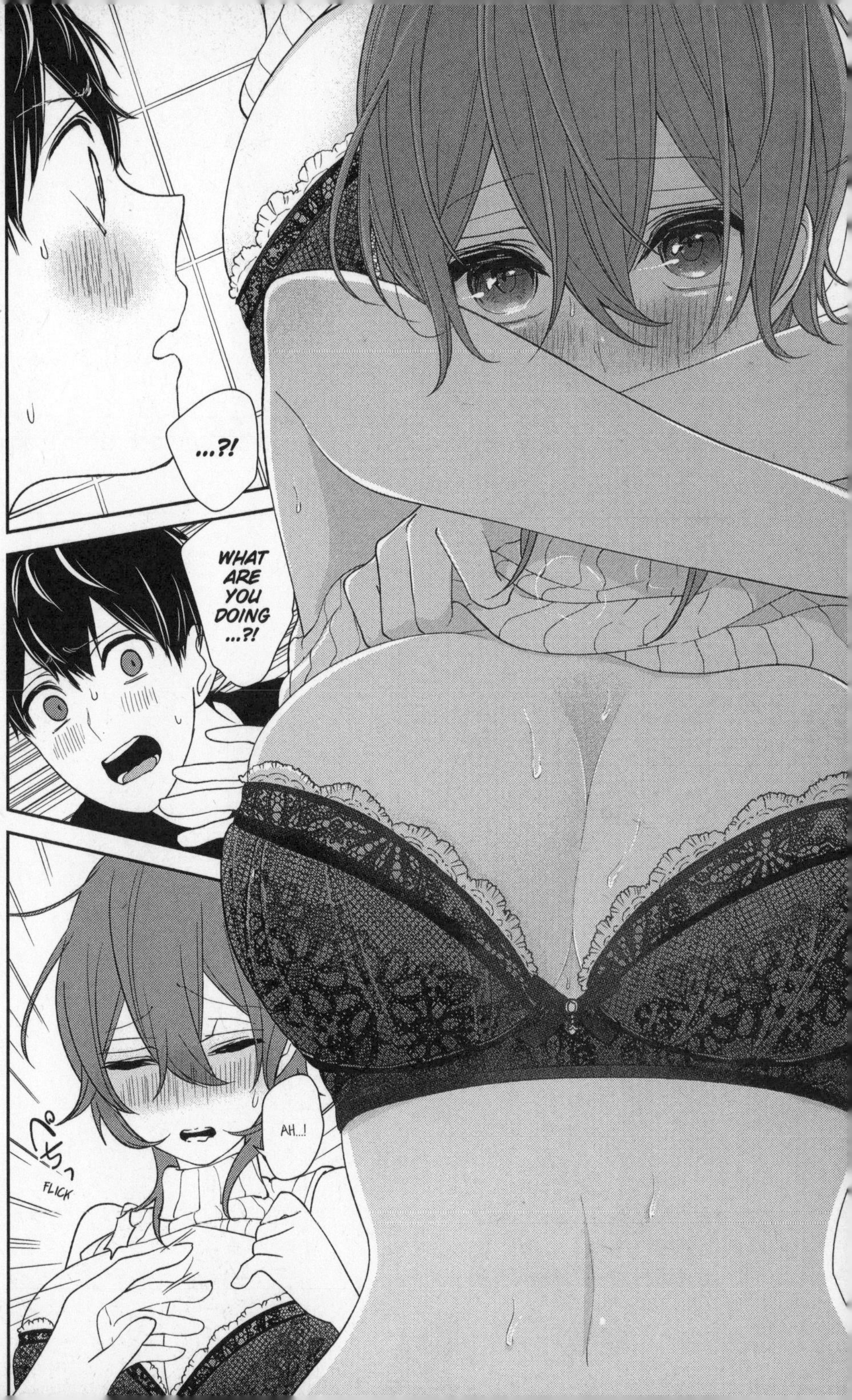
...?!
WHAT ARE YOU DOING ...?!
AH...!
FLICK

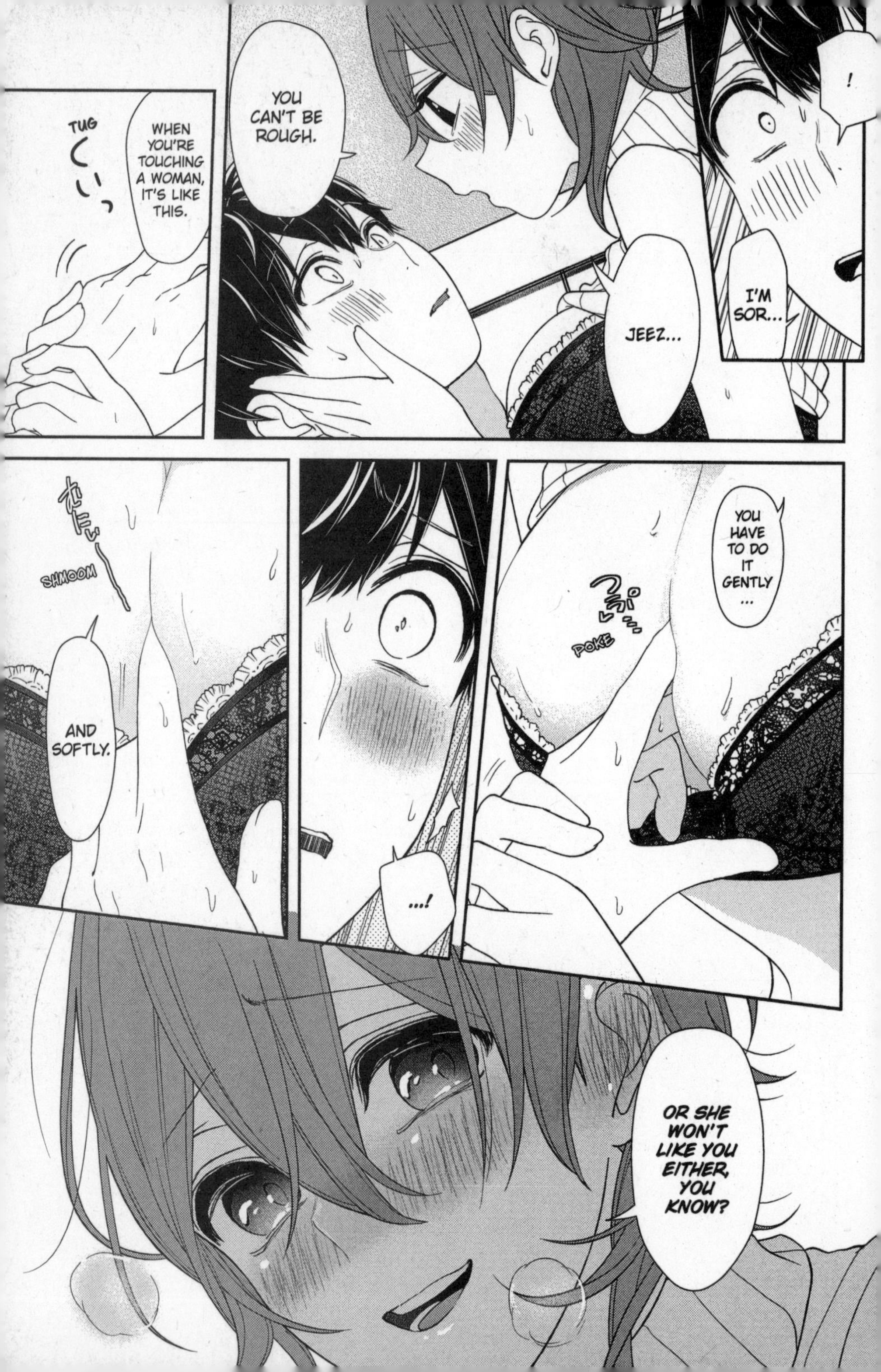
!
I'M SOR...
JEEZ...
YOU CAN'T BE ROUGH.
TUG
WHEN YOU'RE TOUCHING A WOMAN, IT'S LIKE THIS.
YOU HAVE TO DO IT GENTLY ...
POKE
...!
SHMOOM
AND SOFTLY.
OR SHE WON'T LIKE YOU EITHER, YOU KNOW?

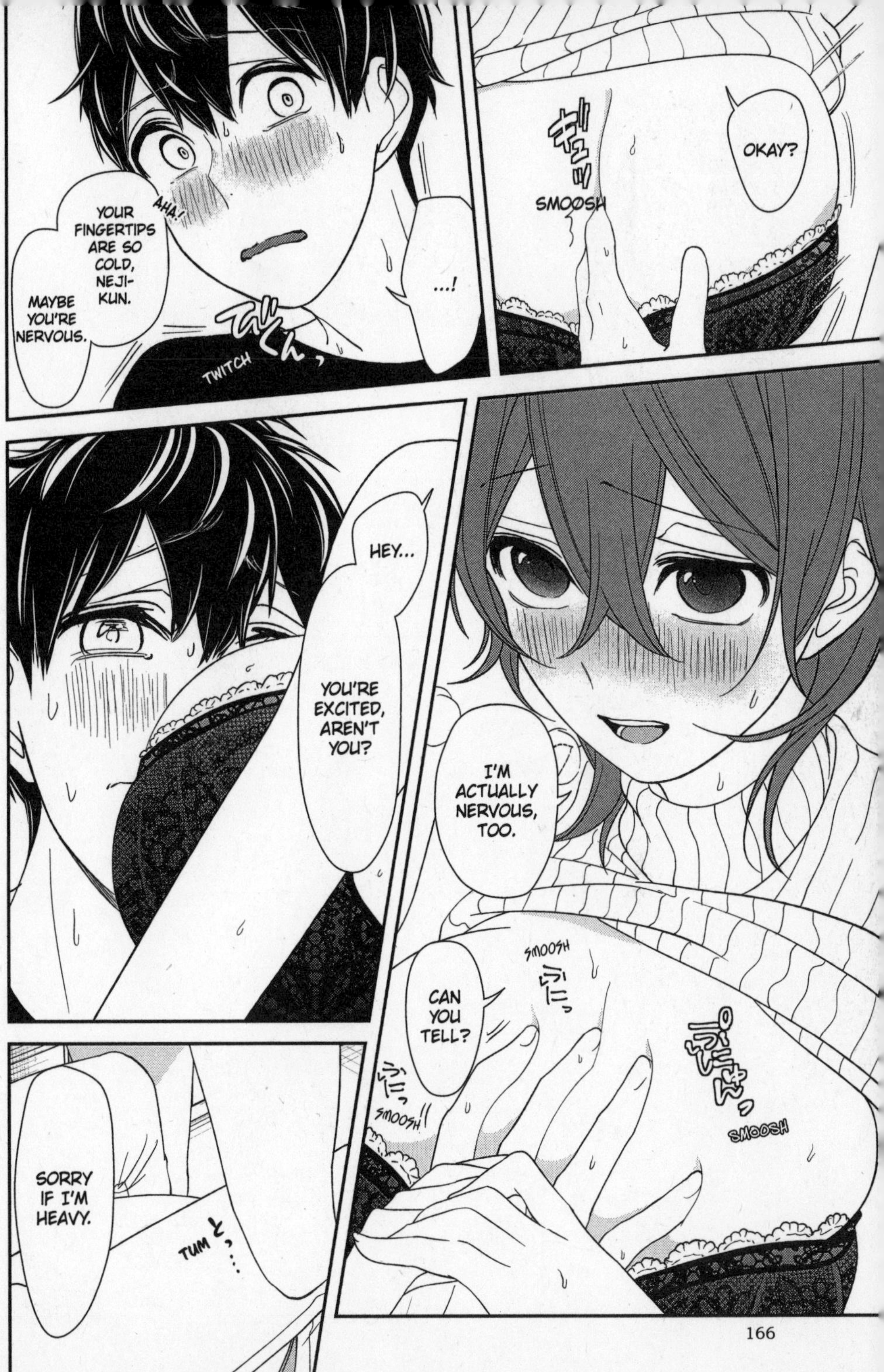
OKAY?
SMOOSH
...!
AHA!
YOUR FINGERTIPS ARE SO COLD, NEJI-KUN.
MAYBE YOU'RE NERVOUS.
TWITCH
I'M ACTUALLY NERVOUS, TOO.
SMOOSH
CAN YOU TELL?
SMOOSH
SMOOSH
HEY...
YOU'RE EXCITED, AREN'T YOU?
SORRY IF I'M HEAVY.
TUM

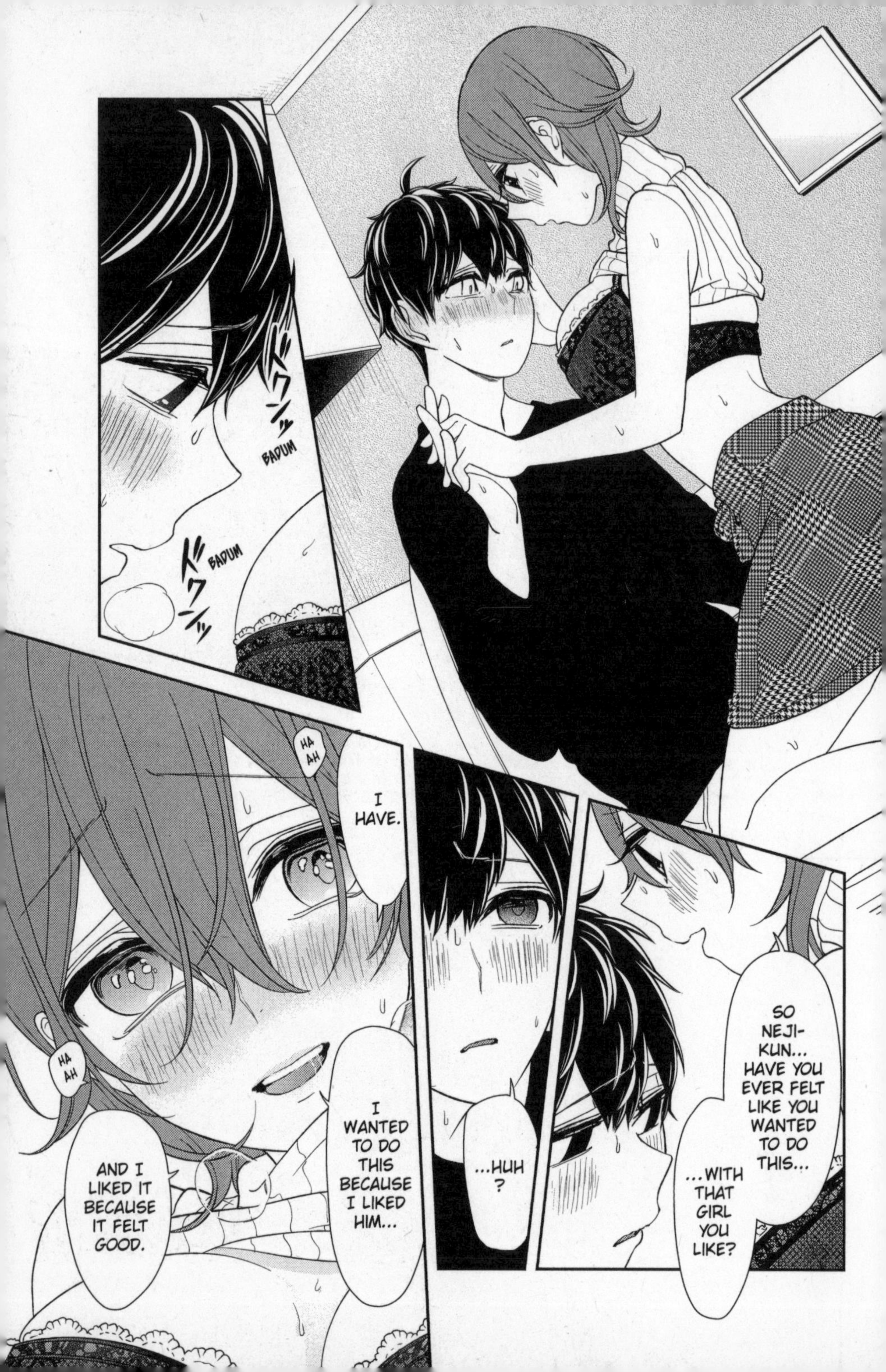
ドクンッ
BADUM
ドクンッ
BADUM
SO NEJI-KUN... HAVE YOU EVER FELT LIKE YOU WANTED TO DO THIS...
...WITH THAT GIRL YOU LIKE?
...HUH?
HA AH
I HAVE.
I WANTED TO DO THIS BECAUSE I LIKED HIM...
AND I LIKED IT BECAUSE IT FELT GOOD.
HA AH

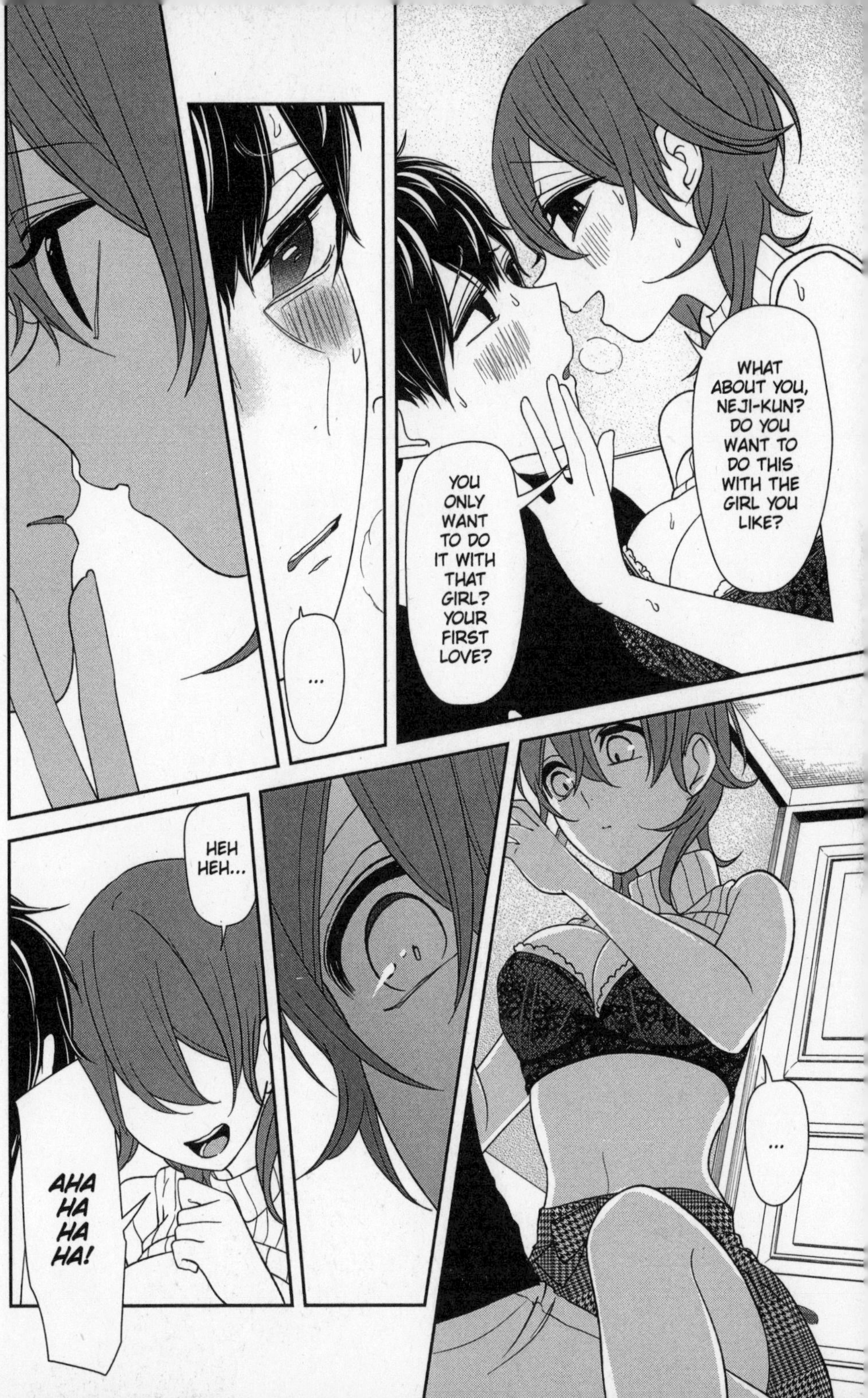
WHAT ABOUT YOU, NEJI-KUN? DO YOU WANT TO DO THIS WITH THE GIRL YOU LIKE?
YOU ONLY WANT TO DO IT WITH THAT GIRL? YOUR FIRST LOVE?
...
...
HEH HEH...
AHA HA HA HA!

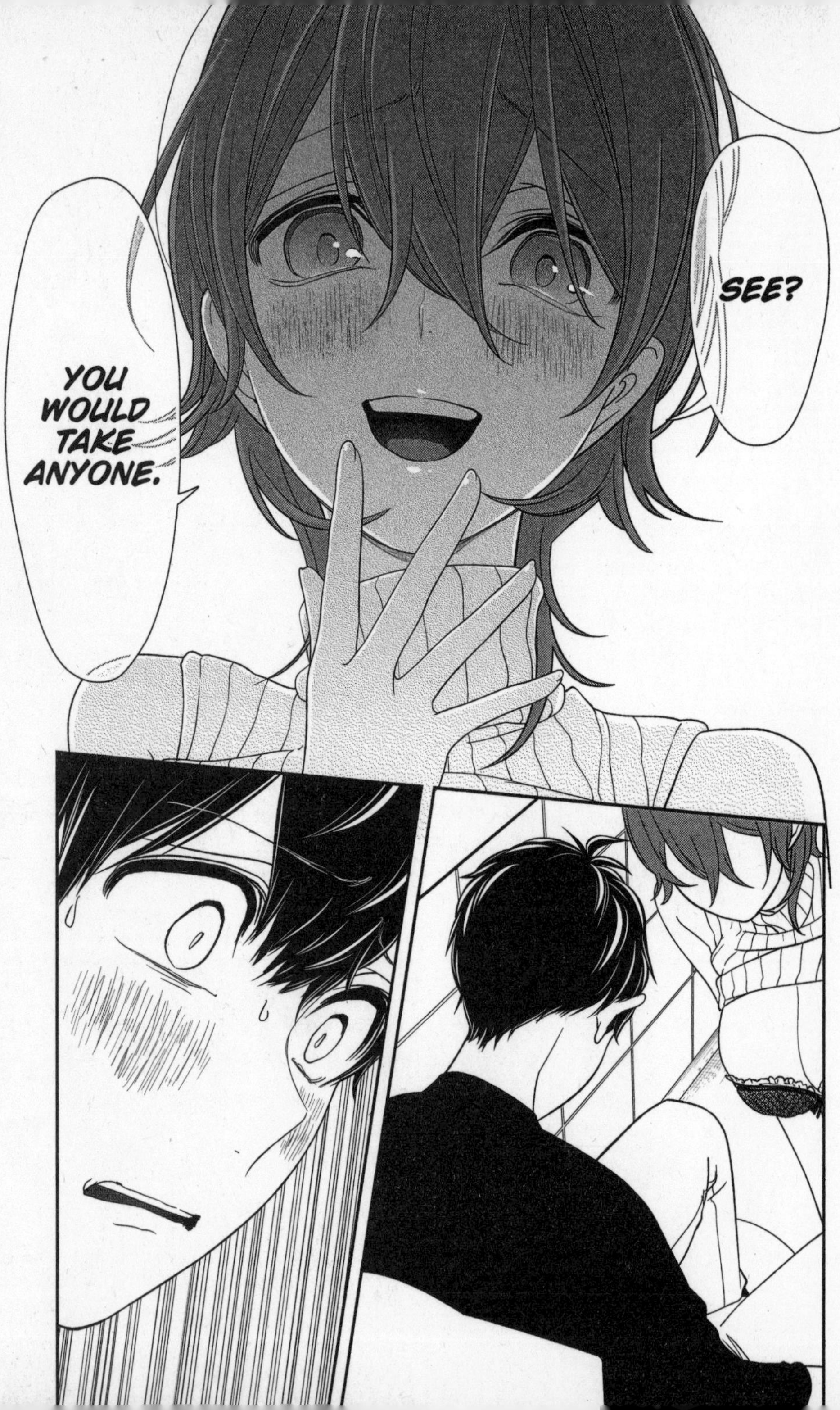
SEE?
YOU WOULD TAKE ANYONE.

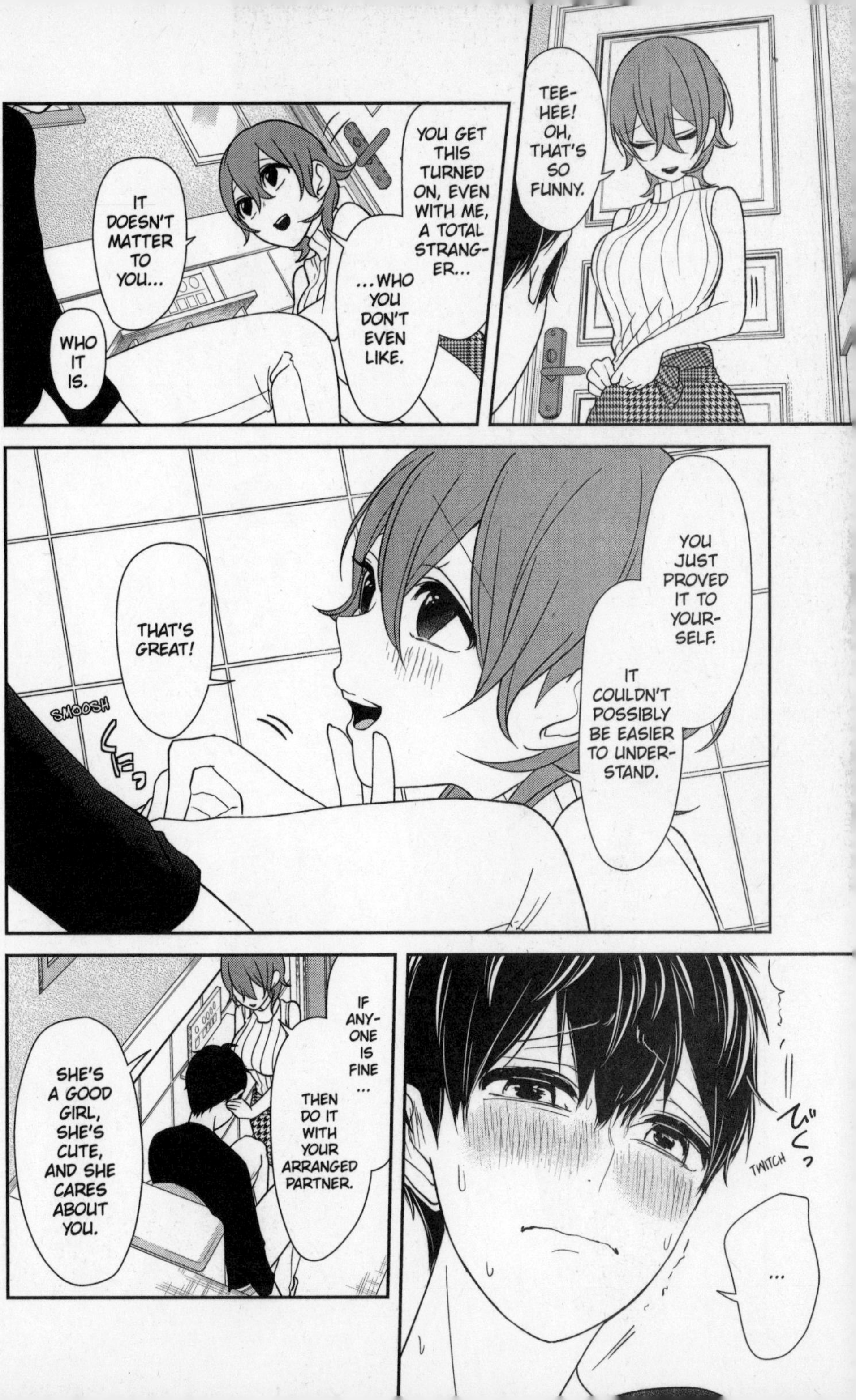
TEE-HEE! OH, THAT'S SO FUNNY.
YOU GET THIS TURNED ON, EVEN WITH ME, A TOTAL STRANGER...
...WHO YOU DON'T EVEN LIKE.
IT DOESN'T MATTER TO YOU...
WHO IT IS.
YOU JUST PROVED IT TO YOURSELF.
IT COULDN'T POSSIBLY BE EASIER TO UNDERSTAND.
THAT'S GREAT!
SMOOSH
TWITCH
...
IF ANYONE IS FINE...
THEN DO IT WITH YOUR ARRANGED PARTNER.
SHE'S A GOOD GIRL, SHE'S CUTE, AND SHE CARES ABOUT YOU.

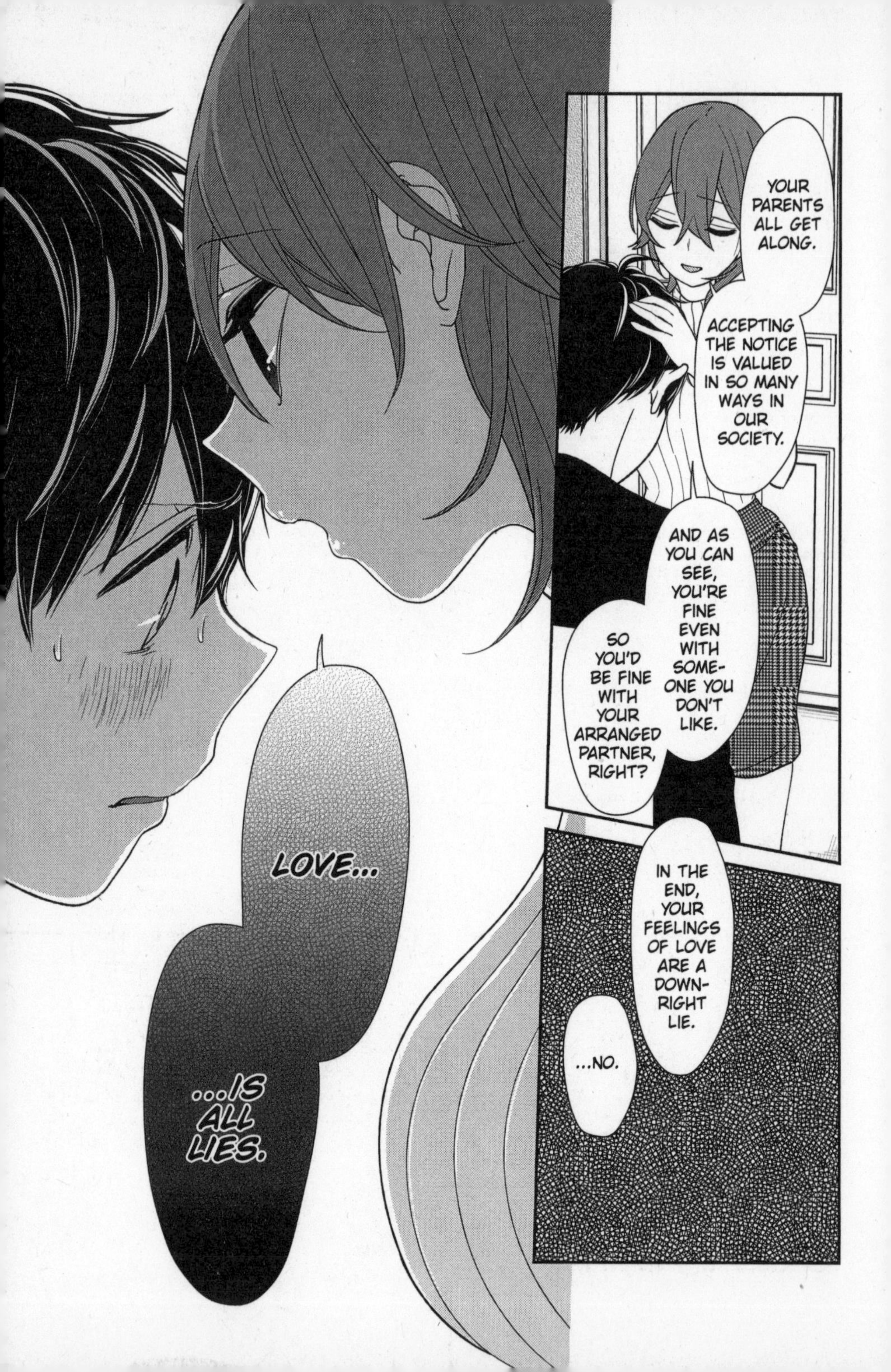
YOUR PARENTS ALL GET ALONG.
ACCEPTING THE NOTICE IS VALUED IN SO MANY WAYS IN OUR SOCIETY.
AND AS YOU CAN SEE, YOU'RE FINE EVEN WITH SOME-ONE YOU DON'T LIKE.
SO YOU'D BE FINE WITH YOUR ARRANGED PARTNER, RIGHT?
IN THE END, YOUR FEELINGS OF LOVE ARE A DOWN-RIGHT LIE.
...NO.
LOVE...
...IS ALL LIES.

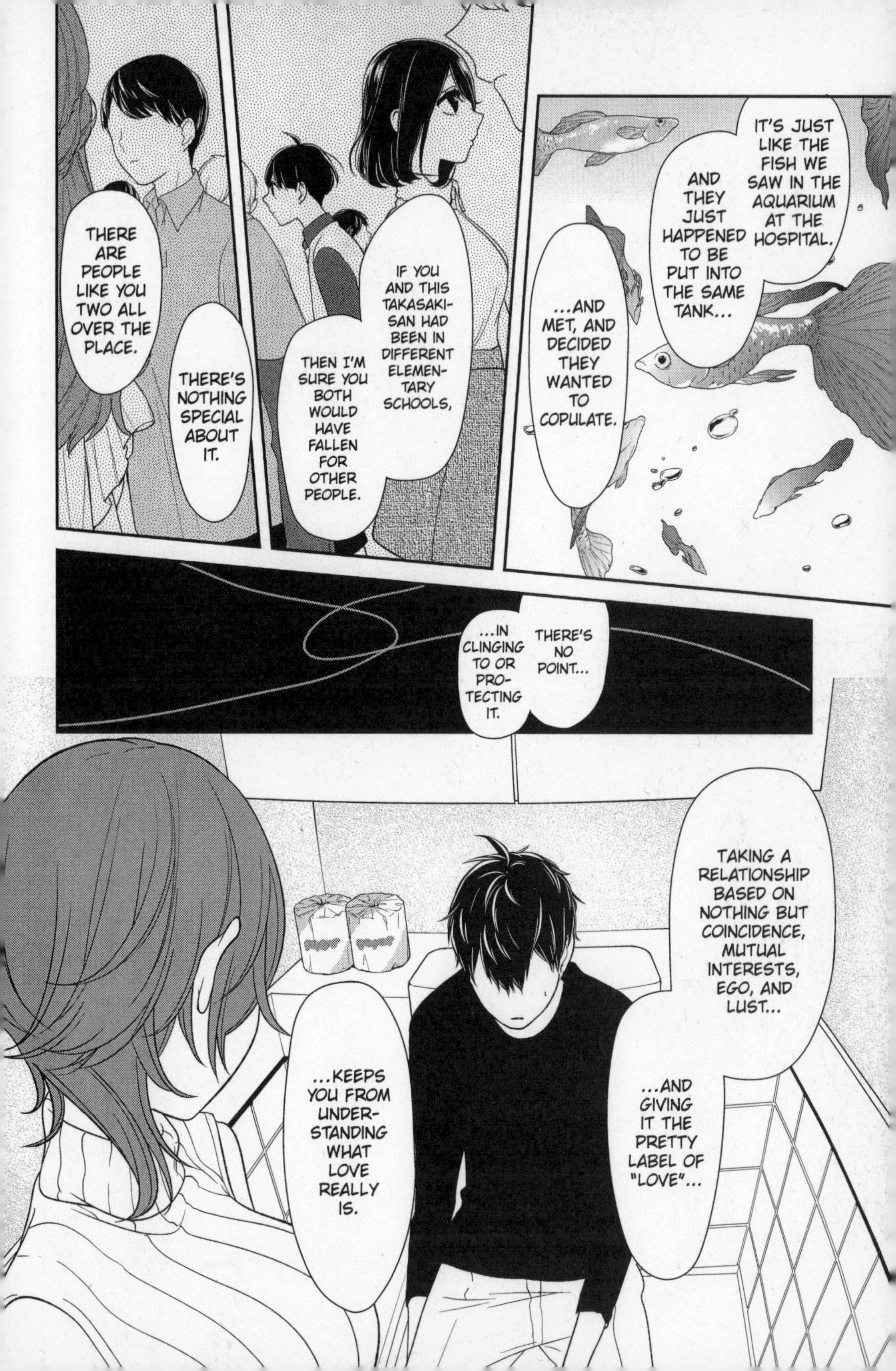
IT'S JUST LIKE THE FISH WE SAW IN THE AQUARIUM AT THE HOSPITAL.
AND THEY JUST HAPPENED TO BE PUT INTO THE SAME TANK...
...AND MET, AND DECIDED THEY WANTED TO COPULATE.
IF YOU AND THIS TAKASAKI-SAN HAD BEEN IN DIFFERENT ELEMEN-TARY SCHOOLS,
THEN I'M SURE YOU BOTH WOULD HAVE FALLEN FOR OTHER PEOPLE.
THERE ARE PEOPLE LIKE YOU TWO ALL OVER THE PLACE.
THERE'S NOTHING SPECIAL ABOUT IT.
THERE'S NO POINT...
...IN CLINGING TO OR PRO-TECTING IT.
TAKING A RELATIONSHIP BASED ON NOTHING BUT COINCIDENCE, MUTUAL INTERESTS, EGO, AND LUST...
...AND GIVING IT THE PRETTY LABEL OF "LOVE"...
...KEEPS YOU FROM UNDER-STANDING WHAT LOVE REALLY IS.

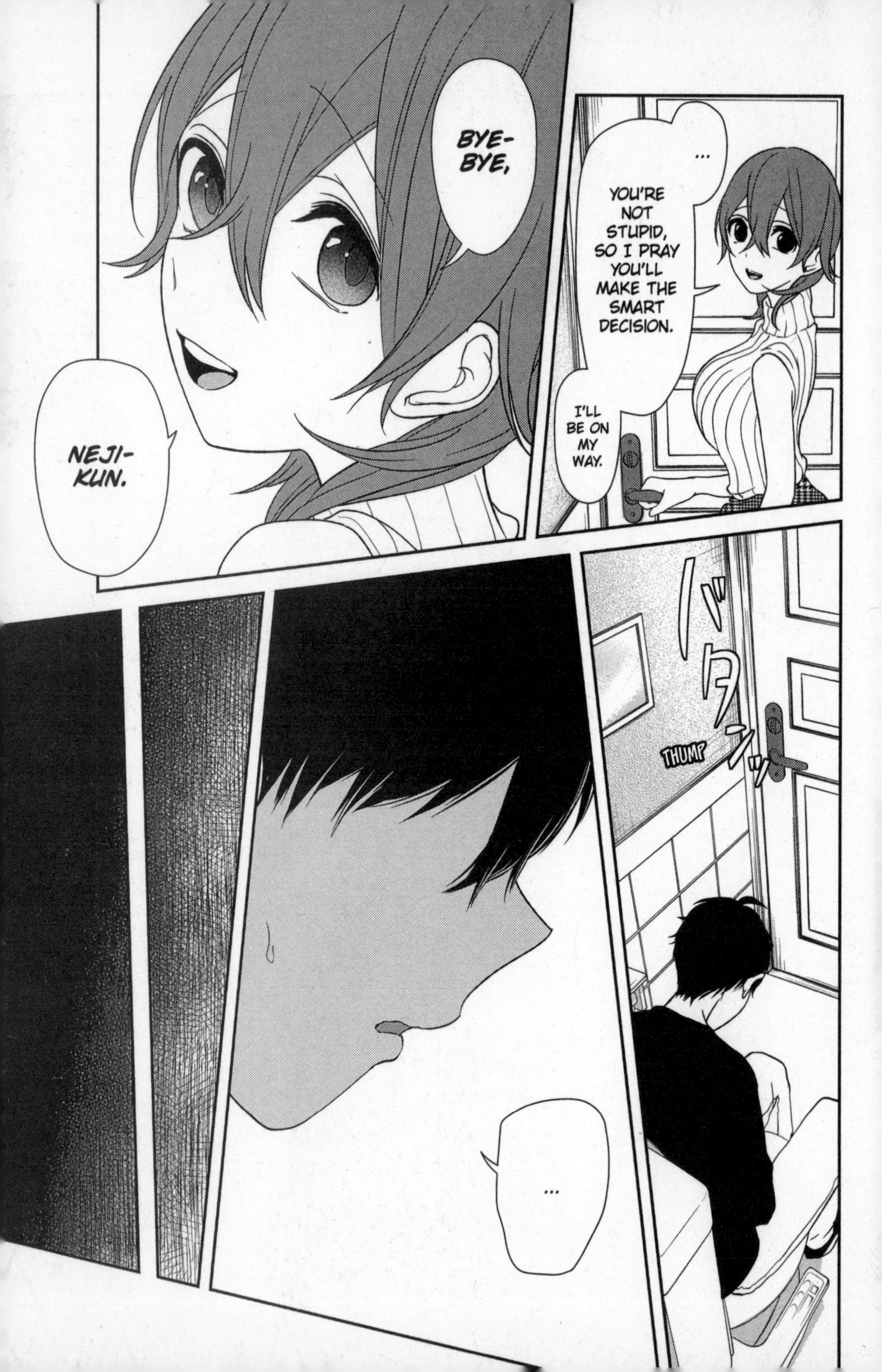
...
YOU'RE NOT STUPID, SO I PRAY YOU'LL MAKE THE SMART DECISION.
I'LL BE ON MY WAY.
BYE-BYE,
NEJI-KUN.
バタンッ
THUMP
...

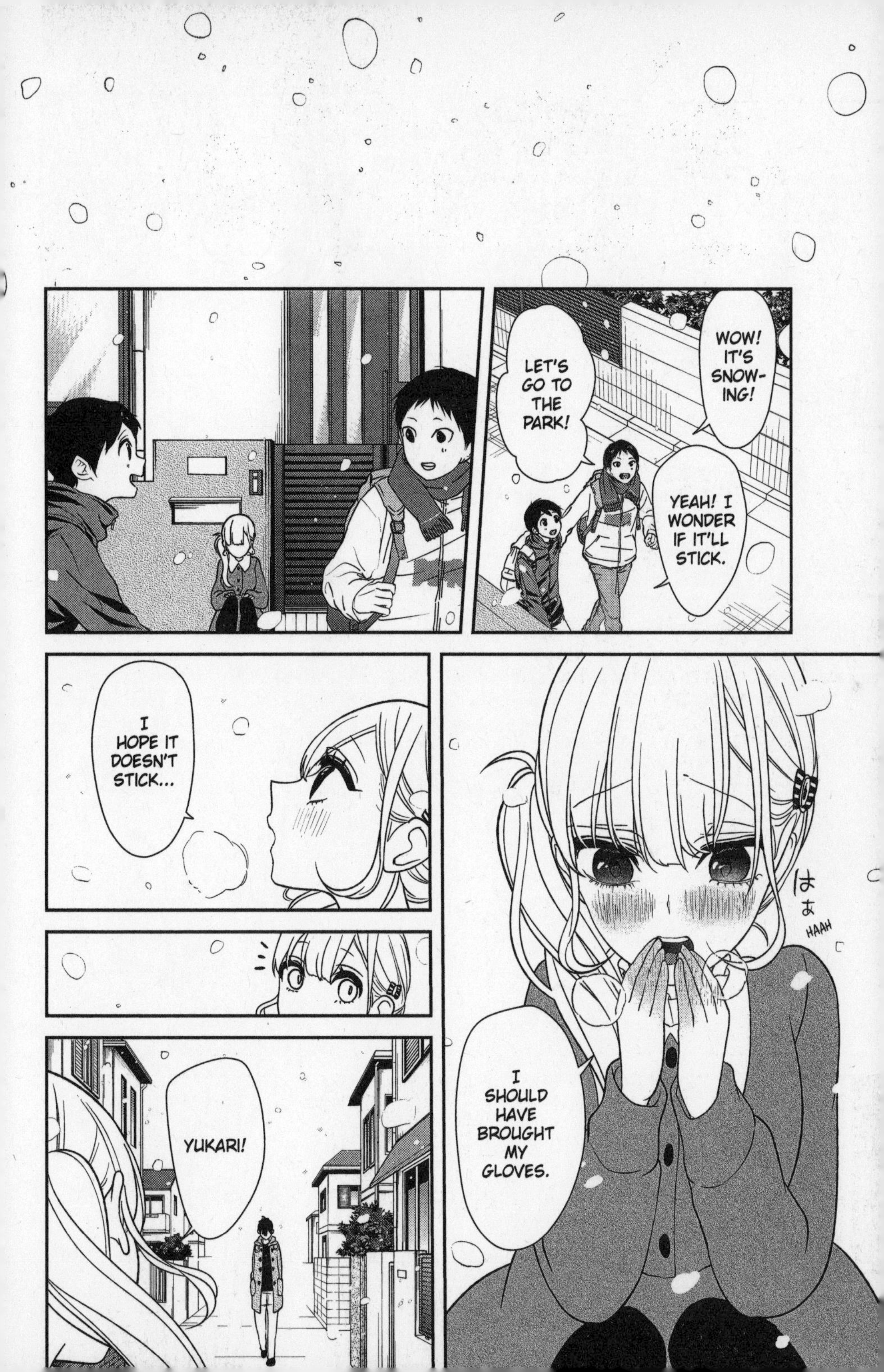
WOW! IT'S SNOW-ING!
LET'S GO TO THE PARK!
YEAH! I WONDER IF IT'LL STICK.
はぁ
HAAH
I SHOULD HAVE BROUGHT MY GLOVES.
I HOPE IT DOESN'T STICK...
YUKARI!

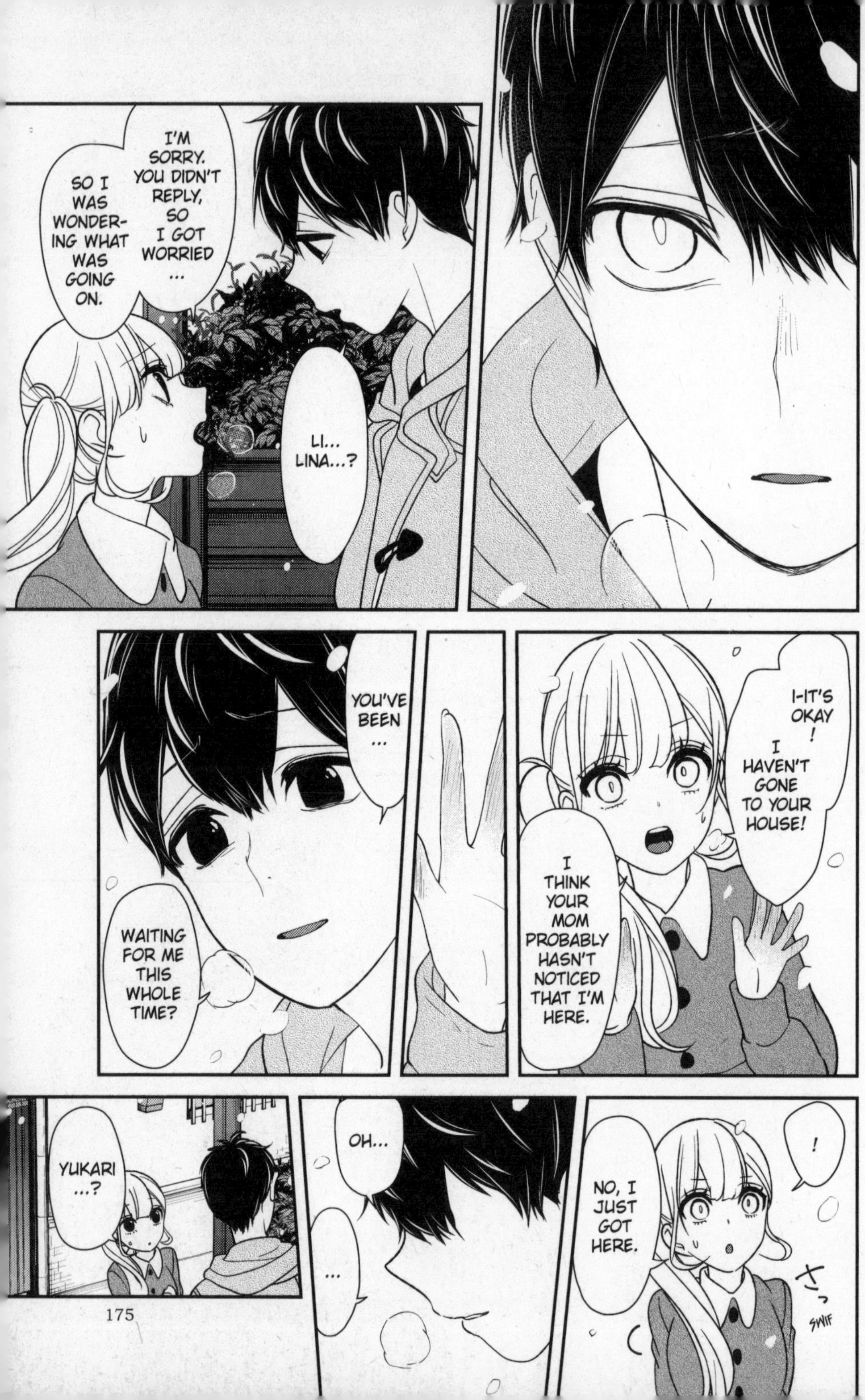
I'M SORRY. YOU DIDN'T REPLY, SO I GOT WORRIED...
SO I WAS WONDERING WHAT WAS GOING ON.
LI... LINA...?
I-IT'S OKAY! I HAVEN'T GONE TO YOUR HOUSE!
I THINK YOUR MOM PROBABLY HASN'T NOTICED THAT I'M HERE.
YOU'VE BEEN...
WAITING FOR ME THIS WHOLE TIME?
!
NO, I JUST GOT HERE.
SWIF
OH...
...
YUKARI...?

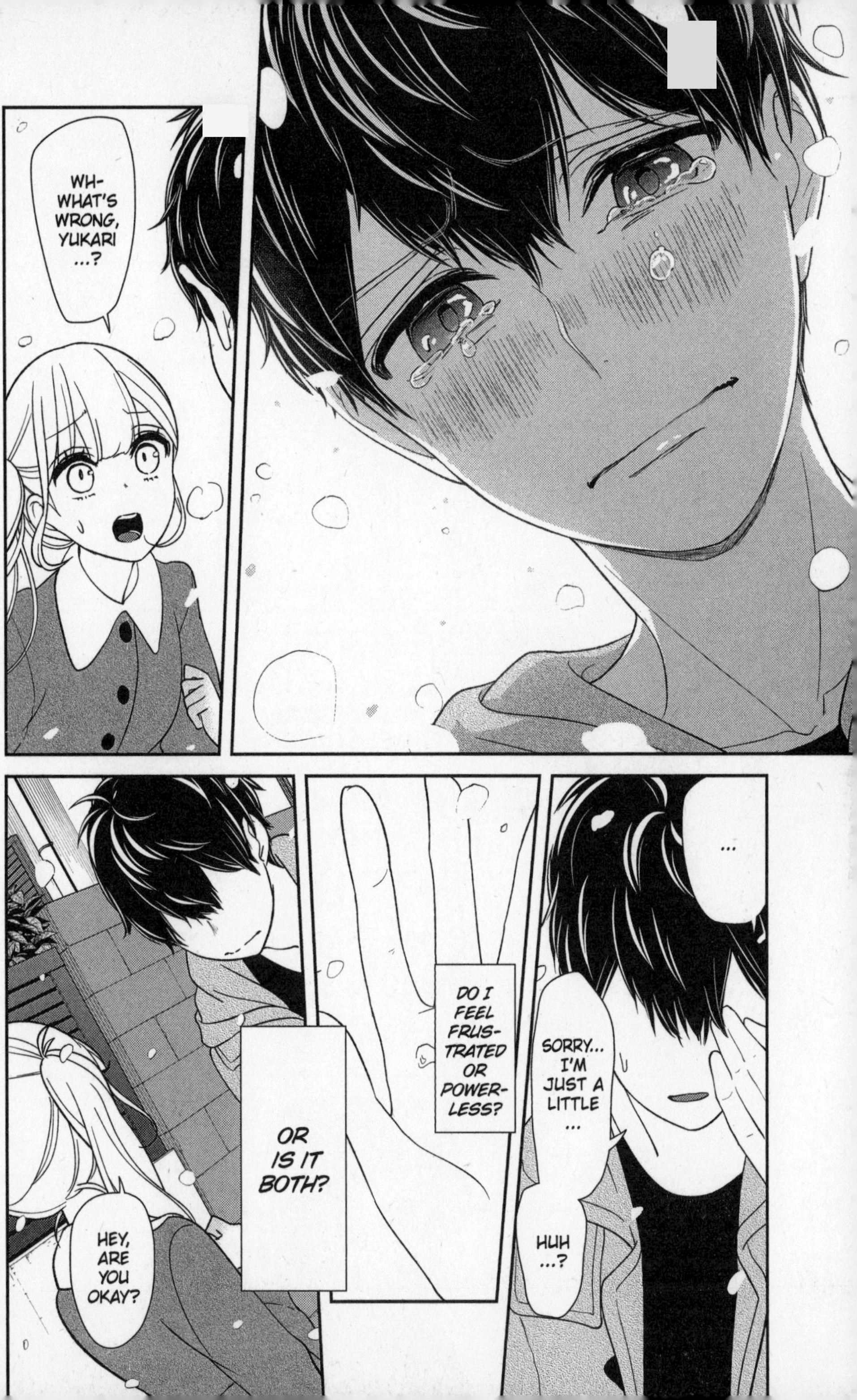
WH- WHAT'S WRONG, YUKARI ...?
...
SORRY... I'M JUST A LITTLE ...
HUH ...?
DO I FEEL FRUS-TRATED OR POWER-LESS?
OR IS IT BOTH?
HEY, ARE YOU OKAY?

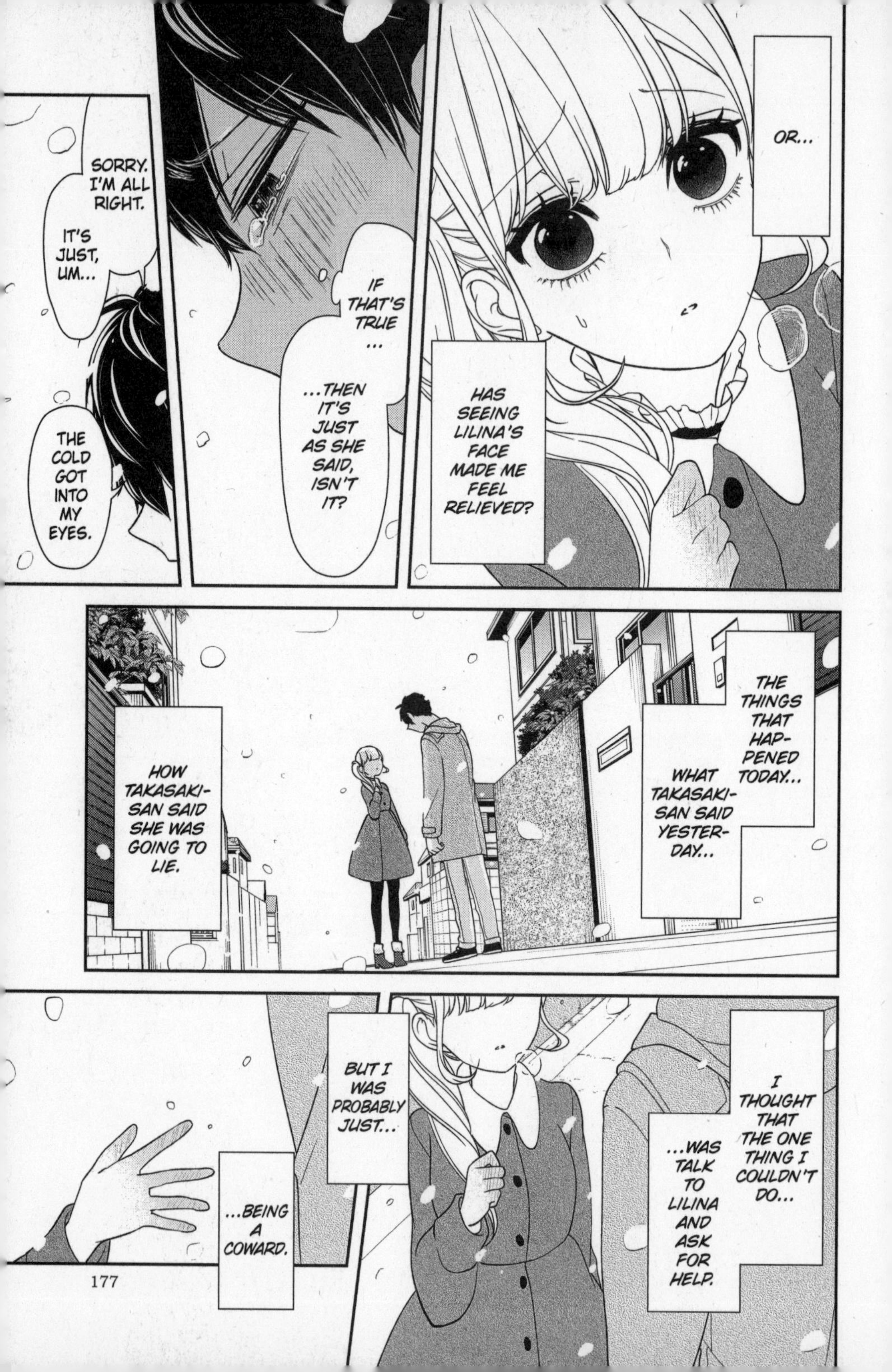
OR...
HAS SEEING LILINA'S FACE MADE ME FEEL RELIEVED?
IF THAT'S TRUE...
...THEN IT'S JUST AS SHE SAID, ISN'T IT?
SORRY. I'M ALL RIGHT.
IT'S JUST, UM...
THE COLD GOT INTO MY EYES.
THE THINGS THAT HAPPENED TODAY...
WHAT TAKASAKI-SAN SAID YESTERDAY...
HOW TAKASAKI-SAN SAID SHE WAS GOING TO LIE.
I THOUGHT THAT THE ONE THING I COULDN'T DO...
...WAS TALK TO LILINA AND ASK FOR HELP.
BUT I WAS PROBABLY JUST...
...BEING A COWARD.

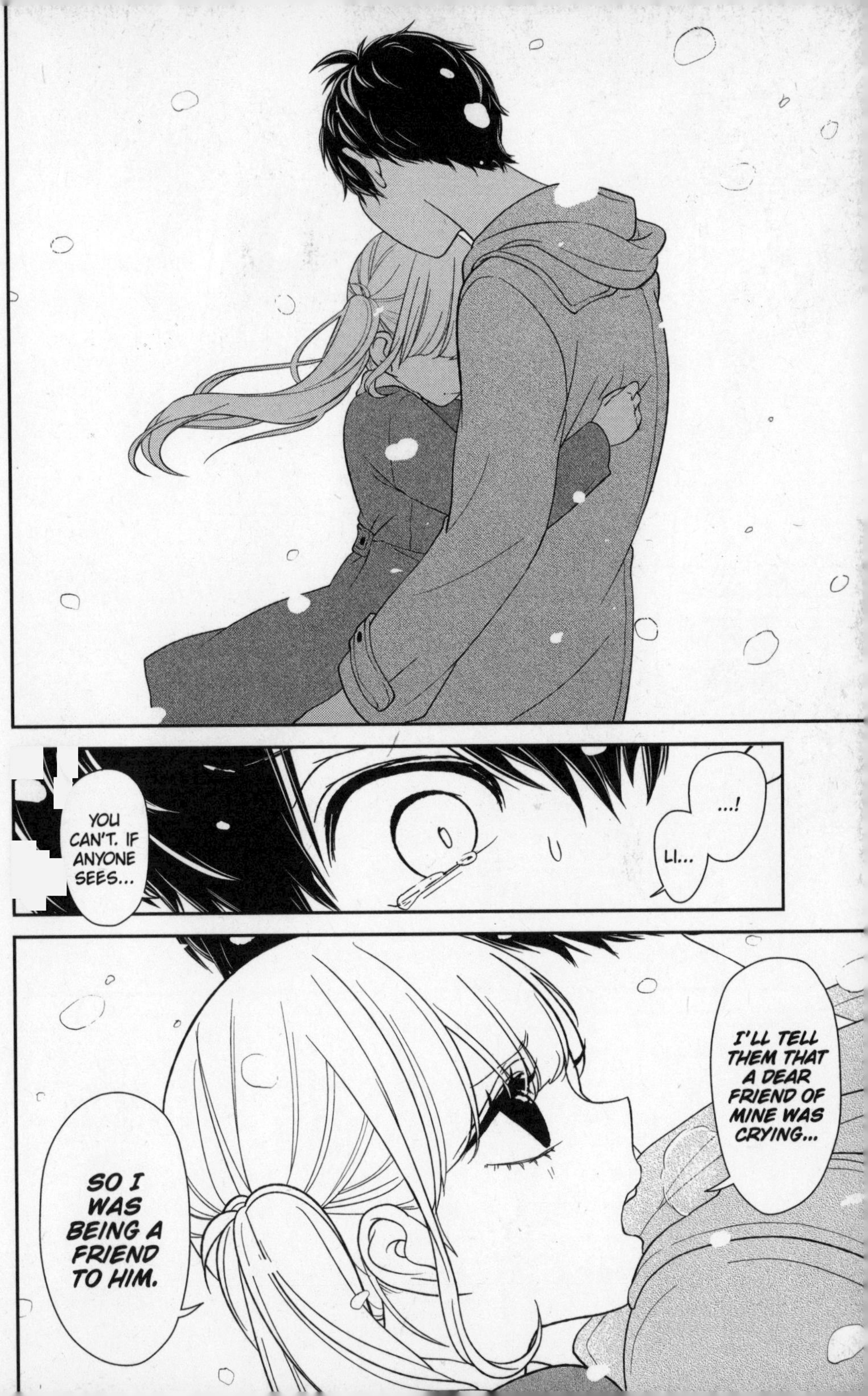
...!
LI...
YOU CAN'T. IF ANYONE SEES...
I'LL TELL THEM THAT A DEAR FRIEND OF MINE WAS CRYING...
SO I WAS BEING A FRIEND TO HIM.

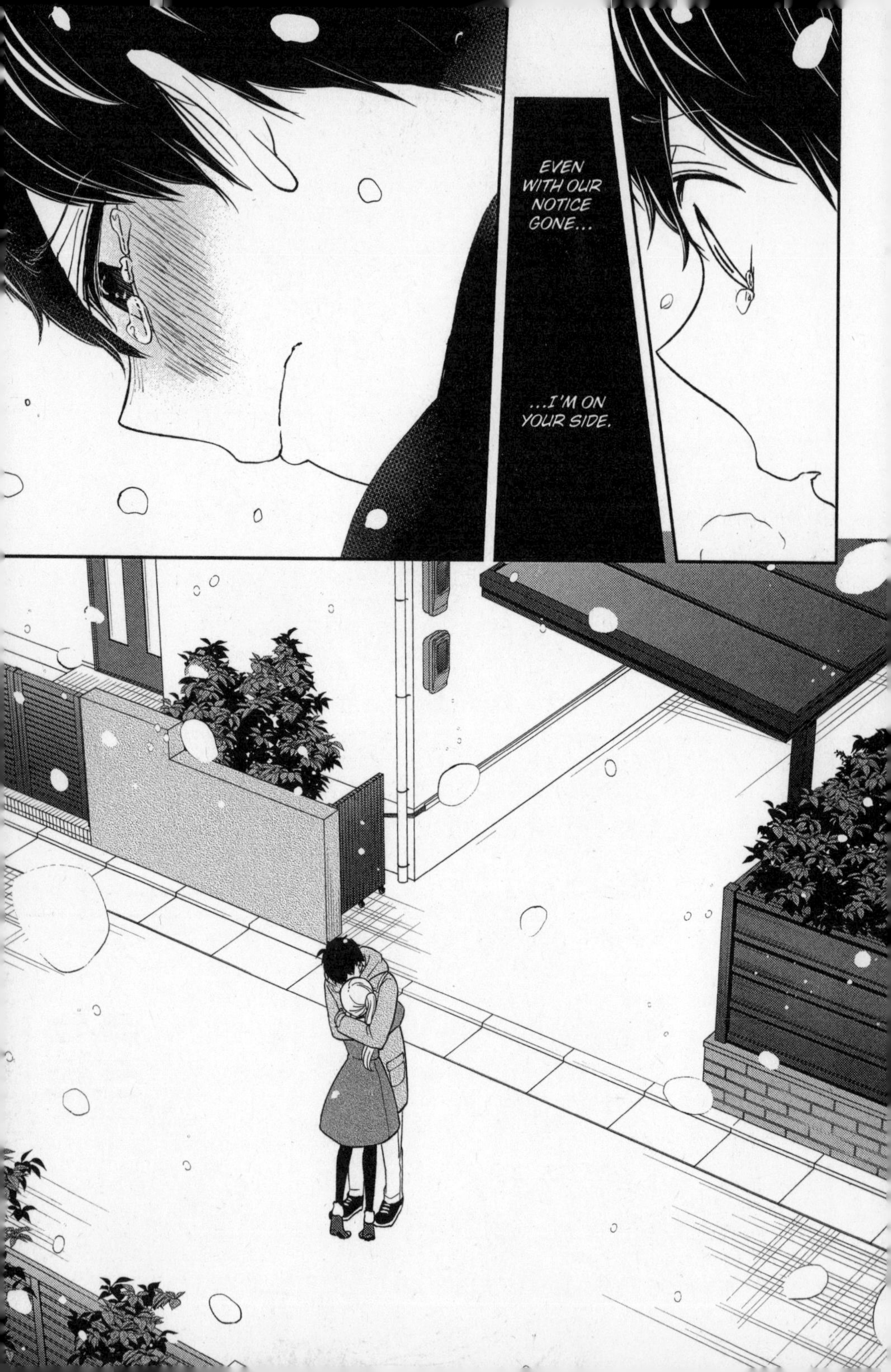
EVEN WITH OUR NOTICE GONE...
...I'M ON YOUR SIDE.

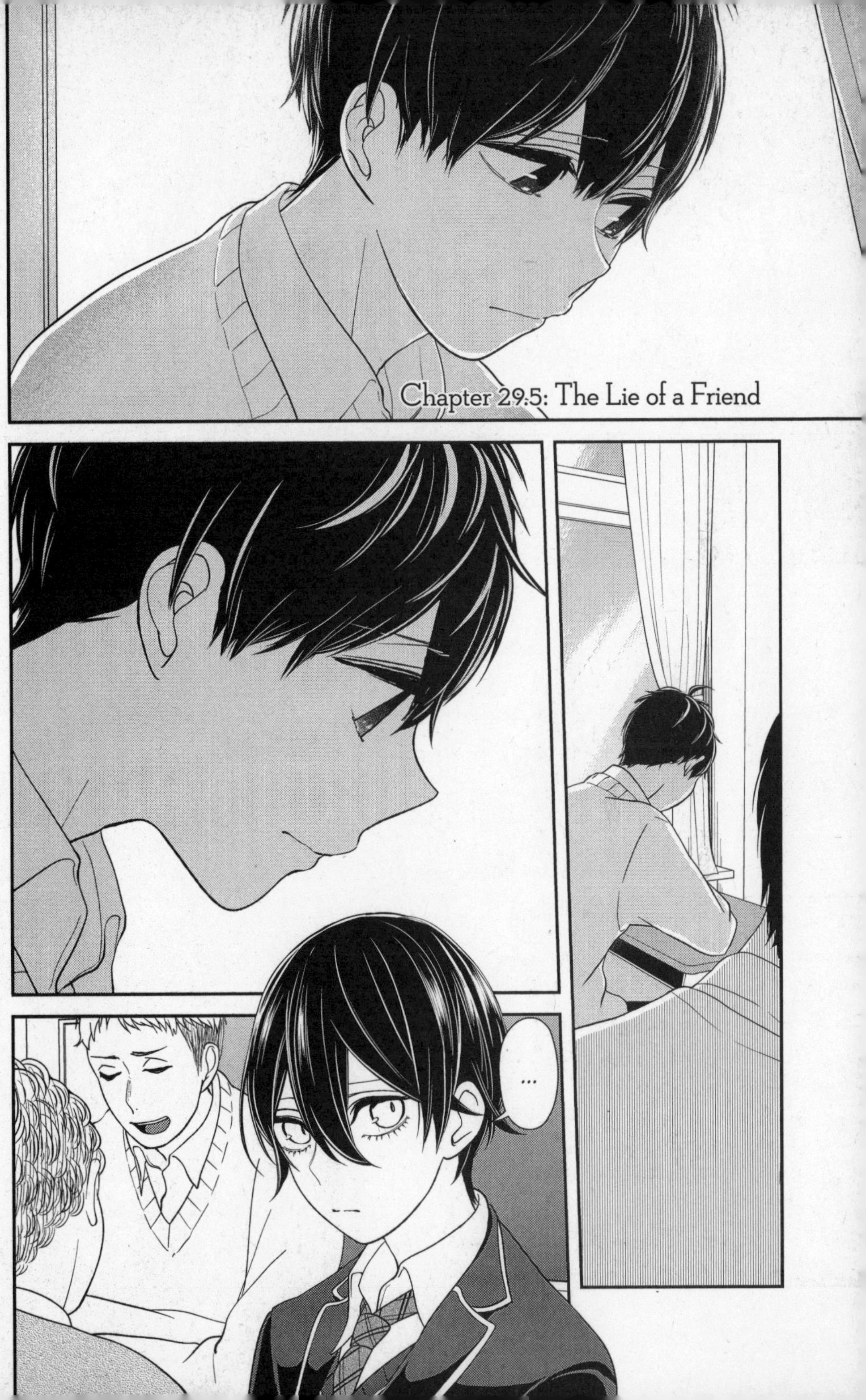
Chapter 29.5: The Lie of a Friend
...

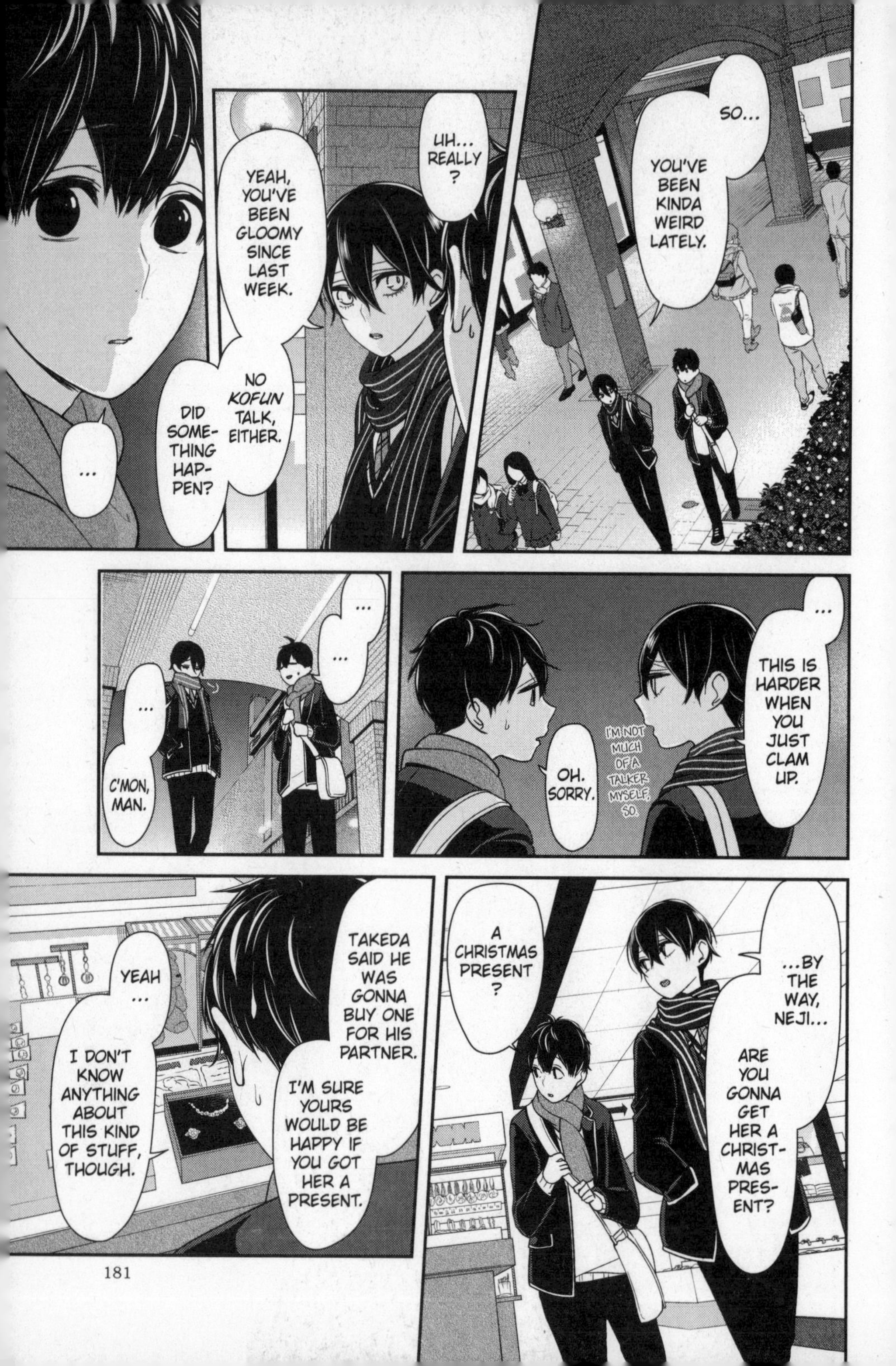
SO...
YOU'VE BEEN KINDA WEIRD LATELY.
UH... REALLY?
YEAH, YOU'VE BEEN GLOOMY SINCE LAST WEEK.
NO KOFUN TALK, EITHER.
DID SOMETHING HAPPEN?
...
...
THIS IS HARDER WHEN YOU JUST CLAM UP.
I'M NOT MUCH OF A TALKER MYSELF, SO.
OH. SORRY.
...
...
...
C'MON, MAN.
...BY THE WAY, NEJI...
ARE YOU GONNA GET HER A CHRISTMAS PRESENT?
A CHRISTMAS PRESENT?
TAKEDA SAID HE WAS GONNA BUY ONE FOR HIS PARTNER.
I'M SURE YOURS WOULD BE HAPPY IF YOU GOT HER A PRESENT.
YEAH...
I DON'T KNOW ANYTHING ABOUT THIS KIND OF STUFF, THOUGH.

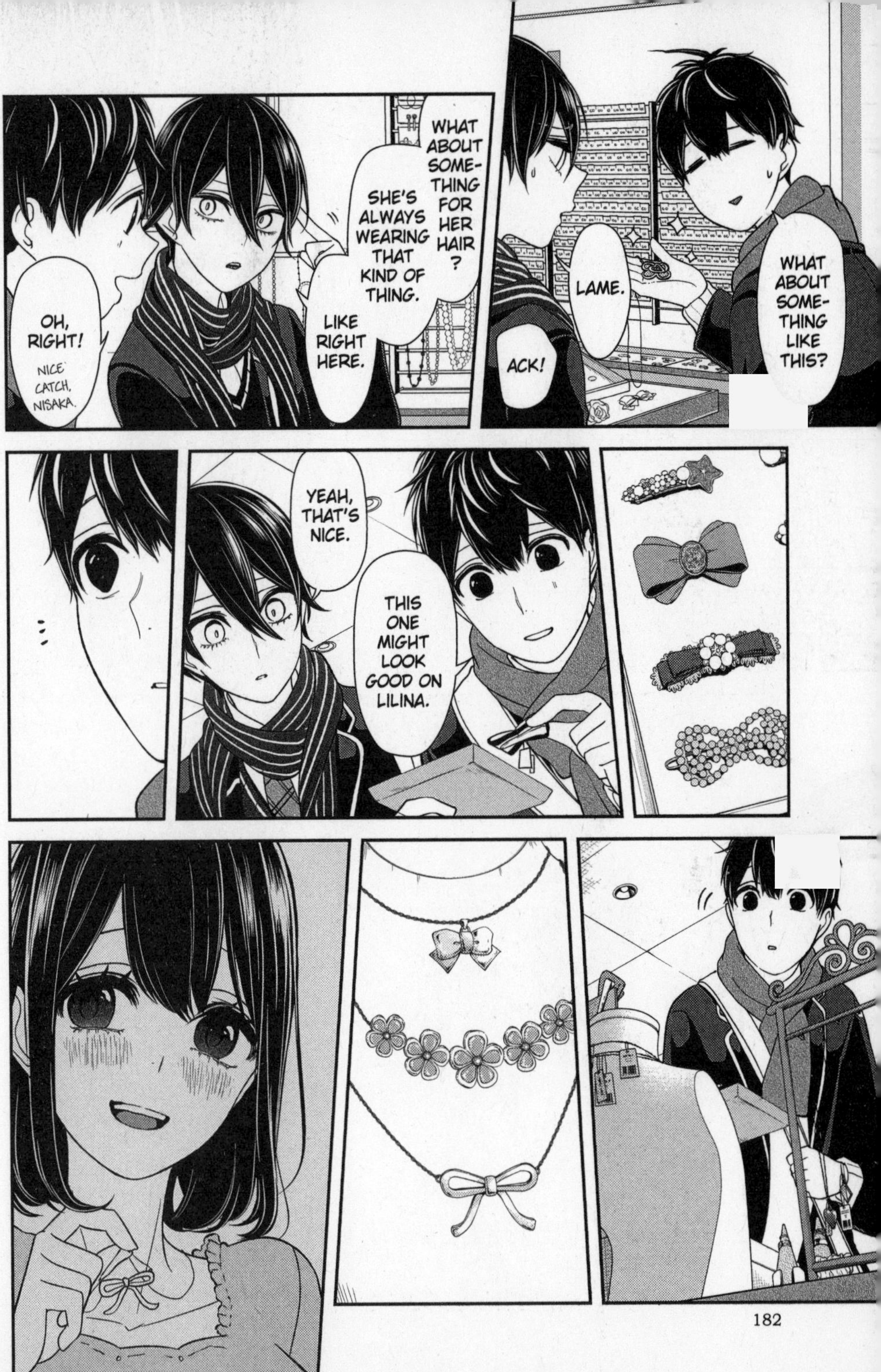
WHAT ABOUT SOME-THING LIKE THIS?
LAME.
ACK!
WHAT ABOUT SOME-THING FOR HER HAIR?
SHE'S ALWAYS WEARING THAT KIND OF THING.
LIKE RIGHT HERE.
OH, RIGHT!
NICE CATCH, NISAKA.
THIS ONE MIGHT LOOK GOOD ON LILINA.
YEAH, THAT'S NICE.

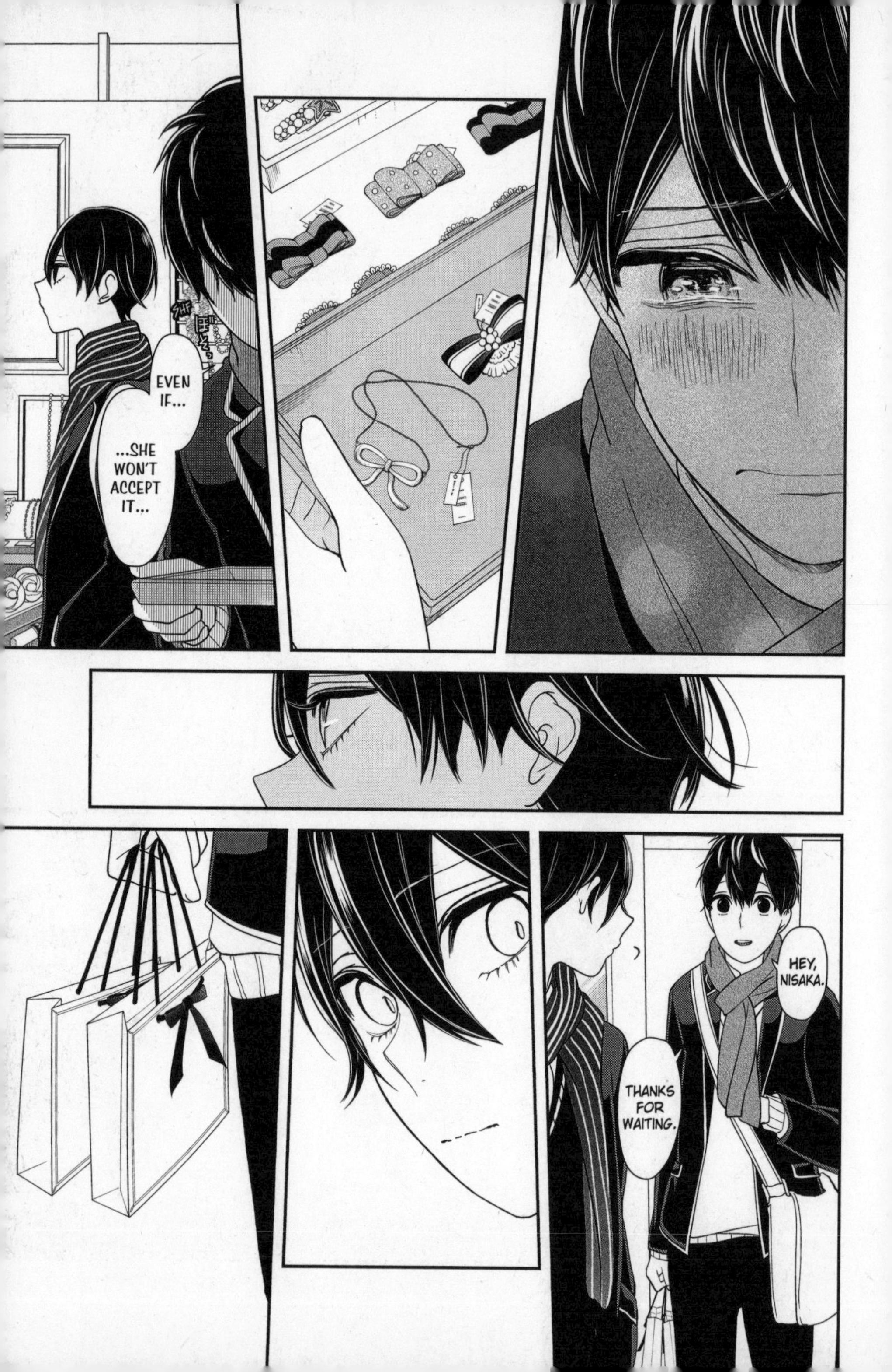
SHF
EVEN IF...
...SHE WON'T ACCEPT IT...
HEY, NISAKA.
THANKS FOR WAITING.

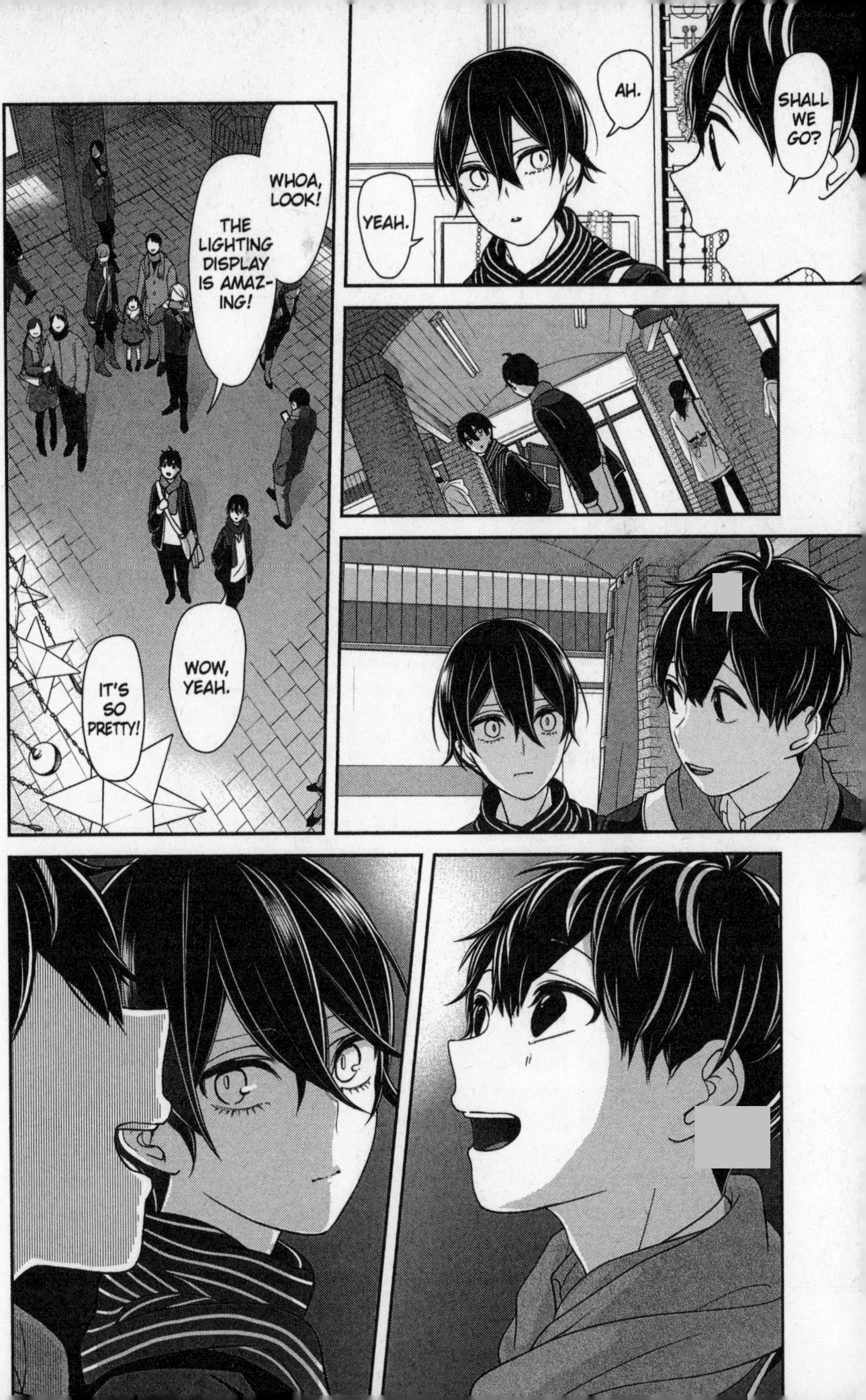
SHALL WE GO?
AH.
YEAH.
WHOA, LOOK!
THE LIGHTING DISPLAY IS AMAZ-ING!
WOW, YEAH.
IT'S SO PRETTY!

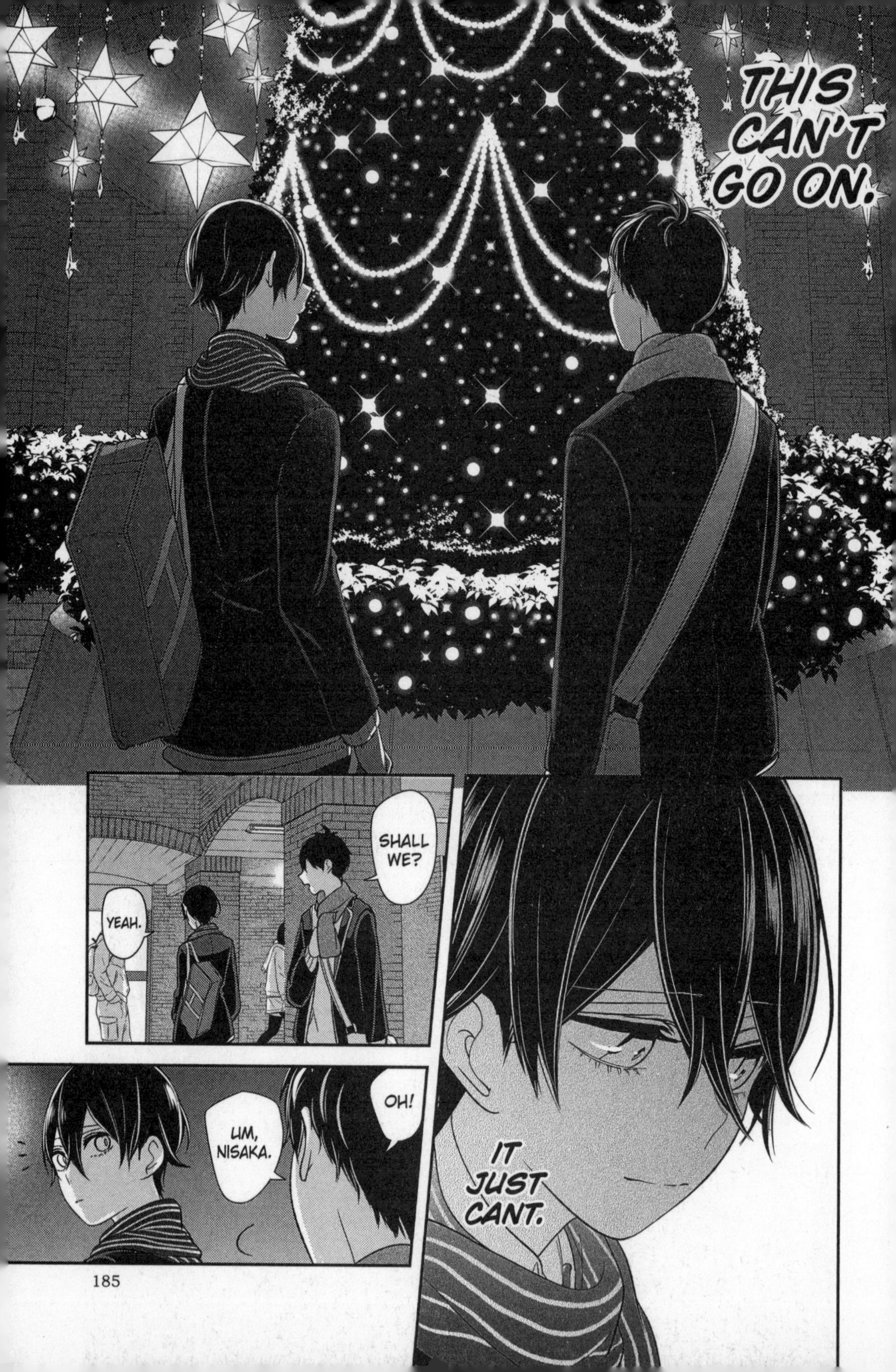
THIS CAN'T GO ON.
IT JUST CANT.
SHALL WE?
YEAH.
OH!
UM, NISAKA.

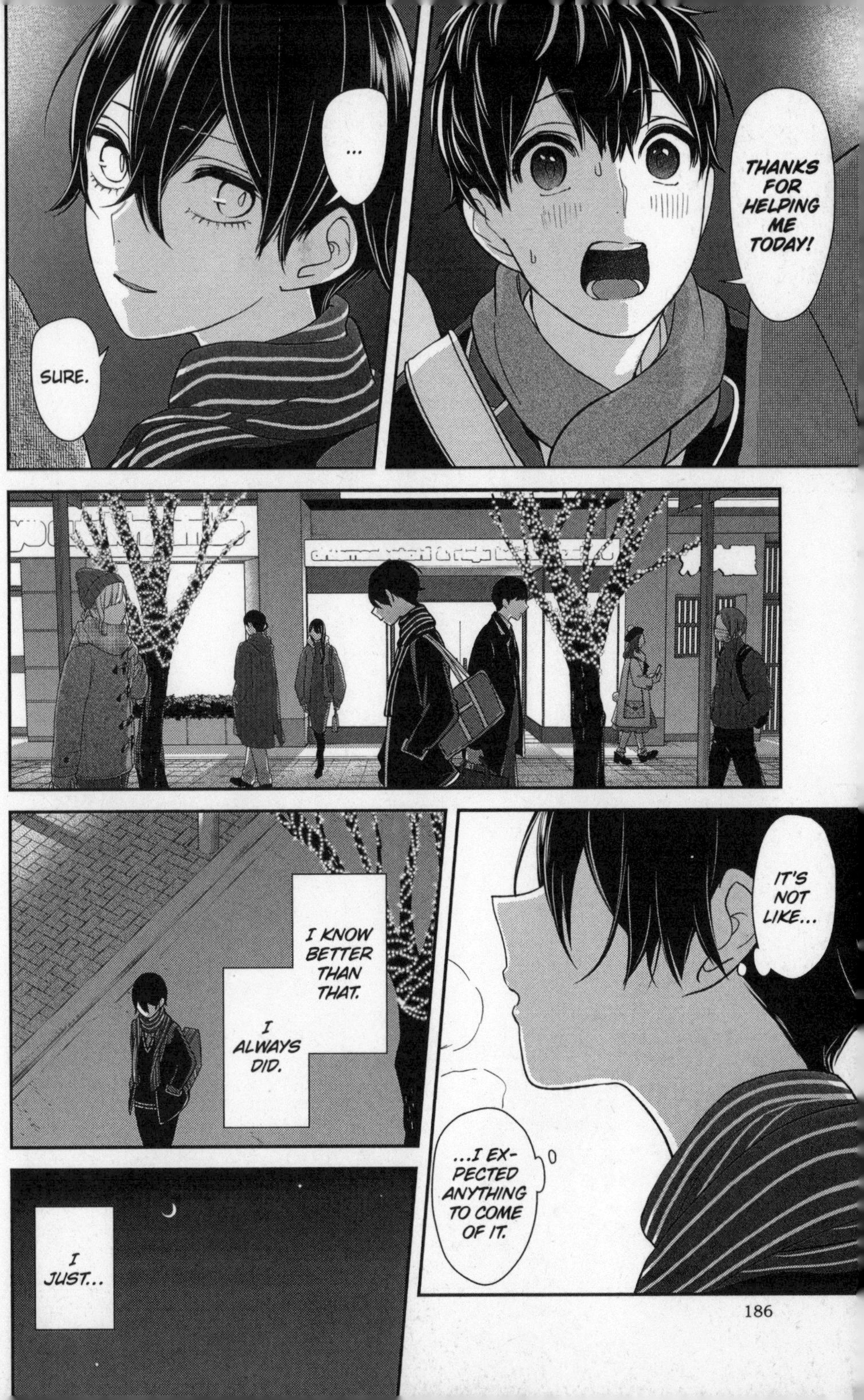
THANKS FOR HELPING ME TODAY!
...
SURE.
IT'S NOT LIKE...
...I EX-PECTED ANYTHING TO COME OF IT.
I KNOW BETTER THAN THAT.
I ALWAYS DID.
I JUST...

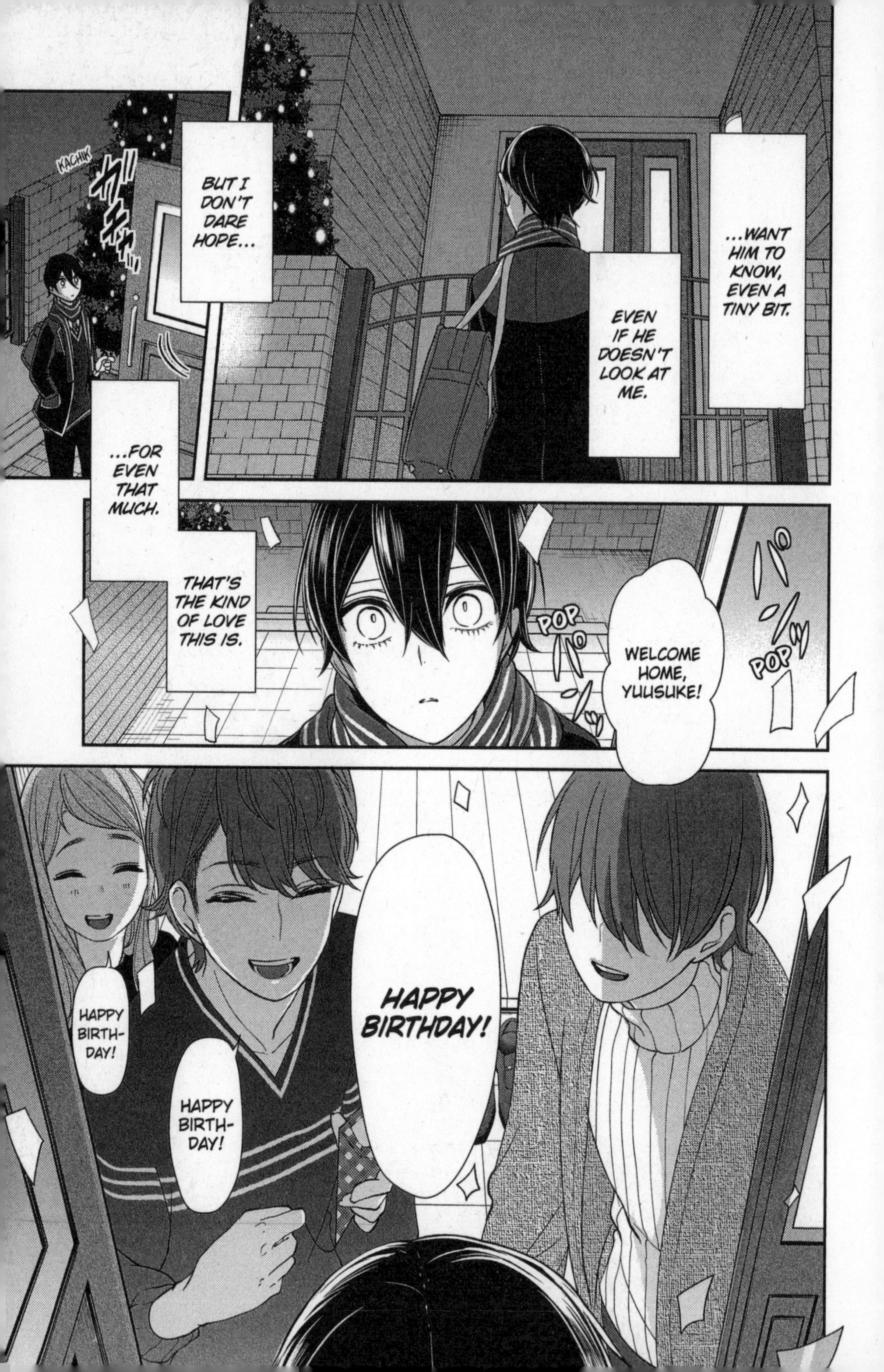
...WANT HIM TO KNOW, EVEN A TINY BIT.
EVEN IF HE DOESN'T LOOK AT ME.
KACHIK
BUT I DON'T DARE HOPE...
...FOR EVEN THAT MUCH.
THAT'S THE KIND OF LOVE THIS IS.
POP
POP
WELCOME HOME, YUUSUKE!
HAPPY BIRTHDAY!
HAPPY BIRTH-DAY!
HAPPY BIRTH-DAY!

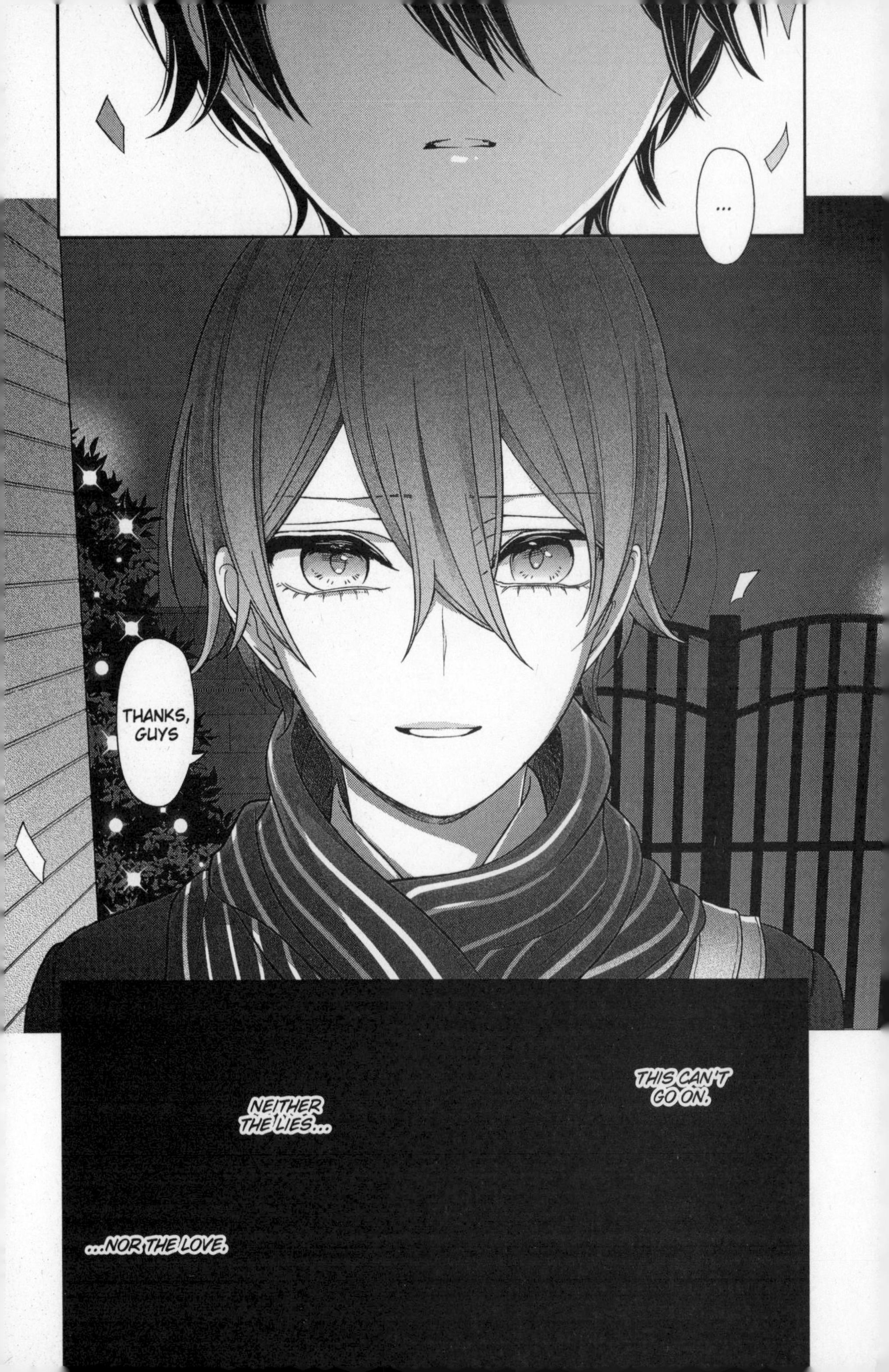
...
THANKS, GUYS
THIS CAN'T GO ON.
NEITHER THE LIES...
...NOR THE LOVE.

Love & Lies

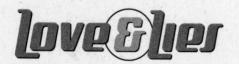

Next volume...

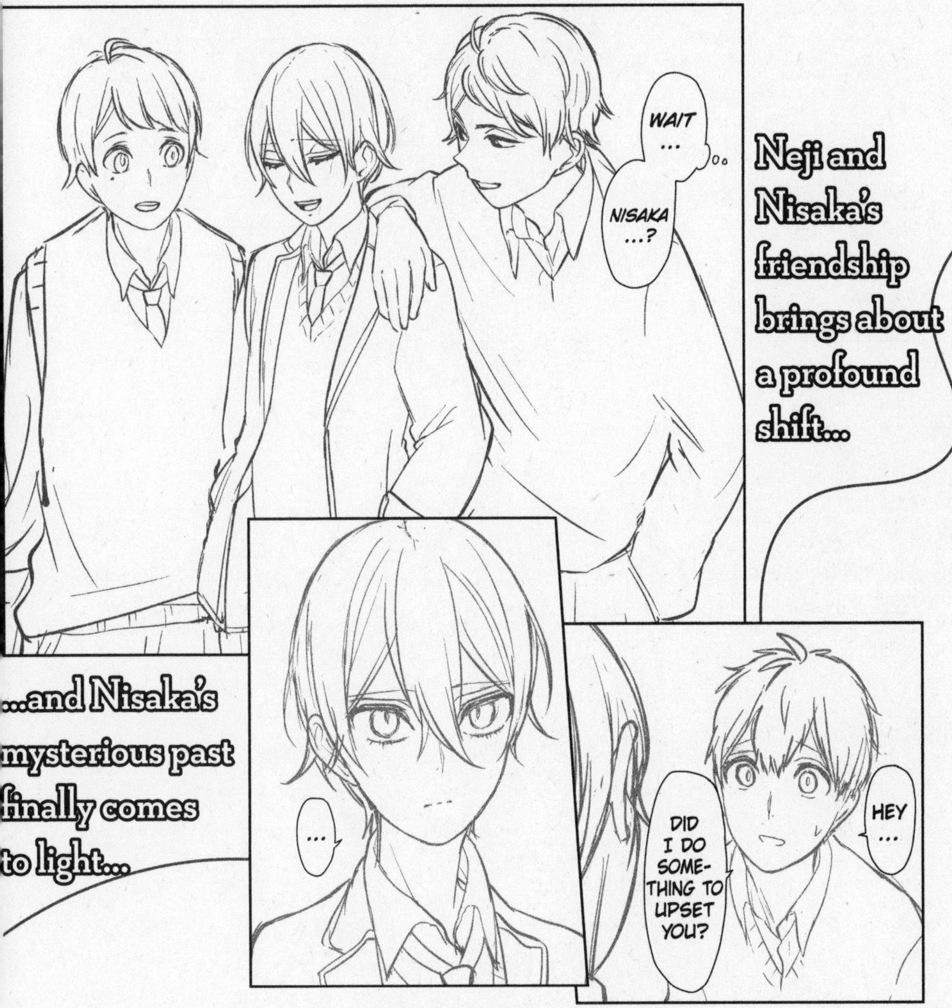

Neji and Nisaka's friendship brings about a profound shift...
WAIT ...
NISAKA ...?
HEY ...
DID I DO SOME-THING TO UPSET YOU?
...
...and Nisaka's mysterious past finally comes to light...

LOVE, LIES, AND PAIN: THE TANGLED LOVE STORY OF THESE BOYS AND GIRLS IS ABOUT TO CHANGE...

Love & Lies

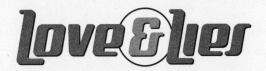

Volume 8
coming soon!

★ SPECIAL THANKS ★

SHINOHARA-SAMA
YOSHIMURA-SAMA
FUJI-SAMA
HANAWA-SAMA

JUU SUDOU-SAMA
MANARU AMAGAWA-SAMA
KOKONATTSU-SAMA
FUKU-SAMA
KEI KOBAYASHI-SAMA
YAYOI HAYASEGAWA-SAMA
UTSUNOMIYA-SAMA
SAYU-SAMA

EVERYONE IN
MY FAMILY

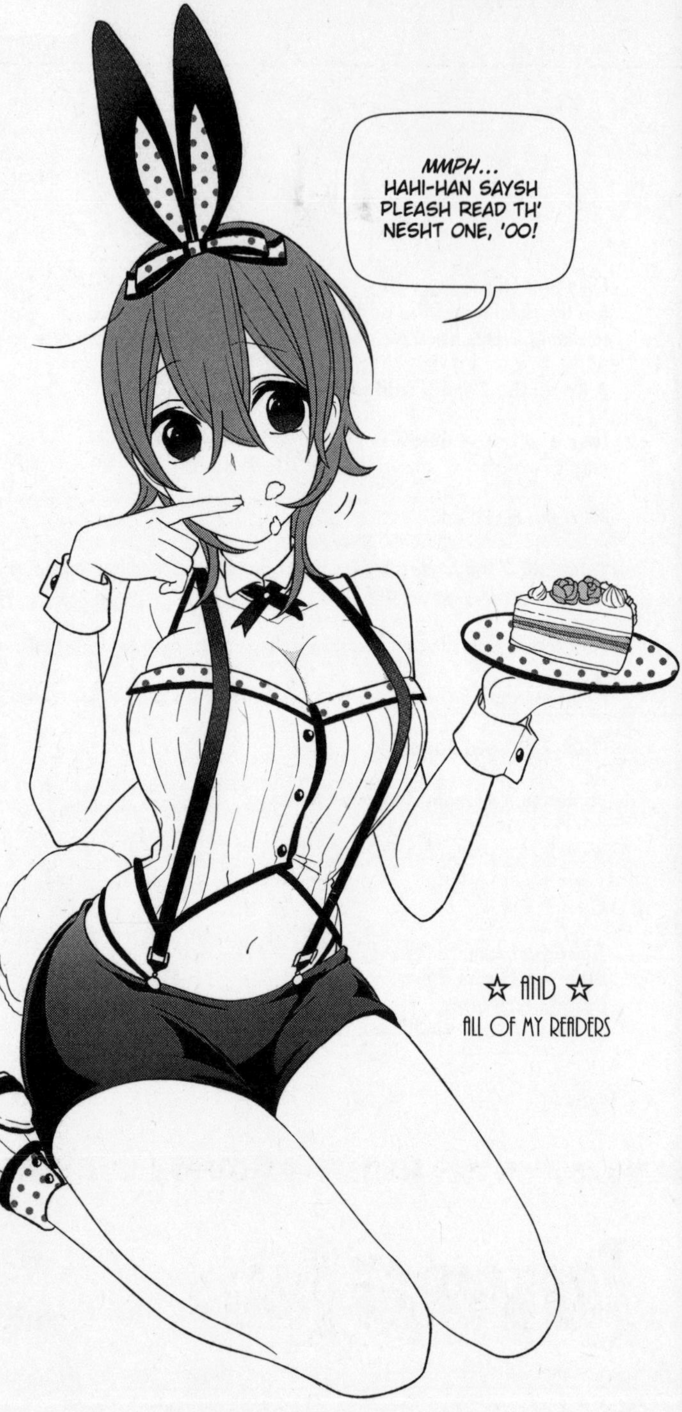
MMPH... HAHI-HAN SAYSH PLEASH READ TH' NESHT ONE, 'OO!

☆ AND ☆

ALL OF MY READERS

Love and Lies volume 7 is a work of fiction. Names, characters, places, and incidents are the products of the author's imagination or are used fictitiously. Any resemblance to actual events, locales, or persons, living or dead, is entirely coincidental.

A Kodansha Comics Trade Paperback Original.

Published in the United States by Kodansha Comics, an imprint of Kodansha USA Publishing, LLC, New York.

Publication rights for this English edition arranged through Kodansha Ltd., Tokyo.

First published in Japan in 2018 by Kodansha Ltd., Tokyo, as *Koi to Uso* volume 7.

ISBN 978-1-63236-626-9

Printed in the United States of America.

www.kodanshacomics.com

9 8 7 6 5 4 3 2 1

Translator: Jennifer Ward
Lettering: Daniel CY
Editing: Paul Starr
Kodansha Comics edition cover design by Phil Balsman